People, Environment,

Disease and Death

This book is dedicated

with love and thanks

to my wife Pat

People, Environment,

Disease and Death

A MEDICAL GEOGRAPHY OF BRITAIN

THROUGHOUT THE AGES

G. Melvyn Howe

UNIVERSITY OF WALES PRESS

CARDIFF

1997

British Library Cataloguing-in-Publication Data.
A catalogue record for this book is available from
the British Library.

ISBN 0-7083-1373-6

Typeset by Action Typesetting Ltd., Gloucester
Printed in Great Britain by The Cromwell Press, Melksham

On Airs, Waters, and Places

I. Whoever wishes to investigate medicine properly, should proceed thus: in the first place to consider the seasons of the year, and what effects each of them produces ... Then the winds, the hot and the cold, especially such as are common to all countries, and then such as are peculiar to each locality. We must also consider the qualities. In the same manner, when one comes into a city to which he is a stranger, he ought to consider its situation, how it lies as to the winds and the rising of the sun; for its influence is not the same whether it lies to the north or the south, to the rising or to the setting sun. These things one ought to consider most attentively, and concerning the waters which the inhabitants use, whether they be marshy and soft, or hard, and running from elevated and rocky situations, and then if saltish and unfit for cooking; and the ground, whether it be naked and deficient in water, or wooded and well watered, and whether it lies in a hollow, confined situation, or is elevated and cold; and the mode in which the inhabitants live, and what are their pursuits, whether they are fond of drinking and eating to excess, and given to indolence, or are fond of exercise and labour, and not given to excess in eating and drinking.

Hippocrates

Contents

Plates

Figures

Tables

Preface

A great deal has happened in the study of people and their relationships with the environment since the first edition of this book was published a quarter of a century ago under the title *Man, Environment and Disease in Britain*. Advances in molecular biology, population genetics and gene therapy, ever-increasing insight into the numerous physical, biological and socio-cultural hazards to health in the environment, more up-to-date statistics relating to morbidity and mortality in the several regions of Birtain, and an ever-increasing interest in local and regional variations in the incidence of disease have, together, prompted this revised and restructured edition.

The Human Genome Mapping Project, whereby all human genes will be mapped precisely to their respective positions on the chromosomes and their DNA sequences identified, is now well advanced. This will facilitate a more refined atlas and unlock more secrets of the human genetic blueprint. This project is complemented by the Medical Research Council's new initiative, Genetic Approach to Human Health. In the context of the present book, however, it is the *faulty* genes that are of special interest – those responsible for inherited diseases. Cystic fibrosis and haemophilia are cases in point and appear now as potential candidates for gene therapy.

Environmental hazards to health are either natural or man-made. They include radon, ultraviolet light, stratospheric ozone depletion, dioxins, dietary habits, work-induced stress and several recently emerging infectious diseases. Distribution maps, which display the spatial elements of the incidence and prevalence of disease are used to highlight areas where there are unfavourable interactions between communities and their environments.

Local and regional differentials in morbidity and mortality are demonstrated with maps. These answer the question 'Where?', that is, they show the localities where there is conflict or lack of adjustment of communities or individuals to hazards in the environment. The result in such cases is *dis*-ease (ecological disequilibrium). On the other hand, where there is a balanced relationship between body and mind, where adjustment to the environment is complete (ecological equilibrium) there is health. It is the search for explanations for the nature (genetic inheritance)/nurture (environment) conflict, and for possible or tentative answers or explanations to the further question 'Why there?' that represents the purpose of this multidisciplinary study. The highlighting of differences in disease incidence between regions and localities within Britain will shed light on the diffusion of the infectious diseases of the past and, at the same time, contribute to the further understanding of the mechanisms or aetiology of the deadly diseases which affect British society at the present time. By offering a geographical, environmental or 'real world' approach to problems it is hoped to provide a counterpoint to the essentially anthropocentric viewpoint of the clinical and laboratory techniques usually employed by medical researchers.

G.M.H.
April 1997

Acknowledgements

This updated and extended edition has benefited greatly from the guiding comments of several friends and colleagues much more expert in certain areas than I would ever claim to be. They have given generously of their time to review various sections of the book and comment on early drafts of relevant material. I am particularly grateful to Dr Brian Dicks who advised me on aspects of the early historical sections of the book, Dr Sally Davies who made comment on items relating to genetics, Emeritus Professor Andrew Learmonth and Dr John Giggs for informed suggestions relative to Chapters 14 and 15, and Dr J. H. Thomas for valuable comments.

I owe a special debt to those who have helped me with the several maps and diagrams. I am particularly indebted to Elizabeth Harvey and Sharon Galleitch in the Cartographic Section of the Department of Geography, University of Strathclyde, who drew the maps, and to Steven Tagg and Ann Mair of the Social Statistics Laboratory, University of Strathclyde, who kindly provided computer assistance. Judith Howells typed the manuscript on to disk for subsequent transfer to the printed page.

Sincere thanks are due to my editors, Susan Jenkins and Ceinwen Jones of the University of Wales Press for their patience and insight. My wife, Patricia, deserves special mention. Without her unfailing patience, encouragement and constant support this volume would never have been completed. It is with gratitude that I dedicate the book to her.

G.M.H.
April 1997

The author and publishers would like to thank the following publishers, organizations and individuals for permission to reprint or reproduce in modified form, copyright material in various figures, tables and plates as indicated below. Every effort has been made to identify the original sources but, if there have been accidental errors or omissions, apologies are extended to those concerned.

Publishers

Her Majesty's Stationery Office; Central Statistical Office for Annual Abstracts of Statistics and Digest of Environmental Statistics; Office of Population Censuses and Surveys for: Population Trends, Social Trends, Regional Trends, General Household Surveys, National Food Surveys; *Punch or the London Charivari.*

Organizations

British Library; British Museum; CERAM Research; The Pepys Librarian, Magdalene Collage, Cambridge; The Wellcome Centre Medical Photographic Library; Office of Health Economics; General Register Office (Scotland); General Register Office (Northern Ireland); General Register Office (England and Wales); Department of Health and Social Security; National Environmental Technology Centre; Public Health Laboratory Service – Communicable Disease Surveillance Centre; International Agency for Research on Cancer; World Health Organization Government Actuary's Department; Meteorological Office; National Radiological Protection Board; Child Growth Foundation; British Airways; Greenpeace; Office of National Statistics; Greater Glasgow Health Board; The Jenner Museum, Gloucester; Duckworth Collection, University of Cambridge.

Individuals

Drs Gerald F. Pyle and K. David Patterson, University of North Carolina – Charlotte, USA; Dr J. Whitelegg, University of Lancaster; Lise Moore; Mr A. Yale, Radiology, University Hospital of Wales; Dr M. D. Crane, Radiology, Llandough Hospital and Community NHS Trust; Professor M. H. Kaufmann, University of Edinburgh; Dr Charlotte Roberts, University of Bradford.

1

Introduction

The World Health Organization has defined health as follows: 'The WHO concept of health as a state of physical, mental and social well-being and not only the absence of disease and disability views health as a positive condition involving the whole person in the context of his/her situation.'[1] Health is not an absolute quantity, but a concept whose standards are continually changing in different lands with the acquisition of knowledge and the establishment of cultural objectives. To be truly healthy a person should enjoy a balanced relationship of the body and mind and be in complete harmony with the external environment (ecological equilibrium). In this context 'environment' (nurture) refers to the whole gamut of influences which impinge on individuals and affect their well-being: it includes the physical surroundings of land, sea and air, the viruses, bacteria and other organisms of the biological environment together with the socio-economic complexities of the human environment. The term embraces not only direct exposure, such as may occur in the workplace or be derived from cultural habits, but also the complex interplay of all hazards or stimuli which modify the individual's reaction to his environment.

In contrast, sick or *dis*eased persons represent maladjustment or maladaptation in the environment (ecological disequilibrium). Disease is a reaction between individuals and the stresses, strains and other adverse factors of their physical, biological and social milieu, the response being conditioned by the genetic make-up (i.e. the *internal* environment or inborn constitution; nature) of the individual.

The present study examines the main diseases which, at one time or another, throughout the ages, have affected the people of Britain. It is a multidisciplinary study, but since the emphasis is on the spatial spread of disease, spatial variability of disease and spatial relationships and inter-relationships of environmental and aetiological factors, it is best considered a study in medical geography rather than in epidemiology or human ecology. Medical geography may be defined as the comparative study of the spatial distribution of diseases and their possible causes. Different ethnic, national or social groups may be involved. The subject is closely related to epidemiology and disease ecology, except that in medical geography the emphasis is on location or place, on patterns of disease distribution and on the spatial aspects of environmental interrelationships.[2]

Much of the subject matter of medical geography is as old as Hippocrates, and his *De aere, aquis et locis* (On Airs, Waters and Places) is well known. Even the term 'medical geography' has been current in Britain for ninety or so years, and was used by Dr Alfred Haviland in his *Geographical Distribution of Disease in Great Britain* (1892). Medical geography itself was somewhat usurped after Pasteur introduced the germ theory of infectious disease and heralded the science of bacteriology in the late nineteenth century. Now, however, with the increasing control or eradication of infectious diseases and, in so-called developed countries such as Britain, the ever-increasing concern with the degenerative diseases of later and middle life, the new methods and techniques of medical geography are being called upon to determine the geographical distribution of these diseases in an attempt to relate differences in incidence to local environmental and behavioural factors which may afford pointers to possible causal relationships.

Human beings are, and always have been, part of the ecosystem.[3] They are but one species in relation to the total evolutionary history. Even so, differing from other members of the animal kingdom which have either suffered extinction or undergone genetic evolution as a result of changes of environment, the human race has undergone cultural development which, in large measure, has overtaken its genetic evolution. Instead of the environment shaping their genetic destiny, people now shape their environment. Of the changes they have brought about, some, such as improved housing, water supply and sanitation, have been good, some, such as atmospheric and water pollution and excessive noise, are obviously harmful; others, such as nuclear explosions, might well prove catastrophic. Nuclear radiations are measurably significant, not only in their capacity for environmental change but also for their effects on man's health and genetic stability.

Infectious diseases have been controlled in Britain chiefly by a combination of enlightened environmental changes, health legislation and education; and secondly by therapeutic advances. Health problems now are of a more chronic kind and include heart disease, cancer, bronchitis, mental illness and accidents. In large towns people live in a polluted atmosphere to which their lungs respond with respiratory disorders and cancerous growths. The tempo of life is such as to create mental tensions and stress which can, in their turn, encourage heart disease. Overcrowding in large communities assists the spread of droplet infections; motor vehicles constitute an ever-present accident hazard, and there is persistent and irritating noise. War itself now approaches the annihilation stage, for it includes nuclear devices, germs and chemicals.[4]

Yet technology helps modify and control the environment, medical care and research have taken the terror from many of the diseases that were once fatal, and there are simple means of birth control for regulating the size of the population. No longer in Britain is there a poor, ignorant and rural population exposed to hunger, malnutrition and the killing diseases of infancy, childhood and early adult life as there was in previous centuries. Instead, the population is relatively affluent, informed and largely urbanized and industrialized. Even so, it is scourged by diseases of the cardiovascular system, respiratory system, by cancer and mental illness.

Environmental improvements, particularly in housing, nutrition and health education, together with improvements in health care have resulted in a far greater life expectancy for the average person. The people of Britain today are bigger and healthier than ever before. Expectation of life increased from about 18 years in prehistoric times to about 33 years in the Middle Ages. Now, in the closing years of the twentieth century, it is well beyond the biblical three score years and ten. In the 1860s expectation of life at birth for a boy was little more than 43 years; in the 1960s it was about 68 years. In the 1990s it is 75 years for men and 79 years for women in England and Wales, in Scotland it is 71.5 and 77 years respectively, while in Northern Ireland the figures are 72.5 years for men and 78.4 for women (Fig. 1.1). Expectation of life at birth is currently increasing by about two years every decade. Such increases in longevity provide a good indicator of the health and status of the nation, though 'days of absence from work' or 'the number of visits to the general practitioner' probably represent more satisfactory indices. Disease is rarely the result of a single factor ('specific aetiology', see p.169) but rather a combination of related factors. For instance, at a WHO conference on the prevention and control of cardiovascular diseases, a group of at least eight risk factors was deemed to be significant in coronary artery disease: high cholesterol or blood lipid levels (lipid being a general term that includes fats and fatlike compounds), hypertension, cigarette-smoking, physical inactivity, overweight or obesity, alcohol, nervous stress, diabetes mellitus, and genetic factors.[5] Much speculation exists as to the role played by each of these factors and their relative importance. The obese are more prone to diabetes; people under stress take little exercise; racial and genetic differences are often associated in diet. Obesity, exercise and diet are themselves all interrelated. When examining the interaction and correlation between human diseases and individual environment or genetic factors, it is more or less inevitable that other factors will interfere with the conclusions. Causes of disease or illness are rarely simple or even static; rather, they are multi-factorial. Neither are diseases immutable throughout history. What is clear now is that modern descriptions of a disease need not necessarily conform to its course throughout history.

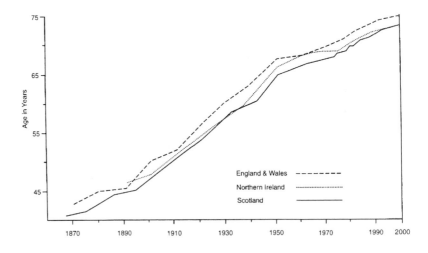

Fig. 1.1(a) Expectation of life (in years) at birth, 1870–2000: males (data from the Registrars General for England and Wales, Scotland, and Northern Ireland)

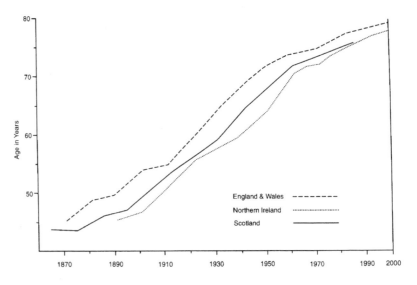

Fig. 1.1(b) Expectation of life (in years) at birth, 1870–2000: females (data from the Registrars General for England and Wales, Scotland, and Northern Ireland)

At one time diseases were thought to be associated with corrupt air (due to putrid effluvia from corpses of men and animals, miasmas from the ground, marshes, stagnant air in narrow streets etc.), at others with eclipses, storms, comets and exotic meteorological events. Such views assumed illness to be exogenous, i.e. coming from outside the body. In Hippocratic theory 'temperaments' and 'humours' were invoked. Temperaments were considered to reflect the balance between the natural elements (air, fire, earth and water), and humours were part of an individual's make-up (blood, phlegm, yellow bile and black bile) (see p.105). With the discovery of the microbe and the elaboration of Pasteur's model of specific aetiology (i.e. the disease-specific approach) all medical conceptions of illness or disease were transformed and hygienics acquired a new content. In the closing years of the twentieth century life-style or the modern way of life appears to predispose to illness and is the prime paradigm for the causality of illness. It is an integrating concept with an infinite number of possibilities and an infinitely variable content. Analysis of the interrelationships between the different variables permits an advancement in the understanding of disease.

In a broad sense every disease is caused either by environmental factors or by genetic factors. Since human response to environmental hazards is conditioned by the inborn constitution or genetic make-up of the individual, a brief outline of Britain's racial history and gene geography is first presented (chapter 2). There follows consideration of a selection of those environmental hazards or risk factors thought likely to promote disease (chapters 3–5). In the remaining chapters (6–15) a synthetic or holistic approach is adopted. Attention in this, the larger part of the book, is directed to a demonstration of the synthesis of relationships and interrelationships of people, environment and disease at selected stages in British history. For each stage or 'period-picture', a normality[6] or normal state is assumed during which the populace and environment are considered to be in a state of symbiosis or mutual equilibrium. It might be questioned if such a state exists or ever really existed, and if it did, how it should be measured. A range of normal values for individual characters of structure or formation is accepted and defined by statistical constants, but a man or woman is something more than his or her parts. Assessments of a normal person vary from age to age, and also among clinicians, actuaries, sociologists, psychologists and the various branches of the health service. In each case 'normality' implies fitness for a purpose. But for what purpose? A primitive hunter may have been adjusted to a life of hunting wild beasts but hardly for work in a twentieth-century city office; similarly, a bank clerk is not well fitted for coal-mining, sheep-shearing, mountaineering, or polar exploration. A definition of normality is elusive. For the purposes of this book the average person's expectation of life at birth is thought to be a reasonable yardstick.

Throughout history, people must have become better adapted to their ever-changing environments or else must have adapted their environment immeasurably better to themselves. There is either a strong argument for the survival of the physically fitter person or the survival of the civilly fitter society. Either the individual man or woman is constitutionally fitter to survive today or is mentally fitter, that is, better able to organize their social surroundings. Both conclusions point definitely to an evolutionary progress.

The selection of 'period pictures' in chapters 6–15 has been a matter of some difficulty and is open to criticism. It is known that there is much in common between one period and another; equally there is a great deal that is different. It is thought that the selection presented offers a reasonable insight into the general evolution of patterns of human disease in Britain from pre-Norman times to the present.

2

People in Britain

To examine human health and disease simply in terms of a person's relationships with the external environment is like discussing the working of a machine without reference to the material which it will have to process. Environmental influences act on people, but their responses, in almost every case, are limited by hereditary or genetic factors. It is necessary, therefore, to gain some insight into the human material which makes up the population of Britain.

Through the centuries Britain has been the final landfall and focus of fusion for emigrating people from Europe. Not much is known about the earliest settlers of this country except that they came from the Mediterranean. The hunters, fishers and gatherers of Palaeolithic and Mesolithic times were few in number and of low stature, averaging 5 foot 3 inches. The first farmers of Neolithic times were also small, with dark hair and long heads. Some anthropologists maintain that these physical characteristics are still prevalent in populations in parts of Wales and other areas of western Britain. After 2000 BC, broad-headed Bronze Age peoples intermixed with them (Fig. 2.1).

Celts began to settle fairly peacefully in the lowlands of southern and eastern England from about 750 to 500 BC after pressure of increasing population had pushed them out of their homelands in the north German plain and the Rhinelands. A major wave of Celtic immigration to Britain came about 300 BC from northern France and Brittany. These people farmed and traded in southern England and on the hillsides of west and north Britain. A third wave of Celtic peoples came into south-east England after 100 BC. These were mainly Belgic tribes, retreating before the advancing Roman conquerors of Gaul.

The Celts remained virtually undisturbed in Britain until the main Roman invasion, planned by the Emperor Claudius, in AD 43. In many respects this invasion was militarily only partially successful. Throughout the greater part of what was to become Scotland the indigenous population lived virtually undisturbed during the period of the Roman 'conquest'; the Roman advance and presence there was a short-lived affair.

This was probably the case in many of the remote parts of what are now

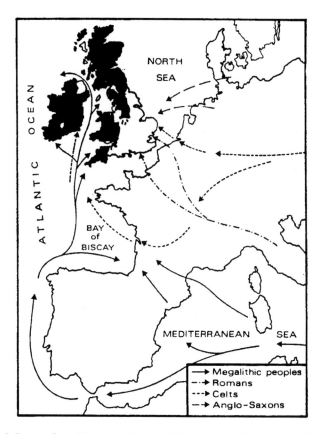

Fig. 2.1 Routes from Europe to Britain followed by early peoples. The shaded areas comprise the 'Highland Zone' of Britain

northern England and Wales. Even in the lowlands of south and east England, the Civil Zone of Roman Britain, the population remained basically Celtic, though Romano-British is the double adjective used to describe them.

West Gloucestershire and east Somerset were well populated at this time, but there were large tracts of the Midlands, particularly Warwickshire, which were very thinly inhabited. The comparatively densely populated areas of north Kent and the Sussex coast immediately adjoined the Kentish and Sussex Weald, where Romano-British remains hardly occur.

Early in the fifth century the east coast of Britain suffered invasions by Angles, Saxons, Jutes and Friesians, mainly fair people who were basically Teutonic (i.e. Germanic). These earlier invasions were followed by movements of colonizers who have left their old tribal names in East Anglia (East Angles), Essex (East Saxons), Sussex (South Saxons), Wessex (West Saxons), etc. Wessex, particularly around the time of Alfred, became an

Fig. 2.2 Scandinavian settlement of the eighth, ninth and tenth centuries –
Danes in the east and Norse by way of the western seas

influential kingdom but was frequently challenged by Mercia which occupied much of the Midlands and the Welsh borderland. Here the great
earthwork of Offa's Dyke[1] formed a treaty boundary between Anglo-Saxon
England and the Celtic provinces of Wales.

Except for parts of its south, particularly its south-east coast, much of
Scotland remained undisturbed by the Anglo-Saxon invaders and colonists.
Yet the area was open to other incursions, particularly from the Scots
(Scotti) who originated in what is now Ulster (Northern Ireland). In the
fifth century they crossed into Argyll and founded the kingdom of
Dalriada. In the eighth century the Scots of Dalriada joined the
Caledonians or Picts (who appear to have been a mixture of Celtic and
earlier peoples) and founded the territory to which they give their name –
Scotland. In the south and west of Scotland was another Celtic group – the
Britons of Strathclyde – whose language and general cultural affinities were

with the people of north-west England, Wales and the south-west peninsula of England.

Norsemen (Vikings) were established in Orkney by the eighth century and from there colonized the north of Scotland and the Hebrides; later they reached the Isle of Man and Ireland, and from Ireland spread to south-west Scotland[2] and south to the Cheshire coast. They were not just warriors, but farmers and their families. They brought with them their language and law, and their cultural influence has remained to this day.

From the ninth century, Danes plundered and later colonized much of eastern England from the Tees to the Thames and set up the Danelaw (Fig. 2.2). They proved a great threat to the Saxon kingdom of Wessex.

The next and last successful invasion of Britain was made by Normans from France, who themselves were of Viking or Scandinavian origin. This meant little more than the replacement of English nobles by Norman nobles and the introduction of French as the language of the upper classes. The feudal system was introduced into south-eastern England, and some common grazing lands and forests were enclosed as hunting grounds for nobles, not least the New Forest of the Hampshire Basin.

Environmental contrasts between the 'Highland Zone' in the north and the 'Lowland Zone' of the south and east (Fig. 2.1) played a part in developing important socio-cultural differences in the population of Britain. Many of these differences remain to this day, despite the very considerable mobility of people and the levelling influence of such mass media as the newspaper, radio and television. The Highland Zone, which in the past was remote and difficult to invade and conquer, continues to preserve characteristics of the ancient peoples who lived there. In many ways it was and continues to be a region of cultural absorption; the Lowland Zone, on the other hand, easy of access across the Channel, is one of cultural replacement. The people of the Lowland Zone of Britain reflect in large measure the characteristics of succeeding waves of invaders and of the immigrants who have settled there.

The south-east of England continues to receive incomers from Scotland, Ireland and Wales, various parts of Europe, white, coloured and black immigrants from Australia, New Zealand, the Caribbean, Africa, India, Pakistan and Bangladesh. More recent migration within the UK has seen a number of the coloured immigrants establishing themselves in Greater London (e.g. Brent, Tower Hamlets, Hackney, Newham), Leicester, Slough, the West Midlands, the Pennine conurbations, Liverpool and Glasgow. Many of their children have been born in this country. Britain, the focus of fusion of so many racial strains, is today a country of considerable ethnic diversity and is as much a creation of immigration as is the USA.

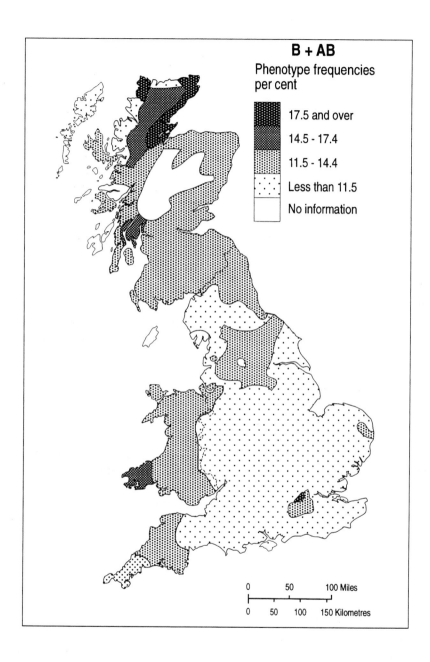

Fig. 2.3 Distribution of blood group A in Britain (based on Kopec (1971), Brown (1965) and unpublished data supplied by Glasgow and West of Scotland Blood Transfusion Service)

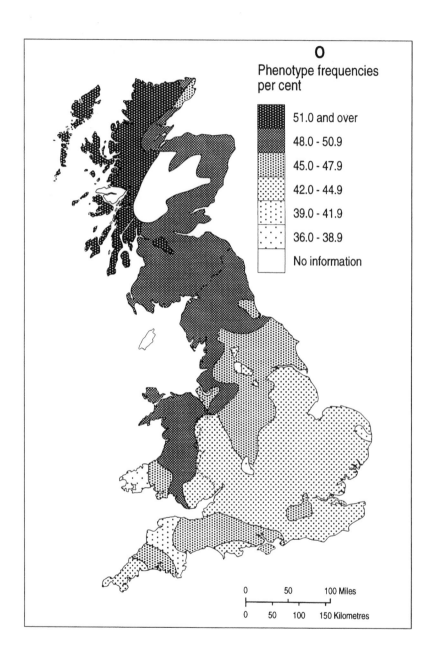

Fig. 2.4 Distribution of blood group O in Britain (based on Kopec (1971),
Brown (1965) and unpublished data supplied by Glasgow and West of Scotland
Blood Transfusion Service)

The ancient patterns of distribution of ancestral populations in Britain have become blurred by movements and intermarriage of people, but the different frequencies of blood groups in the different parts of the country (based on blood donor evidence) continue to lend support to the above summary of the peopling of these islands.

In respect of certain substances on the red cells, blood may be classified into four types, respectively O, A, B, AB. These blood types are determined by heredity and so their frequencies in a population are a useful pointer to its ancestry. AB is uncommon in Britain but, with group B, may be found locally in 5 per cent of the people in eastern England and up to 25 per cent in western Britain. Most people have blood of type O or type A. In England, south of a line running from North Yorkshire to the Mersey and Severn estuaries and also in south Pembrokeshire ('Little England') up to 40 per cent of the population has blood of group A (Fig. 2.3). Similar proportions occur in the populations of countries in Europe from which Anglo-Saxon and Viking invaders and settlers came to these parts of England and Wales.[2] Elsewhere in Britain the percentage of the population with blood group A decreases to the west and north.

The O gene is irregularly distributed over much of western Europe but there are some areas with figures of 60–70 per cent. In Scotland there are a few localities where 60 per cent of the population is of blood group O but elsewhere the values are between 43 and 50 per cent (Fig. 2.4). Values decrease from west to east and from north to south. High frequencies of O group may indicate survival of characteristics of Neolithic and later prehistoric settlers who came to Britain along the western sea routes. Similar high figures occur among the Icelanders, the Basques, in parts of north-west France and in Sardinia. High frequencies of blood group O in southern Scotland and parts of south Lancashire are probably accounted for by relatively recent Irish immigration.

The B blood group gene occurs with frequencies of 5 to 10 per cent over the whole of Britain although there is a rise in frequency in the north and west in more difficult and remote areas which were preferred by prehistoric but not by later peoples (Fig. 2.5). In the interior moorlands of Wales (the Black Mountains of Carmarthenshire, the Plynlimon plateau of Central Wales and the Hiraethog moorlands of Denbighshire) high frequencies, 16.9 per cent, 13.8 per cent, and 9.5 per cent respectively compared with the national average of 6 to 7 per cent, suggest the survival of characteristics which may go back into prehistory.

In anthropometric terms people in blood group A are usually slightly taller and more round-headed than average, usually with blue eyes and fair pigmentation. Shorter, longer-headed and darker-pigmented people are usually of blood group O.

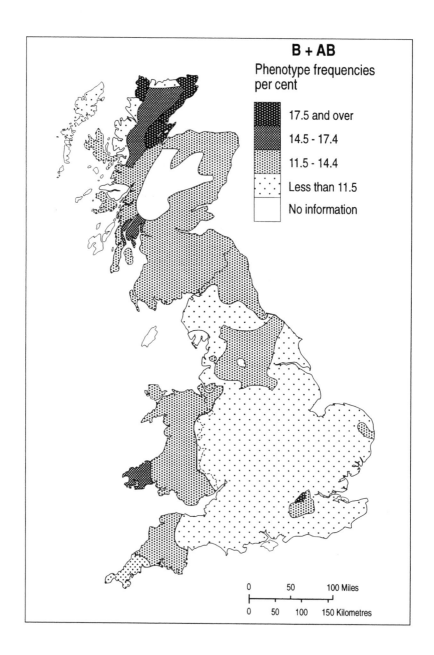

Fig. 2.5 Distribution of blood groups B and AB in Britain (based on Kopec (1971), Brown (1965) and unpublished data supplied by Glasgow and West of Scotland Blood Transfusion Service)

Some associations between the ABO blood groups and disease have been tested beyond all reasonable doubt. The evidence for three associations appears to be overwhelming. The incidence of peptic ulcer is 40 per cent higher in persons of group O than in those belonging to groups A, B and AB. The increased risk attaching to group O is about 25 per cent commoner in gastric ulcer. It has been established that cancer of the stomach is about 25 per cent more common in persons of group A than in those of other groups. Pernicious anaemia, a disease related to the digestive tract, has a similar group A association. Blood group A also appears to have an association with diabetes. Table 2.1 summarizes the known claims for disease and blood group associations. Side by side with the positive results have been negative findings for ABO blood groups in the case of a number of other diseases. These include cancers of various sites not listed in Table 2.1, toxaemia of pregnancy and hypertension.

It is questionable whether the demonstrated associations are truly causal in the sense that a person of group A is intrinsically more liable to cancer of the stomach or whether persons of other blood groups are protected against the disease. Similarly it may not be that group O carries a liability to peptic

Table 2.1 Associations between blood group phenotypes and disease

Disease	Associated ABO phenotype
Broncho-pneumonia	A or AB
Bubonic plague	O
Cancer of the cervix	A
Cancer of the pancreas	A
Cancer of the prostate	A
Cancer of the stomach	A
Diabetes mellitus	A
Duodenal ulcer	O
Gastric ulcer	O
Infantile diarrhoea	A
Influenza virus A$_2$	O
Paralytic poliomyelitis	B
Pernicious anaemia	A
Pituitary adenoma	O
Plague	O
Rheumatic fever	A, B
Salivary gland tumours	A
Smallpox	O
Syphilis	B and AB
Tumours of the ovary	A
Typhoid and paratyphoid	O

ulcer but that other groups have a special protection against it. At present it seems possible that the associations are directly causal,[3] although Weiner is of the opinion that they are almost all fallacious.[4]

Differences of ABO blood groups are at least as old as the human species, and the definite perpetuation of a polymorphism of this kind must depend on a balance of selective forces favouring the existence of a mixture of different genetic types in the population. The balance of equilibrium is of a dynamic rather than a static kind, an equilibrium moreover which is liable to be changed, albeit slowly, by changes in environmental conditions. Researches into the synthesis of amino acids related to the origins of life have shown that the very existence of the chemicals which influence or constitute heredity depend on certain conditions and stimuli. They require the existence of a particular environment. Furthermore, the basic laws of random variation and natural selection ensure that only the creatures that can withstand their environment will pass on their genetic characteristics, as only they will survive to do so. Genes and environment, nature and nurture, interact together throughout life with an intimacy and complexity yet to be fully understood. Are environment and heredity therefore really irreconcilably opposite poles or are they one and the same thing?

Blood-group types, gene frequencies and the science of gene geography support the documentary evidence of the movement into these islands of the Celts, Romans, Anglo-Saxons, Jutes, Normans and Vikings, and also of the more recent migrations of Afro-Caribbeans and Asians who, in their turn, brought with them their own patterns of gene frequencies. Subsequent inter-marriage and assimilation among the white-skinned people and the coloured races with white have brought about the considerable biological pot-pourri and heterogeneity of the present population of Britain, which by a mid-1995 estimate totalled 58,605,760 (48.9 million in England, 5.1 million in Scotland, 2.9 million in Wales and 1.6 million in Northern Ireland).

The differentiation of the blood groups has been followed by spectacular advances in the study of genes. Genes are segments or strands of the chemical deoxyribonucleic acid (DNA) found in chromosomes in all body cells. They contain coded instructions to make the genetic blueprint or building blocks of life, i.e. heredity. Genes carry their biological heritage or ancestral history, though, through constant conflict with the external environment, there is much inherited variation. As with blood groups, every person's DNA profile is different. There is a genetic basis to every human characteristic, from eye colour to personality.

In the context of this book the diseases resulting from *imperfect* or altered genes are of special interest. They are inherited diseases. Imperfections in genes follow from alterations in the genetic code and mutational events. Altered genes give rise to a variety of inherited disorders which traditional medicine has so far failed to cure. They include such conditions as cystic fibrosis, muscular dystrophy, haemophilia and Huntington's disease. These are caused by a defect in a single gene. Other inherited diseases such as childhood diabetes, mental illness, cancer and heart diseases reflect the interaction of several ('polygenic') genes with factors related to the external environment. Predisposition or susceptibility on the part of individuals interacting with external (exogenous) risk factors can, in the course of time, cause the diseases to manifest themselves. Cystic fibrosis is the most prevalent single gene disorder in Britain. In it, alteration in mucus reduces the lung function and interferes with breathing. In sex-linked muscular dystrophy there is progressive weakening of the muscles. This condition often begins in childhood. Haemophilia is caused by a sex-linked recessive gene which affects males and is transmitted by apparently normal females. Blood clots very slowly in this disease and haemorrhaging is very difficult to control. Queen Victoria (1819–1901) was a carrier and, through her daughters, passed on the disorder to other European royal families. Huntington's disease is a hereditary neuro-degenerative disorder which strikes people in middle age.

Other inherited diseases include Down's Syndrome, Tay-Sach's Disease, Phenylketonuria (PKU), Alzheimer's Disease, and amyotrophic lateral sclerosis. Down's Syndrome is a congenital condition originally called mongolism. It is strictly a chromosome abnormality caused by the inheritance of three copies of chromosome 21 instead of the normal two. Tay-Sach's Disease is a single-gene recessive disorder which strikes before the age of four. It is untreatable and fatal. Children born with the PKU gene are at risk of suffering severe mental retardation, phenylketonuria, unless commenced on a special diet soon after birth. Senile dementia of the Alzheimer type (SDAT) is a neuro-degenerative condition but not straightforwardly genetic. The famed British mathematician and physicist, Professor Stephen Hawking, is a victim of the untreatable nerve disorder amyotrophic lateral sclerosis (ALS) which has a genetic component in a percentage of cases.

Considerable research is currently under way with the object of identifying the altered genes responsible for inherited diseases. Results will enable predictive testing of asymptomatic individuals and in certain cases, make gene therapy a possibility. This involves the manipulation of an individual's genetic material. Modifications can be made which involve inserting a missing gene or else eliminating a pathogenic gene. There is, however, a downside. Adverse test results can provide upsetting knowledge and involve detrimental psychological effects and emotional pitfalls for individuals and families.

Gene therapy, involving genetic engineering for the treatment of inherited disease, holds great promise, so much so that several companies are endeavouring to buy and patent specific parts of genes (DNA fragments). It is fervently to be hoped that ethical values will be fully respected and that genetic engineering itself will be governed by respect for life and human dignity.

3

Health Hazards of the Physical Environment

The air, water and land are physical factors of the environment. From the time of Hippocrates, climatic factors have been postulated as influencing, either favourably or unfavourably, a person's well-being. Well-known British historical treatises in this field include Goad's *Astro-meterologica* (1686), Arbuthnot's *An Essay Concerning the Effects of Air on Human Bodies* (1733), Huxham's *Observationes de aere et morbis epidemicis* (1739), and Clarke's *The Influence of Climate in the Prevention and Cure of Chronic Diseases* (1830).

The difficulty all along is to isolate, from the many components which constitute 'climate', specific factors for detailed analysis. The position of Britain on planet Earth, between latitudes 50°N and 60°N, east of the Atlantic Ocean and west of the great land mass of Eurasia, is the most important factor in both its weather and its climate. The net (*not* prevailing) air movement in these latitudes is from west to east, and since air moving in this direction has normally had a long track over the ocean the climate is generally rainy and equable. There are no marked dry seasons as in, say, tropical or subtropical latitudes. Average annual temperatures are relatively high, though they vary appreciably with latitude, altitude, proximity to the sea, exposure, shelter, and other local features. In the Scilly Isles the average temperature is 8.3°C in January and 16°C in July. London is less equable: the January average is 5°C and the July average is 17.2°C. The more northerly latitude of Aberdeen is reflected in its lower average (January 3.3°C) and July (13.9°C) temperatures (Figs 3.1–3.3).

The effects of temperature on the human body are largely a matter of metabolism and respiratory fatigue. Because internal heat generated by metabolic functions must be dissipated, any impediment to heat loss such as occurs with the high temperatures of tropical climates can depress body functions, lower general vitality and predispose a person to infectious disease. Conversely, greater ease of body heat loss associated with the lower temperatures of temperate latitudes directly stimulates vitality and quickens body functions. Minimum metabolism is observed at 20°C to

Fig. 3.1 Average actual daily mean temperature for January in the British Isles

25°C. Below 20°C and above 25°C there is a tendency to increased metabolic rate.[1] It is possible to predict with certainty only that the extremes of heat and cold are definitely harmful and that moderately hot conditions increase susceptibility to intestinal diseases and moderately cold conditions increase susceptibility to respiratory diseases. Injury produced by excessive heat includes prickly heat, tropical neurasthenia, heat exhaustion and heat stroke, but these are rare in Britain. Cold injury includes chilblains, frostbite and hypothermia.[2] British winters are commonly associated with an increase in upper respiratory infections and deaths due to heart disease and stroke. Cold and lack of natural light curtail many forms of outdoor recreation in winter, and there is a tendency for people to crowd together more in places of public entertainment. Natural ventilation in such places,

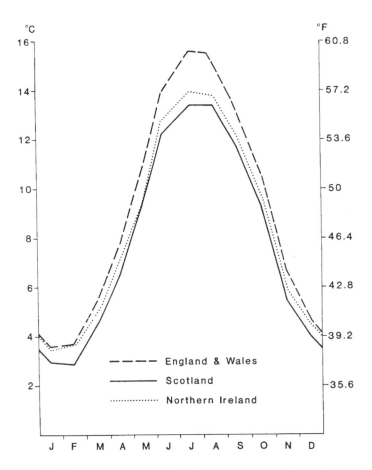

Fig. 3.2 Mean daily temperatures at sea level, 1951–80, in England and Wales, Scotland and Northern Ireland

as indeed in the home, factory, office, bus and train, is frequently reduced to conserve heat, and at the same time there is a tendency to excessive central or artificial heating. Conditions of overcrowding, underventilation and overheating are particularly favourable for droplet infections. The common cold, arguably the most widespread infectious disease, is not necessarily associated with cold weather. It is the world's most prevalent illness and comprises a whole series of infections caused by several viruses which are quick to mutate or change.

Rainfall is highest on the high ground of the north and west of Britain. Similarly, the number of rain days is greater in the west (Fig. 3.4). There are more than 250 rain days a year on the extreme western coast and fewer than 175 in some parts of the east. Throughout most of the high ground

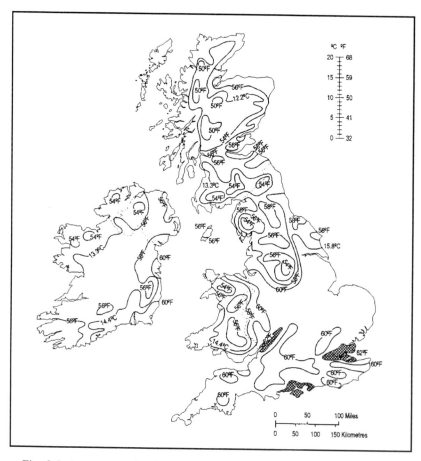

Fig. 3.3 Average actual daily mean temperatures for July in the British Isles

in the north and west the average is over 200 rain days a year. Figure 3.5 shows the seasonal incidence of rainfall in England and Wales, Scotland and Northern Ireland. Popular opinion holds that damp increases individual susceptibility to infection, but volunteers at the Common Cold Research Unit, Salisbury, sitting in draughty passages and wearing damp clothing, were none the worse for their experience. Rheumatic disorders in their several manifestations have long been associated both by the general public and the medical profession with dampness or sudden change of temperature.

It is not generally appreciated that, although the winter half of the year is the wettest in Britain, the *absolute* humidity (i.e. the amount of water vapour in the atmosphere) is actually at its lowest during this period and at its

Fig. 3.4 Average monthly rainfall, 1951–80, in England and Wales, Scotland and Northern Ireland

maximum in July. Waddy[3] has suggested that this seasonal low absolute humidity might exercise a drying action on the mucosa of the upper respiratory tract and lower its vitality and resistance to infection. Boyd[4] found weekly respiratory mortality to be associated equally closely with temperature and absolute humidity, but the very high correlation between these two variables prevents discrimination as to their relative importance.

Winds can impair acoustal comfort. The noise they generate ('unwanted sound') causes degrees of nervous irritation even if it is merely audible. Gales and hurricane-force winds cause structural damage leading to injury and loss of life from collapsing buildings, crashing trees, overturned motor vehicles and motor cycles.

The qualities which make some parts of the country 'relaxing' ('sedative'),

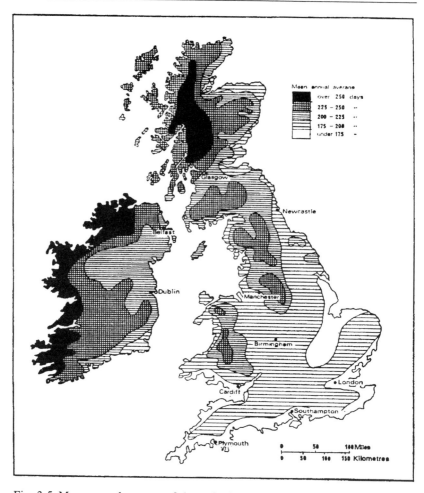

Fig. 3.5 Mean annual average of days of rain in the British Isles (days on which 0.01 inch or 0.25 mm or more of rain is recorded)

and others 'bracing' are not well understood. Wind, humidity, temperature and negative ions[5] are probably involved, though the frequency of weather changes locally is another consideration.[6] Figure 3.6 shows those parts of Britain which are considered tonic and those which are sedative. There are five categories: *very bracing* – Orkney, Shetland, the Grampian Mountains, the east coast of Scotland (Aberdeen, Dundee, Edinburgh), the north-east coast of England (Newcastle-upon-Tyne, Middlesbrough, Hull) and the north Antrim coast in Northern Ireland; *bracing* – the north-west Highlands, Grampian Mountains and southern uplands in Scotland, the whole of the east coast, part of the Sussex coast, and the north coast of Devon and Cornwall in England, the Cambrian Mountains in Wales, northern parts of

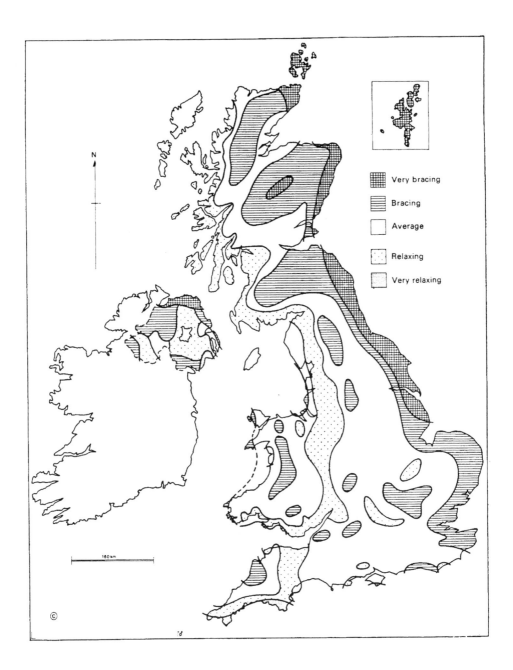

Fig. 3.6 Bracing and relaxing climates in Britain (based, in part, on Brooks, 1954)

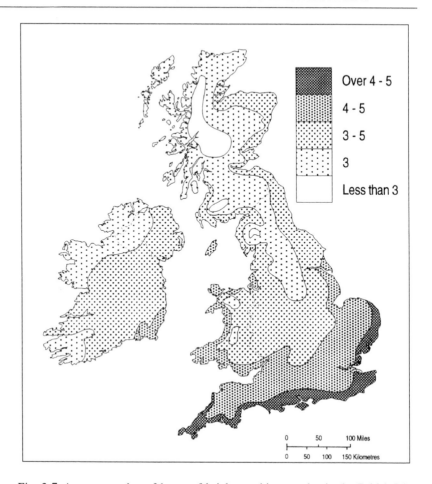

Fig. 3.7 Average number of hours of bright sunshine per day in the British Isles

Londonderry and south of the Antrim Mountains in Northern Ireland; *average* – widespread; *relaxing* – the south coast of Cornwall, Devon, south Wales and the Welsh borders and most of the low ground in the western half of England; *very relaxing* – a relatively small area on the western part of the south coast of England and an enclave between the Mourne Mountains and the sea in Northern Ireland. The main factor in a sedative climate in Britain is the moist, equable west or south winds from the Atlantic whereas exposure to east and north-east winds from the North Sea gives rise to tonic conditions.

'Relaxing' and 'bracing' qualities cannot be clearly and definitely differentiated; certainly they are not measurable.[7,8,9] The cooling power of the atmosphere, essentially a function of temperature, humidity and wind speed (their variations rather than their average values) might provide an appro-

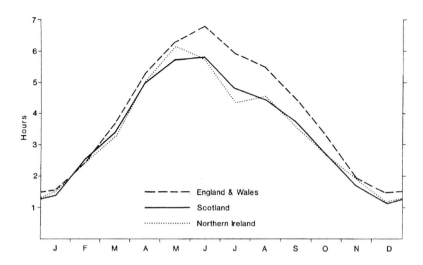

Fig. 3.8 Mean daily sunshine in England and Wales, Scotland and Northern Ireland

priate index of these qualities, with wind probably the most important.

'Windchill' is a term used to describe the cooling effects of air movement and low temperature, i.e. the dry convective power of the atmosphere. Since it is a good measure of about 80 per cent of total body heat loss, windchill correlates more closely with sensations of cold than crude temperatures. The chilling produced by a 45 mph (72 kph) wind at −7°C is about the same as that of a wind moving at 5 mph (8 kph) with a temperature of −30°C. The strong and bitterly cold winds which affected Britain in late December and early January of 1996–7 reduced already low absolute air temperatures (that is, actual thermometer readings) from 0°C to wind-chill temperatures of −21°C in parts of southern England.

Sunshine causes marked changes in a person's subjective sensations of health. Sick or well people, other than those over-sensitive to sunlight, feel better when the sun is shining. The formation of vitamin D, essential for the prevention of rickets, is stimulated by sunlight (ultra-violet rays) on the skin. Alternatively, excessive exposure to these rays during sunbathing is considered by many to be the strongest risk factor for melanoma (Figs. 3.7–3.8). Chlorofluorocarbons (CFCs) and foam plastics (polystyrene) and solvents used in the electronics industry have been reducing the concentration of ozone gas in the stratosphere. This thinning of the high-altitude ozone layer will lead to increased ultraviolet light levels, raise the incidence of some forms of skin cancer (malignant melanoma) and blindness (eye cataract), and weaken the immune system. Of the skin cancers which

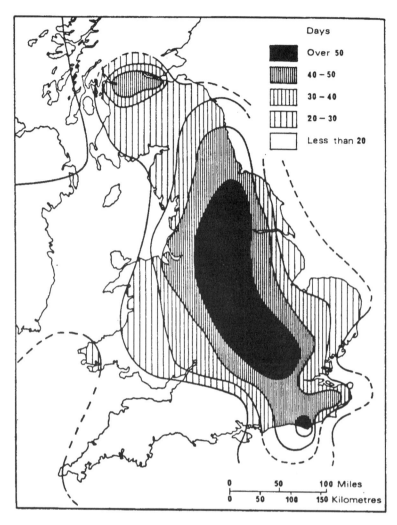

Fig. 3.9 Annual average number of occasions of thick fog in Britain (visibility less than 220 yards at 0900 hours), 1934–43 (adapted from *Climatological Atlas of British Isles 1952*)

follow prolonged exposure to the sun the majority are non-malignant melanoma ulcers.

Fog is the one weather condition in Britain which is undoubtedly and specifically responsible for an increase in morbidity and mortality (Fig. 3.9). A period of fog is always followed by an excessive number of deaths from diseases of the respiratory system and road accidents. Three types of natural fog are distinguished: (a) *radiation fog* which occurs on clear, calm evenings and is most frequent in wide damp river valleys such as the lower

Thames, Severn, Trent or Clyde valleys; (b) *hill fog* which is simply cloud with base below the level of the highest ground in an area and may form at any time of the day; (c) *advection fog* which occurs when warm moist air drifts over cold ground. It often occurs along coasts and is generally associated with a thaw after frost.

Fog is most frequent in autumn and winter, particularly over the low-lying parts of the English Midlands where the air gathers in hollows, and in the polluted parts of cities. Fogs are densest when skies are clear and winds are light (radiation fog); they are less common in coastal regions and in the Highlands of Scotland and Ireland, since autumn and winter winds are generally strong.

Until the time of the Industrial Revolution the emphasis was on fog as the embodiment of damp, causing rheumatism, 'agues' and 'fevers', but during the last century and as recently as the 1950s town fogs or smog (i.e. *smoke–fog*) had become synonymous with atmospheric pollution (see pp.32 and 52ff.).

Climate has undoubted repercussions on the patterns of human disease, but the relationship is not straightforward. In Britain, which experiences very variable and unpredictable weather conditions, it is the meteorological

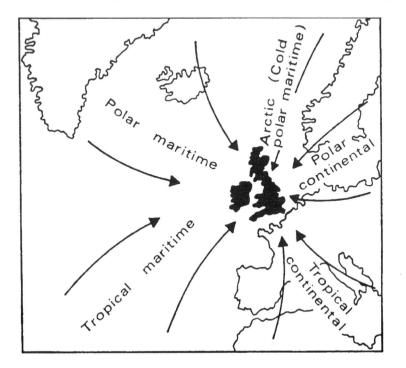

Fig. 3.10 Air masses commonly occurring in Britain

extreme rather than the mean which is important in disease, especially extremes of solar radiation, temperature, humidity and wind. The notoriously fickle character of Britain's weather arises from the frequency with which the air overlaying the country is replaced. Three main types of air, known as air masses, influence the weather of Britain – maritime tropical masses and maritime polar air masses from the Atlantic which reach the country from the south-west, west or north-west, and continental polar air masses from Europe (Fig. 3.10). The air masses arrive as air-streams, having acquired their original characteristics in distant source regions. Maritime tropical air masses from beyond the Azores bring warm, humid, settled weather in summer and unseasonal warmth in winter. When such air masses are cooled by rising over a range of hills they may produce rain. Maritime polar air masses from Greenland and the North Atlantic are very variable and turbulent, usually moderately warm at ground level but cold at higher altitudes. They are associated with brisk, gusty winds, broken cloud and plenty of sunshine. Rain associated with these air masses comes mostly in heavy showers interspersed with sunny intervals. Continental polar air masses are almost entirely limited to the winter months. They come to Britain from Scandinavia, Eastern Europe or Russia as biting east or northeast winds. They are infrequent but tend to persist for several days, bringing with them dry, bitterly cold conditions. Tropical continental air masses from southern Europe or North Africa are uncommon in Britain. When present they bring hot, dry weather, possibly a heatwave.

Progressing air masses bring their contrasting weather, though with local variations resulting from relief differences, proximity to coasts, and the presence of urban settlements. Consequently temperature, atmospheric pressure, humidity and wind velocity can vary greatly over short periods of time. Britain is rarely influenced by one air mass at a time. It is usual for the weather to be the result of two or more air masses in conflict, and it is along the boundary or 'front' between two different air masses in an area of low atmospheric pressure (i.e. a depression) that weather changes are most marked. Such fronts, especially 'cold' fronts (where a warm air mass is replaced by a colder one), are often accompanied by electrical disturbances. Nervousness, mental unrest and nervous disease such as epileptic fits have been reported as increasing on the approach of a cold front. The most extreme form of this effect is the close correlation between the number of suicides and the passage of a weather front. Some of the observed effects of the approach of disturbed weather, such as sleeplessness, may be due to the effects of rapid fluctuations of barometric pressure acting on the bloodstream. Once again, the extreme form is a proved relation between the frequency of blood-clot blockage of the arteries (thrombosis or embolism) and the passage of fronts.[10] Table 3.1 presents

Table 3.1 Reported effects of the influence of weather and climate on diseases (abridged from Tromp (1963) and assembled by Maunder (1970))

Shorter periodical effects	Long periodical effects (seasonal or pseudo-seasonal)

Lung diseases

Tuberculosis: haemoptysis suddenly increases in clinics after oppressive warm weather before thunderstorms, föhn, humid cold foggy weather or sudden heatwaves.

Increased sensitivity to tuberculin test in March and April; low during autumn.

Asthma (bronchial): increases with sudden cooling (particularly if accompanied by falling barometric pressure and rising wind speed); during high barometric pressure and fog (in W. Europe) very low asthma frequency.

Low in winter, suddenly increasing after June, maximum in late autumn (W. Europe).

Bronchitis: increasing complaints during fog (particularly in air-polluted areas) and specially if accompanied by atmospheric cooling.

High in winter, low in summer (in W. Europe).

Hay fever (and various forms of rhinitis): allergic reactions often increase during atmospheric cooling.

Hay fever is related to flowering of certain plants or grasses, different for different countries. In W. Europe usually maximum complaints in May–June.

Cancer

Skin cancer: more common with increasing number of sun-hours and increased exposure of skin to the sun.

—

Rheumatic diseases

Most forms of arthritis react on strong cooling (falling temperature; strong wind). Humidity seems to have no direct effect, only indirect through cooling.

Arthritis complaints particularly common in autumn and early winter (W. Europe).

Heart diseases

Coronary thrombosis, myocardial infarction and angina pectoris: occur more frequently shortly after a period of strong cooling.

Highest mortality in January–February (in W. Europe and northern USA), lowest July–August. In hot countries (e.g. southern USA) highest mortality in summer, lowest in winter.

Infectious diseases

Common cold: weather changes affecting thermoregulation mechanism, membrane permeability, and growth and transmission of several common cold viruses seem to initiate the diseases (e.g. very cold period followed by sudden warming up).

Maximum in February–March; increasing September–March (in W. Europe).

Influenza: relative humidity below 50 per cent and low wind speeds seem to favour the development and transmission of influenza virus.

Maximum in December–February; increasing from September–March.

a summary of the reported effects of the influence of weather and climate on diseases.

There are probably few diseases whose distribution is not affected by climate. Apart from the direct action of the elements there is the indirect action, since climate and climatic conditions determine in part the nature of the foods eaten, the quality of sanitary methods and appliances, the structure of homes, offices and factories, social and family organizations, the viability of pathogenic micro-organisms outside the body, the viability and vitality of insects and other animal factors which carry these micro-organisms. These are, in effect, the major direct and indirect agents of disease. It is hardly surprising, therefore, that it is seldom possible to isolate the influence of climate on disease.

Climatic conditions themselves have varied throughout the ages. They have changed slightly and subtly since people first arrived in Britain. Such changes may have affected their way of life and pattern of disease. Prehistoric cultivators arrived in Britain about 3000 BC, when Europe was experiencing a post-glacial climate optimum with temperatures 2°–3°C higher than now. A gradual deterioration followed which became abrupt about 500 BC, with the setting-in of a cool rainy period, though possibly with mild winters. The climate gradually became drier and probably rather warmer during the Roman period until a secondary optimum was reached between AD 800 and 1000. The recording of thirty-eight flourishing vine-yards in England, in addition to those of the king, in the Domesday Book (1085)[11] might imply summer temperatures perhaps 1°–2°C higher than at present, although there are a number of vineyards in southern Britain to this day. From the late twelfth century to around the middle of the four-teenth another climatic decline set in, but with a partial recovery thereafter to the turn of the sixteenth century. Between 1550 and 1850 the seasons were cooler; they were also drier, particularly in winters during the first half of the eighteenth century.

This cool period is often called the 'Little Ice Age'. The bad weather damaged many harvests, particularly in the early part of the period. This may be one reason for the widespread hardship and distress during the sixteenth century (p.100). The first half of the twentieth century saw an improvement in the climate and an increase of temperatures, particularly in winter although this was accompanied by increased rainfall and reduced sunshine. Experience after the 1940s suggested that the climate was start-ing to deteriorate, with a tendency to colder springs, cooler, wetter summers, somewhat warmer autumns and colder winters. In recent years the consensus among climatologists is that the man-made pollution of the atmosphere by a range of gases (carbon dioxide, nitrous oxide, methane, low-level ozone, factory emissions etc.), opaque or relatively impervious to outgoing long-wave radiation, acts as a barrier and creates a 'greenhouse effect', causing a rise in temperatures (global warming).

It seems unlikely that future climatic change (showing clearly in statistics yet probably barely susceptible to the individual) brought about by the 'greenhouse effect' and damage to the ozone[12] layer, will markedly influence the future pattern of disease in Britain,[13] but see chapter 15 (p.259). Nevertheless it is salutary to be reminded that Britain's climate is always changing, often subtly, usually temporarily, or often in different directions at different times of the year. It is the occasional weather extreme rather than any long-term change in normal or average conditions which is the more significant in terms of morbidity or mortality. The frequency with which weather extremes overlap critical threshold values and trigger off chain reactions, thereby encouraging or inhibiting certain kinds of infections or other diseases, is of greater importance than any slight climatic change, whether it be amelioration or deterioration.

Apart from its weather and climate, Britain represents an amazing variety of other physical environmental conditions. This is particularly true in the variations in general height and form of the land. Nevertheless a broad dichotomy or dualism is clearly recognizable. The dividing line follows an irregular course from the mouth of the River Tees in the north-east to the north of the River Exe in the south-west. West and north of the line lies Highland Britain; to the east and south is Lowland Britain (Fig. 2.1). In Highland Britain occur the major mountain and hill masses. These cool, humid, wind-swept and waterlogged uplands with thin and generally acid soils contrast markedly with conditions to the south and east. In Lowland Britain the land is seldom more than 100 metres or a few hundred feet above sea level and comprises broad plains, low-lying plateaux and scarplands. Conditions on the Mesozoic and Tertiary rocks and the less lime-deficient soils of this part of the country are, in general, more favourable to human settlement than those on the Palaeozoic rocks of Highland Britain.

Historical and cultural contrasts between the Highland and Lowland Zone have been noted. Differences in 'background radiation', in the trace elements in the soil, and in the water supply relate to differences in basic rock structure, rock type, and general relief of the land. Radiation is the term applied to a wide spectrum of energies including radio frequencies, microwaves, infra-red, visible, ultraviolet light and lasers, 'ionizing radiation', gamma and X-rays. All forms of radiation, if intense enough, may produce adverse effects on humans (i.e. damage biological molecules), but ionizing radiation is the greatest hazard. Sources of ionizing radiation are principally the members of the uranium and thorium series. They produce a background gamma-radiation and vary markedly from one locality to

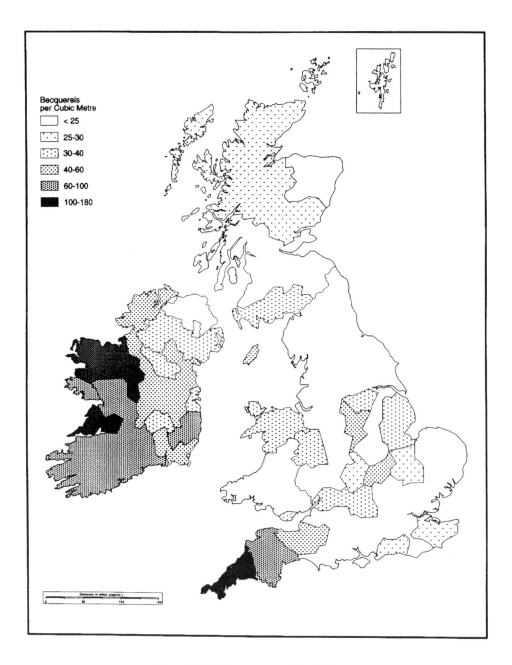

Fig. 3.11 Radon concentration indoors
(*Source*: National Radiological Protection Board)

another. Sedimentary rocks have a lower content of the radioactive elements uranium and thorium, and provide less gamma-ray background than igneous rocks. Consequently gamma-ray background from, say, the chalk in Kent or the limestone of the Cotswolds is far less than that from the granites or other igneous rocks of south-west England (Devon, Cornwall and Somerset), northern Scotland or County Down and County Armagh in Northern Ireland, which contain more uranium than elsewhere. This source of radiation is particularly significant since the cancer-causing gas, radon,[14] and its decay products can be inhaled into the lungs. In fact radon is second only to cigarette-smoking in terms of public-health impact. It delivers higher doses of radiation than nuclear power. The gas disperses quickly in the open air but quite high levels of radon can develop in confined spaces or where there is limited ventilation, as inside houses, schools, offices or in mines. Under such conditions the sensitive bronchial tissues receive substantial exposure (Fig. 3.11). Of the total annual radiation exposure, a person living in Britain typically receives 85.5 per cent from natural sources; the remaining 14.5 per cent comes from man-made (mainly medical) sources.

Rocks, together with overlying soils, can have anomalous trace-element or micro-nutrient contents. The essential trace elements are more important in the nutrition of the individual than their organic micro-nutrient counterparts, the vitamins. They cannot be synthesized as can most vitamins but must be present in the environment within a relatively narrow range of concentration. Both deficiencies and excesses kill. Soils derive their trace elements from the soil parent material, applied fertilizers, agricultural dusts and sprays, and pass on their trace-element characteristics to vegetable matter growing in them. Vegetable matter used as food may thus reflect the trace element peculiarities of the soil and of the parent geological material. Scientific evidence suggests that the presence of the inorganic elements lithium, chromium, fluorine, calcium, magnesium, sodium and potassium may make the difference between health and disease. An excess of trace elements such as mercury, lead, cadmium or selenium, whether eaten in vegetable matter or animal foods, can seriously affect health. Deficiencies of elements such as copper, iron, manganese, zinc, iodine, fluorine, cobalt and molybdenum give rise to nutritional problems.[15] Trace-element anomalies of rocks and soils may be transferred to the water supply.

Rain-water contains small quantities of dissolved atmospheric gases, particularly from oxygen, and weak-acid from carbon dioxide. Occasionally traces of other acids are present as when nitric acid droplets are formed during thunderstorms. In industrial areas, as a result of atmospheric pollutants (sulphur dioxide, nitrogen oxides, hydrogen chloride,

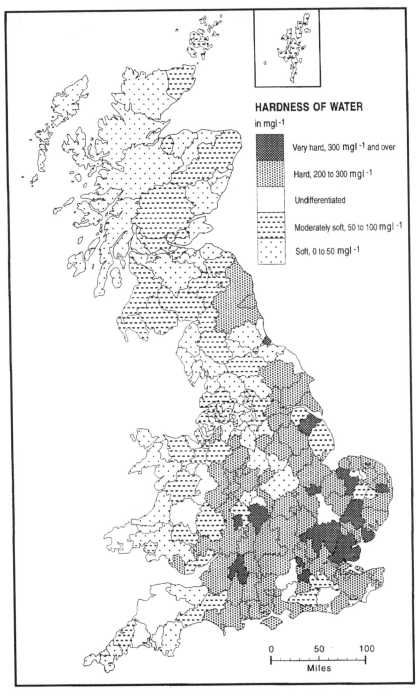

Fig. 3.12 Level of hardness (CaCO$_3$) and softness of public water supplies

etc.), rain-water may contain sulphuric acid, organic and inorganic dust and other objectionable impurities, giving so-called 'acid rain'. In Britain, the greatest average acidity of precipitation occurs in Yorkshire and Humberside and the northern part of the West Midlands. Once on the ground, rain-water may also pick up humic acids formed by decaying vegetation. Penetrating into the rocks, this acidulated water sets up slow chemical decay of the rock minerals and removes much material in solution.

The quality of the water supply, and in particular its level of hardness ($CaCO_3$), is related to the difference in chemical composition of the rocks from which the water is obtained. Hard and very hard water is usually obtained from underground water-bearing formations such as the Chalk, Bunter Sandstone and Pebble Beds, and the Carboniferous Limestone; soft and moderately soft water comes from surface supplies, particularly from the peat-covered uplands in the west and north of the country. Hardness, due to the presence of sulphates of calcium and magnesium, if present in slight degree, is usually considered good from a hygienic point of view although there is a vague and indefinite association between thyroid abnormalities such as goitre and certain types of hard water (Fig. 3.12). The frequency of occurrence of goitre in the Carboniferous Limestone county of Derbyshire led to its old name of 'Derbyshire neck'.[16] Goitre, cretinism in its various forms and hypothyroidism are manifestations of gross iodine deficiency. A lack of iodine can also result in mental retardation, physical stuntedness, deafness and muteness.

Most people appear to prefer soft water both for drinking and for domestic purposes, yet such waters have been associated by some with higher death rates from cardiovascular disease both in Britain[17] and the USA[18] (see pp. 310-11). The problem presented here is whether it reflects other factors with which both water, mortality and morbidity are associated. Hard categories of water seem to dominate the area south-east of a line from the Wash to the River Exe. The softer categories are dominant in the south-west peninsula of England, in upland Wales, much of the Pennines and the Lake District and in Scotland. Water may also acquire other chemical characteristics from the rocks through and over which it flows. Acidity, for instance, will make a solvent for certain metals, as is the case of lead piping used for plumbing in some older households. It has been suggested that sub-clinical lead exposure from drinking-water is a factor in the development of hypertension in man. Either way lead is one of the commonest toxic substances in the environment.

The spoil heaps of defunct lead, zinc and copper mines in central and north Wales[19] contain residual amounts of these metals, generally as sulphides which are changed to more soluble form by aerial oxidation and the action of acidic waters. Untreated acidic water supplies polluted by effluent from these mines have been associated with the high incidence of stomach cancer in north and mid-Wales. This association may also apply in the Leadhills of southern Scotland. Certain mineralized waters, as at Harrogate, Bath,[20] Buxton, Llandrindod, Strathpeffer and Bridge of Allan, contain agents which are thought to be of medical value. Communities living in areas where the drinking-water has a high (but less than one part per million) fluorine content have a low incidence of dental caries.

There are parts of East Anglia and the Severn–Trent area where, as a result of intensive farming methods and the extensive use of artificial fertilizers, the waters have a high nitrate content which, entering crops and the food chain, may produce adverse health effects such as gastric cancer.[21] Exploitable ground-water resources (some 30 per cent of public water supply in England and Wales is sourced from ground water) are vulnerable to contamination from activities such as intensive agriculture, slurry, silt, pesticides, fertilizers and waste dumping.

The health hazards of water are not limited to impurities in solution. Those in suspension – whether living or dead – are also dangerous. Of the living, pathogenic organisms are more important than plankton. The former cause cholera, typhoid, paratyphoid, infectious hepatitis, dysentery and gastroenteritis; others are beneficial because they play an essential role in natural purification processes. Dead impurities in suspension may consist of organic matter of decayed leaves, carcasses, animal excrement and certain industrial wastes, or of mineral matter such as fine sand or clay or industrial wastes. Clear sparkling water is often suggestive of contamination by organic matter, opalescent water indicates the presence of colloid material, yellowish water may mean sewage contamination, black-brown water the presence of vegetable matter, and red-brown the presence of iron compounds.

Such is the present demand for water in Britain that the reuse of water is being constantly extended. Two-thirds of London's water comes out of the River Thames at Laleham for purification. At this point the river has already been through the sewage systems of several Thames Valley towns. York drinks water out of the River Ouse after its tributaries have drained a number of North and West Riding towns. Nottingham takes water from the Derwent below the outflow from Derby and a large chemical works. Rivers provide most of Britain's water supply, and in inland communities they take back most of the waste from human bodies, households and factories. Modern methods of water purification (e.g. introducing chloramine, a mixture of chlorine and ammonia into the system) and the capacity of rivers for self-purification make possible the reuse of water, and where water is in short supply, second-hand water is regularly drunk and so far without ill effect.

4

Health Hazards of the Biological Environment

Throughout history vengeance of the gods for wrongdoing, corruption of the air by noxious vapours (*mal-aria*), arrows shot at victims by elves (elfshot) and imbalance of the four humours of the body (blood, phlegm, yellow bile, black bile) have been used to explain ill-health. In the early nineteenth century the miasmatic theory was evoked at a time when environmental (sanitary) reform was being introduced (p.169) but it was with the discovery of 'germs' and the advent of bacteriology a century or so ago that the mystery of infectious disease seemed to be swept away (p.169).

Despite an apparent aloofness from the biological world, a man or woman fundamentally is still an animal. *Homo sapiens* is a primate. Together they occupy a place in the economy of nature and are part of the ecosystem.[1] Together or separately they exercise a vast influence and much control over their environment but they, in their turn, are influenced by it and, as with other animals, have to contend with natural enemies. They use many species of plants and animals for food but in turn their bodies provide a rich ground for many parasites. There are several parasites that live in or within people permanently, without causing any structural change or functional disturbance. On the skin there are the staphylococci, in the mouth non-pathogenic strains of streptococci, and in the colon coliform organisms of the bowel, the *E (scherichia) coli*. In the atmosphere are pathogenic bacteria and pathogenic viruses which are responsible for the majority of human diseases. Bacteria are among the smallest living creatures. They are very much smaller than the body cells into which they penetrate or by which they are engulfed. They can be grown outside the body on laboratory media. Viruses are even smaller than bacteria. They are the most minute pathogenic organisms known, and the largest can only just be seen under the strongest power of the ordinary microscope. They exhibit the highest known degree of parasitism and cannot reproduce outside living cells.

Most micro-organisms have, in general, an exceptionally active metabolism. Most reproduce by merely dividing into two when they reach a certain size, as do most of the cells of the body. But unlike body cells, each of the new daughter cells is capable of further division. Most micro-organisms multiply at a much faster rate than the cells of higher organisms. A typical time for such a doubling is 20 minutes; thus in a single day a bacterium will reproduce 48 to 50 generations. The single bacterium thus could theoretically produce a million million cells a day. If, for instance, there is an infection of a cut by a thousand cells of a virulent streptococ-cus, these will produce something like 10 to 100 million streptococci in twelve hours if left to grow unchecked in the wound and blood. This number is sufficient to kill a man. If the reproduction rate is halved then the number of cells is reduced to nearer several thousand. The significance of bacteriostatic drugs such as the sulphonamides and antibiotics (peni-cillin, streptomycin and tetracyclines) is that they decrease the reproduction rate of infecting bacteria.

What is most interesting about the micro-organisms which can attack humans is their natural history and the ways in which they are transmitted from one person to another. It is here that the relationship between disease agents and the disease they cause on the one hand, and the physical and human environments on the other, is most clearly seen. Bacteria, rick-ettsiae and viruses may be introduced to the human body directly by inhalation, ingestion or through abrasions and wounds (as with cholera, epidemic meningitis, tetanus, typhoid fever and tuberculosis) or indirectly by a carrier or vector (as in the case of malaria, yellow fever and African sleeping sickness).

For cholera, little more than a name in Britain now but a very serious disease in the nineteenth century (pp.153ff.), there is a two-factor complex, causative organism and host. The causative organism, the vibrio cholerae (discovered by Koch in 1883) is introduced into the human body directly and, as far as is known, only man can be infected by it. Factors or stimuli thought to correlate with, and possibly govern, cholera endemicity are high temper-atures, low-lying lands, ponds and lakes, and other bodies of water rich in organic matter and salts, and shelter from the rays of the sun and from rain. These conditions are common in the Indian subcontinent where cholera is thought to have existed from the beginning of recorded history.

Smallpox, now completely eliminated from the world, is another example of the two-factor complex (pp.143ff). This acute, infectious disease, caused by the variola virus, arises from either direct or indirect contact with a preceding case of the disease. There are no natural animal carriers or natural propagation of the virus outside the human body; the virus does not live long outside the body unless it is carried more than a few feet through the air. There were serious epidemics of smallpox in the sixteenth century such as that in 1561–2 (see p.105), followed by others at various times during the seventeenth and eighteenth centuries (see pp. 119ff). The disease was present in Britain from 1840 to 1870 but the epidemic of 1900–5 was the last considerable outbreak of smallpox in these islands.

The venereal or sexually transmitted diseases (STDs) provide a further example of the two-factor complex. They are caused by spirochaetes (syphilis), bacteria (gonorrhoea), viruses (venereal warts), protozoa (trichomoniasis), fungi (thrush) and parasites (scabies) and traditionally occur among seamen and soldiers, through the medium of prostitutes.

Since 1981 there has been much concern about the spread of the human immunodeficiency virus HIV-1 which is believed to cause the acquired immune deficiency syndrome (AIDS).[2] As with STDs AIDS relates closely to the behavioural element, and more particularly with the activities of homosexual males (gays) and intravenous drug abusers (IVDA). Sexual contact is the predominant method of passing the virus from one person to another, primarily via semen and blood, but the spread can also take place in the course of therapeutic use of infected blood or blood products. Heat treatment of factors VIII and IX blood concentrates (begun in April 1985 in the ·UK) have effectively limited this mode of transmission, but not before many haemophiliacs were infected. Those who inject drugs intravenously may acquire HIV by sharing a needle or syringe with someone who is infected by the HIV-1 virus. The number of HIV-1 infected persons in the UK is probably far greater than the 28,447 positive tests for the human immunodeficiency virus antibody reported to the Communicable Disease Surveillance Centre in London up to the end of December 1996. The cumulative total of United Kingdom reports of AIDS cases (January 1982 to the end of December 1996) was 13,720, of whom about 90 per cent were males. There were 9,678 AIDS-related deaths (that is, 70.5 per cent of reported AIDS cases) in the same period.

Plague, now extinct in Britain, is a disease caused by a bacillus *Yersinia pestis*. It causes endemic infection in certain rodents and may be transmitted to humans by the bite of the rat flea *Xenopsylla cheopsis*. It is a complex of three factors: bacillus, rodent and man. Bubonic plague, the commonest form of the disease, occurs in this way. In human epidemics infection may spread from man to man by coughing up sputum producing a more rapidly fatal form which affects the lung (see pp.88ff.). The last death from plague in Britain was in 1962 when a worker at the Chemical Defence Experimental Establishment, Porton Down, Wiltshire, became accidentally infected, presumably from laboratory cultures with which he was working.

Under the name ague[3] malaria was endemic in marshy districts of England (the Fens in East Anglia, the Isle of Sheppey in the Thames estuary, along the south coast as far as the Isle of Wight and certain other more isolated areas such as the Bridgwater area of Somerset) until the beginning of the twentieth century. The last case of typical English malaria was reported in 1911. Thereafter, for a variety of reasons, indigenous malaria disappeared from Britain (Table 4.1).

Cases are now occurring among non-immune tourists and other travellers returning to Britain who do not normally reside in those parts of the Indian subcontinent and Africa where malaria is endemic. The number of cases of malaria rose from 300 in 1970 to 1,500 in 1985, with 8-10 deaths each year. In 1994, 1,800 people returning from malarious areas developed the disease and 11 died. The risk of fatality is much greater for those infected by *P. falciparum*, the most virulent of the malaria parasites, than by the other species of the parasite. A disturbing feature in some endemic areas for malaria is that there are now strains of *Plasmodium* which are resistant to prophylactic drugs (chloroquine, prognuanil and pyrimethamine) used for treatment and prevention.

The distribution of malaria and its degree of endemicity are closely related to the distribution of the various species of mosquitoes of the genus *Anopheles* which, in turn, have different bionomics, ecological characteristics and breeding habits. The disease is transmitted to humans through the injection of the sporozoites of the malaria parasite of the genus *Plasmodium*. This takes place when an infected female mosquito bites a person. Malaria represents a three-factor complex: host (man)–causative organism (*Plasmodium*)–vector (mosquito), the last two having close and direct relationships with water, air temperature and other climatic conditions. There were plenty of mosquitoes in England capable of transmitting the parasites, and there were at certain times, people in the south-east of England with malarial parasites in their blood. But the mosquitoes were, so to speak, kept too cold and sporozoites cannot develop in them. Sporozoites occasionally developed in mosquitoes in England and local people were infected by malarial parasites taken up by the mosquitoes from the blood of others. This occurred after both World Wars when many servicemen returned to Britain with malarial parasites in their blood. The species of the parasite that people were most likely to acquire in Britain were *Plasmodium vivax* and *P. malariae*; this was because the sexual cycle of these species could be completed in the mosquito at lower temperatures than can the sexual cycles of the other species of the parasites. Land drainage and reclamation have long since deprived the mosquito of its habitat in parts of the south-east of England, and malaria has been eliminated.

Typhoid, caused by a bacterium *Salmonella typhosa*, usually enters the body through the mouth in contaminated food, milk or water. Water

Table 4.1 Selected transmissible diseases which occur, or have occurred, in Britain, together with their biological and other relationships

Disease	Causative organism	Modes of transmission
Acquired immune deficiency syndrome (AIDS)	Retrovirus (HIV)	Semen, cervical and vaginal secretions, infected blood, venereal contact, intravenous drug abuse
Ankylostomiasis (hook worm)	Helminth (*Ankylostoma duodenate*)	Skin penetration
Botulism (food poisoning)	Bacterium (*Clostridium botulinum*)	Contaminated cooked meat dishes, gravies, stews, pies
Chicken pox (varicella)	Virus	Inter-person contact
Cholera	Bacterium (*Vibrio cholerae*)	Water-borne; discharges from bowels of sufferers
Common cold (acute rhinitis)	Rhinovirus (with over 100 different and common forms)	Droplet infection
Diphtheria	Bacterium (*Coryne bacterium diphtheriae*)	Infective droplets via the respiratory tract
Dysentery	Bacterium (*Shigella sp*)	Water or food
Gonorrhoea	Bacterium (*Gonococcus*)	Venereal contact
Herpes zoster (shingles)	Virus (*Herpes*)	Inter-person contact
Infectious hepatitis (A, B, C)	Hepatitis B virus	Food or drink contaminated by food handlers
Influenza	Orthomyxoviruses (H and N)	Infective droplets via the respiratory tract
Listeriosis	Bacterium (*Listerium*)	Unwashed vegetables, cook-chill and chilled processed foods, soft cheese
Malaria	Protozoa (*Plasmodium vivax*, *P. falciparium*, *P. ovale*)	*Anopheles* mosquito
Measles (morbilli)	Virus (Myxovirus group)	Infective droplets via the respiratory tract
Meningitis	Virus Bacteria (*Meningococcus*)	Droplets from the upper respiratory tract
Mumps (epidemic parotitis)	Virus	From the mouth along the parotid duct
Pertussis (whooping cough)	Bacterium (*Bordetella pertussis*)	Direct by cough droplets
Plague	Bacterium (*Yersinia pestis*)	Flea (*Xenopsylla cheopis*)
Streptococcus pneumonia	Bacterium (*Streptococcus pneumoniae*)	Infective droplets via the respiratory tract
Poliomyelitis (infantile paralysis)	Virus	Enters the system through the nose or mouth
Rubella (German measles)	Virus	Infective droplets via the respiratory tract
Salmonellosis (food poisoning)	Bacterium (*Salmonella*)	Raw milk, eggs, poultry, meat, etc.
Scarlet fever	Bacterium (*Streptococcus pyogenes*)	Infective droplets
Smallpox (Variola)	Virus	Inter-person contact
Syphilis	Bacterium (*Treponema pallidum*)	Venereal contact
Tetanus (lockjaw)	Bacterium (*Clostridium tetani*)	Skin penetration
Tinea (ring worm)	Fungus (*Microsporon*)	Direct contact
Tuberculosis	Bacterium (*Mycobacterium tuberculosis*)	Infective droplets via the respiratory tract
Typhoid	Bacterium (*Salmonella typhi*)	Water, milk and food
Typhus	Bacterium-like (*Rickettsia prowazeki*)	Louse, flea, tick, mites

contaminated by infected sewage provides a major means of spread. At one time bovine tuberculosis thrived in cows, but because of the eradication of the disease in cattle and the widespread pasteurization of milk, transmission of the disease in milk from infected cows is now extremely rare in Britain.

Certain loathsome parasitic worms (*Trichinella spiralis*) live in pigs and can infect people who eat pork sausages and other pig meat which has been insufficiently cooked; others live in dogs (*Toxicara canis*) and cats (*Toxicara cati*). The body louse (*Pediculus humanus corporis*) is an important vector of the organisms that cause endemic typhus fever, trench fever and European relapsing fever, Endemic typhus occurs in people confined in unhygienic and crowded prisons or in armies, or in people suffering from famine. The lice, infected by feeding upon a person sick with the disease, readily spread under these conditions from one person to another and transmit the causative organism of the disease as they do so.

Sewer rats can constitute a serious risk to the health of an individual. They carry in their urine the virulent Weil's Disease which can be caught by people with open wounds who come into contact with infected water. In the last decade, there has been an increase of 20–30 per cent in the rat population of Britain, which is now estimated to be 60 million.

The distribution of infectious and parasitic diseases becomes extremely difficult to explain, because the different hosts of the pathogenic viruses, pathogenic bacteria and parasitic organisms may be differently affected by geographical conditions and controls. Furthermore, the disease agent itself may be affected by these geographical controls when in the alternative host, especially if it is a cold-blooded (poikilothermic) creature such as an insect. And finally, the disease agent, as happens with malaria, may be carried by different vectors in different parts of its range (Table 4.1).

Insects are probably the most important disease vectors. They may transmit the disease agent mechanically, as in the case of flies, beetles and cockroaches, which pollute human food or skin with their feet, saliva or faeces; or through their bite, as occurs in the case of fleas, lice, ticks and mosquitoes. The geographical distribution of the different species of vectors is regulated by such critical factors as temperature and humidity. Each species has a wide range of temperatures between cold stupor (beyond which lies dormancy, hibernation and finally death) and temporary heat stupor (culminating ultimately in heat paralysis and death) within which it can perform its normal functions. Towards the limit of this range growth or reproduction or some other function may be adversely affected. Some point in the middle of the range is sometimes described as the optimum or preferred temperature where all activities are vigorous. The optimum zone may vary with humidity. The louse *Pediculus*, for example, has a preferred temperature of about 29°C (84°F), a hungry female mosquito *Culex fatigans* prefers temperatures down to 15°C (59°F) over higher temperatures.[4]

Optimum temperatures for insect activity and reproduction are normal in most months in the tropics. Such temperatures are, however, reached only during the summer in Britain. The rapid rate of insect reproduction in the tropics results in several periods of injurious activities by a single species each year, whereas in Britain, certain species of insect may reproduce themselves only once a year. Their activities are accordingly restricted, as noted in the case of malaria.

Whether it be the causative organism of a disease (bacterium, spirochaete, rickettsia virus), intermediate host or vector, each has its own specific environmental requirements. Each element in a disease complex, including humans, is inescapably bound up with the geographical environment. Disease in any given locality is the result of a combination of geographical circumstances which bring together disease agent, vector, intermediate host, reservoir and man or woman at the most auspicious time. Knowledge of these relationships and of each element in the complex is a prerequisite to an understanding of infectious disease, its distribution and control. Furthermore relationships are rarely simple or static. They are highly complicated, far more than the foregoing illustrations suggest or was realized by the proponents of a 'scientific' germ theory of infectious diseases. Pathogenic organisms evolve following mutation or more drastic alterations in genetic constitution. In consequence, descriptions of a disease at the present time may not necessarily conform to the course of that disease throughout history.

The modern attack on microbial diseases centres on either stopping the spread of infecting micro-organisms or interfering with their reproductive potential within a host by means of drugs. The modern antibiotic streptomycin, the synthetic iso-nictinoyl hydrazide, and para-amino salicylic acid have proved so successful against tuberculosis that sanatoria have been closed or used for other purposes. The spread of the causative organism of malaria in the tropics has been restricted by campaigns against the vector *Anopheles* using residual insecticides such as DDT[5] or BHC. Unfortunately certain strains of *Anopheles* have developed a resistance to DDT and other specific insecticides. One of the most successful alternative insecticides for DDT-resistant mosquitoes has been dieldrin. Drug resistance of *Plasmodium falciparum* has increased in both geographical distribution and intensity. Travellers to malarious areas now take either chloroquine, mefloquine or other appropriate chemoprophylaxis.

Treatment with antibiotics means that rheumatic fever, chorea and erysipelas are now rare. Immunization against diphtheria and poliomyelitis has resulted in a marked reduction in these diseases. German measles (rubella) and whooping cough (pertussis) too have declined rapidly since the introduction of vaccines and antibiotics.

Pursuing the relationships of people and their environments, and with the animals with which they associate, there is currently concern about a possible link between the animal disease 'scrapie' in sheep, bovine spongiform encephalopathy (BSE, 'Mad Cow Disease') in cows and a new variant of Creutzfeldt-Jacob Disease (NVCJD) in humans. Controversy abounds concerning the likelihood of BSE crossing the species barrier from infected cows and cattle products contaminated with brain and spinal chord, to human populations. There is, as yet, no proof of any link.[6]

Rabies (hydrophobia), another zoonosis, is a virus disease transmitted to humans via the saliva of an infected animal entering an open wound. It is usually inflicted by the bite of an infected dog, but almost any warm-blooded animal can be infected and so carry the disease. The disease does not occur in Britain owing to strict quarantine regulations, though these seem likely to be abolished in the near future. Of the rabies strains the endemic European variety is restricted to foxes. Should a rabid fox bite a dog, the dog will contract rabies and could then pass on the disease to humans.

Some people are hypersensitive to a wide range of pollens, and in spring and summer suffer from 'hay fever' and rhinitis. In Britain each year half a million people suffer from severe 'hay fever' or similar allergy symptoms caused by grass or tree pollens, mould spores and dust, or dandruff or hairs from pet dogs and cats. Bracken (*Pteridium aquilinum*) spores, spread in the wind from July to October, contaminate pastures and water supplies. Milk from cows feeding on such pastures may dispose to gastric cancer.

Humans are also subject to fungus infections. The contagious group includes ringworm and *tinea pedis*, commonly known as athlete's foot. The occupational disease 'farmer's lung' (*allergic alveolitis*) has symptoms similar to the North American 'maple bark disease' and to the 'paprik-splitter's disease' of Hungary. This is a pulmonary condition resulting from the inhalation of mouldy hay or grain, itself a complex material consisting of innumerable fungal spores, hyphae and bacteria, and fragments of vegetable matter. The critical fungal spores are actinomycetes (*Thermopolyspora spora*), a simple form of organism which lives in the soil, and whose spores are liberated in dry weather.

In the century or so since Louis Pasteur, Robert Koch and others spearheaded the triumphant series of successes in incriminating pathogenic microbes (bacteria, viruses and other microscopic forms of life) as causes of disease, the theory of specific aetiology – the notion that particular diseases have particular causes (a one-to-one relationship) – has permeated most branches of medical science and practice. The prospect of fabricating corresponding chemical weapons ('magic bullets') to deal with them has become compelling. But, at a time when most people in Britain are likely to die of so-called degenerative diseases such as coronary heart disease (pp.205ff.), cancer (pp.213ff.) or suffer mental illness (pp.188–9), the exclusively biological or biomedical approach to disease is no longer valid. Multiple-factor aetiology, holistically embracing physical, biological, socio-economic and behavioural life-style factors, is the more appropriate stance.

In contrast to the health hazards presented by some aspects of the biological environment, attention might be directed to those aspects which are more beneficial. For instance, the large-scale brewing of beers, wine-making and the making of leaven bread, cheese and certain pickles depend wholly or partly on microbes for their special properties and for the subtle flavours of the resultant foods and beverages. Brewing and bread-making depend on a sophisticated microbiological technique in which yeast must be preserved from batch to batch. Should this culture be contaminated by certain other bacteria or micro-organisms there will be vinegar instead of beer, or the bread becomes sour and inedible. Microbes are also used to modify natural products occurring in industrial and city wastes. Such wastes are often made less toxic, and some toxic substances may even be converted into useful products.

Hirudo-medicinalis, the blood-sucking leech, notorious for its medicinal uses in the nineteenth and earlier centuries, is still used in some cases of phlebotomy (blood-letting). Micro-surgeons use it to keep blood flowing to a newly sewn-on (reattached) ear, nose or finger, or to the skin in a way no drug can imitate. The saliva of such leeches contains a cocktail of powerful chemicals that can dissolve dangerous blood clots or even stop them forming.

5

Health Hazards of the Human Environment

Hazards of the human, or socio-cultural environment, are essentially man-made. They relate to people and include the distribution, density and mobility of population, housing, diet, pollution, agricultural practices, industrial processes and cultural traits.

Prior to the Industrial Revolution, the population of Britain was largely rural and not as mobile as in later years. Industrialization intensified the process of urbanization which had been initiated by improvements in agriculture and food storage techniques associated with the 'agricultural revolution'. Urbanization brought additional disease hazards in its wake. The new industrial towns of nineteenth-century Britain suffered from severe overcrowding and possessed only rudimentary sanitation.

Outbreaks of grave infectious disease such as typhus, cholera and other bowel complaints, and smallpox, particularly among the child apprentices (some would consider child 'slaves' to be a more appropriate description) in mines and textile mills, were recurrent. So great was the need for labour in the factories that the high death rates put the spotlight on the value of human life. It was the Report of the earnest Benthamite reformer, Edwin Chadwick, in 1842[1] (see p.146) which precipitated improvements in housing, sanitation, and the provision of clean, public water supplies.

More than 91 per cent of the present population of Britain is urbanized or semi-urbanized. Not, however, in the densely packed, grossly overcrowded dwellings devoid of drainage, water closets and other basic facilities such as were to be found in nineteenth-century Liverpool, Glasgow, Manchester, Birmingham, Leeds, Sheffield, Bradford, Nottingham, Newcastle-upon-Tyne and other big cities. Such housing has been largely replaced by modern high-density local-authority houses or multi-storeyed blocks of flats. Whereas in 1951 over a third of the households in Britain lacked a fixed bath or shower, and around 8 per cent possessed neither an internal nor external flush toilet, at the time of the 1991 census less than 0.5 per cent lacked either a bath or shower, and a similar proportion lacked an internal flush toilet. Air-conditioning and central heating of stone, concrete or brick-built houses and offices provide congenial living and working conditions, in stark contrast to conditions in early Victorian times or to the foul and verminous dwellings of medieval Britain.

The artificial interior climates of many of the modern buildings are quite different from the climate outside. Artificial climates are now commonplace in the country's hospitals, office blocks, department stores and supermarkets. Such conditions might well prove detrimental to health through their monotony if the people concerned lived under such conditions for the whole of their time rather than for the working day. Whether such artificial climates are optimal for a person's physical or mental functioning is not known. It was thought that air-conditioning would provide relative freedom from infection for the occupants of buildings where it is installed, through both the withdrawal of infected air and the filtration of incoming air. On the other hand there is increasing evidence that air-conditioned offices do not necessarily provide the controlled, healthy environment for which they were intended. Reports of dry, gritty and painful eyes, symptoms of nasal stuffiness, itching and rhinorrhoea, dry throats, dryness of skin, headaches and lethargy – the 'sick-building syndrome' – are commonplace.

Food can provide a hazard to health. Over the centuries there has been a change in food and food habits, and in particular, a reduction in the amount of protein and an increase in carbohydrates. Some authorities would argue that, compared with the total evolutionary history, the relatively short time since man changed from the protein-rich diet of the hunter to the contemporary carbohydrate-rich diet has not permitted adaptation.[2] This being the case, it seems unlikely that the people of Britain are fully adapted or adjusted to some of their diets. Sugar is used in ever-decreasing quantities while emulsifiers, colouring agents, flavour-enhancers, artificial sweeteners, preservatives (sodium benzoate, E211, sodium metabisulphite, E223 etc.) and stabilizers are added to food and drink to improve palatability and shelf-life appearance. Cyclamates, derived from benzine, long used as a substitute for sugar, have now been banned, as have many artificial colourings.[3]

During the Second World War, when food rationing was enforced, the findings of nutritional science were applied to the task of feeding the population. It became necessary to provide bread of high nutritive value, to increase the consumption of potatoes, oatmeal, cheese and green vegetables, to supply not less than a pint of milk per day to expectant and nursing mothers, and to all children up to the age of fifteen years, and to fortify margarine with vitamins A and D, in order to maintain a balanced diet. This was achieved. At the end of the war the national diet suffered temporarily following the termination of American Lend-Lease but since about 1953 it has been of a very high order.

Within the last thirty or so years, largely on the advice of nutritionists and doctors to eat fewer fats containing fatty acids, to avoid high levels of cholesterol in the blood and the risk of heart disease (see p.209) there has been a switch in the household consumption from butter, firstly towards margarine, and more recently to low and reduced-fat spreads. The consumption of whole milk has declined and that of skimmed and semi-skimmed risen, so that now virtually the same amounts of each are drunk. The national consumption of poultry has risen appreciably and that of fresh fruit slightly, but that of beef, veal, pork, mutton and lamb has fallen. The recent upward trend in favour of wholemeal bread to increase the supply of dietary fibre essential to a healthy diet, has slowed down slightly because of the availability of a wider variety of white bread, including soft-grain loaves. Eating habits too are changing with a shift to 'healthy eating' and convenience foods (instant soups, frozen ready meals etc.) in association with microwave cooking (Fig. 5.1).

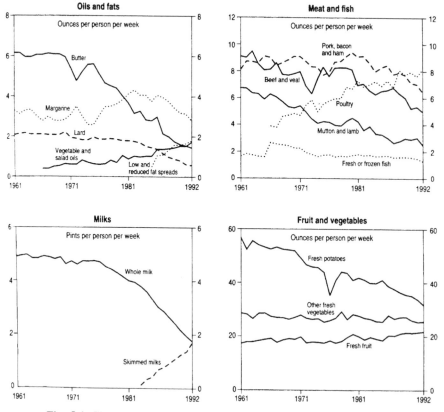

Fig. 5.1 Changing patterns in the consumption of food at home in Britain
(*Source*: Ministry of Agriculture, Fisheries and Food)

There are still, however, interesting regional variations with household consumption in the London area generally in excess of the national average for all selected items of food except margarine, cakes and biscuits. People there tend also to eat more fresh fruit and vegetables and buy more pre-packed food than people in the Midlands and the north of England. Consumption in Scotland is below the average for the same items except margarine, cakes, biscuits and beef. Wales is characterized by high consumption of butter, the north-west and north-east of England by high consumption of margarine but few fresh green vegetables and fresh fruit, and the Midlands by potatoes, pork and more fruit, vegetables and salads than in the past. Such regional variations in household consumption are tending to disappear now that most people buy food from supermarkets which purvey nation-wide similar mass-produced, factory-made foods which are often over-processed and nutritionally depleted.

Battery and deep-litter systems of egg and poultry production, the 'sweat box' system of rearing pigs, the intensive systems of livestock husbandry and other intensive methods of food production contrast markedly with traditional free-range and mixed farming methods. The use of drugs, growth-promoting implants and additives to the food of livestock reared under intensive methods can introduce unsuspected residual hazards and possible adverse consequences for health. The lacing of food of young animals with traces of broad-spectrum antibiotics has been such that Britain's cattle and fowl stocks have become reservoirs of drug-resistant germs.[4] Chloramphenicol, the only drug effective against typhoid, could become useless following the vogue for giving it to broiler fowls. Changes in farm practices must not pass unnoticed in the context of man-made health hazards.

Soil, a complex system of mineral, chemical and biological components, is the substance in which plants grow and is the main source of food for man and his animals. The maintenance of soil fertility is a basic requirement for the continuation of human life and is achieved through the combination of the application of farmyard manure, compost, mineral matter, or the practice of crop rotations. Chemical fertilizers such as super-phosphates and ammonium nitrates are being applied to the soil in increasing amounts to boost crop production. The application of excessive amounts of such chemical fertilizers causes eutrophication of nearby surface waters and pollution of ground water supplies,[5] and affects soil structure. It is thought not to have a deleterious effect on human health. On the other hand, the unrestricted use of powerful chemical insecticides based on organophosphorous compounds and chlorinated hydrocarbons, while revolutionizing chemical warfare against harmful insects and pests (and at the same time destroying earthworms, honey bees and a host of beneficial insects, flowers and wildlife) upsets the balance of the soil ecosystem and may prove a serious source of contamination of food and water supplies (Fig. 5.2).

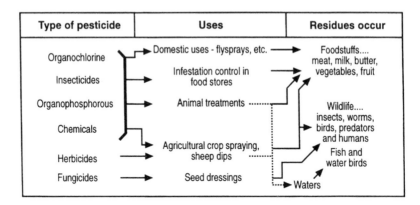

Fig. 5.2 Pesticides, their uses and the location of residues (after Abbott and Thompson, 1968)

It should not go unnoticed that the farmer is responsible for much environmental pollution in the form of agricultural discharges of dung, slurry, silage and piggery effluent – all of which eventually finds its way into streams and rivers.[6] The mechanization of agriculture has changed the farmyard scene tremendously over the last forty to fifty years and led to many accidents caused by machinery. There were 46 deaths in farm accidents in Britain in 1994/95 caused by machinery. This annual fatality compared with 3 in coal-mining and 2 in quarrying.

The modern town, the social habitat of industrialized humankind is characterized by high-density living and overcrowding, by petrol and diesel fumes, smoke and sulphur dioxide, and by the noise of heavy traffic. The pollution over cities and industrial areas, grit, dust, smoke and gases such as sulphur dioxide, carbon monoxide, hydrocarbons and fluorine (Table 5.1) was, until the introduction of the Clean Air Acts and smoke-free zones in cities in 1956 and 1958, sufficient to reduce the duration of sunshine in such cities as London, Leeds, Sheffield, Glasgow, Sunderland and Manchester in winter months to less than half that of outlying districts. The reduction in average bright sunshine in central London compared with areas outside the metropolis amounted to a loss of 44 minutes a day. In Glasgow the loss in the centre was 20 minutes compared with the western outskirts. The introduction of smoke-free zones in the industrial towns of Britain has been most successful and given rise to a far clearer atmosphere. London and other large cities are far less smoky, sooty and foggy now than they were forty or more years ago (Plate 1).

Table 5.1 Atmospheric pollutants in the outdoor environment and their sources

Atmospheric pollutants	Main source	Diseases or disorders commonly associated with them or thought to be caused by them
Asbestos (crocidolite)	Insulation and fireproofing	Asbestosis, bronchial cancer, mesothelioma
Carbon monoxide	Chiefly exhausts from motor vehicles (not diesel-engined vehicles)	Aggravation of respiratory disorders
Dioxins	Waste and hospital incinerators, paper bleaching plants, chemical industry (used by the Americans in the Vietnam War in the 1960s in the herbicide Agent Orange)	Cancer, reduced male sperm counts, disruption of the immune system and regulatory hormones
Exhaust products	Diesel-engined vehicles	Lung cancer
Fluorides	Enamelling works, some steel plants, artificial fertilizer plants, bauxite processing, pottery kilns, brickworks, aluminium smelters	Irritation of skin and mucous membranes Fluoridosis in animals grazing on contaminated pastures
Hydrocarbons	Oil refineries and gases (unburned petrol) from motor vehicles	Cancer of the lung
Inhalable dust and sulphur dioxide	Coal and oil heating	Bronchitis and/or irritation of mucous membranes of respiratory system
Methane (marsh gas)	Decaying household and commercial refuse buried in the ground	
Nickel (carbonyl)	Refining process, furniture, boot and shoe industries, sheep dips	Nasal sinus cancer, life-threatening heart condition
Oxides of nitrogen	Motor vehicles	Aggravation of respiratory disorders
Ozone	Not ascertained – probably the interaction of ultra-violet rays and products of combustion in the presence of a catalyst	Bronchitis and/or irritation of mucous membranes of respiratory system
Pollen	Ragweed	Hay fever
Polycyclic organic compounds (especially 3.4 benz-pyrene) also contain aliphatic hydrocarbons	Incomplete combustion of hydrocarbons	Factor in cancer of the lung
Polyvinyl chloride (PVC)	Manufacture of PVC	Angiosarcoma of the liver
Radon	Gamma radiation from granites or other igneous rocks	Cancer-causing
Sulphur dioxide	Industry, electricity generating stations	Irritation of respiratory disorders

Plate 1: Stoke-on-Trent, 1910 and 1969
(by permission of CERAM Research)

Visible atmospheric pollution has certainly abated, but this is not so for insidious, invisible pollution like sulphur emissions not covered by the Clean Air Acts of 1956 and 1958. This pollution, from power stations such as Drax, Europe's largest coal-fired station in Yorkshire, Ratcliff-on-Soar in the Midlands and Fiddler's Ferry, Merseyside, causes the so-called 'acid rain' which, in turn, is thought to kill forest trees and plants and fish life in streams and lakes. Hydrocarbon gases, especially carbon dioxide (from burning fossil fuels), are responsible also for the 'greenhouse effect' (p.258) leading to a warming of the atmosphere (Figs. 5.3–5.5).

The classic example of atmospheric pollution in Britain was 'the great smog' which engulfed London from 6 to 10 December 1952. An inversion of temperature[7] had checked the upward drift of chimney products and greatly increased the intensity of impurities in the stagnant air near the ground. Sulphur dioxide levels at Monk Street in the City of Westminster and in Golden Lane in the City of London reached 7,000 or 8,000 microgrammes per cubic metre, eight to ten times the normal December levels. Although at first the dire results of this massive pollution were not appreciated, it is now thought to have caused the deaths of 3,500 to 4,000, mostly elderly persons, from chronic bronchitis, heart and lung diseases. London's longest and most severe foggy episode since 'the great smog' occurred in December 1962, when over a thousand people died. But for the Clean Air Acts the death toll could have been ten times greater.

There are pollutants of more local importance, associated with industrial processes in the manufacturing industry and of domestic importance associated with vaporizing fly-killers, washing-up detergents and weed-killers. These present a range of health hazards in the form of absorption or contact with poisonous or deleterious substances. As early as 1775 Percival Pott drew attention to soot as a cause of scrotal cancer in chimney-sweeps. Silicosis is a risk in quarrying and glass manufacture, and there is an above-average incidence of pneumoconiosis among coal-miners. Lead, mercury, arsenic, fluoride, chromium, asbestos and benzene are among the recognized toxic materials used in modern industry. These, and hundreds more new chemicals are being introduced into the environment each year. Diseases or disorders commonly associated with atmospheric pollutants and thought to be aggravated by them include chronic bronchitis, pneumonia, lung cancer, emphysema, mesothelioma and asbestosis. Financial cost is used by industrialists as justification for inaction on a wide range of issues such as power station and car emissions, toxic waste, river pollution and the dumping of sewage into the sea.

In contrast to times past, the tempo and tensions of life in the large, modern, urban communities of Britain are such as to lead to 'stress' believed by some physicians to be a factor in producing coronary heart

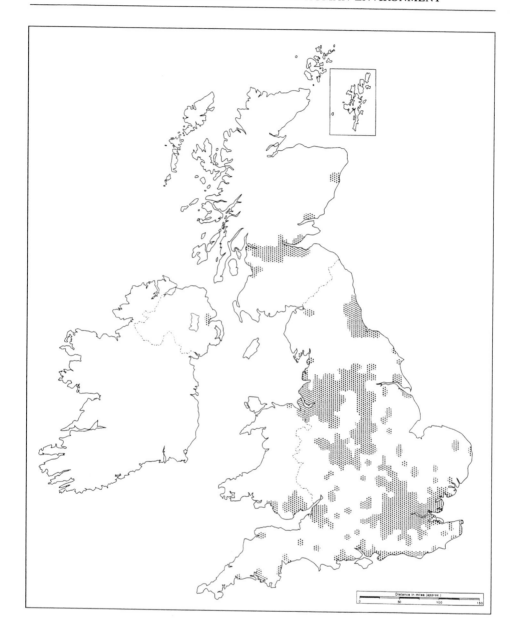

Fig. 5.3 Emissions of carbon monoxide in the UK, 1993 (simplified from *National Atmospheric Emissions Inventory*)

Fig. 5.4 Emissions of sulphur dioxide in the UK, 1993 (simplified from *National Atmospheric Emissions Inventory*)

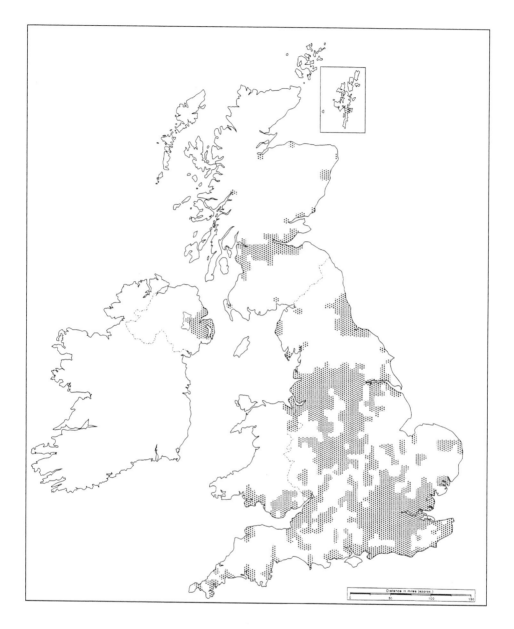

Fig. 5.5 Emissions of nitrogen oxides in the UK, 1993 (simplified from *National Atmospheric Emissions Inventory*)

disease, cerebro-vascular disease ('stroke') and some cancers. Deaths from these causes are considered to be premature and give cause for concern. Stress is a nebulous factor. It is a response in reaction to a wide range of physical and emotional situations such as bereavement, divorce, being made redundant, unemployment, change in financial and social roles, drink, drug abuse and so on, which occur throughout life. The body responds to a stressful situation by increasing the production of such hormones as cortisol and adrenaline. This increase in hormones leads to changes in heartbeat, blood pressure, metabolism and physical activity. Such changes can, in turn, disrupt a person's ability to cope. Individuals most likely to experience stress are usually hard-working, assertive, competitive, ambitious and impatient (Personality Type A).[8] *The Annual Review of Public Health* (1994) lists stress as the second most common cause of absence from work lasting more than twenty-one days. Three out of ten people suffer from stress at work, with rates rising higher when staff are threatened with redundancy or during labour disputes. How much mental illness is due to the stresses of modern life, to genetic causes or to influences in early years in the Freudian sense is still unknown.

Some workers in industries which use or produce dangerous materials, such as chemicals or industrial dust, become ill as a direct result of their occupation. Many modern industries have machines that are excessively noisy, and a person working with them for any length of time is likely to suffer from impaired hearing (Fig. 5.6). Furnacemen, glass-blowers, miners, steel workers, welders and many others have to work in very high temperatures. As a result they may suffer from heat fatigue (sweating, thirst, headache, irritability) or cramp. Workers exposed to chemicals, metals and metallic compounds, essential materials in many industries and processes, have to guard against poisoning. The grinding, cutting, drilling and crushing of metals, stone and coal produces dust which can cause lung disorders among industrial workers. Insulating fireproofing with asbestos causes the lung disease, asbestosis.

Male occupations are used as a basis for subdividing Britain's society into social classes. The social grading system recognized by the Registrar-General (OPCS) is given in Table 5.2.

Class differences reflecting occupation, income, nutrition, education, ethnicity and much else, are a feature of the entire human lifetime. They are found at birth during the first year of life, childhood, adolescence and adult life. Relationships between social class and ill-health have been demonstrated. At birth and in the first month of life twice as many babies born to families of unskilled manual workers (Class V) die compared with those born to families in the professional class (Class I), and in the next 11 months of life four times as many boys and five times as many girls

Table 5.2 Registrar-General's social grading system

Social class	Description	Example	Percentage of population
I	Professional/ upper-middle class	Accountant, judge, doctor, professor, lawyer	6
II	Intermediate/ middle-class	Teacher, manager, journalist, nurse	20
IIIn	Skilled non-manual lower-middle class	Clerical worker, secretary, shop assistant	15
IIIm	Skilled manual/ skilled working class	Bus driver, butcher, carpenter, plumber, miner	33
IV V	Semi-skilled/ unskilled working class	Agricultural worker, bus conductor, postman, assembly-line worker, hospital porter, labourer	19
	Those at lowest levels of subsistence	Old-age pensioners, widows and those totally dependent on social security through long-term unemployment or sickness	7

die. For both men and women the risk of death before retirement is two-and-a-half times as great in Class V (unskilled manual workers and their wives) as it is in Class I (professional men and their wives).[9]

To a large extent social divisions structure most human relations and form the background against which the biological processes that lead to illness and death operate. Socio-economic differences are thus mortality determinants, but of a different type from such factors as nutritional intake, cigarette-smoking or quality of drinking-water. Health and mortality levels can be affected not only through specific health and medical action but also through changes in the class structure of society, and in particular, by bettering living conditions among the poorest and most disadvantaged groups.

Noise is a major health hazard. Excessive noise in towns from motor vehicles, building-site machinery, pneumatic drills, jet aircraft, and, to a lesser extent, ice-cream vendors' chimes, TV sets, radios, record and tape players, and discos can be damaging to health and a contributory cause of serious nervous disease (Fig. 5.6). In the countryside the offenders include tractors, combine harvesters, chainsaws and crop-spraying aircraft. The noise of winds in high-rise blocks of flats produces tension from the fear of actual physical harm. On the other hand the comparative quiet of rural areas, low-density suburbs or the more spacious new towns can sometimes cause stress among those not accustomed to it.

Increasing use of water closets in the nineteenth century instead of the earth midden led to the direct pollution of streams, rivers and coasts with

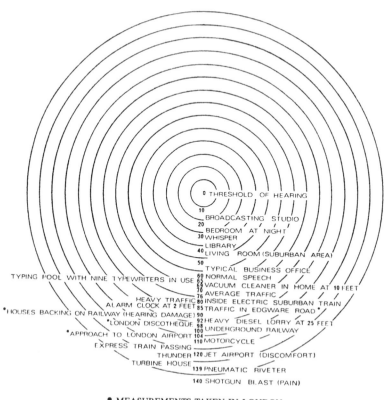

0 THRESHOLD OF HEARING
10
BROADCASTING STUDIO
20
BEDROOM AT NIGHT
30 WHISPER
LIBRARY
40 LIVING ROOM (SUBURBAN AREA)
50
TYPICAL BUSINESS OFFICE
TYPING POOL WITH NINE TYPEWRITERS IN USE 60 NORMAL SPEECH
65 VACUUM CLEANER IN HOME AT 10 FEET
70
76 AVERAGE TRAFFIC
HEAVY TRAFFIC 80 INSIDE ELECTRIC SUBURBAN TRAIN
ALARM CLOCK AT 2 FEET 85 TRAFFIC IN EDGWARE ROAD *
*HOUSES BACKING ON RAILWAY (HEARING DAMAGE) 90
*LONDON DISCOTHEQUE 92 HEAVY DIESEL LORRY AT 25 FEET
98
100 UNDERGROUND RAILWAY
*APPROACH TO LONDON AIRPORT 104
110 MOTORCYCLE
EXPRESS TRAIN PASSING
THUNDER 120 JET AIRPORT (DISCOMFORT)
TURBINE HOUSE
139 PNEUMATIC RIVETER
140 SHOTGUN BLAST (PAIN)

● MEASUREMENTS TAKEN IN LONDON

Fig. 5.6 Sound levels in decibels

sewage. Indeed the condition of the water and foreshore of the Thames in the middle of London in the nineteenth century was so foul that sheets soaked in disinfectant (chloride of lime) were hung in the Houses of Parliament in an attempt to counteract the stench (Plate 15).[10] Water was, and is, also contaminated from other sources. In particular, wells are subject to seepage from manure heaps, silage heaps, cesspits or the more recent septic tank.

Sanitation in most parts of Britain is now of a far higher standard than in the last century, and, except for towns and cities near the sea, sewage is generally treated and neutralized before it is disposed of. But rivers, and ultimately the sea, continue to function as the cheapest industrial lavatory in the world, with raw sewage and consumer waste occurring on many of Britain's shores and holiday beaches. In addition, the sewage, industrial effluents (including such toxic substances as phenols, oils, heavy metals and detergents), together with agricultural discharges (including silage liquors which are twenty times more polluting than sewage) find their way into streams and rivers. Pulping plants release sulphate and kier liquors, and mines pump out highly mineralized waters containing sulphates, chlorides and calcium and magnesium compounds. A survey of river quality in England and Wales, conducted by the Department of the Environment and the Welsh Office[11] in 1985 revealed stretches of the Tyne, Tees, Ouse, Aire, Calder, Don, Irwell, Mersey, Weaver, Rother, Dow, Idle, Erewash, Tame, Nene, Cam, Gipping, Thames, Avon, Ebbw, Taff, Ely, Tawe and Fal to be of poor to bad quality owing mainly to either sewage effluent, overloaded sewage treatment works, animal slurries, silage liquors or industrial discharges from factories, coke works and collieries. Untreated sewage and industrial waste, together with radioactive and chemical wastes (Fig. 5.7) discharged into the seas around Britain through hundreds of pipelines, cause shellfish in some areas to be unfit to eat and fish to be diseased.

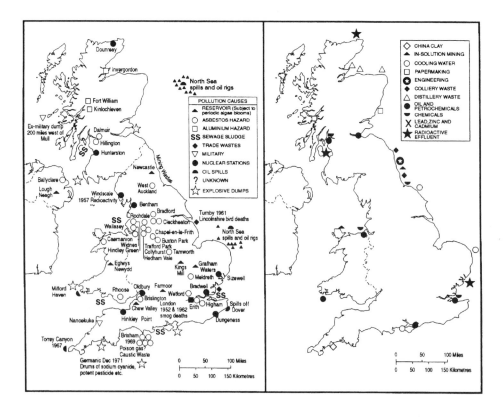

Fig. 5.7 Coastal and other discharges of industrial and other waste

Radiation from rocks (e.g. radon gas produced by the decay of the trace amounts of uranium that occur in virtually all rocks but more particularly in granites and other igneous rocks) and any cosmic sources constitutes a perfectly natural part of man's environment and varies from one part of the country to another. Human populations have adapted themselves to such background radioactivity and to its regional variations. 'Man-made radiation' on the other hand is likely to increase from nuclear power stations, nuclear processing plants and other nuclear facilities. Radio-nuclides from such sources (e.g. iodine 131, caesium 137 and caesium 134) may cause thyroid cancer and other malignancies. Radioactive mate-rials in Britain associated with the nuclear fuel cycle are well protected at source but are nevertheless potentially highly dangerous. Reactors to gener-ate electricity are located at Sizewell (Suffolk), Bradwell (Essex), Dungeness (Kent), Hinkley Point (Somerset), Oldbury (Avon), Wylfa (Anglesey), Hunterston (Ayrshire), Torness (E. Lothian), Heysham (Lancashire) and Hartlepool (Durham), and there are installations at Calder Hall (Cumbria), Sellafield (Cumbria), Springfields (Lancashire) and Chapelcross (Dumfriesshire) for enriching, fabricating and reprocess-ing nuclear fuels. Considerable radioactive waste is or was discharged from establishments at Dounreay, Windscale, Springfields, Culcheth, Culham, Amersham, Burghfield, Winfrith and Harwell which support research and developments. Reactors are always enclosed and fully protected within 'biological shields' and radioactive contamination is extremely unlikely. Accidents can happen, however, as in the case of a fire at the Windscale reactor in 1957 which resulted in serious contamination of the local atmos-phere with radioactive iodine 131. The disposal of radioactive waste from decommissioning and dismantled nuclear reactors is currently posing a major problem.

Radioactive material inhaled from the air, ingested in food and water or absorbed through the skin is particularly dangerous. Ionizing radiation can be damaging to the genetic material contained in the cells of the human body. Currently the largest area of exposure to 'man-made' radiation is from medical sources (diagnostic X-rays and nuclear medicine procedures) Radioactive isotopes advance medicine both in investigation and in therapy especially for cancer (e.g. of the thyroid). There is currently concern that exposure to electromagnetic radiation from high-tension electric power lines may result in an increased risk of cancer and degenerative diseases.

Technological advances such as cars, lifts, computers, and automation generally have made work and life-styles increasingly sedentary. They have also contributed to redundancies, unemployment, enforced idleness and/or the doubtful benefits of increased leisure time. In theory leisure time should be beneficial, but it is, in fact, fraught with social problems when employed passively rather than actively. Reduced physical activity can have unfavourable effects on physiological mechanisms. The way in which the weekend and holiday exodus to seaside resorts, the countryside and airports contributes to road traffic jams is but one illustration. Evidently the manner in which leisure is used not infrequently involves mental strain, frustration, stress and little genuine relaxation. Automation has brought about important changes in the social environment and it seems evident that increasing attention needs to be directed to the planning of facilities for exercise, recreation, entertainment, and hobbies for those unable to plan their own.

The smoking of cigarettes is a social habit of long standing. It has been praised variously, as a stimulant for work, as a sedative for relaxation, as a cure for colds and catarrh (so common in Britain) and indispensable for social intercourse. More accurately it must be damned as a serious health hazard. It is a major aetiological factor in coronary heart disease and chronic bronchitis, and the increased incidence in lung cancer observed since the 1930s has resulted in cigarette-smoking and atmospheric pollution being associated with that disease epidemiologically. Carcinogenic hydrocarbons, notably 3–4 benzpyrene among others, have been isolated from tars of cigarette smoke and from soot of polluted atmospheres. Why this relatively recent awareness of the association when seemingly the dangers were appreciated as early as the sixteenth century?

> Od's me, I marle what pleasure or felicity they have in taking this roguish tobacco. It's good for nothing but to choke a man, and fill him full of smoke and embers: there were four died out of one house last week with taking of it, and two more the bell went for yesternight; one of them, they say, will never scape it, he voided a bushel of soot yesterday, upward and downward. By the stocks, an there were no wiser men than I, I'd have it present whipping, man or woman, that should but deal with a tobacco pipe: why it will stifle them all in the end, as many as use it; it's little better than ratsbane or rosaker. (Cob, in *Every Man in His Humour* by Ben Jonson)

Royal disapprobation of tobacco, 'the new drug from the Indies', was offered also by King James I in *A Counter-Blast to Tobacco* in 1604.

At the beginning of the twentieth century, 80 per cent of the tobacco consumed in the country was used in pipe tobacco and only about 12 per cent in cigarettes. By 1914 cigarettes were fast catching up with pipe tobaccos, and by the end of the First World War had overtaken them. Since that time cigarettes have gone ahead rapidly. In 1972, when quantitative information about the incidence of cigarette-smoking in Britain first became available, 52 per cent of men and 41 per cent of women aged sixteen and over smoked cigarettes; by 1980 this had fallen to 42 per cent for men and 33 per cent for women. A further fall to 31 per cent for men and 29 per cent for women in 1990 continued this trend.[12] Twenty or thirty years may need to elapse before the ill-effects of cigarette-smoking become manifest, and it was not until the 1930s and the alarming rise of male deaths from lung cancer in the 1940s that the full dangers were realized. It is now almost universally accepted that cigarette-smoking is addictive and a major risk factor in the aetiology of cancer of the lung, mouth, oesophagus, cervix and bladder, and that it is involved in heart disease and peptic ulcer. There is no doubt that smoking is Britain's largest single cause of premature death, 'the most lethal instrument devised by man for peaceful use' (G. Godber, 1976).

The prejudice against cigarette-smoking by women was first broken in the First World War, but it was not until the late 1920s and 1930s that smoking by women started to become general in Britain. Now women account for nearly one-third of the total consumption of cigarettes in the country, and 29 per cent of the female population aged sixteen years and over are smokers. Regrettably the lung cancer mortality pattern for women is following that of the male population. Seemingly, pipe- and cigar-smoking produce a relatively small risk of lung cancer, possibly because pipe- and cigar-smokers seldom inhale the irritating alkaline smoke produced, whereas cigarette-smokers inhale the slightly acid smoke of cigarettes.

Male and female smokers in the professional socio-economic group now have a lower average consumption than smokers in other groups.[13] Such differentials are reflected in the incidence of lung cancer. Furthermore, breathing other people's cigarette smoke ('passive smoking') is considered by many to be a health hazard.

Other human life-style habits have associations with disease. Chronic alcoholism results in mental deterioration in the form of impaired thinking and psychoses, and extends to actual physical deterioration in the form of gastritis and cirrhosis of the liver (Table 5.3), to marital discord, to the breaking up of families, and much misery. Alcoholism is considered by many to be the third major health hazard in Britain after heart disease and cancer. It is the cause of numerous road accidents and possibly of industrial and home accidents. In contrast the *British Heart Journal* (73 (1995), 8–9) proclaims the cardio-protective effects of alcohol and advises the public to 'consume one or two drinks a day, preferably with meals, and perhaps red wine'.

Britain in the late 1990s, in common with several other 'developed' countries, appears to be caught up in an epidemic of drug abuse and dependence in the amphetamine, cannabis ('hash'), heroin, cocaine, crack, steroid Ecstasy ('white doves', 'disco burgers', 'New Yorkers'), LSD

Table 5.3 Liver cirrhosis mortality amongst British males in different occupations

Occupational group	Mortality rate
Average occupation	100
Publicans	1,017
Foremen, ships, lighters and other vessels	900
Deck, engine-room hands, bargemen, lightermen and boatmen	873
Barmen	612
Managers of hotels, clubs etc. and in entertainment and sports	553
Waiters and bar staff	461
Deck, engineering and radio officers and pilots (ship)	417
Electrical engineers (as described)	387
Hotel and residential club managers	342
Officers (ships and aircraft), air traffic planners and controllers	337
Innkeepers	315
Officers, UK armed forces	303
Catering supervisors	297
Fishermen	296
Bus conductors	277
Chefs, cooks	265
Restaurateurs	263
Authors, writers, journalists	261
General labourers	247
Travel stewards and attendants, hotel and hospital porters	245
Drivers' mates	225
Actors, musicians, entertainers, stage managers	222
Winders, reelers	202
Bakers, flour confectioners	157
Judges, barristers, advocates, solicitors	155
Salesmen, sales assistants, shop assistants, shelf-fillers, petrol-pump forecourt attendants	147
Other domestic and school helpers	141
Garage proprietors	140
Clergy, ministers of religion	131
Pharmacists, radiographers, therapists	127
Medical and dental practitioners	115
Nurse administrators, nurses	108

Source: OPCS, combined tables from M. A. Plant (London, 1987), 92, and Labour Research Department, Bargaining Report (December 1986), 11.

(acid), benzodiazapine tranquillizers range. The taking of drugs seems to be particularly prevalent among those under the age of thirty. Solvent-sniffing (solvent-based glues, butane gas, aerosol sprays, etc.) is another form of drug-taking by young people. There is a large range of drugs – some illegal, some not – that can be misused with varying effects. The long-term health effects are impossible to assess.

Sexual behaviour in the permissive society frequently leads to venereal diseases. Sexually transmitted diseases (STDs) are commonplace; transmission of the HIV virus (causing AIDS, see p.41) is effected mainly by sexual (particularly, but not exclusively, homosexual) intercourse.

At a time when the population of Britain was mainly rural, people remained in the same locality for the greater part of their lives. Today people are mobile to a remarkable degree and there is a marked slackening of close family and social relationships. Many urban dwellers have moved farther away from the centres of towns and their places of work and taken up residence in suburbs, in nearby market towns and villages and in 'new towns' such as Crawley, Milton Keynes, Lower Earley, Stevenage, Basildon, Corby, Peterlee, Cwmbran, East Kilbride and Cumbernauld. In theory, the 'new towns' were intended to reduce the journey to work, but there is still considerable mobility of workers. Such changes of place of residence involve not only a physical disturbance but also a social disturbance, since people are obliged to create entirely new social environments for themselves. There is also the inevitable journey to work. This may be long or short, but it involves extra energy and takes toll of physical and mental reserves. What in theory may be a five-day week of 40 working hours may, because of the journey to work, amount in practice to 45–50 hours. Bus or rail travel to work involves waiting and standing; car driving often involves heavy traffic, delay and frustration. The increased mobility of the present population of Britain associated particularly with the motor car and motor cycle, highlights the hazard of the road accident. In contrast, agricultural communities and some working-class communities in the industrialized quarters of our towns which are not obliged to commute find certain endearing qualities in their environments. They enjoy a sense of 'belonging' and hand down traditions from parents to children.

The high degree of internal mobility which characterizes the population of Britain in the final decade of the twentieth century is matched by ever-increasing movement of people between this country and other parts of the world. Movement of people in association with trade has existed since time immemorial. Men, goods and animals have followed the main trade routes of the world; so too have the germs of disease (see pp.88 (plague), 153 (cholera) etc.). Contributory factors, involving human contacts, have included commercial exchanges, caravans, pilgrimages, movements of labour and migration in search of pastures and water for livestock. Germs have passed between humans, from animal to animal, or from animal to human being, or indirectly through carriers. Human lines of communication have long been the pathways of infection.

India, for instance, suffering from conditions of extreme overcrowding, undernourishment, lack of hygiene and grinding poverty, has endemic cholera, plague, malaria, typhoid and dysentery. China is an endemic centre for leprosy and has been the cradle of two plagues, bubonic and pneumonic, and of several epidemics of influenza. South America is the home of yellow fever. Communication between these disease foci and Europe and Britain in the past were by sea, and the journey to Britain was usually longer than the incubation period for most infectious diseases. This was an effective protection for Britain against infection. However, the increase in the volume and speed of modern air travel has broken down this protection and exposed Britain to the danger of direct transmissions of old and emerging infectious diseases. The last half-century or so has witnessed an appreciable amount of movement of citizens of the Old Commonwealth, New Commonwealth and others into this country, drawn particularly to London, Birmingham, and some of the major cities. Not infrequently these people have presented serious health risks in that some are carriers of tuberculosis, typhoid and other infectious diseases.

The discovery of the effectiveness of antibiotics, particularly strepto-mycin and tetracyclines, had almost eliminated the risk of death from bacterial infectious diseases, but it may be wondered whether medicine's present advantage over infection is going to last. Some drugs themselves are often poisonous – penicillin can kill people who have become sensitive to it. Some drugs often work too well. They can eliminate other organisms that are, in fact, protecting the body. Then there are certain organisms (e.g. *Mycobacterium tuberculosis*, *Gonococcus* and *Plasmodium falciparum*) with antibiotic-resistant strains. It is a fact that more and more bacteria are becoming resistant to common antibiotics. One strain of the staphylococci that are the most common cause of skin boils, wound and bloodstream infections, has a reputation for its ability to pick up resistance against drugs. The most serious is the antibiotic-resistant bacterium MRSA – methicillin resistant *staphylococcus aureus*.[14] The constant indiscriminate use of drugs inevitably produces drug-resistant strains like *Pseudomonas*, a hospital-bred organism, which, when established, has an 80 per cent mortality rate.

Many modern drugs have powerful adverse side-effects in some patients which, though rare, may be more serious than the original illness. Such effects, called 'iatrogenic' or 'nosocomial' illnesses, result from orthodox medical treatment. It has been suggested that 30 per cent of patients in the acute wards of NHS hospitals are there for this reason. Resistant strains are countered in turn by new drugs, and the pharmaceutical industry is hard-pressed simply to maintain the status quo.

It would appear that forms resistant to antibiotics are likely to be branded one of the most serious problems facing the British and global medical community. The rapidly changing social environment associated with Britain's late twentieth-century technological civilization is bringing a whole host of new and unsolved health and allied problems in its wake. Are we about to witness the Armageddon of medicine's search for new antibiotics?

6

Pre-Norman and Norman Times

1

Before considering the diseases thought likely to have been prevalent in the Norman and pre-Norman period it is necessary to examine briefly the environment of Britain's earliest people. The landscape provided the physical stage on which the drama of British history was to be performed. The actors were the prehistoric, Romano-British, Anglo-Saxon and Scandinavian populations, joined during the eleventh century by the Normans.

Living in a highly industrialized and urbanized society, and occupying a countryside which has been very much modified by the hand of man, we find it difficult to visualize what the scene was like in Britain in times past. What is certain is that there are few, if any, places in the country which look today as they did in Norman times.

Pine forests established themselves throughout the greater part of Britain during the milder conditions which followed the retreat of the ice of the last glacial epoch. The lowlands of Britain were later covered with heavy forests of oak, elm, beech and ash, and the uplands with pine and birch up to the heights of 1,500–2,000 feet (450–600 metres). Limestone ridges and chalk lands carried only a light forest cover. The marshes, bogs and fens of the lowlands carried scrub. Beyond the forested heights came the open moorlands covered with expanses of tundra-type vegetation.

Britain's virgin or primitive landscape was, to say the least, inhospitable to early man, and yet, as already noted, the country was destined to become a final landfall for several migrating European peoples.

Following the physical separation of Britain from the Continent successive groups, including traders in copper, tin and gold, and husbandmen in search of new pastures and soils, reached such areas as present-day Cornwall, Dyfed, Gwynedd and the west coast of Scotland from the Mediterranean. Others, of different stock, took the shorter crossing and entered Britain at its south-east corner. The newcomers brought knowledge of cultivation and the domestication of animals, the hoe, the grinding stone, of weaving clothes and fashioning clay pots. They were small, dark, slender Mediterranean or Iberian colonists, few and scattered at first, who tended to group around the western shores of the country. Their habitations were stone, or wooden huts covered with branches and surrounded by small fields hewn or burnt out of woodland.

In the fulness of time came the Celts or Gaels, tall, blue-eyed folk, who crossed Europe from the east and settled in Gaul or present-day France. They came first as small bands and families, later as large tribal groups. Early Celts built hill-forts occupying strategic and defensive sites, and other settlements. Their forts may not have been much more than an enclosure surrounded by a single ditch and bank; at other times the protective works may have comprised multiple lines of earthworks and drystone walling. The Celts used iron tools and created permanent fields and villages. They used small wooden ploughs drawn by oxen to till light chalk soils for crops of wheat, barley and oats. Celtic peoples who came later into south-east Britain introduced a heavier plough which, with coulter and mould-board, was capable of undercutting and turning over the sod of the heavy clay lands. Increasing control over the environment through the use of iron for tools enabled the settlers to utilize land which was open or thinly forested for flocks, herds and crops, and to attack 'damp' oakwood forests which covered the low-lying clay lands. It is considered now that prehistoric populations made significant contributions to Britain's landscape evolution.

Certainly agriculture and the appearance of settled villages are thought by some to have represented a 'revolution in human life comparable in magnitude with the effects of the industrial revolution of the nineteenth century'.[1]

The population of the country increased only gradually during the Celtic occupation. It totalled little more than a quarter-million and was unevenly distributed. Indeed, no more than a fifth of Britain was occupied, and this was mainly in the south-east.

During their stay in Britain (mid-first century BC to the end of the fourth century AD) the Romans left a visible imprint on the landscape. They introduced towns, agricultural 'villas' and a network of roads and yet, relative to the wilderness that was Britain (Fig. 6.1), such man-made features of the landscape were minimal. Roman Britain had three culture zones. First, the Civil Zone of southern and eastern England, with all the signs of a peaceful occupation. Second, the Military Zone, comprising Wales, northern England and, for a short time, southern Scotland between Hadrian's Wall and the Antonine Wall[2] where the military occupation was maintained by forts. Much of Scotland north of the Central Lowlands could be regarded as a non-Romanized zone. Here, the Roman occupation was

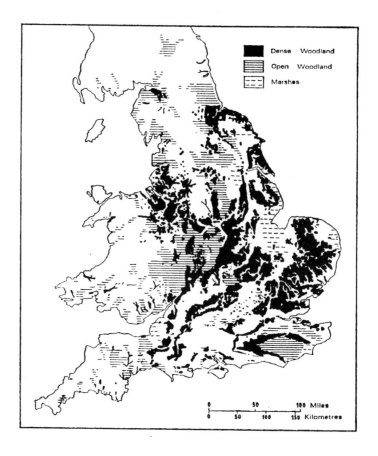

Fig. 6.1 Woodland and marsh in Britain in Roman times (based on a map of
Roman Britain published by the Ordnance Survey)

short-lived, and the indigenous peoples retained their traditional habits and
customs.

Municipal life was a feature of Roman civilization, and at the height of
the Roman occupation there were about fifty towns in southern Britain.
The largest, London (Londinium), which was to replace Colchester as the
leading trading centre of the country, may have had 20,000 inhabitants. By
modern standards the other towns were small, with no more than
2,000–5,000 inhabitants. St Albans, Winchester, Colchester, Lincoln,
York, Gloucester, Caerwent, Chester and Bath may have averaged 3,500
each. There were about a dozen other towns with 2,000 or so inhabitants
each, and forty to fifty other places with about 1,000 each. Fleure[3] has
suggested a total urban population of 120,000 and says, 'if it was about 20

per cent of the whole, this gives a total of 600,000 for prosperous times in the areas south of Hadrian's Wall.' North of Hadrian's Wall the figure would have been a mere fraction of this amount.

The streets of the Roman towns were broad and well paved. They ran straight and parallel and crossed at right angles. Houses were usually of the single-storey type, each detached and standing in a garden. The Romans excelled in their stone buildings. They were solid, well designed and ventilated. A unique feature was the hypocaust or heating chamber built beneath the floors, from which warm air was distributed by means of a system of pottery flue pipes into the walls of the main living room.

The Romans built public water supplies and paid attention to the purity of the water. At certain points in the aqueducts were built settling basins, in which suspended solid matter was able to sediment out. The Romans were presumably not aware of the fact, but such storage of water in a relatively quiet state was effective in ridding it of some of its harmful bacteria. There were also bath-houses and sewers for the prompt disposal of excrement. In fact there were latrines in Hadrian's Wall (e.g. at Housesteads), flushed by running water from storage tanks or surface water. The realization of the importance of a clean and ample water supply and the prompt disposal of polluted water after use must have been of incalculable value in terms of public health. It meant that water-borne diseases such as typhoid fever were reduced, and typhus and relapsing fever curbed through personal cleanliness and the accompanying discouragement of lice.

Scattered within the countryside of the Civil Zone were farmsteads or villas, worked by Romanized Britons, on which wheat, barley and other crops were grown. These substantial structures contrasted with the foul and verminous conditions of the rude thatched shelters with straw-covered floors and smoke-laden atmospheres which housed most of the Celtic farmers.

The Romans introduced poultry, pheasants, pears, cherries, figs, mulberries and a wide variety of herbs into Britain, together with such vegetables as cabbage, onions, turnips, lettuce and parsnips. In parts of southern England, e.g. the Isle of Wight, they also introduced vines. Nutritionally they had a more balanced and healthy diet than the native British population.

The departure of the Roman legions was followed by a period of disorder among the native population. This encouraged foreign invasion. Angles, Saxons and Jutes from northern Germany and Denmark entered England by way of the Wash and the Humber, Thames and Solent estuaries. They came first as raiders but later as settlers, and by AD 600, they predominated in all but some western and northern areas. Celtic tribes held out in Cornwall, Wales, Strathclyde and other parts of Scotland, but elsewhere Romano-British inhabitants were submerged under or assimilated with the Anglo-Saxons. The Angles, Saxons and Jutes were illiterate, heathen peoples. They destroyed towns and villages, overthrew the Christian Church and, by displacing the Latin language, suppressed the art of writing and also the men who could practise it. There is in consequence such a lack of written records for this period that the title Dark Age would seem appropriate.

The natural harbours of the east coast provided easy landfalls for the invading Anglo-Saxons who occupied sites along river banks or on the lower slopes of the valleys. These land-hungry people evidently recognized the good ploughlands and waterside flood plains which would make the best grazings. Indeed the river systems provided the key to much of the distribution of settlement in Anglo-Saxon times. Fox[4] has suggested that 'it is archaeologically possible to see the Saxon farmer at work, turning the valley bottoms into water meadows, the forest margins into arable and pasture.' Evidently they came as settlers determined to till the land.

Anglo-Saxon and Scandinavian settlement spread over some twenty generations prior to AD 1066. During that time there was a valleyward movement of people consequent upon the progressive clearing of woods and draining of marsh. Indeed within Lowland Britain there was a slow change-over from what was dominance of the environment to the dominance of man. But the task was immense. Forests were dense and many, and the numbers of people engaged in clearing very small. Roads were few, mainly ridgeways along the downs and those Roman roads which were still usable. In consequence there were few if any facilities for communications and each district was more or less dependent on its own resources (Fig. 6.2)

In the west and north of the country Celtic tribes maintained a traditional way of life. They grazed their cattle and sheep on bleak open moorlands in summertime, but their permanent homes were small farms or communal enclosures on the open slopes of valleys or the brows of hills above the tangle of forest and undergrowth in the valley bottoms, or on the coasts. Christianity persisted among them at a time when Saxon heathendom prevailed in the south and east of the country. Contact with Rome and Christian settlements in the Mediterranean was maintained along western sea-ways linking Wales, Ireland and south-west England with Brittany and Spain. Christian teachers, the Celtic saints, established a large number of semi-monastic settlements and showed other less venturesome people how the forest lands might be tamed and planted with grains or reclaimed as a pasture. Saints, such as St Columba, St Ninian, St Samson and St David, were among the pioneers of the valleyward movement and village settlement in the west and north of Britain. Estimation of the total population of Britain at this time is necessarily guesswork, but with the reservations

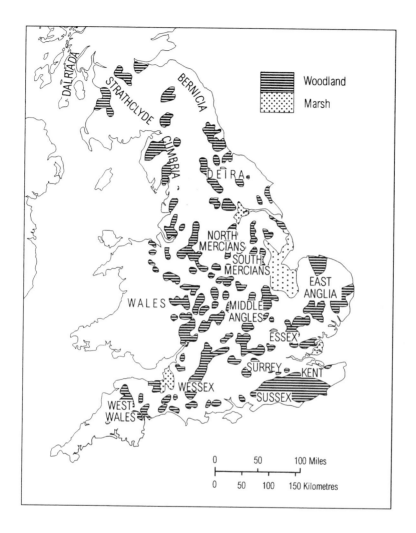

Fig. 6.2 Woodland and marsh in Britain in the late seventh century (based on R. H. Hodgkin, *A History of the Anglo-Saxons*)

that befit such an estimation it would seem that there were still less than a million people in the country.

Viking invasions in the eighth, ninth and tenth centuries resulted in the seizure of not only parts of East Anglia but lands to the south of what is now Essex, Hertfordshire, Bedfordshire and possibly Buckinghamshire. Danes also held land in Yorkshire, Lincolnshire, Leicestershire, Nottinghamshire, Northamptonshire and Derbyshire. Other Viking raids and the invasion and colonization of the Orkneys, the north of Scotland and

the Hebrides heralded a later expansion into Ireland. From there and from
their kingdom on the Isle of Man they reinvaded England and the Scottish
Lowlands (Fig. 2.2). These activities along the northern and western sea-
ways coincided with a general improvement of climate which was, in
general terms, dry and warm. This particular climate amelioration reached
its optimum probably between AD 800 and 1000.

The last successful invasion of Britain was by the Normans in AD 1066.
However, their arrival was, in effect, little more than the transposition of an
aristocracy into Britain and not a folk movement of people in search of a new
homeland. The Normans merely reinforced and replaced by their own feudal
system an aristocracy which had already been established by Anglo-Saxon
and Danish dynasties. The Welsh coastlands yielded slowly to the Norman
advance, but northern England remained a frontier province as during the
Dark Ages. Mainland Scotland was nominally united under one king.

The great achievement of the Anglo-Saxons and the Vikings was their
progressive clearing of the natural woodland, though a great deal still
remained even in Norman times, as the Domesday Survey (1086) bears
witness. There were also lands converted to 'forest law' to preserve the king's
hunting, and much devastated land following the Norman Conquest, particularly in Yorkshire. Even so, arable land continued to increase at the expense
of woodland throughout England and in the Celtic lands of the north and west.
There were inroads, too, on the marshlands of the Thames, Fens, Somerset
Levels, Humber Lowlands, Holderness, the mosslands of Lancashire and
Central Scotland (especially the Vale of Menteith and Carse of Gowrie), and
other local improvements following the drainage of floodable valleys.

Population distribution continued to show a fairly close relationship to
agricultural productivity, the greater part being located in Lowland Britain,
especially south of a line from the Wash to the middle Severn (Fig. 6.3).
There were, however, wide variations in the density of the population, since
thousands of square miles remained forested or untouched by the plough.
The average density of the population in England was about 15 to 20 per
square mile, although parts of East Anglia might have had as many as 20
to 40 per square mile. It is doubtful if the average was more than four
people per square mile over the whole of northern England. In Wales and
Scotland it was probably less. Hoskins[5] says that Norfolk (95,000), Lincoln
(90,000), Suffolk and Devon (70,000 each) were the most populous counties, followed by Kent, Hampshire, Sussex and Wiltshire, each with
40,000–50,000 people. What is certain is that the country was still very
sparsely populated. The population for the whole country at the time of
the Domesday Survey was little more than 1½–2 million. In England small
nucleated villages had evolved within the forest clearings and 'towns'
appeared, or reappeared in rudimentary form. In the north and west of the

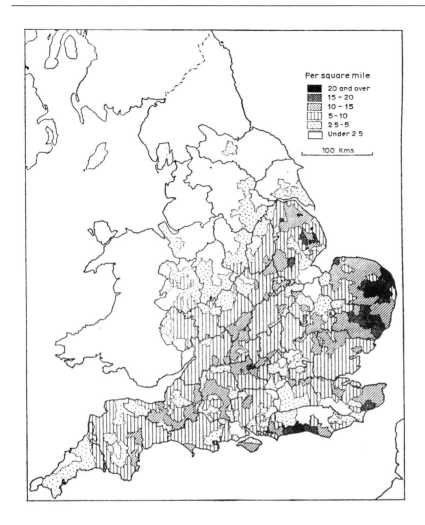

Fig. 6.3 Distribution of population in England at the time of Domesday (after
H.C. Darby, *An Historical Geography of England before 1800*)

country, however, the characteristic settlement pattern was that of the scattered hamlet or single farmstead surrounded by a few small fields.

The urban life introduced by the Romans suffered a temporary set-back
with the withdrawal of the garrisons. The initial Anglo-Saxon period was
not one of town life. Indeed the sites of a number of Roman towns (e.g.
Silchester, Wroxeter) became deserted.

Following the firm establishment of the Anglo-Saxons and later
Scandinavian settlers, there once more came into being centres with an
economy different from that of the surrounding agricultural countryside.

Some of these towns grew up as market centres serving as foci for the villages around, and those favoured by location became regional capitals for wider areas. Others, along the coast (but also inland), developed as protective burghs against Danish invasion, and later some became ports with overseas connections. A number of towns originated as seats of administration for king, army or Church (Exeter, Chichester, Norwich). Such were some of the Midland boroughs, each surrounded by a shire to which it gave its name, e.g. Bedford, Leicester, Nottingham. Several existing settlements gained borough status by charter.

Society, based on the manor or barony, was feudal. Nine-tenths of the peasant cultivators were tied to the land and lived in small villages. Elsewhere they occupied isolated farmsteads.

Words such as beef (*boeuf*), mutton (*mouton*), and pork (*porc*) were introduced into the English language by the Normans, but these items of food were characteristic of the meals of nobles rather than of peasants. Ox, sheep, swine, were the names used by the herdsmen who tended the animals rather than fed upon them. Feeding farm animals presented serious problems with the approach of winter. There was virtually no fodder, so that it was necessary to slaughter old and weakly beasts in the late autumn.

2

The amount of reliable material relating to disease in Britain up to and including Norman times is lamentably small, and when information is available, it lacks detail. During the Roman occupation it is assumed that their society included physicians, surgeons, oculists and others to care for the health of the population, but few traces of their existence and activity remain. Very little is known about the diseases of the time. The Dark Ages are darker to the student of disease than to the historian. What little information there is, is based on palaeopathological material[6], on state documents, and, since literacy was associated with monastic clergy, on documents which survived the Viking invasions or the destruction and disposal of monastic libraries in the time of Henry VIII.

Because they leave few traces on early human skeletons, some of the diseases of prehistoric times are difficult to study. Other diseases, however, leave skeletal manifestations which permit of diagnosis. Palaeopathologists, including Brothwell, Møller-Christensen, Wells, Sandison, MacArthur and Roberts and Manchester, have studied thousands of early British skeletons and, on the basis of inferential evidence indicate the presence of leprosy, syphilis, tuberculosis, osteo-arthritis, osteomyelitis, weapon injuries, tumours and dental caries in the pre-Conquest population of this country.

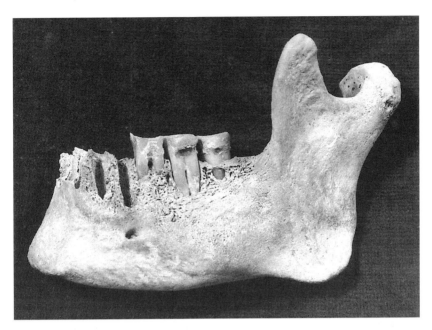

Plate 2: Mandible from an Anglo-Saxon individual from Raunds,
Northamptonshire, with carious lesions in the molars and evidence of
inflammation and recession of the bone consistent with leprosy (by permission of
the Department of Archaeological Sciences, University of Bradford)

It is not possible to indicate the frequency of leprosy from the contemporary historical records because available descriptions do not provide convincing evidence that what was called 'leprosy' was in fact influenced by the *Mycobacterium leprae*. The medieval conception of leprosy was strongly influenced by the biblical usage of the word. In the Bible 'leprosy' (*zara'ath*) is more a generic word embracing a number of different diseases. It also implied 'moral uncleanliness', which explains the present-day overtones of the word leper. MacArthur[7] sums up the confusion in diagnosis in early records as follows:

In the past 'leprosy' and its equivalents had a multitude of meanings. It was used for the true disease and for every disorder that was formerly supposed to be leprosy. The Greek form of the word was *lepra* (lepros, scaly), and was applied by the Greeks themselves to scaling skin diseases of the psoriasis type, and never to leprosy for which they used the word 'elephantiasis' because of the thickening and corrugation of the skin. Unfortunately 'lepra' was adopted as the classical medical term for leprosy with the result that, by suggestion of the word itself, a host of skin conditions associated with scales or scabs, which have no connexion with real leprosy, were identified as manifestations of this disease.

Leprosy began to make its appearance in Europe in the sixth century and it seems likely that the disease was introduced into Britain later in the same century. The lazar house (*leprosarium*) on the island of Tean in the Isles of Scilly has been dated to the seventh century. Doubtless the so-called lazar houses included among the inmates genuine cases of leprosy but the word 'lazar' signifies 'a poor and diseased person, especially a leper' and derives from the Lazarus of the Gospels. MacArthur says that there is no scriptural record 'that either the symbolic beggar of Christ's parable or the real Lazarus of Bethany, suffered from leprosy ... The beggar was *ulcerosus*, full of sores, which then suggested leprosy only.' Lazar houses, therefore, such as, for example, the early Hospital of St Peter and St Leonard at York, founded in AD 936 by King Athelstane,[8] were not necessarily built to halt the spread of the disease.

During the winter months the lack of fresh foods, meat, fruit and vegetables might be expected to have caused a serious deficiency of vitamins A and C. This would give rise to increased liability to septic infections of the skin, to rough and dry skin or to mild scurvy. But this is inferential since there is no direct bone evidence. Famines were frequent, and it has been suggested that the skin disease might have been pellagra, a dietary (vitamin B) deficiency disease, and not leprosy. Either way, personal hygiene during Anglo-Saxon times, and indeed until the mid-nineteenth century, was of a low order (where, except in literature, does one find evidence for unpleasant but medically important environmental facts such as the ubiquity of infestation by human fleas?) and skin diseases were commonplace. There is skeletal evidence of nine cases of leprosy in Great Britain, the oldest dating back to about AD 600. In Scotland, St Fillan, the 'leper', a teacher of the sixth century of peculiar sanctity, was specially celebrated in the cure of the disease[9] (Plate 2).

Investigators into the origin of syphilis have been more cautious in expressing opinions about evidence for the disease in ancient times. Syphilis has to be studied in terms of the treponematoses as a whole, since venereal syphilis, yaws and endemic syphilis cause bone lesions. At present there is no way to differentiate between these three infections in bones, if, bearing in mind the importance of bacterial mutation, they are to be regarded as individual infections by separate organisms. The sole British example in which the diagnosis of advanced syphilis is unquestionable is of a female skull discovered in the graveyard of St Mary Spittle, Spitalfields Market, London in 1926 (Plate 3). There are two skeletons, one from Chadlington, Oxfordshire, and another from near Portsmouth, which provide evidence that tuberculosis was also established in Britain by Saxon times.

As with modern humankind, the earlier peoples of Britain suffered from several varieties of arthritis. The type generally known as osteo-arthritis was seemingly common.

Plate 3: Adult female skull (medieval) showing evidence suggestive of syphilis
(by permission of the Duckworth Collection, University of Cambridge)

Apart from ancient bones there are early literary sources which afford evidence for the presence of certain diseases in Norman and pre-Norman times. Creighton,[10] the nineteenth-century medical historian, tells of a foreign invasion of plague at the time of the Venerable Bede (AD 672–735), of famine, pestilence and some non-famine sicknesses, but there is insufficient information to provide even tentative support for the diagnosis of any of these diseases.

Plague has always been a major scourge of mankind, but in these early days 'plague' was a general word for all diseases with a high mortality. It was in fact by way of being a generic term, rather like 'leprosy', or 'influenza' or 'fever' today. The name may have included true plague (bubonic or pneumonic) but also perhaps typhus or some other disorders for which no specific name existed. The word 'pestilence', too, would refer to almost any kind of acute epidemic. Pestilences were so frequent that only the most virulent and fatal ones would have been recorded. Nevertheless they were important factors in the social history of early Britain. Medical opinion at the present time would say that people do not die of hunger *per se*, i.e. hunger associated with the so-called 'famine pestilence', but rather from disease contracted as a result of undernourishment.

A major difficulty in attempts to interpret medieval and indeed classical medicine from literary documentary evidence is the complete lack of modern terminology and nomenclature. For instance, the Anglo-Saxon word for disease was *ádl*, that for pain was *ádl*, *cóau* or *ece*, and for ache or pain, *waerc*. When the ache or pain was localized in a particular part of the body, or was especially severe or fatal, these words were compounded with others, e.g. *fot-ádl*, a pain in the foot, gout, *ban-coau*, a killing pain, erysipelas. The usual word for pestilence was *máncwealm* (*cwelan*, to die), for cattle murrain *orfcwealm*, and both pestilence and murrain were signified by *wól*. It is clear that there is little evidence to suggest specific knowledge of the interior organs of the body or of their diseases.

In accordance with the beliefs of the times, plagues and pestilences were attributed to a variety of causes including arrows shot at victims by the gods, failure of crops, movement of stars, storms, the effect of drought or floods. In Anglo-Saxon England the sudden onset of disease was often ascribed to 'elfshot', arrows shot by elves. An alternative theory was that pestilence was caused by corrupted air, emanations from marshes or noxious vapours inhaled into the body. St Columba on Iona, seeing a dense cloud arising from the sea on an otherwise clear day, said to one of his monks:

> This cloud will be very harmful to men and to cattle ... it will pour down in the evening a pestilential rain which will cause grievous and festering ulcers to be found on the bodies of men and on the teats of cattle; and by these the sick men and cattle will suffer from that poisonous infection even unto death.

Such views persisted up to the beginning of scientific study of medicine, barely a century ago.

Pestilence appears to have devastated parts of Ireland, Scotland and Wales in the mid-sixth century, but there is no record of it having spread into England. St Brioc is said to have returned to his native Ceredigion (Dyfed) from Brittany to minister to his folk during a local outbreak of pestilence about 526. In 550 the 'Yellow Plague' was roaming through the land in the guise of 'a loathly monster'. A full description of this outbreak of pestilence in Wales is given in the life of St Teilo in the *Liber Landavensis* (quoted by Bonser).[11]

> St. Teilo received the pastoral care of the Church of Llandaff ... in which however he could not long remain, on account of the pestilence which nearly destroyed the whole nation. It was called Pestis Flava, because it occasioned all persons who were seized by it, to be yellow and without blood, and it

appeared to men as a column of watery cloud, having one end trailing along the ground, and on the other above, proceeding in the air, and passing through the whole country like a shower going through the bottom of the valleys. Whatever living creatures it touched with its pestiferous blast, either immediately died, or sickened for death. If anyone endeavoured to apply a remedy to the sick person, not only had the medicine no effect, but the dreadful disorder brought the physician, together with the sick person, to death. For it seized Maelgwyn, King of Guenedoth, and destroyed his country; and so greatly did the aforesaid destruction rage throughout the nation that it caused the country to be nearly deserted.

It is important to view such literary references within their traditional framework, since pestilence at that time was considered to be a living thing which roamed the land. There are several references in Celtic sources to severe epidemics in Ireland in the period 537–77. Mention is made of 'the battle of Camlann, in which Arthur and Medraut fell: and there was a plague (*mortalitas*) in Britain and Ireland', of 'a great mortality in which Mailcun, King of Guededota, reposed', of 'the disease (*pestis*) which is called *samthrosc*', of the 'Great Pestilence called the Boy Connell (buidhe chonnaill)' (in 550), and for the year 555 'a great mortality in this year'.

Scotland was also visited, for Adamnan[12] in his *Life of St Columba*, is at pains to record that the pestilence did not penetrate to those areas of Scotland in which were situated monasteries founded by St Columba. Shrewsbury[13] is of the opinion that these epidemics were spread by Celtic missionaries who carried them from the Continent to Ireland, whence they spread to Wales and Scotland.

The Celtic names for the pestilence, *blefed*, *cron chonnaill* and *buidhe chonnaill*, have given rise to misunderstanding as to the nature of the diseases concerned. Shrewsbury identifies all three words as smallpox, whereas MacArthur[14] suggests bubonic plague, relapsing fever and smallpox respectively. MacArthur is of the opinion that the series of outbreaks of pestilence (*blefed*) in the sixth century, were bubonic plague and related to the pestilence in the Byzantine Empire during Justinian's reign, the first authenticated visitation of bubonic plague in Europe. This epidemic probably originated in the hinterland of south-west Asia in about 540. Pelusium,[15] the great commercial entrepôt of Egypt, served as the major centre from which it is thought the infection spread, probably by corn ships. By 542, the pandemic extension of the great pestilence was under way, and it eventually spread slowly throughout the then known world, dying out towards the end of the sixth century. Western Europe, especially southern France and Germany, were heavily smitten by the *Lues inguinaria* (presumably the buboes of bubonic plague) with far-reaching social and economic results. The view of Procopius,[16] an eyewitness, was that 'no cause for the plague could be given or imagined except God.'

A second series of outbreaks of pestilence began in Britain and Ireland in 664 and continued, with short intervals, for about half a century. Creighton refers to this invasion as the only epidemic in early British annals that could be regarded as a plague of the same nature and on the same scale as the devastation of the continent of Europe brought by the plague of Justinian a century earlier. Community life was disorganized and Bede[17] speaks of the pestilence depopulating the south coast of Britain before spreading north into Northumbria. As with most visitations this pestilence was reputedly heralded by natural phenomena, in this case an eclipse of the sun, and 'it ravaged the country far and wide and destroyed a great multitude of men.' This was the great plague of Cadwallader's time. The East Saxons turned to idolatry on account of it. 'While the plague caused a heavy death roll in the province,' Sighere, who was ruler of the East Saxons under Wulfhere, King of Mercia, and his people 'abandoned the mysteries of the Christian Faith and relapsed into paganism. For the King himself, together with many of the nobles and common folk, loved this life and sought no other, having no belief in a future life.'[18]

The epidemic disease raged with equal severity in Ireland and Scotland. St Cuthbert was seized by the pestilence in the Abbey of Old Melrose. Seemingly he developed the usual swelling in the groin which unfortunately burst inwards so that he suffered from its effects for the rest of his life. Boisil, the prior of the Abbey, succumbed to it.[19]

Pestilence is recorded in Britain and Ireland in the years following 664, particularly in the monasteries. At this time, before the growth of towns, monasteries were among the larger communities; they carried large stores of grain, which would attract rats, the carriers of the plague. It is likely that monks, travelling from infested to uninfested monasteries, spread the pestilence. Certainly monasteries in isolated and unlikely places were afflicted. Bede tells of a decree by Theodore at the Synod of Hertford in 672, forbidding the movement of monks from one monastery to another 'after the Celtic fashion'. Outbreaks in Wales in the early 680s are mentioned in the Chronicle of the Princes (*Brut y Twysogion*) and for Ireland in the Cambrian Annals (*Annales Cambriae*).

There was a series of outbreaks of pestilence in the second half of the eighth century, chronicled in Irish annals, and from the pages of the *Anglo-Saxon Chronicle* came a long record of famine and disease in the ninth, tenth and eleventh centuries. These coincided with the incursions of the Norsemen in northern England and the Danish invasions of East Anglia which ravaged the country, leaving destruction in their train.

In the absence of efficient means of communication, areas devastated by

Viking raiders were unable to obtain even the necessities of life from other districts, and famines were frequent. Thus followed inevitable and local serious mortality among the population, and murrain (not plague) among cattle. Creighton has listed 'famine pestilences' in England for the years 679 to 1322.[20] There were forty-two such pestilences during this period, some lasting a year, others as many as four. An extract from the list for the second half of the eleventh and the first half of the twelfth century is given in Table 6.1.

Table 6.1 Famine pestilences in England between 1069 and 1143 (after Creighton)

Year	Character	Authority
1069	Wasting of Yorkshire	Simeon of Durham, ii. 188
1086 }	Great fever pestilence	Anglo-Saxon Chronicle, Malmesbury
1087 }	Sharp fever	Henry of Huntingdon, and most annalists
1091	Siege of Durham by the Scots	Simeon of Durham, ii. 339
1093 }	Floods, hard winter;	Anglo-Saxon Chronicle, Annals of
1095 }	severe famines; universal	Winchester, William of Malmesbury.
1096 }	sickness and mortality	Henry of Huntingdon, Annals of
1097 }		Margan, Matthew Paris and others
1103 }	General pestilence and murrain	Anglo-Saxon Chronicle, Roger of Wendover
1104 }		
1105 }		
1110 }	Famine	Anglo-Saxon Chronicle, Roger of Wendover
1112	'Destructive pestilence'	Anglo-Saxon Chronicle, Annals of Osney, Annales Cambriae
1114	Famine in Ireland; flight or death of people	Annals of Margan
1125	Most dire famine in all England; pestilence and murrain	Anglo-Saxon Chronicle, William of Malmesbury, Gest. Pont., p. 442, Henry of Huntingdon, Annals of Margan, Roger of Howden
1137	Famine from Civil War mortality	Anglo-Saxon Chronicle, Annals of Winchester, Henry of Huntingdon (1138)
1143	Famine and mortality	Gesta Stephani, p. 98, William of Newburgh, Henry of Huntingdon

There was virtually no increase of population during this period, famines and pestilences being the principal ('Malthusian') checks which kept it down to the level of its scanty means of subsistence. Expectation of life was probably less than thirty years.

Apart from pestilences, the early Anglo-Saxons were familiar with 'spring relapses', a peculiarity of the malaria that flourished in parts of England at that time. In infected persons the parasites tended to lie dormant during the winter, later becoming active with the approach of the longer days in spring. The Fen country, the marshes of the Thames and south-east Kent were endemic centres for malaria, the *lencten adl* (spring ill). MacArthur[21] says that the Venerable Bede in his *Ecclesiastical History*, written in Latin, describes the miraculous cure of a long-continued illness which he calls merely by the general term *febris* (fever). It is of interest to notice that in the Anglo-Saxon translation of this work, attributed to King Alfred, the translator identified the malady as malaria, and instead of employing one of the Anglo-Saxon equivalents of 'fever', he boldly repeated Bede's vague word by the specific *Lencten adl*, malaria. The term 'ague' has been used as synonymous with malaria, but not all agues were malarial. Ague originally meant any acute fever, and later was often applied specifically to typhus, sometimes in the more unequivocal form 'the spotted ague'.

Creighton, an important source of information for this period, also mentions a swift and fatal pestilence which broke out among the Danes in Kent. It was probably of the same form of camp sickness, including dysentery (as the name *dolor viscerum* suggests) as that which occurred in later periods. It is the only instance of this kind recorded in early British history. It occurred in the year 1010 or 1011, when the Danes stormed Canterbury, massacred its inhabitants and carried the remnants captive to their ships at Sandwich. If the disease was dysentery it is now known that the organisms which produce it are widespread in those places where hygiene or sanitation are of a low order. Such conditions are favourable to the spread of the disease, which produces a steady and unrelenting series of infections. Mortality from dysentery depends on the particular variety of organisms involved, but death rates were usually high. Creighton, quoting an early narrative of William of Malmesbury, says, 'a deadly sickness broke out among the Danes, affecting them in troops (*catervatim*) and proving so rapid in its effects that death ensued before they could feel pain. The stench of the unburied bodies so infected the air as to bring a plague upon those of them who had remained well.'[22] Seemingly the pestilence destroyed the Danes by tens and twenties, and a large number perished.

There are scattered references to 'pock disease' and 'the pox' in Norman and pre-Norman times, and these would refer to smallpox, a disease which did not come into prominence until the sixteenth century, and not to 'great pox' or syphilis, which erupted with extraordinary virulence in 1493 and spread with great rapidity. This reached Britain by 1497, and there were victims as far north as Aberdeen.

Though the treatment of disease is not considered, brief mention should be made at this point of the Anglo-Saxon Leech Books, and more precisely to the Leech Book of Bald. Bald, a physician, had a monastic scribe write, between 900 and 950, a medical manuscript which incorporated extensive borrowings from Greek writers such as Paulus of Aegina, Alexander of Tralles, and others of classical medical thought, together with a medley of folk remedies, Christian prayers, magic and pagan material. The Leech Book embodies some of the best medical literature available to Britain and western Europe at that time and also provides an indication of the separation between spiritual and physical conceptions of disease healing. The work is of interest in that it contains characteristic views on medicine in these early centuries.

7

Medieval Times

The invasion of Britain by bubonic plague in 1348 was an episode of exceptional catastrophe. It was a new and terrifying illness and no one at the time had any idea of its fundamental nature, ultimate cause or its method of diffusion. Apocalyptic estimates of the subsequent plague mortality of one-third or even one-half of the population have long prevailed. The 'Great Pestilence' or 'Great Dying', as the disease was called by contemporary chroniclers (the modern pseudonym 'The Black Death' was not introduced until 1823), was a wave of the second pandemic of the disease which had spread out from the Indian subcontinent between 1340 and 1352 to affect Asia Minor, Europe, the Channel Islands, Britain, Iceland and Greenland and parts of North Africa.

In keeping with the general beliefs of those early days, it comes as no surprise to discover that putrefying corpses in China, fogs over Europe, corruption or pollution of the air by noxious vapours, comet-borne miasmas, Jews acting as agents for Satan, and punishment by God for human sins, were among the several explanations invoked as the cause of plague.

The disease is thought to have started its expansion into Europe at Kaffa (Caffa) – the modern Feodosia – a Black Sea town on the Crimea, in 1346 (Fig. 7.1). The town was under siege by the Tartar army of Kipchik Khan Janiberg and 'the beleaguered Christians saw the heavenly arrows strike the Tartars.' It would seem that the Tartars were suffering from plague which they had probably contracted in Central Asia. Gabriel de Mussis says that the Tartars hurled their dead with catapults into the city. This might well suggest a fourteenth-century attempt at bacteriological warfare. Indeed, subsequent events revealed the 'Great Pestilence' to be a particularly vicious attempt on the part of plague parasites to wipe out the human race. From Kaffa the disease was disseminated by rats aboard sailing vessels bound for parts of Europe and North Africa.

Bubonic plague was primarily an infectious disease of certain species of rodents, and plague in humans was the result of a fortuitous invasion of the human body by an internal pathogen of these rodents. The pathogen in question was the bacillus *Pasteurella pestis* (now *Yersinia pestis*), and this produced endemic infection in rats. It was transferred from plague-infested

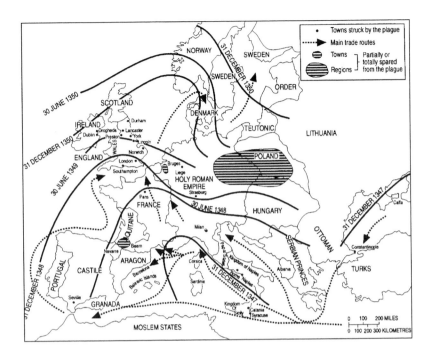

Fig. 7.1 Advance of the Great Pestilence
('Black Death') into west and central Europe, 1347–50
(adapted from E. Carpentier, 'Autour de la peste noire')

rats to individuals through the bite of infected rat fleas (*Xenopsylla cheopis*).
The rodent acted as host to the plague bacillus, and the flea was the carrier
or vector. In medieval times the black or house or ship rat (*Rattus rattus*)
was responsible for the epidemics of bubonic plague. It infested the dark,
unventilated, humid, wattle-and-daub and thatch-roofed dwellings of the
common folk and rarely and reluctantly strayed out of doors. A native of
western Asia, this type of rat was a climbing animal which lived and bred in
close contact with humans. The field rat (*Rattus norvegicus*), which did not
come to Europe until the eighteenth century but now holds supremacy in
these islands, is different from the house rat in that it normally breeds at
some distance from people. Human plague is said to have correlated with
plague in house rats since it was only after the usual rat hosts had been killed
by bubonic plague that fleas sought the blood of individuals. The bite of the
flea was the commonest mode of transmission of the bacillus into the human
bloodstream. This gave the bubonic type of plague. There were certain
conditions, however, in which respiratory droplets infected by the plague
bacillus entered the human body and caused pulmonary or pneumonic

plague. According to Shrewsbury[1] this form could not persist as an independent disease in the absence of the bubonic form.

Bubonic plague ('botch') was characterized by the appearance of buboes (swellings) of the lymph glands, particularly in the groin and armpits. In its final phase the infection took on the septicaemic form in which the bacillus passed directly into the blood. Pneumonic plague, characterized by spitting blood, was localized in the lungs and seems to have thrived under cool or cold conditions. It was directly transmissible from person to person through breathing, coughing or sputum. This is not the place to offer hypotheses or explanations, but it should be noted that 'the few medical historians who have taken cognizance of the detailed evidence of historic outbreaks of plague have tended to come to one conclusion: that bubonic plague was spread by *Pulex irritans* (the human flea) and not the fleas of rats.'[2]

Hirst[3] maintains that the distribution and density of rat populations governs the distribution and density of the human disease, and that the rodent density is decisive because no serious outbreak of bubonic plague can take place in a locality supporting only a small or widely dispersed rat population. The house-rat population of Britain on the eve of the 'Great Pestilence' is not known, but it might be inferred from a study of the distribution and local densities of the human population about which a certain amount of information is available.

Rattus rattus found conditions congenial in the lowly dwelling-houses crowded together in fourteenth-century towns (Fig. 7.2). Stone-built houses of the well-to-do were not so congenial to them. Thus bubonic plague was primarily and principally a disease of the poor. Where dwellings were scattered in the thinly populated countryside, the rat population was too small for plague to become established, and it struck only the occasional house here and there. In consequence, the incidence of bubonic plague in fourteenth-century Britain was very uneven, and many places were spared its ravages. Shrewsbury's view is that 'in the comparatively densely populated region of East Anglia, and in the larger towns that were afflicted by it, 'The Great Pestilence' may possibly have destroyed as much as one-third of the population; in the rest of England and Wales it is extremely doubtful if as much as one-twentieth of the population was destroyed by it. These are not random assertions; they are inherent in the aetiology of bubonic plague.' This might explain why the crisis of 1349 seems to have had less of an effect on the military and political history of the period than on social and economic history.

Bubonic plague entered Britain at the little haven of Melcombe Regis (the modern Weymouth) in Dorset early in August 1348. It came to Europe either via Calais or via the Channel Islands[4] and spread thence with a speed relative to the transport conditions of the day. Fleas were transported about

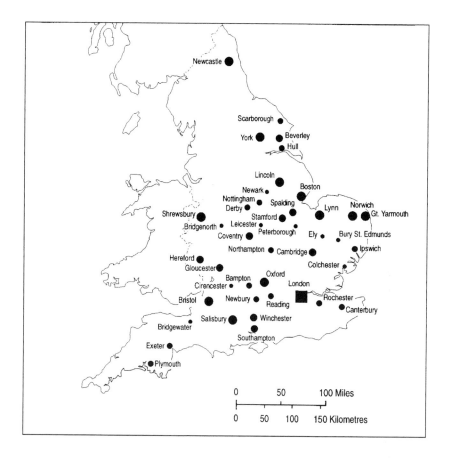

Fig. 7.2 Ranking of the provincial towns of England, 1334 (based on data in
W. G. Hoskins, *The Making of the English Landscape*)

the human person in his belongings while the timid *Rattus rattus* was
conveyed within bulky merchandise. Creighton says the disease spread
from Melcombe Regis through Dorset, Devon and Somerset, and reached
Bristol by 15 August 1348 (Fig. 7.3). It was in Gloucester, Oxford and
London either 'at Michaelmas' (29 September) or 'at All Saints' (1
November),[5] was active in London during the winter months of that year,
an unusual occurrence because in temperate latitudes the rat fleas hiber-
nate and the plague becomes quiescent or is extinguished. The disease also
moved south-westwards through Devon into Cornwall. 'The deanery of
Kenn to the south and south-west of Exeter is believed to have been the
worst-affected in the whole of England: eighty-six incumbents perished
from a deanery with only seventeen parish churches.'[6]

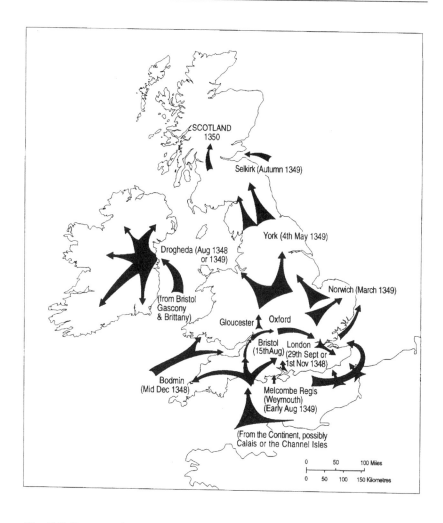

Fig. 7.3 Progress of the Great Pestilence ('Black Death') in Britain in the four-teenth century (based on C. Creighton, *A History of Epidemics* and P. Ziegler, *The Black Death*)

Norwich and the eastern counties were smitten in the spring of 1349 and suffered severely during the summer. York was attacked about the first week of May and suffered until the end of July. The spring and summer of 1349 were seasons of great mortality all over England except perhaps in the southern counties where the outbreaks began.

The disease apparently moved into Monmouthshire before it had run its course through Gloucestershire and Worcestershire. It seems to have trav-elled north along the Welsh border and entered north Wales near Holywell.

Thence the plague spread quickly in the summer of 1349 to such places as Ruthin and Llangollen. The 'Great Pestilence' probably reached Carmarthen by way of the sea.[7]

Of the appearance of plague in Scotland in 1349, John of Fordun wrote: 'By God's will this evil led to a strange and unwonted kind of death, in so much that the flesh of the sick was somehow puffed out and swollen, and they dragged out their earthly life for barely two days.'

The 'pestilence' came to Scotland from Cumberland and Durham. For a time its progress was held up at the Scottish border and 'the foul death of the English' gave the Scots a malicious pleasure. But from a reckless foray into England the Scots brought the plague into their own country, where it was estimated that it destroyed one-third of the population. 'Men shrank from it so much that, through fear of contagion, some, fleeing as from the face of leprosy, or from an adder, durst not go and see their parents in the throes of death.'[8] That Scotland suffered severely is confirmed by Andrew of Wyntoun:[9]

> In Scotland, the fyrst Pestilens
> Begough, off sa gret wyolens,
> That it was sayd, off lywand men
> The thyrd part it destroyid then
> Efftyr that in till Scotland
> A yhere or more it was wedand
> Before that tyme was nevyr sene
> A pestilens in our land sa kene:
> Bathe men and barnys and women
> It sparryd noucht for to kille them.

The disease made only slight progress in Scotland during the winter of 1349, but the following spring advanced with renewed vigour to encompass virtually the whole of the country.

The 'Great Pestilence' in Britain extended over a period of three years: southern England in the latter half of 1348, the whole of England and Wales and the south of Scotland in 1349, and Scotland in 1350.

While plague spread to some remote hamlets its incidence and effect were nevertheless uneven. East Kent, for instance, was only slightly affected, while west Kent experienced heavy mortality. In Dorset one hundred benefices were vacated in seven months. Deaths ran highest in sea and river ports and coastal districts, where presumably rats obtained food most easily; they were lowest in pastoral or sparsely populated hilly areas. Stretches of marshland and fen acted as effective barriers against the disease.

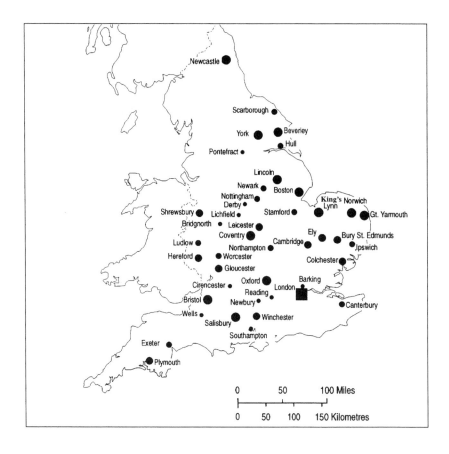

Fig. 7.4 Ranking of the provincial towns of England, 1377 (based on data in
W. G. Hoskins, *The Making of the English Landscape*)

Some authorities are of the opinion that the population of Britain was
halved, others that it was reduced by 30 per cent. Shrewsbury carves the
figure down to one-tenth at most. Studies of manorial documents by Rees[10]
and others indicate that in some parts of England at least scarcely one-tenth
of the inhabitants were left alive. 'Animals wandered about without an
owner, goods lay open on all sides and the harvest remained ungathered.'
In the period 1348–77 the population of England fell from about 3.8
million to 2.5 million.[11] London's population in 1377 was about 35,000.
For York it was 11,000, Bristol 9,500, Coventry 7,000, Plymouth 7,000
and Norwich 6,000 (Fig. 7.4).

The medical profession was virtually helpless in both the prevention and
cure of plague. Later centuries produced a veritable flood of preventive

orders, plague tracts and defensive measures (Plate 5) but the fourteenth century regrettably produced little practical activity on the part of contemporary British physicians. There is evidence of some slight appreciation of quarantine and sanitation problems. For instance, in 1348 Gloucester cut off all intercourse with Bristol. Not improbably other towns adopted a similar practice. Some public authorities such as London devoted special attention to the cleaning of the town's ditches and streets and the carting away of filth.[12]

In addition to the sometimes severe mortality there were important economic and social consequences of the 'Great Pestilence'. For a time art, education, trade and industry were paralysed. Norwich, centre of the Flemish cloth-weaving industry and sixth city of the kingdom, took a generation to recover something of its former prosperity after being struck by the plague. There was an easing of the pressure of population and a retreat from agriculturally marginal lands. Labour was at a premium, and instead of peasants seeking land, landlords were obliged to seek workers and tenants. In many parts scarcity of labour and high wages contributed to a change-over from arable to sheep farming and in some cases to abandonment of villages. The decay of feudalism was accelerated and the villein (agricultural serf) became yeoman-farmer or wage-earner. The new class of yeomen rented their own farms and bought land. Others remained as free labourers able to demand high wages. Parliament was obliged eventually to pass laws in an attempt to stabilize wages. It would seem that the plague contributed to a change in the status of England from a society based on personal service to a money economy dictated by the state. Agitations for higher wages and higher standards of living were persistent. Bean[13] says that the peasants and artisans of late fourteenth- and fifteenth-century England did, in fact, achieve high standards of living following a considerable rise in wages.

Some appreciation, expressed in modern terms, of the magnitude of the experience in which the people of medieval Britain had been involved during the time of the 'Great Pestilence' may be obtained from Thompson's analogy between its after-effects and those of the First World War.[14] In both instances he says, contemporaries complained of 'economic chaos, social unrest, high prices, profiteering, depravation of morals, lack of production, industrial indolence, frenetic gaiety, wild expenditure, luxury, debauchery, social and religious hysteria, greed, avarice, maladministration, decay of manners.'[15]

For three centuries or more after the 'Great Pestilence', plague was not long absent from one part of Britain or another but, taken as a whole, the country was never again affected to the same extent as in the years 1348–50. A so-called 'Second Pestilence' (*Pestis secunda*) occurred in

1361–2. It appears to have attacked in particular the young (hence *Pestis puerorum*), 'pestilence of the children'. Shrewsbury[16] is of the opinion that this was not bubonic plague but epidemic influenza. There is reference to pestilence in Scotland in 1362 with symptoms and mortality similar to those of the 1350 outbreak. A 'Third Pestilence' (*Pestis tertia*) affected England in 1368–9, and a 'Fourth Pestilence' (*Pestis quarta*) in 1375–6 affected the south of England, with an outbreak four years later in northern England and Scotland. *Pestis quinta*, said to have been comparable to the 'Great Pestilence' in its severity, spread through most of England in 1390–1 and into Scotland in the following year.

The seeming ubiquity of bubonic plague in Britain in the fourteenth century must not obscure the fact that other diseases afflicted the population at that time. Most of them were untreatable, spread more readily than bubonic plague and were usually just as lethal. These included fevers, fluxes, running scabs, boils and botches, burning agues, pocks and pestilences. All of these are mentioned by Langland.[17] 'Burning ague' was almost certainly typhus fever (see p.118), a winter disease associated with dirt and destitution. It flourished on the medieval custom of wearing the same underclothing (and therefore the same fleas!) from Michaelmas to Lady Day (29 September–25 March). Pneumonia undoubtedly occurred in epidemic form in the winter months. In all probability, whooping cough, smallpox, measles, diphtheria, the enteric fevers and influenza also occurred in widespread and deadly epidemics.

Talbot[18] draws attention to one of the most curious epidemics to appear in the Middle Ages. The disease involved was called St Vitus's Dance. 'Crowds of people were suddenly smitten with an urge to dance and although they professed to be suffering agonies while doing so, continued their compulsive movements for long periods at a time, even until they fell down and died.' He quotes one of the earliest and most vivid accounts given by Giraldus Cambrensis of events at St Almedha's (St Eiliwedd) Church in the parish of Llanhamlach, a mile east of Brecon, south Wales:

> The saint's day was celebrated again in the same place where it had been celebrated for many years. The day was August 1st. Many people came here from distant parts, their bodies weakened by various diseases, hoping to be healed through the merits of the holy maiden ... Men and women could be seen in the church and churchyard, singing and dancing. Suddenly they would fall down quite motionless, as if in a trance, and then as suddenly leap up again like lunatics to perform tasks that were forbidden on feast days ... One man appeared to have a ploughshare in his hands, another urged forward his oxen with a whip. They accompanied these tasks with songs, but the notes were all out of tune. You could see one imitating a cobbler,

another a carpenter; one pretended to be carrying a yoke, whilst another moved his hands as if he were drawing out thread and winding it into a skein. One man would be walking up and down weaving a net with imaginary thread; another would sit at an imaginary loom, throwing his shuttle to and fro and banging the treadle with jerky movements. Inside the church (which is more surprising), you could see the same people offering gifts at the altar, after which they appeared to rouse themselves from their trance and recover.

There was a continuing climatic decline during the fourteenth century (p.32) with lower temperatures. Britain suffered frequent famines and hundreds of people are thought to have starved. The year 1371 was described as the 'grete de yere'. Another bad year was 1383 when harvests were poor and the fruit crop was badly affected. Many deaths were attributed to starving people having fed on unripe or bad fruit.

Unless they assumed truly catastrophic dimensions and caused terror and panic in the whole population, as in the case of plague, pestilence and famine, disease and death are rarely mentioned in extant records. There is no mention of the common, if not almost universal presence of unrelieved pain from infected wounds suppurating for weeks, bad teeth and toothache, or gastric upsets following the eating of rotten foods. Expectation of life at birth for males was about thirty years, and after surviving the first and critical year it was still only thirty-four years.

Periods of privation and malnutrition must have greatly impaired the resistance of the common folk to disease. However, the economic and social *sequelae* of this period are in course of re-examination.

8

Tudor Times

The 'Great Pestilence' or Black Death was followed by a long series of recurrent outbreaks of plague. The disease was endemic in Britain in the late fourteenth century and fifteenth century. There were at least twelve outbreaks between the Black Death and the succession of the Tudors which affected the whole country, and eight outbreaks which appear to have been confined to London. There is little record of the almost annual ravages of plague in Tudor times, although it is known from letters and a few surviving Elizabethan plague-bills that these were considerable and constituted the most formidable medical problem of the day. Indeed, the official celebration of Queen Elizabeth's accession had to be curtailed because of an epidemic in London which caused the death of over 30,000 people. At first, the visitations were on a national scale but afterwards became more localized, being restricted to towns, and more particularly to the larger towns. The incidence of plague became increasingly urban at a time when most of the population lived in the countryside. Alongside plague were severe outbreaks of typhus, measles, syphilis and 'English sweat'. There were repeated outbreaks of these major infectious diseases which tended to obscure the presence of the common, everyday ailments of the people such as rheumatism, toothache and septic infections of the skin, which were accepted as the normal accompaniment of living.

The sixteenth century was a period when life for the ordinary people was hard and comfortless. Birth rates and death rates were high. Infancy and childhood were marked by fearful mortality, and early life was plagued by several killing and disabling diseases. In epidemic or famine years, death rates exceeded birth rates, and sometimes population growth was at a standstill or even declined. At best the population increased only slowly.

Eighty per cent of the population lived in rural communities and, as in previous centuries, was confined to the more fertile areas. The general changes in the agricultural system from arable to sheep farming led to the enclosure of estates by landlords, particularly in the south-east of Britain. A single shepherd was often all that was required when previously there had been a number of ploughmen. The resulting pressure on the labour market combined with the financial stability of the government of the day and debasement of the coinage led to widespread poverty. The equivalent of the wage rate in terms of consumables reached a particularly low level by the end of the sixteenth century.[1] Town life and industrial life had not developed sufficiently to absorb the new class of vagrant and rootless labourers which was created. It was this great social problem which resulted in the passing of the first Poor Law Act early in the seventeenth century. By this Act local taxes were raised and officials appointed to act as overseers of the poor.

Towns were still relatively unimportant. The average-sized provincial town had perhaps 2,000 to 5,000 inhabitants. London, about the year 1500, may have had about 60,000 people, York, Norwich, Bristol and Edinburgh about 15,000 inhabitants each. Before these came a dozen or so towns such as Exeter and Salisbury, each with between 5,000 and 10,000 people. At the start of the sixteenth century the population of England was just over 3¼ million, of Scotland about ¾ million, and of Wales, ¼ million. A total for Britain of about 4¼ in 1500 rose to between 6 and 7 million by 1600 (Fig. 8.1). Expectation of life at birth was still little more than thirty years.

Methods of keeping livestock had made little progress up to Tudor times. It remained difficult to provide adequate winter feed for the animals and it was still customary to slaughter and salt most of the non-breeding stock in the late autumn. Meat was in short supply during winter, although for a time the pigeon-loft provided a useful source of fresh meat for certain of the gentry along with the birds and beasts that were hunted and trapped. Milk could not be kept for any length of time, and a great deal of it was churned into butter which, though salted, was to a greater or lesser degree rancid by the time of eating.

Apart from London and a few other centres, food for the main towns could be obtained without a great deal of difficulty from the immediate neighbourhood. There was no means of preserving perishable foods apart from drying, salting or pickling. This was serious in the towns, where carcasses of meat or consignments of fish might be several days old before being disposed of. Indeed a contemporary theory of disease was that the smell from stale fish and stinking meat gave 'an odour of putrefaction' which led to outbreaks of plague.

Land enclosure in some areas meant the loss of grazing lands for peasants. They were thus unable to keep the occasional cow to provide them with 'white meat', as dairy produce was called in the sixteenth century. During the second half of the sixteenth century bread was the mainstay of the diet of the English village labourer, supplemented by peas and beans, soups, trapped game and fish. Eggs were generally plentiful, sometimes supplemented by bacon or ham. It is said that the traditional English breakfast of bacon and eggs dates from this period. Oatmeal was an important

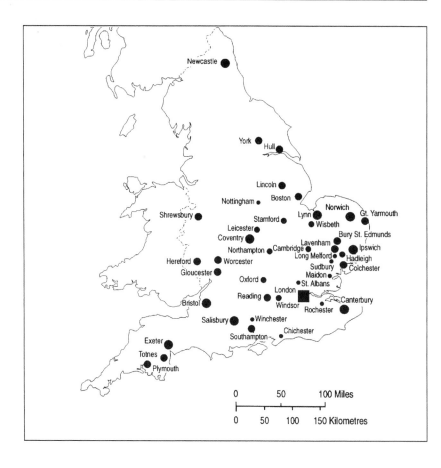

Fig. 8.1 Ranking of the provincial towns of England, 1523–7 (based on data in
W. G. Hoskins, *The Making of the English Landscape*)

item of diet in Scotland. Estienne Perlin in his *Description des royaulmes
d'Angleterre et d'Écosse* (Paris, 1558), after observing that Scotland was
plentiful in provisions 'which are as cheap as any part of the world', wrote
that the poor people 'put their dough between two irons to make it into
bread and then made it into what was esteemed good food in that country
and tolerably cheap'.

On the whole diets were deficient in vitamins A and D, and this is
thought by Drummond[2] to account for the then common occurrence of
stones in the bladder and urinary tract. Vitamin A deficiency might also
have accounted for such eye diseases as night blindness (xeropthalmia).

There were several years of dearth during the second half of the sixteenth
century when malnutrition, if not actual starvation, must have been wide-

spread.[3] Periods of food shortage in the latter part of the sixteenth century were frequently followed by outbreaks of plague and typhus. Indeed, Saltmarsh[4] says that 'more than any single catastrophe this continual sapping of the human resources of England would account for the gradual but continuous decay of her national prosperity.'

The sixteenth century saw the beginning of statistical records in the form of the London Bills of Mortality and the parish register. The Bills, one of the earliest examples of a classification of causes of death, began probably in 1532 and were published thereafter at regular intervals, usually only when plague was epidemic (Plate 6). Between 1563 and 1592 the regular series began. The Bills were compiled by parish clerks[5] from lists furnished every Tuesday by 'Searchers' whose duty it was to inspect the dead and register the cause of death. 'The Searchers, hereupon (who are ancient Matrons sworn to their office) repair to place where the dead Corps lies, and by view of the same, and by other enquiries, they examine by what Disease or Casualty the Corps died.'[6]

The reliability or otherwise of the lists drawn up by the Searchers (who were seldom able to diagnose the cause of death except in obvious and familiar conditions such as trauma or plague) is not relevant here. The Bills, nevertheless, provide some indication of the diseases prevalent at that time. Among these, in addition to plague, may be cited 'sweating sickness', syphilis and 'gaol fever' (typhus).

According to Creighton, a confirmed believer in the miasmatic theory of disease causation (foul odours emanating from decaying bodies, decomposing rubbish and excreta, etc.) and opponent of the newly formulated and rudimentary germ theory, 'sweating sickness' (English Sweat) suddenly appeared in Britain at the end of the fifteenth century. It was in Creighton's view a 'new disease' with a high mortality. Death occurred sometimes within six hours of onset, with sweating, from which the disease took its name, as a prominent symptom. Seemingly, the disease remained localized in various parts of England, and after five epidemics, in 1485, 1508, 1517, 1528, and 1551 respectively, vanished as mysteriously as it had come. The disease was known a few days after the landing of Henry VII at Milford Haven on 7 August 1485, and certainly before the Battle of Bosworth on 22 August. It broke out in London after Henry's arrival in that city and was severe at the end of September and during October, causing great mortality. Among the victims were two mayors and four aldermen.

Nothing was heard again of the sweating sickness until 1507–8 when a second outbreak of the disease occurred. This was less fatal than the visitation of 1485. A third epidemic in 1517 was more severe. Several towns, including Oxford and Cambridge, had a 50 per cent death rate. The disease occurred for the fourth time in 1528 and with great severity. It first showed itself in London at the end of May and spread quickly over the whole of England. Mortality was particularly heavy in the metropolis; the royal court was broken up and Henry VIII left the city, frequently changing his residence.

Sweating sickness spread over England and the rest of Britain, the Low Countries, Germany and France on several occasions in the 1520s, and there were further outbreaks in 1545, 1551 and 1558. The epidemic of 1551 was described with care by the physician John Caius.[7]

The sweating sickness, unlike plague, or typhus, was not especially fatal to the poor, but rather, as Caius affirmed, attacked the richer people and those who led a free life. 'They which had this sweat, sore with the peril of death, were either men of wealth, ease or welfare, or of the poorer sort such as were idle persons, good ale drinkers and tavern haunters.'

Some attributed the sweating sickness to the English climate with its damp atmosphere and fogs, others to the frightful lack of personal and domestic hygiene, still others to the intemperate habits of its victims. More recently it has been ascribed to food poisoning, although a nutritional aetiology is also claimed as a predisposing cause. Neither of these was adequate, either separately or collectively, to produce the disease. The sweating sickness was probably a specific infective disease in much the same sense as were plague, typhus, scarlet fever or malaria. It was a clearly defined entity which ran a dramatic course. Contemporary descriptions of sweating sickness fail to reveal recognizable similarities to influenza as the latter disease is known at the present time, or to descriptions of an epidemic of influenza which occurred in Edinburgh in 1562. There were, in fact, influenza epidemics in Britain throughout the sixteenth century, particularly in 1510, 1557-8 and 1580 (see Fig. 8.2). The 1580 influenza epidemic (called the 'Spanish Flu') crossed the English Channel from the Low Countries and diffused through the British Isles during August, September and October of that year, the last one comparable with the pandemic of 1918. The only modern disease resembling sweating sickness is that known in France as the Picardy Sweat, but there seems little doubt that the Picardy Sweat is not the same disease as influenza. The disease arrived on the English scene after the Wars of the Roses and vanished as mysteriously as it came, never to appear again. In that time, however, it killed more than all the long years of the wars had done.

There was still confusion in medieval times between leprosy, syphilis and smallpox. True leprosy was declining at the end of the fourteenth century, and by the fifteenth was no longer endemic, but the term 'leprosy' continued to be used later to describe a multitude of skin conditions. Creighton's numerous mentions of leprosy (of special note in this context is the Ordnance of Edward III which Creighton quotes and which, addressed to the mayor and sheriffs of London, states that lepers communicated their

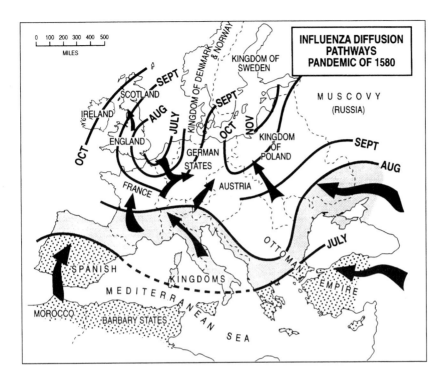

Fig. 8.2 Reconstructed influenza diffusion pathways during the late summer and autumn of 1580. Spanish economic and political ties at that time, including activities within the Netherlands, help explain many of the movement directions (after G. F. Pyle and K. D. Patterson, 1983)

disease by 'carnal intercourse with women in stews and other secret places') were not leprosy but may well have been syphilis.

In the last years of the fifteenth century there was an extraordinary pandemic of syphilis ('French pox' or 'the Great Pox') in Europe. That it reached Britain there is little doubt,[8] yet it makes hardly any appearance in records of that time. 'Wide and deep as the commotion must have been which caused it, it found hardly any more permanent expression than the private talk of the many of those days.'[9] The origin of the European pandemic remains a mystery. Some cite an American origin, believing that it was brought back from America by sailors who accompanied Columbus on his celebrated voyage. Others argue that syphilis had occurred in Europe from time immemorial and that up to the end of the fifteenth century and the beginning of the sixteenth century it had been a less acute and fatal illness and had been confused with leprosy and many other skin diseases.

There were indications of a somewhat unusual prevalence of *lues venerea*

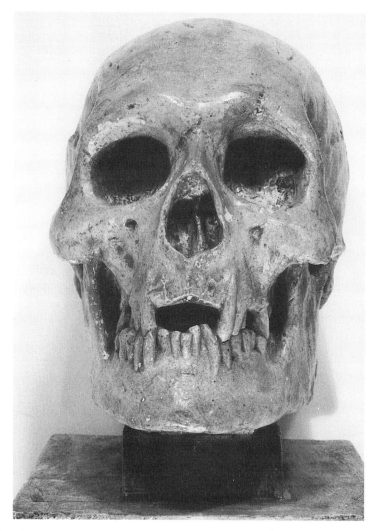

Plate 4: Cast of the skull of King Robert I of Scotland (1306–9) showing evidence
suggestive of leprosy (copyright, Department of Anatomy, University of Edinburgh,
with permission)

(*Morbus Gallicus* or *Morbus Neapolitanus*) in southern France in the autumn
of 1494 and of a spread by contagion to Barcelona and Valencia in Spain.
The expedition (1494–5) of the young French king, Charles VIII, which
passed through southern France *en route* for Naples is said to have started
the malady on Italian soil. There are also theories of a native Italian origin,
and also for a French origin for the disease. Hirsch has drawn parallels, on
a minor scale, to cases of syphilis of severe type and communicable by

unusual means, having been cultivated from quite commonplace beginnings among unsophisticated communities about the Adriatic and Baltic, and concludes that the 'mode of origin and the characteristics of these epidemics of syphilis appear to me to furnish the key to an understanding of the remarkable disease in the fifteenth century – an episode which entirely resembles them as regards its type and differs from them only as regards extent'.[10] At the present time there is doubt concerning a New World origin of venereal syphilis, and yet it is not possible to prove for certain its presence in the Old World in pre-Columban times.

Syphilis was thought to be a punishment sent by God, and theologians maintained that general godlessness was the cause of the scourge. Doctors refused to have anything to do with the 'dirty' diseases and handed over the sick to barbers, bath attendants and charlatans. Syphilis is now known as a social disease, communicated by intimate contact, nearly always by sexual intercourse. The causative organism is the spirochaete *Treponema pallidum* (earlier *Spirochaeta pallida*) which has the important biological characteristic of requiring moisture for life and transmission. Continuous moisture is necessary for the transfer of the organism from one person to another. The socio-economic environment in which the habits, customs and attitudes of people permit them to have sexual relations with infected persons plays an important part in the transmission.

The epidemic of syphilis lasted for about twenty-five to thirty years in Britain, after which the disease reverted to the more endemic form of the present day. By the time William Clowes,[11] surgeon to St Bartholomew's Hospital, London, published his treatise on syphilis in 1579, the disease appears to have lost its terrible severity.

Much points to Henry VIII having had syphilis. The many miscarriages and still-born children of his queens, his own chronic leg sores and a suspected nerve syphilis towards the end of his life suggest as much.[12] Syphilis was supposed to have been the reason for Edward VI's sickliness and early death, Queen Mary's childlessness and a contributory reason why Queen Elizabeth did not marry.

The early history of smallpox in Britain is obscure but it seems to have been a common disease in the sixteenth century. There was an epidemic of smallpox in 1561–2, and Queen Elizabeth herself suffered from a severe attack of the disease.

Medical teaching during the late Middle Ages continued in favour of the Greek doctrine of Aristotle, Hippocrates and Galen.[13] This, a blend of observation, experience and philosophy, was the humoral doctrine. The natural world was assumed to be made up of air, fire, water and earth. Each of these elements had a characteristic quality: air was cold, fire was hot, water was moist and earth was dry. A combination of any of these elements resulted in a blending of qualities or a complexion. Four complexions were recognized and with each was associated an appropriate humour.

Complexion	*Qualities*	*Humour*
Choleric	Hot and dry	Yellow or green bile
Melancholic	Cold and dry	Black bile
Phlegmatic	Cold and moist	Phlegm
Sanguine	Hot and moist	Blood

The complexions determined the individual's appearance and characteristics, but it could be affected by an excess of another humour. Thus a person of phlegmatic temperament would be rendered melancholic if anything occurred to cause an excess of black bile.

Ill-balanced humours were thought to predispose to disease in general, although it was admitted that some diseases such as plague, syphilis, ophthalmia, consumption (tuberculosis), and leprosy were exceptions. No theory had however been put forward to account for these exceptions and certainly no one knew what was transmitted. In 1546 Girolamo Frascatoro (Hieronymus Frascatorius, 1478–1553), who lived most of his life in Verona, published a small book called *De contagione* (Venice, 1546) which contains a theory by which it was thought that 'infection' was due to the passage of minute bodies, capable of self-multiplication, from the infector to the infected. Frascatorius was without doubt long before his time, for his theory bears a superficial resemblance to modern doctrine. Indeed he might even be called the sixteenth-century pioneer of the germ theory. The term 'syphilis' originated with him for he also wrote a long medical poem entitled *Syphilis sive morbus gallicus* (Verona, 1530).

There was much human misery in Britain in Tudor times. The gaols were seriously overcrowded with unwashed wretches, and the lice they brought with them sufficed to transmit the horrifying disease typhus. There were at least three accounts of typhus ('gaol fever tragedies'). They relate to the Cambridge Black Assizes in 1522, the Oxford Black Assizes in 1577 and the Exeter Black Assizes in 1586. In each case lawyers, county gentry and officials, jurors and others died. There is no mention of prisoners dying in the Cambridge episode, but two or three prisoners died in chains a few days before the Assizes in Oxford. In Exeter there had been deaths in the gaols among Portuguese and English felons.

It was not known then that typhus (the causative organism is a rickettsia – *R. prowazekii*) was conveyed from person to person by lice (*Pediculus humanus*). The lice were infected by feeding upon persons sick with the disease. Several explanations for typhus were offered; 'the savour of the prisoners' or 'the filth of the house' were invoked for the Cambridge

Assizes, and in Oxford it was the 'smell of the gaol'. In Exeter 'some did impute it to certain Portingals, then prisoners in the said gaol.' In the history of disease in Britain, typhus figures mainly in connection with the Civil War and as a disease of prisons, though, as noted later (chapter 11) it caused terror among the Irish, following the failed potato harvests of 1846–7. It was also common in the hideous slum quarters of cities like Liverpool, Manchester and Glasgow in the nineteenth century.

Dental caries appears to have increased through time, and to have a marked correlation with the introduction of large amounts of sucrose into the diet. Cane sugar was generally unavailable until the early sixteenth century to the majority of the population (honey was probably the main sweetening agent up to this time), but a study of seventeenth-century British teeth revealed an increase in the caries rate (Moore and Corbett, 1975).

The winter diet of the peasant, made up of salty bacon, bread and peas, and lacking in vitamin C, gave little protection against scurvy. In late winter and spring most of the poor country folk must have been at least in a pre-scorbutic condition. Drummond[14] says there is evidence to support the belief that pre-scorbutic conditions were common in sixteenth-century England. He cites the frequent mention in contemporary herbals of remedies for making 'loose teeth' firm and for 'purifying the blood in spring-tyme'. The majority of the remedies were fresh herbs or extracts from them, fresh gooseberry leaves, raw purslane, elecampane leaves, raw gooseberries, decoctions of bramble leaves, leaves in wine, etc. Scurvy occurs when fresh fruit and vegetables are unobtainable or when people do not appreciate the need to include them in their diet. In the sixteenth century and later the most serious shortages of fresh foods occurred among sailors on long voyages and during military sieges. Under such conditions scurvy became a dreaded and much described menace.

9

Stuart Times

The chief disease events of the seventeenth century were a series of outbreaks of plague and typhus. Historians have left the impression that no serious epidemic of plague attacked Britain between AD 1350 and 1603, and for the seventeenth century only the plague of 1665 has received special mention. Yet in almost any of the years 1348 to 1668 some community or other suffered visitations of these diseases, and on several occasions considerable areas were devastated.[1] Not surprisingly such ravages had an adverse effect on the economy of the country, which in consequence suffered repeated set-backs.

In those early days plague, and epidemics generally, were assumed to be due to supernatural or astral causes, corruption of the air, the conjunction of Jupiter and Saturn, or to popular superstitions such as ghosts, angels, coffins, hearses, flaming swords, and corpses in the air. Modern knowledge makes such theories appear ludicrous and the prophylactics futile (Plate 5) but an awareness and appreciation of such contemporary explanations or theories about disease is necessary for any real understanding of seventeenth-century attitudes towards the infection.

The London experience during the seventeenth century will suffice to illustrate the course of plague. The visitation of 1603 was believed to have been brought from Amsterdam, though it had been reported in Cheshire, Derbyshire and Lincolnshire the previous year. The epidemic attracted little or no attention before the end of April, but thereafter, aided by crowds assembled for the coronation of James I of England (James VI of Scotland), and also hot weather, it acquired a firm grip on the city.

Public and private affairs were completely disorganized during that year. A proclamation postponed the coronation. Gentlemen were not permitted to attend court when it was in London, and when business did not keep them in the city they were obliged to return home. No one was allowed to visit the royal palace or Westminster during the summer or autumn unless certified as having come from an uninfected area. Fairs were not permitted within fifty miles of the city, new building was prohibited and houses that had been recently built were pulled down. The London Companies were forbidden to hold public feasts in their Halls and it was suggested

Prefent Remedies

againft the plague.

Shewing fundrye preferuatiues

for the fame, by wholfome Fumes, drinkes, vomits
and other inward Receits; as alfo the perfect
cure (by Implaifture) of any that are
therewith infected.

How neceffary to be obferued of euery Houfholder, to
auoide the infection, lately begun in fome
places of this Cittie.

Written by a learned Phyfition, for the health
of his Countrey.

Printed for Thomas Pauyer, and are to be fold at his
fhop at the entrance into the Exchange.
1 6 0 3

Plate 5: Title-page of *Present Remedies against the Plague*, published in 1603
(by permission of the British Library)

that a proportion of the money saved should be given towards the relief of the infected poor. All public meetings, feasts and assemblies were postponed. Under such conditions of privation many people took to drink and riotous living, others to the churches. As in previous centuries, physicians and surgeons deserted the city in its hour of greatest need; so did wealthy citizens, aldermen and justices. The Court, attended by a disorderly company, migrated from one part of the country to another and infected the places to which it went. Among these were Southampton, Winchester,[2] Woodstock and Wilton. Plague also put an end to the export trade, particularly of broadcloth, and was equally destructive to domestic trade. With the approach of the colder and shorter days of autumn and winter the disease lost much of its virulence.

That the disease was associated with the flourishing rat population of London was not appreciated until several centuries later and long after plague had finally left the shores of Britain. The question posed at present is whether the 1603 outbreak was due to a recrudescence of a long-standing, smouldering disease, or to the introduction of a new or more virulent or infectious strain of the bacillus *Yersinia pestis* in goods from overseas. Certainly the years preceding 1603 had been years of economic depression. There had been a succession of bad harvests from 1594 to 1598 and again in 1600. The price of corn had risen 40 per cent. There was widespread poverty, and plague is well known as a poor man's disease. It flourished among the ill-fed, ill-clothed and poorly housed, among those living in rat-ridden tenements and insanitary alleys. Rarely was a plague victim one of wealth or rank.

The London epidemic lasted from March 1603 to January 1604 and was responsible for the death of practically one-eighth of its quarter-million inhabitants (Fig. 9.1). Plague also raged fiercely in Bristol, Bath, Chester, Shrewsbury, Manchester, York, Enfield, Cranborne, and Hassington (Northamptonshire), and parish registers record melancholy tales of households being entirely wiped out.

London was not free of plague for the next few years. All the time, the disease was most deadly in the hot weather; in several years its activities were confined entirely to the autumn. There was another disastrous visitation in 1625, with evidence of a pneumonic component. The death toll exceeded that of 1603 by several thousand (41,313 as against 33,347). Like that of 1603 the infection was possibly introduced in goods imported from Holland. All the horrors of that epidemic were experienced and witnessed again, only this time to a heightened degree and the dislocation of commerce was even more severe than in 1603. The author of *Lachrymae Londinenses*[3] summed up the lasting impression of the 1625 epidemic upon the minds of Londoners when in 1626 he wrote: 'to this present Plague of

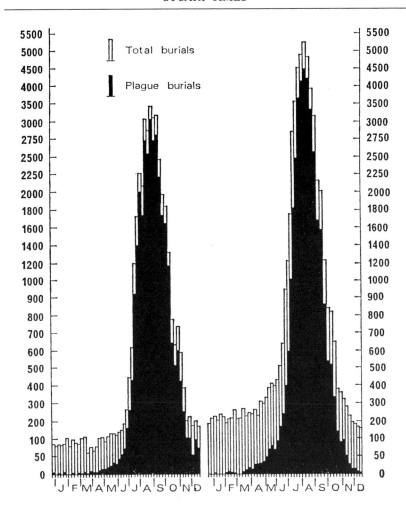

Fig. 9.1 Total burials and plague burials in London in 1603 and 1625 respectively (after J. F. D. Shrewsbury, *A History of Bubonic Plague in the British Isles*)

Pestilence, all former plagues were but pettie ones ... This, to future Ages and Histiographers must needs be Kalendred the *Great Plague*.'

One other London plague of importance between 1625 and 1665 was that of 1636. During that year 10,400 of a total of 23,359 deaths were due to the disease. This particular plague led, among other things, to a mass of official correspondence on the subject of rag-gathering for the making of paper. It was felt that the unwholesome trade in street-refuse for rags spread plague. It was probably as a preventive measure against plague that 'the grant for gathering of rags' was recalled on 15 April 1639.

The words from *Lachrymae Londinenses* proved to be tragically wrong. It was the Great Plague of 1665 which was destined to be the worst, and last, of a centuries-long series of outbreaks in Britain. The epidemic had been anticipated by such auguries as spotted fever (typhus), pleurisy and pneumonia which had flourished since 1658, together with the fact that it was practically thirty years since there had been a plague epidemic. The Great Plague might have represented a revival of a smouldering endemic disease, although the visitation was sometimes credited to infected merchandise routes through Amsterdam. The goods in question were probably cotton, the Levant being at that time the chief source of cotton piece goods and cotton wool.

Crowds of people had flocked to London after the Restoration. Many had not acquired the immunity of those citizens who had survived previous and repeated outbreaks of plague. There were also many more living in conditions more congested and insanitary than ever before. This encouraged rats, whose fleas transmitted the bubonic plague and, once it had broken out, its rapid spread within the city was inevitable.

The plague began unostentatiously in London in the winter of 1664–5, but by early summer it was well established. There were 68,596 deaths from plague in 1665 (Fig. 9.2), 2,000 in 1666, 35 in 1667 and 14 in 1668. Details need not be given since there are classic descriptions written by Samuel Pepys in his Diary[4] and by Daniel Defoe in his historical novel *A Journal of the Plague Year*.[5] Some of the main features, summarized by Hirst,[6] include the awful suffering of the poor, the paralysis of business; the constant tolling of the church bells and the frequent funerals in the early days, giving way when the graveyards were full, to mass burial of corpses, layer upon layer, in the great plague-pits; the flight on foot, on horse and on wagon of multitudes of panic-stricken citizens along the roads from London; all this forms 'one of the saddest chapters in the history of the English people' (Plate 7). Defoe's references to people falling dead in the streets and to death within a few hours of the appearance of 'tokens' suggest either the presence of septicaemic cases of plague or the lack of reliable clinical data. There were in fact remarkably few records of pneumonic symptoms or signs – which would be far more frequent in winter than in summer – during this or any of the seventeenth-century epidemics.

There were several accounts of plague in provincial towns in Britain. Among those affected were Southampton, Chatham, Cambridge, Yarmouth, Salisbury, Colchester, Norwich, Deal, Dover, Canterbury, Maidstone, Bristol and Portsmouth. The south and Midlands of the country were hard hit, but apart from occasional pockets the north and west got off lightly.

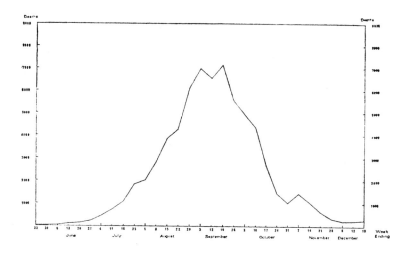

Fig. 9.2 Deaths from plague in London, June–December 1665
(based on text of Creighton, 1965)

York, Newcastle and Hull, for instance, escaped the disease, and even within affected towns deaths were localized and restricted to a small number of families. Yet some towns and villages suffered severely from its devastating impact. One such was the small village of Eyam, during 1665–6.

> The plague was likewise at Eyam, in the Peak of Derbyshire, being brought thither by means of a box sent from London to a taylor in that village, containing some materials of his trade. A servant who opened the aforesaid box, complaining that the goods were damp, was ordered to dry them by the fire, but in so doing it was seized with the plague and died.[7]

The first victim recorded in the Eyam parish register was George Vicars who died on 6 September 1665; apparently it was he who opened the box. Subsequent deaths followed a seasonal pattern consistent with other outbreaks of bubonic plague, a reduced mortality during the winter but rising to a climax the following summer. Several of the wealthier families from the west end of Eyam fled when the presence of the disease was discovered, but over 300 persons remained. In June 1666, under the guidance of the Revd William Mompesson, the rector, and his nonconformist predecessor, the Revd Thomas Stanley, the villagers imposed their own quarantine on the village as a precaution against the plague spreading to neighbouring hamlets.

The Diseases and Casualties this Week.

	Gangrene------1
	Griping in the Guts------22
	Jaundies------5
	Impoisthume------6
	Infants------7
	Kild 2, one at St. Paul Covent Garden, and one by a Horse at S. Sepulchers------2

Abortive------	4	Kingsevil------	1
Aged------	25	Mouldfallen------	1
Ague------	1	Plague------	2
Cancer------	2	Plurisie------	1
Childbed------	5	Purples------	1
Chrisomes------	8	Rickets------	10
Consumption------	79	Rising of the Lights------	8
Convulsion------	33	Scowring------	2
Cough------	3	Scurvy------	2
Dropsie------	33	Spotted Feaver------	14
Drownd 3, two at St. Katharine Tower, and one at St. James Clerkenwell------	3	Stilborn------	5
		Stopping of the stomach------	6
		Suddenly------	1
Feaver------	36	Surfeit------	8
Fistula------	1	Teeth------	22
Flox and Small-pox------	17	Thrush------	4
Flux------	5	Tissick------	4
Found dead in the street at St. Giles in the Fields------	1	Ulcer------	2
		Winde------	1
French-pox------	5	Wormes------	1

Christned { Males---122 Females---107 In all---229 }   Buried { Males---211 Females---187 In all---398 } Plague— 2.

Increased in the Burials this Week------54
Parishes clear of the Plague------129 Parishes Infected------1

The Assize of Bread set forth by Order of the Lord Maior and Court of Aldermen, A penny Wheaten Loaf to contain Ten Ounces, and three half-penny White Loaves the like weight.

Plate 6: A London Bill of Mortality for 15–22 August 1665
(by permission of the Wellcome Institute Library)

Oral tradition offers a guide to the measures taken to deal with the situation when it became serious in the spring of 1666. Men were still greatly influenced by the fifteenth-century idea that plague was not only infectious directly, as in the case of pneumonic plague, but that all who breathed the same air as the sick, or were exposed to their emanations, were carriers of the infection, domestic animals as well as man, and that inanimate objects of all kinds from an infected area could be sources of the disease. It was decided in June 1666 to confine and isolate the village behind the famous *cordon sanitaire*, about half a mile in circuit, with its stones in which news and details of requirements were left and to which provisions

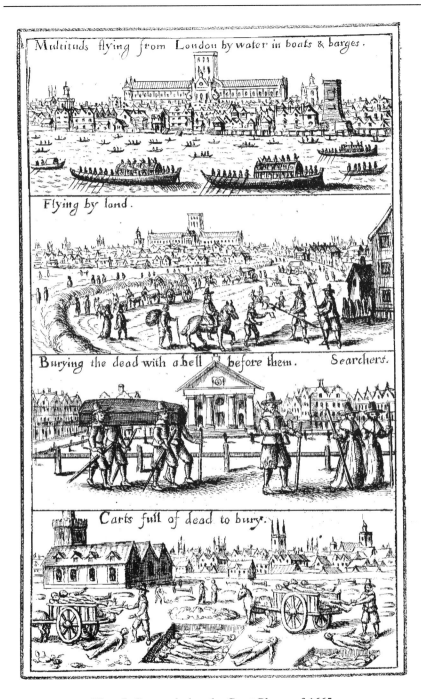

Plate 7: Scenes during the Great Plague of 1665
(by permission of the Pepys Library, Magdalene College, Cambridge)

were brought in accordance with an arrangement which was reached with the Earl of Devonshire, then at Chatsworth. The church was closed and services were held in the 'Cucklet Church', a natural formation in the Dell below the village. Burials no longer took place in the churchyard but in a variety of places around the village; an exception was made when Catherine Mompesson, the rector's young wife died on 25 August. The Mompesson children, George and Elizabeth, aged three and four had been sent to relatives in Yorkshire in June and we have the rector's own testimony in his letter to his uncle of 20 November that he himself was unharmed: 'During this dreadful visitation I have not had the least symptom of disease, nor had I better health.' This same letter testifies to the erection of pest-houses in the village and to the use of chemicals on the sick, sometimes with efficacy: 'My man had the distemper and, upon the appearance of a tumour, I gave him some chemical antidotes which operated and after the rising broke, it was very well.' Letters were not sent directly from the village for fear of contamination: 'I have got these lines transcribed by a friend, being loth to affright you with a letter from my hands,' Mompesson comments to his uncle.[8]

In the words of Creighton,[9] 'shut up in their narrow valley, the villagers perished helplessly like a stricken flock of sheep.' The village was decimated by the death of 259 of its inhabitants. In the light of present-day knowledge, flight from the village would have been preferable to the vain sacrifice behind the *cordon sanitaire* where rats, fleas and people were kept in close contact with one another.

Scotland during the seventeenth century was an extremely poor country. The southern and wealthy part had been laid waste by the wars with England in the middle of the sixteenth century, by internal political troubles associated with the period of the Reformation, by efforts made in 1650 on behalf of Prince Charles (later Charles II), by heavy fines subsequently imposed by Cromwell, and by plague. Plague continued in the south of the country in the early years of the seventeenth century after a long period of plague years during the second half of the sixteenth. In 1606, 'it raged so extremely in all the corners of the kingdom that neither burgh nor land in any part was free.'[10] After the storming of Newcastle by Scots Covenanters in October 1644, the plague appeared in Edinburgh, Kelso, Bo'ness, Perth, Glasgow, St Andrews, Aberdeen and other places. The disease was serious in Glasgow and made havoc from 1645 until the autumn of 1648.

The last case of plague in Scotland was in 1648;[11] in the south-west and north-west of England it was about 1650; and in Wales probably 1636–8. The absolute last of its provincial prevalence in England was in Peterborough in the early months of 1667.

In the late twentieth century, at a time when there is a threat of mass human extermination by very rapid means, happenings during both the Great Pestilence (Black Death) of the fourteenth century and the Great Plague of the seventeenth century shed interesting light on human behaviour under conditions of what, at the time, seemed to be universal catastrophe. A fundamental reaction throughout was flight.[12] Kings and their households, physicians, surgeons, merchants, lawyers, the clergy, professors, students and the rich generally were all involved in mass migration from the towns, leaving the ordinary folk to their own devices. Strenuous efforts were made to segregate those who were forced to remain in the towns by quarantining houses, closing off entire streets and erecting gallows to warn against the violation of regulations.[13] Many people of all classes gave themselves up to carousing and ribaldry, and even Samuel Pepys and his wife indulged in a 'great store of dancings'. London and Oxford experienced much 'lewd and dissolute behaviour'. There was also a wave of violence and crime. Some people were driven to a complete abandonment of morality, others resorted to religious extravagances. That there was profound disturbance of people's minds by ubiquitous and chronic grief and by the immediacy of death is unquestionable.

The main plague epidemics of the seventeenth century in London (including the liberties and out-parishes) and their associated mortalities were:

Year	Plague deaths
1603	33,347
1625	41,313
1636	10,400
1665	68,596

The popular nursery rhyme

> Ring-a-ring o' roses
> A pocket full of posies
> A-tishoo! A-tishoo!
> We all fall down

takes its origin from the Great Plague.[14] A rosy rash, it is alleged, was a symptom of the plague. Posies of herbs were carried as protection, sneezing was a final fatal symptom, and 'all fall down' was exactly what happened.

The Paracelsist physician Dr G. Thomson[15] in his *Loimotamia* tract on the London Plague of 1665, describes how he cured himself of plague by applying to his stomach a large dried toad sewn up in linen cloth 'where after it had remained some hours, became so tumified, distended (as it were blown up) to that bignesse, that it was an object of wonder to those who believed it.' Toads were thought to exert a special influence on plague and could draw out the poison.

Examination of the Bills of Mortality which gave the probable reasons for the death of citizens of London in the seventeenth century shows that, in addition to plague, 'consumption and cough', 'ague and fever', 'cold and cough', 'quinsy and sore throat', 'flux and smallpox' figured prominently.

'Consumption' was the heading for various wasting diseases under which pulmonary tuberculosis (phthisis) appeared in the Bills of Mortality. It was, and had been, a common disease, accounting for 15–20 per cent of all deaths in London at the time, but it had not been epidemic in the sense of it being more prevalent at one time than at another. Tuberculosis is now known to be due to the invasion of the tissues of man or animals (especially cattle) by *Mycobacterium tuberculosis*,[16] but in early records tuberculosis was confused with other diseases. Even so, environmental conditions necessary for the active spread of the disease were undoubtedly present in areas of persistent overcrowding in close-packed dwellings. A low standard of living is known now to be another predisposing association. The susceptibility of the poorer people must have been greatly increased by malnutrition. Death rates from pulmonary tuberculosis in Britain are thought to have reached a peak about 1800.[17] For this reason more detailed consideration of the disease will be given in chapter 11.

'Epidemic agues', 'hot agues', 'new agues' and 'quartan agues' were widely prevalent in different years of the seventeenth and earlier centuries, but they were not related to the endemic fevers of malarial districts such as the Isles of Sheppey, the Fens and the Somerset Levels. Ague really referred to any acute fever, and most commonly to 'continued fever' such as typhus (putrid malignant fever) or enteric (typhoid, or 'slow, nervous fever').

Typhus was a constant visitor to London in particular, and less frequently to smaller towns of the country. During the Civil War there were severe epidemics of this disease. Worthy of mention was the experience in Reading (Berkshire) in 1643. The royal army in the town had been besieged for eleven days by parliamentary forces under Essex. When the beleaguered garrison surrendered, Essex found Reading infected and 'a great mortality ensued among his men.' Dr Thomas Willis (1621–75), royal physician, wrote:

In both armies there began a disease to arise very epidemical; however they persisted in that work until the besieged were forced to surrender, this disease grew so grevious that in a short time after, either side left off and from that time for many months fought not until the evening, but with the disease, as if there had not been leisure to turn aside to another kind of death.[18]

Among the causes mentioned were 'putrid exhalations from stinking matters, dung, carcasses of dead horses and other carrion'. In particular there was the filth of 'unshifted apparel' and the associated body lice which transmitted the organism *Rickettsia prowazekii*. The following year (1644) Tiverton (Devon), which had been occupied by both the royal and parliamentary armies, suffered a serious epidemic of typhus from August to November.

Seemingly, there were no epidemics of typhoid, paratyphoid or dysentery as there were of typhus, but since the causal micro-organisms for the enteric fevers and typhus were then unknown the diseases were assumed to be related. There is no doubt but that with bad water supplies and defective sanitation, typhoid, paratyphoid and dysentery were endemic diseases during the seventeenth and earlier centuries.

The seventeenth century witnessed the rise to prominence of smallpox and measles. In early English medieval writings the two diseases – *variola* and *morbilli* – were inseparable companions, but by the time of the London Bills of Mortality in the first half of the century they were distinguished as independent diseases.

There were several smallpox epidemics in London, for example in 1628 and 1634, and according to later experience, a high mortality in London in any one year meant a general epidemic elsewhere in the country in that or the following year. This appears to have been so for the period following the Restoration, but details are lacking. Epidemics are known to have occurred in various parts of the country between the late 1660s and 1670s. In Taunton in 1658, 1670, 1677 and 1684, in Norwich and Halifax in 1681, in Cambridge in 1674 and Bath in 1675. The Duke of Gloucester and the Princess of Orange, both children of Charles I, died of smallpox within a few months of each other in the year of the Restoration (1660). Queen Mary died from the same cause in 1694. Smallpox reached its peak in Britain in the eighteenth century, and is discussed at greater length in chapter 10.

Measles ('mezils') was first recognized as an independent disease by the English physician Sydenham. It was particularly virulent and fatal in seventeenth-century London, and struck in epidemic form in 1664, causing 311 deaths. The Bills of Mortality record 295 deaths from measles in 1670[19] and 795 deaths in 1674. Thereafter, there was a long interval of low mortality until 1705-6. There is no mention of epidemic measles elsewhere in the country in the seventeenth century.

That summer diarrhoea in infants ('griping of the guts' or 'convulsions') and probably dysentery were common in London in the latter half of the seventeenth century, and particularly in the populous working-class liberties and outparishes, is well testified by the works of Harris.[20] He refers to epidemics as follows: 'From the middle of July to the middle of September these epidemic gripes of infants are so common (being the annual heat of the season doth entirely exhaust their strength) that more infants, affected with these, do die in one month than in any other three that are gentle.' There was a serious mortality in 1669 and in subsequent years to 1672, in 1675, 1676, 1678–81 and 1688–9. Seemingly, these years had hot dry summers and autumns, and the diarrhoea incidence rose during August and fell again in October. The climate fluctuated then as now, and one year's weather might well have differed considerably from long-term characteristics. There is no reason to suppose that there were not occasional exceptionally hot dry summers, e.g. 1666, 1667, 1676. Pepys notes 5 July 1666 as 'Extremely hot ... oranges ripening in the open at Hackney'[21] and John Evelyn (1620–1706) refers to the dry year of 1681 as follows: 'June 12. There still continues such a drought as has hardly ever been known in England.' In 1684 he wrote: 'July 2. An excessive hot and dry spring and such a drought continues as is not in my memory.' In 1685 there was another drought, and on 14 June Evelyn wrote, 'such a dearth for want of rain as never was in my memory.' The causal relationships, direct or indirect, between infant diarrhoea and hot dry summers are not fully understood, although the consensus of twentieth-century opinion is that outbreaks were due to some particular kinds of bacillus coli, possibly fly-borne and possibly associated with animal manure.

The influenza pandemics of 1889–92 (p.170) and 1918–19 (p.172) are milestones in the history of influenza in Britain. The disease was present in the seventeenth century, although it was not known by that name until the eighteenth century. There were occasional outbreaks in the first half of the century but Creighton[22] makes particular mention of influenza epidemics in 1657–9, 1661–4, 1675, 1678–9, 1688 and 1693. Influenza was given such names as 'new disease', 'hot ague', 'new ague', 'new fever', 'new ague fever', 'new pestilence', 'new distemper', and in Derbyshire 'the new delight'. There were two catarrhal epidemics or of influenza proper in the spring of 1658[23] and 1659 respectively set within a two-to-three-year period of epidemic agues. Their overall effects were afterwards viewed as a 'little plague' and popularly spoken of as a warning of the Great Plague of 1665. The epidemic of the spring of 1658 arrived suddenly in April 'as if sent by some blast of the stars',[24] after a long winter of intense frost. Willis's explanation of the epidemic was related to the constant north wind which 'checked the natural action of the blood in spring'. Sydenham, known for the accuracy of his observations, considered the epidemic between 1661 and 1664 to be malaria or 'intermittent fever'. Molyneux's account of the influenza of 1693 in Dublin states,[25] 'It spread itself all over England in the same manner as it did here, particularly it seized them at London and Oxford as universally and with the same symptoms as it seized us in Dublin, but with this observable difference that it appeared three or four weeks sooner in London, that is, about the beginning of October.' There seems no doubt also that the influenza was present in Scotland in the seventeenth century. As early as 1173 there was a reference in the *Chronicle Melrose* to a bad kind of cough, unheard of before, which affected almost everyone from far and wide, 'from which pest' many died.

John Evelyn reminds us of some of the endemic ills of seventeenth-century London in his *Fumifugium*[26] (Plate 8), dedicated to King Charles II (Founder of the Royal Society). Evelyn, concerned with the pollution of London's atmosphere by 'Sea-Coale' brought in from Newcastle for use in domestic fires and by 'brewers, dyers, soap-boilers and lime-burners' and in 'glasshouses, foundaries and sugar bakers', wrote:

And what is all this, but that Hellish and Dismall Cloud of SEA-COALE? which is not onely perpetually imminent over her head; For as the Poet, *Conditus in tenebris caligne coelum*; but so universally mixed with the otherwise wholesome and excellent Aer, that her *Inhabitants* breathe nothing but an impure and thick Mist, accompanied with a fuliginous and filthy vapour, which renders them obnoxious to a thousand inconveniences, corrupting the lungs and disordering the entire habit of their Bodies, so that *Catharrs, Phthisicks, Coughs* and *Consumptions* rage more in this one City, than in the whole Earth besides ...

London, 'tis confess'd, is not the only City most obnoxious to the Pestilence; but it is yet never more clear of this Smoake which is a Plague so many other ways, and indeed intolerable; because it kills not at once, but always, since still to languish, is worse than even Death itself. For is there under Heaven such *Coughing* and *Snuffing* to be heard, as in the London Churches and Assemblies of People, where the Barking and the Spitting is uncessant and most importunate ...

England, Wales and Scotland supported about 4 million people at the beginning of the seventeenth century and 6½ million at the end, distributed in close relationship to productive agricultural lands (Fig. 9.3). The greater part of the population was country-bred and confined largely to lowland England, especially south of a line from the middle Severn Valley to the Wash. There were, however, some areas of greater density of population, associated with the growing textile, iron and coal industries. Most of the people lived at subsistence level or hardly above it, even by the low

FUMIFUGIUM:

O R,

The Inconvenience of the A E R,

A N D

SMOAKE of LONDON

D I S S I P A T E D.

TOGETHER

With some REMEDIES humbly propofed

By J. E. Efq;

To His Sacred MAJESTIE,

A N D

To the PARLIAMENT now Aſſembled.

Publiſhed by His Majeſties Command.

Lucret. l. 5.

Carbonumque gravis vis, atque odor infinuatur
Quam facile in cerebrum?-

L O N D O N :
Printed by W. GODBID, for GABRIEL BEDEL, and THOMAS
COLLINS ; and are to be ſold at their Shop at the Middle
Temple Gate, neer Temple Bar. M.DC.LXI.
Re-printed for B. WHITE, at Horace's Head, in Fleet-ſtreet,
M DCCLXXII.

Plate 8: Title-page of *Fumifugium* by John Evelyn, published in 1661
(by permission of the British Library)

standards of the time. Expectation of life was now about forty years, though Evelyn has the following to say about London, which in 1603, had a population of 250,000, increasing to 320,000 in 1625, 460,000 (Graunt), and 530,000 in 1690 (King):

> there is a waste of near ten thousand people who are drawn every year from the Country, to supply the room of those that *London* destroys beyond what it raises. Indeed the supply that the Town furnishes towards keeping up its own Inhabitants appears so very small to the ablest Calculators and most rational Enquirer[27] unto this subject that he owns he was afraid to publish the result. But without the use of Calculations it is evident to every one who looks on the yearly Bill of Mortality, that near half the children that are born and bred in *London* die under two years of age. Some have attributed this amazing destruction to luxury and the abuse of Spirituous liquors. These, no doubt, are powerful assistants, but the constant and unremitting Poison is communicated by the foul Air, which, as the Town still grows larger, has made regular and steady advances in its fatal influence.

The seventeenth century was a period of economic readjustment, particularly in respect of corn production (arable) and wool production (pastoral). High prices for corn favoured by some good summers encouraged many farmers to expand corn tillage. This brought down the price of corn, although with inevitable fluctuations after poor harvests. For the mass of the population times were hard, and there was much unemployment and distressing poverty in the towns well into the middle of the century. Thorold Rogers writes: 'But I have never noticed in any earlier century such a continuity of dearth as from 1630 to 1637, from 1646 to 1651, from 1658 to 1661, from 1693 to 1699, in each case inclusive.'[28] During such times the poor people suffered severely from the high price of food. Indeed, according to Drummond[29] the state of the lower classes in England during the latter part of the century seems to have become progressively worse. The main food of the working class, according to contemporary accounts, was bread, beef, fish, home-brewed beer or ale[30] and cheese. There was a tendency for people in the south and especially in the towns to give up dark rye and coarse-meal breads for white bread (the product of 'high milling' which removed the bran). In Lancashire and the Pennines the peasants ate oaten cakes. Beans were reputed to constitute an important item of diet in Leicestershire and the local population was labelled with the rude name 'bean belly'. In Scotland, lean years kept recurring with monotonous regularity, culminating from time to time in periods of acute starvation. A climax was reached in the dreadful famine of 1698–9, with the heaviest mortality

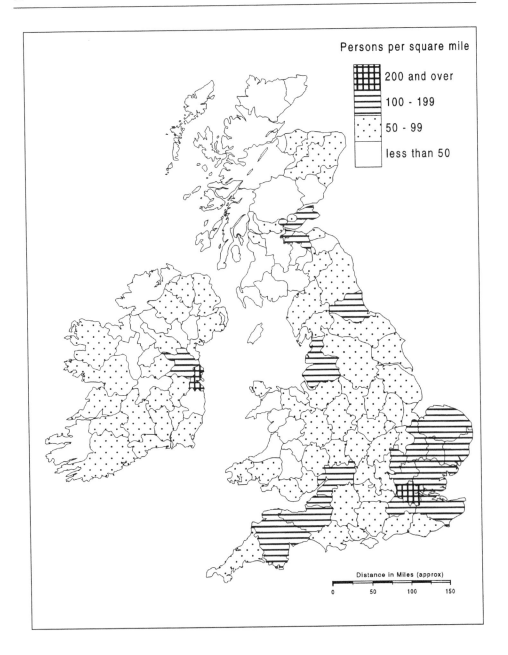

Fig. 9.3 Distribution of population in the British Isles, 1670 (adapted from *Reader's Digest Atlas of the British Isles*, 1965)

for a century, 'King William's III Years' as they were called in the folk memory.[31]

Reference must be made to what was called a 'new disease' which came to Scotland in the middle of the seventeenth century. It was named *sibben*[32] and was said to have been brought into the country by Cromwell's soldiers. It spread up the east coast at first and reached Orkney and Shetland, and then moved gradually south-west to reach the Solway Firth. The similarity between sibbens and syphilis was noted from the beginning; subsequent research confirmed that sibbens was, in fact, syphilis.

10

Hanoverian Times

The eighteenth century in Britain saw the beginning of the change from the basically subsistent simple agricultural economy of previous centuries, with local associations and peasant occupations, to a complicated industrial society with world-wide connections. It witnessed the introduction of steam (raised by coal) as a source of power for new mechanical inventions, the start of a new and intense concentration of large-scale industry on the coal-fields, and also of the labour force to man such industry. The eighteenth century was, in effect, the curtain-raiser to the Industrial Revolution and to the Steam Age of the nineteenth century. Above all, it saw the trend towards a rapid growth in population which, continuing through the nine-teenth century, is only now, in the late twentieth century, showing signs of slowing down.

At the turn of the eighteenth century Britain was still largely rural and agricultural (Fig. 10.1). It exported some grain and certain raw materials, but its only major industrial export was woollen cloth. A rather lengthy process of agricultural improvement had been taking place since the late sixteenth century, associated with such names as Jethro Tull, 'Turnip' Townshend, Thomas Coke and Robert Bakewell. The Norfolk or four-course rotation in arable agriculture had been replaced by a three-year rotation, and there had been a speeding up of land enclosure. Open fields had gradually disappeared and much moor and fen had been reclaimed and brought under cultivation. Enclosure had caused local hardship, but the higher food production which followed improved agricultural techniques would not have been possible under the previous open-field system. Wheat, barley, clover and beans were grown increasingly. Wheat yields in 1735 at about twenty bushels to the acre were twice those of the medieval period, and exports continued until such time as the rise in population associated with developments in manufacturing industry absorbed all the food grown in the country. Root crops were grown to provide essential winter fodder for cattle which were no longer killed off in the autumn through lack of feeding stuffs.

By the eighteenth century the face of southern Britain had attained a mature agricultural-rural pattern, and for the first fifty years fortune smiled

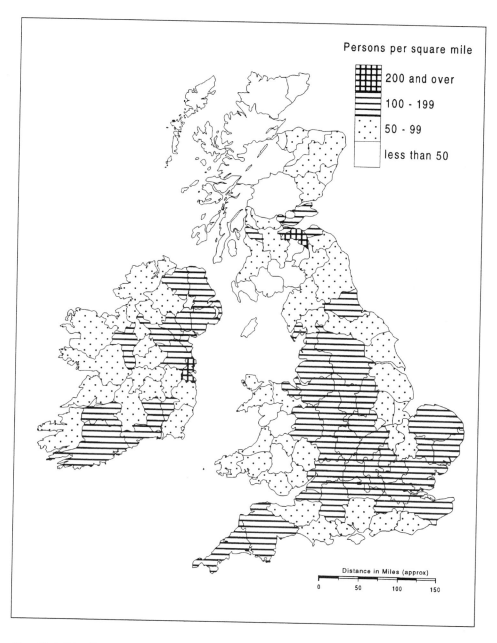

Persons per square mile

200 and over

100 - 199

50 - 99

less than 50

Distance in Miles (approx)

0   50   100   150

Fig. 10.1 Distribution of population in the British Isles, 1750 (adapted from *Reader's Digest Atlas of the British Isles*, 1965)

Plate 9: Portrayal of eighteenth-century gluttony by Thomas Rowlandson (1788)
(copyright © British Museum)

on its people. There were occasional bad years, such as 1718, 1728, 1741 and 1757, but there were no long and lasting famines after the turn of the century. Improved communications made it easier to transport food to the needy in the event of local crop failure. Food prices after 1730 were relatively lower than previously, and it appears that most people fed well and amply. Unless portrait painters and cartoonists such as Rowlandson and Gillray misrepresented their victims grossly, the consequences of gluttony were not apparently considered unaesthetic (Plate 9). There was also much heavy drinking among all classes of the community, particularly of cheap

Plate 10: James Gillray's cartoon of gluttony in 1792
(copyright © British Museum)

'gin' and other forms of raw crude spirit. The overall impression is of an age of heavy eating and heavy drinking in both town and country (Plate 10). Artisans and labourers lived well, and gout,[1] traditionally supposed to have been a disease of the rich and over-indulgent was commonplace.

After about 1765 the poorer people knew hard times. The French wars (1756–63), a disastrous sequence of wet seasons and bad harvests during the period 1764–75, the interruption of trade (including foodstuffs and wines) at the time of the French Revolutionary wars, a financial crisis and a disastrous harvest in 1793 all contributed to a progressive worsening of

Plate 11: *Gin Lane* by William Hogarth
(copyright © British Museum)

conditions as the nineteenth century approached. The barest necessities of life became scarce and expensive, and discontent, which was widespread, occasionally culminated in lawlessness and riots. By the end of the eighteenth century a large proportion was suffering depression, disaster and death.

Population growth was relatively slow, increasing from 5½–6 million in 1700 to 6–6½ million in 1750. Webster's[2] first census of Scotland in 1755 gave the population of that country as 1.3 million. Birth rates and death rates were high by modern standards, and yet there were occasional years between 1720 and 1740 when the death rate exceeded the birth rate. After about 1750, however, there was an increase of population, variously ascribed either to a reduction in the death rate[3] or a rise in the birth rate, or a shorter-run recovery or else 'compensatory fluctuation' from a rate of growth which previously had been abnormally low (caused by unusually high mortality earlier in the century) (Fig. 10.2). Two-thirds of the people still worked on the land, distributed in close relationship with agricultural productivity. There were, however, areas of more dense population developing in the industrial parts of Yorkshire, north-east England and Lancashire. Dominating the populous areas of England were regional centres and market towns which included Plymouth, Exeter, Bristol, Birmingham, Coventry, Nottingham, Norwich, Hull, Leeds, Sheffield, York, Newcastle, Liverpool and Manchester. London was by far the largest city and largest port. Bristol and Norwich were possibly second to London at this time. In Wales, where the settlements were still small, the main centres were the county and market towns, of which the largest was Carmarthen with about 10,000 inhabitants. In Scotland, Edinburgh and Glasgow were growing rapidly, the central Lowlands, especially the eastern side, having the highest overall density.

A quickening tempo of industrialization occurred after 1750, but radical social and economic changes did not become particularly evident until early in the nineteenth century. Industrially, eighteenth-century Britain was not unimportant, for she had woollen industries in East Anglia and the West Country, flax spinning and linen weaving in Renfrewshire and Lanarkshire, silk weaving in London, Coventry, Macclesfield and Norwich, cotton in east Lancashire and in the Clyde Valley. Metallurgical industries were widespread and varied, and newer industries such as pottery, glass-making and paper-making had developed considerably from the seventeenth century (Fig. 10.3). Even so, industry was still generally small-scale and domestic in character, with water the main source of power. Manufacturing industry was geared mainly to satisfying the demands of the home market, and workers engaged in it worked under generally free and easy conditions,

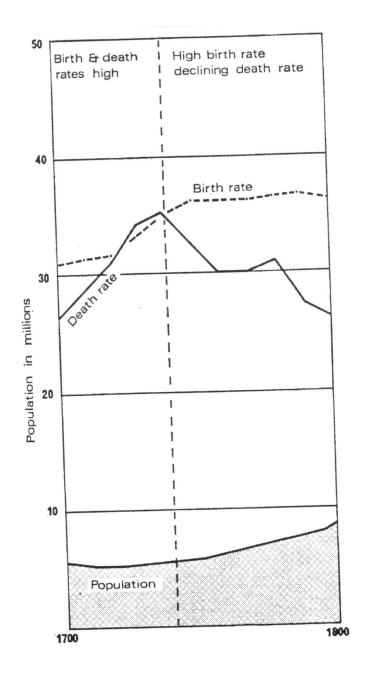

Fig. 10.2 Birth rates, death rates and population totals in Britain, 1700–1800

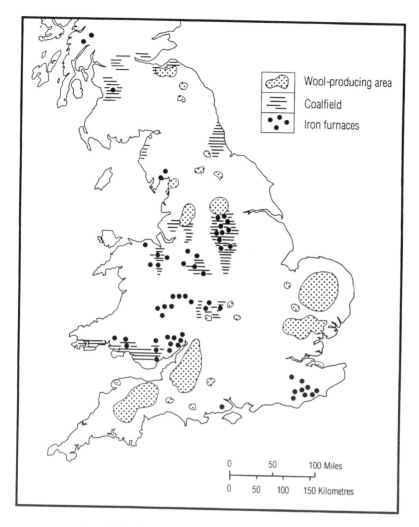

Fig. 10.3 Distribution of industry in Britain, 1750

either in their own homes or in small workshops. It was not until water power was applied to bigger textile machines that the large factory became an element in the landscape. Even then the textile mills needed to be confined to more or less remote places. Similar considerations applied to Abraham Darby's ironworks at Coalbrookdale, Josiah Wedgwood's pottery at Burslem, Richard Arkwright's spinning mill at Nottingham, and the Lombe brothers' silk mill at Derby. The modern industrial landscape was only just beginning to take shape; the real blighting of the environment with factories, industrial towns, atmospheric pollution, stream and river fouling in the coalfield areas came with the Steam Age of the nineteenth century.

Such was the industrial environment of eighteenth-century Britain. What were the diseases of the period, the maladjustments to environmental hazards? Plague, more or less endemic in Britain from the time of the 'Great Pestilence' (Black Death) in the fourteenth century to the Great Plague of the seventeenth century, had ceased. Why the Great Plague should have proved to be the last of a centuries-long series of outbreaks has yet to be convincingly explained. The tremendous mortality, the 'sum of individual tragedies' of previous centuries was repeated in the eighteenth century, but this time the result of another deadly disease, smallpox.

Smallpox had been a scourge upon society for untold centuries. It had been described accurately by the great Persian physician Rhazes in the tenth century, although it had evidently been known in China and India long before. Creighton, misusing the evidence relating to the early history of the disease in the sixteenth century, says incorrectly, that smallpox in Britain came slowly into prominence and that it hardly attained a leading place until the reign of James I (1603–25). He omits from his narrative the epidemic of 1561–2, despite the well-known fact that Queen Elizabeth herself suffered from such a severe attack of smallpox that it was thought by many at Court necessary to contemplate the appointment of a successor. Seventeenth-century epidemics in England, when young adults seem to have borne the brunt of the attacks, have been mentioned. There are also reports of an outbreak in Aberdeen in the summer of 1610: 'There was at this time a great visitation of the young children with the plague of the pox.'[4]

Smallpox was the most widespread and fatal disease throughout eighteenth-century Britain. Outstanding epidemics occurred in 1722, 1723 and 1740–2, but the disease kept returning, time and time again, after relatively short intervals, to the major industrial towns, after longer intervals to the market towns, and after even longer intervals to the villages. Peak years in London were 1723, 1725, 1736, 1746, 1752, 1757, 1763, 1768, 1772, 1781 and 1796, each with over 3,000 deaths from smallpox. Edinburgh lost over 2,700 of its 40,000 inhabitants in the course of the two years 1740–2, more than half the deaths being of children under the age of five years. During the last quarter of the eighteenth century, nearly 19 per cent of all the deaths in Glasgow were due to smallpox.

The disease is an adverse reaction between humans and the smallpox virus or variola. It is an acute infectious disease which can be picked up anywhere, but only if there are other cases or carriers of the infection in the vicinity. Cases of smallpox arise from contact, direct or indirect, with a preceding case of the disease. The main mechanism of infection is by the inhalation of infected droplets; even then the virus is not ordinarily carried more than a few feet through the air. There are no natural insect or animal vectors, nor natural propagation of the virus outside the body. The virus ordinarily does not live long outside the body, yet it would appear that it can be picked up from bed linen or clothing. The theory of the day was that the disease was the result of social and soil conditions.

Smallpox disfigured the faces of many of those whom it did not kill, and caused much of the blindness of the eighteenth century. Thanks to keen observation and persistence in experimentation, Edward Jenner (1749–1823), a country doctor of Berkeley, Gloucestershire, gave to the medical world a method of combating the disease: vaccination.[5] Early in his career Jenner had been impressed by the insistence of dairymaids suffering from sores and from mild reactions to cowpox that thereafter they would be safe from smallpox. Medical men believed this to be an old country folk saying; but the idea intrigued Jenner. He collected examples of persons who had had cowpox and afterwards had escaped smallpox, or who, having had cowpox, did not react successfully to smallpox inoculation. Of this methodical work E. Ashworth Underwood and A.M.G. Campbell say:[6]

> Even at this early stage he [Jenner] seems to have been obsessed by the feeling that cowpox *ought* to give complete and permanent immunity to smallpox. This is indeed strange, since every practitioner knew that smallpox did not always give complete and permanent protection against itself ... Jenner set out to show that cowpox protected against smallpox, and also that cowpox could be transmitted from one human being to another just as smallpox could ... that cowpox naturally acquired, could be transmitted artificially from *person to person* so that there would result an increasing reservoir of persons who had been given the opportunity of becoming ... immune ... to smallpox ... That was the cardinal factor in Jenner's doctrine and it was an idea which had probably not occurred seriously to anyone before, at least no one had attempted to put it into practice.

The first vaccination against smallpox was performed by Jenner in 1796. Exudate from a cowpox pustule on the hand of dairymaid Sarah Nelmes was inserted into scratches on the arm of an eight-year-old boy, James Phipps. The vaccination proved to be effective protective therapy. Jenner was unable to repeat his successful discovery before 1798, when he published his famous *Inquiry into the Cause and Effects of the Variolae Vaccinae*. When it was realized that vaccination was a sure protection against smallpox the disease began to recede as an important cause of death and disfigurement in Britain (Plate 12).

The Cow-Pock __ or __ the Wonderful Effects of the New Inoculation !__

Plate 12: *The Cow Pock – the Wonderful Effects of the New Inoculation*, by James Gillray, 1802 (by permission of the Wellcome Institute Library)

'Fever', probably chiefly typhus,[7] was as important, if not more important than smallpox during the eighteenth century. It was a constant visitor to London in particular and less frequently to smaller towns. It was highly fatal in its epidemic form and was transmitted from person to person by the body louse (*Pediculus humanus corporis*). Lice took up the causative micro-organism, *Rickettsia prowazekii*, from the blood of people sick with the disease, and were themselves fatally infected in the process. The lice had about a week in which to transfer the infection to another subject before they died. Predisposing environmental conditions providing stimuli for the disease included the crowding together of poor, undernourished, unwashed and filthily clad people. Typhus was especially common in the gaols and was often spread by contagion among court officers when prisoners were brought in for trial. 'Black assizes' comparable to those of Cambridge, Oxford and Exeter in the sixteenth century (see p.106) took place in the Old Bailey in London in April 1750. The disease was normally unknown among the more affluent citizens, but fifty or so people, including the Lord Mayor of London and several court officials died following contact with dirty, neglected and wretched prisoners.

It was ironic that, at a time when most people seemed to enjoy relative prosperity and general well-being, an occasional poor harvest still gave rise to widespread distress. There were epidemics of typhus, called *synochus*, following bad harvests in 1718, 1728 and 1741. But in addition it was a time of sloth, drunkenness and thriftlessness. The particularly severe typhus epidemic of 1741–2 in London marked the climax of a number of years of severe fever mortality. The epidemic came after a long hard winter,[8] a dry spring, a hot summer and a deficient harvest, although a complex of other environmental conditions also contributed to the spread of the disease: the gross overcrowding of dwellings, separated by narrow alleys and courts, especially in the City itself, sealed or deliberately blocked windows (resulting from the window tax), cesspools beneath houses, stinking indoor privies, poor personal hygiene, drunkenness, low moral standards and privation. It is small wonder that the London house in which Jonathan Swift then lodged had 'a thousand stinks in it'.

London mortality had never been so high as at this time. In 1741 typhus accounted for 7,500 deaths or about a quarter of the total deaths in the metropolis. Creighton described the disease as 'a curiously correct index' of the lowly condition of the working classes and the unwholesomeness of towns. It might have been appropriate, but this description should be related to Creighton's own social, political and medical beliefs. The 1741–2 epidemic, said to have reached Plymouth and Bristol from Ireland in the autumn of 1740, spread from there to Worcester and Exeter. Its subsequent diffusion throughout much of Britain may have been stimulated by the comings and goings associated with a General Election.

London was not the only one of the big towns to be struck by typhus in the eighteenth century. Liverpool, Britain's second city (population 56,000 in 1790) housing 7,000 people in cellars and 9,000 in back-to-back houses, was equally troubled. So, too, were the poorer citizens of Edinburgh, Newcastle, Leeds, Hull, Carlisle, Lancaster, Manchester, Warrington and Chester, and of the counties of Oxfordshire, Gloucestershire, Worcester, Wiltshire, and Buckinghamshire. It is said that the death rate from typhus in Manchester in 1773 was twice that of the surrounding countryside. This city had further outbreaks of typhus in 1794–5.

Scotland, like England, was sorely troubled by typhus. In 1741, for example, following a year of famine, the disease inflicted itself on top of the other miseries of the people. In Edinburgh that year deaths from typhus amounted to nearly 20 per cent of all deaths. Then, during the 1745 rebellion government troops returning from the Low Countries brought the fever with them and passed it on to the inhabitants in several parts of Scotland. Privation among the people during the latter half of the century was invariably associated with outbreaks of fever.

> Ye ugly creeping blastit wonner
> Detected, shunn'd by saint and sinner
> Robert Burns, *Ode to a Louse*

Cold weather, bad harvests, food scarcity, heavy drinking, filth, over-crowding, dirty clothes and badly ventilated houses all contributed to the spread of the louse.

Enteric fever (typhoid, paratyphoid), one of the 'continued fevers', was, like typhus, familiar to everyone in the eighteenth century. It was a common, almost 'natural' cause of death, and in its endemic form was a constant menace and serious problem in public health. In the twentieth century enteric fever is generally spread by infection introduced from abroad[9] and may affect a wide area, but in the eighteenth century it was pre-eminently a water-borne disease. The infection was spread by contaminated water (sewage) or by contaminated food, but neither water nor food was the cause. The cause was a bacterium, *Salmonella typhi* (*Bacillus typhosus*) and the fever was due to the ingestion of the micro-organism in water or food. Not until the late nineteenth century, when pure water supplies became available, sewers were substituted for privies and more personal hygiene and cleanliness adopted, did typhoid decline.

Up to the beginning of the nineteenth century it was virtually impossible to diagnose the nature of the many throat infections mentioned in medical writings. In particular it was difficult to disentangle scarlet fever from measles or diphtheria. Fothergill[10] and Huxham[11] described epidemics of sore throat in London (1746–8) and Plymouth (1750–1) respectively, but Fothergill's description was of diphtheria and Huxham was speaking of a more or less concurrent outbreak of scarlet fever. In Scotland it may have been that causes of 'putrid sore throat' were, in fact, cases of diphtheria. The disease was said to prevail chiefly in damp situations in cold and rainy seasons, and more especially, near the sea; Stirling and Cupar in Fife were said to be particularly vulnerable. Both diphtheria and scarlet fever were serious infectious diseases in the eighteenth century, especially of childhood, and were a frequent cause of death. It is now known that diphtheria ('croup') is caused by *Corynebacterium diphtheriae*. There are three types, *intermedius*, *gravis* and *mitis*; the two former are severe forms, the latter mild. Predisposing environmental conditions doubtless included over-crowding in people's workplaces and in their homes.

Scarlet fever, known also as scarlatina, occurred in epidemic form on several occasions. The disease had been clearly differentiated by Sydenham in 1676. 'The skin is marked with small, red spots, more frequent, more diffuse, and more red than measles. These last two or three days. They then disappear, leaving the skin covered with brawny squamulae as if powdered with meal.' In the context of scarlet fever 'rash' and 'scarlet' were synonyms. Modern knowledge of streptococcal sore throat tells that the disease was due to infection with haemolytic streptococci, spread chiefly by droplet infection. For young children living in the close and crowded homes of the poor, scarlet fever was especially common.

Creighton writes of sore throat distempers (diphtheria and scarlatina) in Edinburgh in 1733, in Devon and Cornwall in 1734, in London late in 1739,[12] Sheffield in 1745. London (Bromley, near Bow) in 1746–8, St Albans in 1748, Cornwall in 1748, Kidderminster in 1748, Plymouth in 1751–3, London in 1776–8, Birmingham in 1778, Aberdeenshire in 1791, and again in London in 1796–1805.

Confusion persisted, also, between scarlatina and measles (mezils), but there were undoubted epidemics of measles ('black measles') throughout the eighteenth century. The more severe epidemics of measles came to those communities which had lost their immunity through having been free of the disease for a long interval. The Bills of Mortality for London recorded 319 deaths from measles in 1705 and 361 in 1706, mainly among children. These fatalities were related to one continuous epidemic extending from October 1705 to April 1706. Further epidemics recurred, those of 1718–19, 1733, 1742, 1755, 1758, 1763, 1766, 1768, 1778, 1786, 1789 and 1792 were outstanding. The main victims were infants and young children. Creighton says, 'measles caused by its direct fatality not more than a sixth part of the deaths by smallpox in Britain generally.'[13] In Scotland the disease appears to have been more common than scarlatina. The view of the College of Physicians in Edinburgh at the time was that the heavy drinking of spirits on the part of parents, together with their general ill-health, rendered offspring weak, feeble, distempered and predisposed to infectious diseases. The real cause of this extremely infectious disease is a virus which is apparently spread through the secretions of the eyes and respiratory passages of the infected.

A further serious complaint among children, already present in the seventeenth century was infantile diarrhoea. It is not known if the causal micro-organism then was the same as that which causes fatal diarrhoea in infants in the present century. What is known is that it caused enormous mortality among children in the summer months, July and August. Drummond's view was that 'the mortality among infants was in no small measure due to the heavy spirit drinking in the towns, particularly in the first half of the century. Wet nurses were all too often gin tipplers and the practice of giving spirits to quieten the infants was very general.'[14]

In the second half of the century, poverty, dearth and high food prices added to life's misery. Thousands of children were abandoned, others were farmed out to foster-mothers, only to die after a few months' 'care'. Under the insanitary conditions of the poorer parts of towns, or in such places as workhouses where large numbers of people were herded together, it was small wonder that infant mortality was high. One modern theory for the high mortality rate among infants in the eighteenth century implicates horse manure. It holds that infantile diarrhoea was a fly-borne disease and associated with heaps of horse manure, an ideal breeding ground for flies. That horse manure was present in the streets and alleys there is no doubt, but also present were muckheaps in private premises, dead dogs and cats, the entrails and bones of cattle thrown on the streets, gutters choked with refuse and pigs fouling the streets. Everywhere there was filth and the menace to health was manifest (see pp. 146ff.).

Whooping cough (chin-cough) was not only a common and distressing malady of children but also a consistent contributor to the mortality of children in the eighteenth century. In his *Treatise on the History, Nature and Treatment of Chin-Cough*, Robert Watt, in 1813, recorded that 'Next to the Smallpox formerly, and the Measles now, Chincough is the most fatal disease to which children are liable.'

Influenza, sudden in appearance, equally sudden in withdrawal and rarely lasting more than a few weeks at a time, was common in Britain in the eighteenth century. There were outbreaks in 1712, 1727–9, 1733, 1737, 1743, 1762, 1767, 1775, 1782 and 1788. One epidemic which reached Britain in April 1782, though no more outstanding in terms of character or mortality than the previous ones, may be mentioned since it was selected as the subject of two collective inquiries. It formed part of a pandemic which started in Asia and spread westwards through Siberia into Russia by December 1781. From there it attacked Germany and Finland in February 1782, Denmark, Sweden and England in April, and then France, Italy and most of the remainder of Europe. In England its first foothold was Newcastle, but it spread rapidly southwards, reaching London, the eastern counties, Surrey, Portsmouth, Oxford and Chester by May, Yarmouth, Ipswich, Devon, Liverpool and York by early June. Northwards it was in Edinburgh by May and Glasgow by June, and affecting the whole of Scotland and Ireland by July. Some 75 to 80 per cent of the adult population were affected by the epidemic, yet old people and children were generally spared. 'People are variously affected by it, with swelled faces, sore throats, dizzy heads, coughs, violent pains and feverishness; for remedy is prescribed a decoction of 2 oz lint-seed, 2 do. of Liquorish-stick bruised and boiled over a slow fire in a pint of water to half-do., then strained and mixed with 4 oz powdered sugar candy, also some lemon juice, brandy or rum; take frequently a spoonfull thereoff etc.'

There was a progressive increase in the death rate from consumption (pulmonary tuberculosis) during the eighteenth century. Migration to the developing industrial towns was taking place on a scale without precedent and the accommodation provided to meet it was hopelessly inadequate. Lack of transport facilities and the need to live reasonably close to places of employment led to overbuilding of sites and overcrowding of houses. Domestic overcrowding offered ideal conditions for mass infection of susceptible people. Tuberculosis developed into a chronic, endemic disease. However it is as a scourge of nineteenth-century Britain that consumption is remembered and so will receive further consideration in chapter 11.

By the time of the first census in 1801 the population of the British Isles had increased to 10½ million (Fig. 10.4). This increase has been variously ascribed either to a fall in the death rate or to an increase in the birth rate. Griffith[15] suggests that medical measures introduced during the eighteenth century had a substantial effect on the death rate. This view is not acceptable to McKeown and Record,[16] and they are probably right. These two authors review the value of eighteenth-century surgery. In the case of midwifery they say that 'the introduction of institutional confinement had an adverse effect on mortality', and that such medicines as mercury, digitalis and cinchona had no appreciable influence on mortality trends. Of hospitals and dispensaries they said, 'the chief indictment of hospital work at this period is not that it did no good, but that it positively did harm.' The only disease upon which specific preventive therapy could have had a substantial effect at this time was smallpox, but since vaccination was not introduced by Jenner until 1796, McKeown and Record point out that 'it is hard to believe that inoculation can have been responsible for a reduction in the incidence of smallpox large enough to have had a substantial effect on national mortality trends', and conclude that the rise of population was the result of an improvement in economic and social conditions. A substantial increase in the birth rate was considered unlikely to have occurred during the eighteenth century, except as a secondary result of a reduction of mortality. It seems therefore, that despite reports of a deterioration of living conditions in the last quarter of the eighteenth century, the economic developments of the period probably brought a general advance in the standard of living in their wake. The effectiveness of medical therapy as a factor influencing the increase of population in the latter half of the eighteenth century can be discounted.

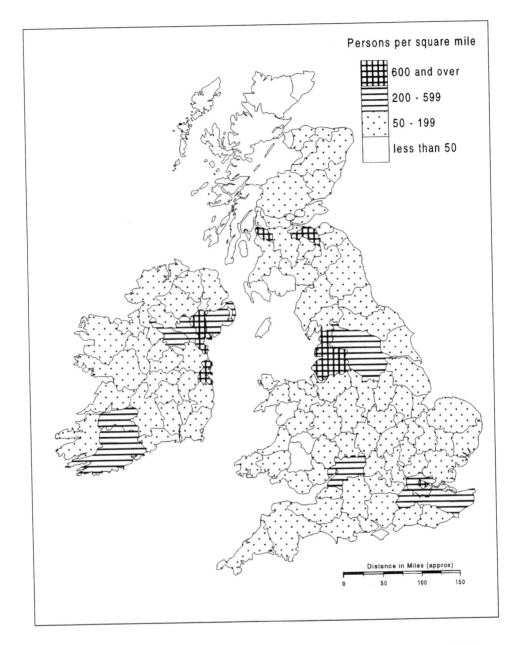

Fig. 10.4 Distribution of population in the British Isles, 1801 (adapted from *Reader's Digest Atlas of the British Isles*, 1965)

11

Early Victorian Times

The age to which Queen Victoria gave her name was so long (1837–1901) that it cannot be thought of as one but several ages. It was an Age of Steam. It was also an age of high birth rates,[1] declining death rates and rapid growth of population, an age of social reform and substantial improvements, particularly in real wages.

The rapid growth of population which had begun in the second half of the eighteenth century continued into the nineteenth century. At the time of the first census in 1801 the population of Britain was 10½ million; by 1831 it was 16.3 million. But not only did the population increase in numbers, its distribution was also changed in response to the developing cotton industry in Lancashire, the woollen industry of west Yorkshire, the knitwear industry of the east Midlands, and the coal-mining and metallurgical activities of the coalfields of the Midlands, and the textile industries and coal-mining of Scotland. The Northumberland and Durham coalfields, the Yorkshire–Derbyshire–Nottinghamshire fields, those of the Black Country and along the Welsh border had been exploited since the late 1500s, but were further stimulated during the nineteenth century. Instead of the populous zone extending in broad fashion across the southern half of England as in earlier centuries· and related to a largely rural society, there was now an axial belt extending from London to Liverpool and also across the central lowlands of Scotland, related essentially to an industrial and urban society. London retained and even increased its national pre-eminence and with its suburbs had a population of nearly 1 million by 1801. In contrast, eastern, southern and south-western England (though showing substantial growth) had declined in relative importance. Bristol and its hinterland at the western end of the former zone of relatively dense population were eclipsed in importance by Liverpool, the second port of the country and the industrial hinterland of Lancashire. In fact, Bristol was surpassed in population by Birmingham, Liverpool and Manchester-Salford, although none as yet had populations over 100,000 (Fig. 11.1).

Industrial developments had also taken place in south Wales and in the central lowlands of Scotland. In south Wales urbanization expanded with

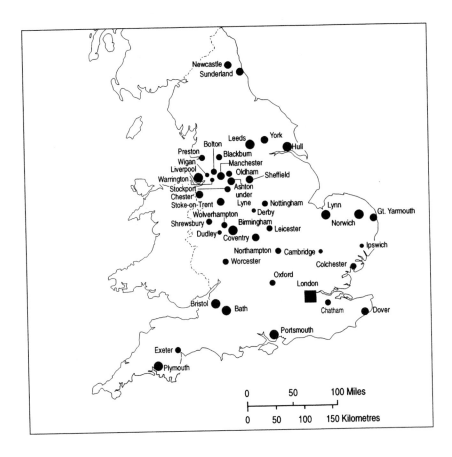

Fig. 11.1 Ranking of the provincial towns of England, 1801 (based on data in
W. G. Hoskins, *The Making of the English Landscape*)

developments in the metallurgical industries and in coal mining; in Scotland
there was a gradual shift of emphasis from the east to the west in association with the very rapid growth of Glasgow and the surrounding district.
Everywhere the new industrial towns created unprecedented social problems
and hardships for the working classes.

The lack of employment opportunities for local population growth in the
rural areas and a rising demand for labour in expanding industrial and
mining areas resulted in a high volume of migration within the country.
There was a general townward movement of the younger, more active age
groups and a high rate of natural increase in the towns to which they went.

The class system in Britain which evolved from this movement of population was complex, but in broad terms resolved itself into two systems of

authority, conflicting, complementary or interdependent. The one was derived from the land and its traditional power, the other from developing industry. But the conflict was not one of equals: in the countryside there were the landlords as well as landless labourers; the towns had their industrialists and their factory operatives. The contrasts in experience of rich and poor were stark.

The struggle against Napoleon's France ended in 1815 with Britain in a thoroughly exhausted condition. Poverty, distress and discontent were rife among the working classes. To the ill-effects of war and financial and trade disturbance were added the grave consequences of a sequence of indifferent harvests. The country came very close to real famine in 1812, but two bumper harvests in 1813 and 1814 brought the price of wheat down. Farmers protested that cheap corn would ruin home agriculture, and the Corn Law of 1815 (forbidding the import of foreign wheat and keeping home-grown wheat prices artificially high) was passed to placate them. There was a considerable increase in unemployment in Britain following the closing of war industries after the French wars, and this, combined with three bad harvests in 1817–19 caused poverty, distress, hunger, death and widespread rioting. The culmination was the breaking up by force of a public meeting in Manchester – the tragic Peterloo massacre – on 16 August 1819. The numbers of killed and wounded were disputed; 600 authenticated cases are known.

The proportion of population engaged in agriculture fell to about 30 per cent, but productivity increased. Even so foodstuffs had to be imported in years of bad harvest. For the first twenty-five years of the century the conditions of the poorer people in both town and country remained bad. In Scotland many people were driven to desperation by the terrible struggle for existence after the repeal of the Salt Tax[2] and braved the hardships of long sea voyages to Australia and North America rather than endure the misery at home. There was particularly large-scale emigration from Britain to the New World and Australia between 1840 and 1850.

The large provincial industrial town was the unprecedented social phenomenon of early Victorian times. It usually grew from quite a small nucleus. Bradford in Yorkshire, a typical example, had little more than two streets at the beginning of the nineteenth century, each about a quarter of a mile long, converging on a bridge. According to the *Bradford Observer* for 9 June 1836 it was 'a town which previous to the introduction of machinery, was a miserable looking place, certainly not much more than a thousand souls, destitute of almost any public convenience or accommodation, its streets narrow and irregular, its buildings jumbled together without a design, or as if they had been dropped together by accident'. When it came, much of its early population growth was absorbed within the existing nucleus of the town. Single or double rows of cottages were erected in the long gardens or crofts of existing houses, and reached by narrow passages frequently arched over. This irregular early development gave rise to 'the old slums'. The earliest industries established themselves on the edge of the original nucleus where all too many of them stayed. In the 1830s, developments on a larger scale began around the nucleus with the building of terraces of two-storey working-class houses – a typically English form of habitation. Back-to-back houses were built in repeated rectangular blocks, perhaps 70 to 75 yards by about 35 yards, completely enclosing airless central courts reached only by tunnel entries. These soon merited the description 'the new slums'. It is possible to level criticism at such developments, but it is important to appreciate the scale of the problem. Between 1841 and 1851 the population of Bradford increased from 66,718 to 103,786. And Bradford was no exception, the huddled courts in the original nucleus, surrounded by rows of back-to-back houses were repeated in practically every industrial town in the North of England.[3] In Scotland three- or four-storeyed tenements were more typical.

Conditions in these towns were worse than in London, since few had any form of local government capable of ensuring even the most elementary standards of public hygiene. Many lacked the supply of such basic public amenities as water, sanitation, paving and street cleansing, and harboured innumerable hazards to good health. Edwin Chadwick in his *Report on the Sanitary Conditions of the Labouring Population of Great Britain* (1842) gave insight into the situation in these towns and provided disturbing evidence of the general living standards of the working people. In the *Report* one reads of ill-constructed houses, often mud-walled, with ill-ventilated rooms, neither boarded nor paved, and generally damp, of the retention of refuse inside the houses in cesspools and privies. Near at hand were reeking dunghills and accumulations of filth; alongside habitations ran open drains oozing with sewage and animal and vegetable refuse, pigsties attached to dwellings, rubbish thrown alongside dwellings, and open slaughterhouses where the refuse and filth were allowed to accumulate for weeks without removal. In this way were the slums born.

Descriptions, in their own words, of the experiences of men, women, young people and children, who lived in and through the Industrial Revolution in Britain, are given in the following selection of quotations.

England's Manufacturing Population – Housing Arrangements
One of the circumstances in which they are especially defective is that of drainage and water-closets. Whole ranges of these houses are totally undrained or only very partially ... The whole of the washings and filth from these consequently are thrown into the front or back street, which

being often unpaved and cut up into deep ruts allows them to collect into stinking and stagnant pools, while fifty, or more even than that number, having only a single convenience common to them all, it is in a very short time completely choked up with excrementitious matter. No alternative is left to the inhabitants but adding this to the already defiled street, and thus leading to a violation of all those decencies which shed a protection over family morals.[4]

Manchester

The greater portion of those districts inhabited by the labouring population ... are untraversed by common sewers. The houses are ill-soughed (drained), often ill-ventilated, improvided with privies, and in consequence, the streets which are narrow, unpaved and worn into deep ruts, become the common receptacle of mud, refuse and disgusting ordure ... surrounded on every side by some of the largest factories of the town, whose chimneys vomit forth dense clouds of smoke, which hang heavily over this insalubrious region.[5]

Liverpool

As in all large towns, the borough of Liverpool has its share of courts and alleys for the working population. Many of these, constructed within the last 10 or 15 years, are open, and afford comfortable dwellings, are well drained and clean, and are consequently healthy; others are of a very different class ... The houses are generally built back to back, but this does not present a sufficient ventilation, as each has three openings, viz. a door, a window, and a chimney; some of the courts are closed, some open; the cleansing of the courts is left to the inhabitants themselves, and some of these will be found to be as clean as the most favoured parts of any town, whilst others, inhabited by the idle and dissolute, are as filthy.[6]

Birmingham

The courts of Birmingham are extremely numerous; they exist in every part of the town, and a very large proportion of the poorer inhabitants reside in them ... The courts vary in the number of the houses which they contain. From four to twenty, and most of these houses are three storeys high and built as it is termed back to back. There is a wash-house, ash-pit, and a privy to the end, or on one side of the court, and not frequently one or more pigsties and heaps of manure. Generally speaking, the privies in the old courts are in a most filthy condition.

... a few of the circumstances in which Birmingham, perhaps, differs from the most of those large towns in which fever constantly prevails and in which its ravages are so formidable. These are – the elevated situation of the town – its excellent natural drainage, and its abundant supplies of water –

the entire absence of cellars used as dwellings – the circumstances of every family having a separate house – and lastly, the amount of wages received by the working classes, which may be regarded as generally adequate to provide the necessities of life.[7]

Bradford

In some streets a piece of paving is laid half across the street, opposite one man's tenement, whilst his neighbour contents himself with a slight covering of soft engine ashes, through which the native clay of the subsoil is seen protruding, with unequal surface, and pools of slop water and filth are visible all over the surface. The dungheaps are found in several parts of the street and open privies are seen in many directions.[8]

Sheffield

Sheffield is one of the dirtiest and most smokey towns I ever saw ... One cannot be long in the town without experiencing the necessary inhalation of soot, which accumulates in the lungs, and its baneful effects are experienced by all who are not accustomed to it. There are, however, numbers of persons in Sheffield who think the smoke healthy.[9]

Leeds

By far the most unhealthy localities of Leeds are close squares of houses or yards as they are called, which have been erected for the accommodation of working people. Some of these, though situated in comparatively high ground, are airless from the enclosed structure and being wholly unprovided with any form of drainage, or convenience, or arrangements for cleansing, are one mass of damp and filth ... The ashes, garbage and filth of all kinds are thrown from the doors and windows of the houses upon the surface of the streets and courts ... The privies are few in proportion to the number. They are open to view both in front and rear, are invariably in a filthy condition, and often remain without the removal of any portion of the filth for six months ...[10]

Nottingham

I believe that nowhere else shall we find so large a mass of inhabitants crowded into courts, alleys and lanes, as in Nottingham, and those too of the worst possible construction ...[11]

Bath

... diseases showing here and there with a predilection for particular spots, are settling with full virulence in Avon Street and its off sets ... Everything vile and offensive is congregated there ... and to aggravate the mischief, the refuse is commonly thrown under the staircase; and water more scarce than any quarter of the town.[12]

Greenock

In one part of market street there is a dunghill – yet it is too large to be called a dunghill. I do not mis-state its size when I say it contains a hundred cubic yards of impure filth, collected from all parts of town. It is never removed; it is the stock-in-trade of a person who deals in dung; he retails it cartfuls.[13]

Glasgow

It is my firm belief that penury, dirt, misery, drunkenness, disease and crime culminate in Glasgow to a pitch unparalleled in Great Britain.[14]

Eyewitness accounts can sometimes enliven the sober pages of *Parliamentary Papers*. In his *Rural Rides*, compiled between 1822 and 1830, William Cobbett describes the conditions of agriculture in southern England in a tone of passionate indignation. This is what he writes of life in the village of Cricklade (Wiltshire):

The labourers seem miserably poor. Their dwellings are little better than pigsties, and their looks indicate that their food is not nearly equal to that of a pig. Their wretched hovels are struck upon little bits of ground *on the roadside*, where the space has been wider than the road demanded. In many places they have not two rods (11 yards) to a hovel ... Yesterday morning was a sharp frost; and this had set the poor creatures to digging up their little plots of potatoes. In my whole life I never saw human wretchedness equal to this; no, not even among the free negroes of America.[15]

Living conditions in early Victorian times were bad. But Dr Guy, a physician of King's College Hospital, London, giving evidence to the Health of Towns Commissioners, said that, bad as they were, the apartments of the poor were more wholesome than their place of work.[16]

Factories multiplied, first alongside streams and rivers but within the towns after steam power was adopted. It was in the towns of the industrial belt of the Scottish lowlands, Manchester, Yorkshire, the Midlands and south Wales that the British proletariat was born. Gaskell's description of workers employed in the great cotton mills reads as follows:

Their complexion is sallow and pallid – with a peculiar pattern of feature, caused by the want of a proper quality of adipose substance to cushion out the cheeks. Their stature low – the average height of four hundred men, measured at different times, and in different places, being five feet six inches. Their limbs slender and splaying badly and ungracefully. A very general bowing of the legs. Great numbers of girls and women walking lamely or awkwardly, with raised chests and spinal flexures. Nearly all have flat feet, accompanied by a down trend, differing very widely from the elasticity of action in the foot and ankle, attendant upon perfect formation. Hair straight and thin.[17]

Of the food habits of the early years of the nineteenth century the chief features were the increased consumption of potatoes and tea. Bread was still 'the staff of life'. It was white bread and all too often alum-whitened. In years of want much of it was baked with flour of very inferior quality, known as 'seconds', frequently mixed with potato flour, garden beans, barley bran and other products which darkened the loaf. Alum was added to make it white. It was not only the bread that was adulterated. Copperas was added to ale and beer, capsicum to mustard, wine was faked (much of it was made with spoiled cider), artificial tea was made from blackthorn leaves, and 'Radical Coffee' (so called because it was favoured by some of the disaffected) made from horse beans, rye or wheat, partially carbonized and ground down.[18] The quality of milk too was unbelievably bad and supplies were heavily infected with tuberculosis. Much of the butter was rancid, meat was tainted and fish stank.[19] Major regional differences in diet tended to disappear with the increasing dependence on purchased food, and the diet of the vast majority of town-dwellers became more uniform.

The water supplies in many towns came from wells, and many of these were polluted. Infected wells proved a serious menace to community health, as the incident of the Broad Street pump in London indicates (see p.161). Rivers too were often little better than 'elongated cesspools'.

Such, briefly, was the environment of the early years of the Victorian age. Expectation of life at birth in 1841 was about 40 for a boy and 42 for a girl, but with considerable regional variation and also differences between the social classes (Table 11.1).[20]

The main causes of death in early Victorian times were typhus, commonly called 'fever', smallpox, cholera and tuberculosis. Lack of adequate protection against secondary infection also rendered some of the common fevers of childhood a serious threat to life, and infant mortality was high.

Typhus, still confused with the enteric group of fevers, was endemic and epidemic in Britain in the early nineteenth century. In previous centuries it had been associated with famines and undernourishment; now it was the constant accompaniment to life in the courts, closes and wynds of the industrial towns. It was the poor person's disease ('that unerring index of destitution'), the product of squalor, insanitation, overcrowding and verminous conditions, a concomitant of working-class housing. It was persistent and devitalizing. It smouldered, but occasionally broke out with renewed virulence whenever a new crop of susceptible people came within its reach. There were outbreaks in 1817–19, 1826–7, 1831–2, 1837 and 1846–8.

Table 11.1 Average age of deceased persons, by social class, in selected localities in England in early Victorian times

Localities	Professional persons or gentry and their families	Tradesmen and their families	Labourers, artisans, servants etc. and their families
Unions in the Country of Wilts.	50	48	33
Kendal Union	45	39	34
Derby	49	38	21
Strand Union	43	33	24
Truro	40	33	29
Kensington Union	44	29	26
Whitechapel Union	45	27	22
Leeds Borough	44	27	19
Bethnal Green	45	26	16
Bolton Union	34	23	18
Liverpool	35	22	15

The epidemic of 1817–19 visited almost every town and village of the United Kingdom. The fever was generally typhus in England, but in Scotland it was to a large extent relapsing fever. The outbreak in 1826–7 had a distinctly more relapsing character in Scotland, although this was not altogether unobserved in London, Bristol, or anywhere else in England. Glasgow, Edinburgh, and Dundee had an epidemic of typhus in 1831–2 and a steady prevalence thereafter. The year 1837 witnessed yet another climax in Glasgow and Dundee,· followed a year later in Edinburgh and Aberdeen. The corresponding epidemic in England, 1837–8, was almost wholly typhus.[21] It led to the death of 6,011 people in London in the space of eighteen months. Other large towns affected – mainly in the latter half of 1837 – were Liverpool, Manchester, Salford, Birmingham, Bolton, Sunderland, Leeds, Sheffield, Bradford, Stockport, Dudley, Wolverhampton, Newcastle, Wigan, Chorley, Swansea, Halifax, Macclesfield and Norwich.

Typhus deaths in the four largest towns of England were:

	1838	**1839**
Manchester-Salford	627	416
Liverpool	573	358
Leeds	245	150
Birmingham	123	141

Several of the outbreaks of typhus were associated with the Irish immigrations which followed potato famines in that country. The disease was endemic in Ireland and in times of stress, as accompanied the failure of a harvest and food shortage, it almost invariably produced an epidemic. That of 1846–7 was by far the worst outbreak and was one of the consequences of the ghastly Irish Potato Famine. The very wet and cool summers of 1846 and 1847, and the unbroken expanses of susceptible cultivated varieties of potatoes in the Irish fields were ideal for the small fungus *Phytophthora infestans*, which came in from America, the original home of the wild potato, on some infested tubers and spread with great rapidity. For two years the potato harvest on which the peasants depended almost exclusively for their food supply failed almost completely. Local workhouses or emigration either to Britain or to North America were the only alternatives to death from starvation. US ports were effectively closed to Irish emigrants at this time and it was left to Canadian authorities to deal with the influx. The tiny Canadian quarantine station on Grosse Ile, near the mouth of the St Lawrence River was the receiving place and all too often the final resting place for many of the incomers. Over 5,000 fell victim to the ravages of famine, typhus or ship fever. A simple white memorial stone on Grosse Ile refers mournfully to 'the mortal remains of 5424 persons who, flying from Pestilence and Famine in Ireland, in the year 1847, found in America but a grave' (*The Ottawa Citizen*, October 31 1996). In no time the disease, called 'famine fever', spread to the remainder of the British Isles, with dire consequences in the overcrowded cellar-dwellings of Liverpool and Manchester and the slum tenements of Glasgow.

The years 1847–8 were particularly bad for typhus in Britain. Liverpool, Manchester, Birmingham, Dudley, Wolverhampton, London, Shrewsbury, Leeds, Hull, York, Sunderland, Edinburgh and Glasgow were seriously affected. The experience in Glasgow, as described by Chalmers, will serve as an illustration:

> From 1816, indeed, until the early seventies of last century, the closes and wynds of the city were devastated by recurring epidemics of infectious diseases of several kinds, and of considerable magnitude. Nor did these stand alone; they formed only the higher peaks of an elevated table-land of disease, which was capable of maintaining an annual death-rate, oscillating frequently between 30 and 40 per 1,000, and of rising in occasional years, under the influences of epidemic prevalences to 46, as in 1832, during the first cholera epidemic, and 56, as in 1846, when typhus fever alone caused a death-rate approaching 14 per 1,000 or only a little lower than the average rate for all causes at the present time.[22]

Glasgow was possibly the filthiest and unhealthiest of all the towns of Britain at this period. Immigration into the city had occurred on a scale without precedent and the accommodation provided to meet it was hopelessly inadequate. There was a general lack of transport facilities, and this, coupled with the need to be living in close proximity to places of employment, led to overbuilding of sites and overcrowding in houses. Nor was there an effective system of refuse removal. The pollution of water supplies and of gross surface impurity near houses was inevitable.

> Pauperism, or destitution worse than pauperism, which demanded relief and failed to obtain it, was not only much greater in Scotland than any other European country similarly situated, but ... it was greatly increasing, and this increase together with the influx of rural and Irish pauperism, into our great towns, had brought them into a condition greatly more favourable than they had ever been before for the spread of epidemic disease and had accordingly raised their mortality far above the level of the corresponding towns in England and on the Continent.[23]

The situation in other cities was little better. In Liverpool, for instance, there were, even as early as the decade 1787-96, an average of 3,000 or more typhus cases each year.[24]

Cholera presented a picture which was very different from that of typhus. This was a disease of rapid onset, dramatic course, highly lethal while it lasted, and exceptionally contagious. The pathogenic agent, *Vibrio cholerae*, on reaching the intestine, causes diarrhoea, which can be fatal within two to six days through acute dehydration of the affected person. It is transferred from person to person either by stools which contaminate clothing, linen or the hands, allowing transmission through contact, or more usually through the intake of water or food contaminated by the excrement of cholera patients.

Cholera, the classic epidemic disease of the nineteenth century, spread throughout China, Burma and Ceylon during the eighteenth century, propagated largely by pilgrims, military personnel and traders. In the nineteenth century there were some great epidemics, occasionally developing into pandemics, which originated in an endemic source in Asia – essentially Lower Bengal and Indonesia but with secondary sources in India-Pakistan, Burma and southern China. Descriptions of these Asian epidemics had been given by European settlers, but cholera did not spread westwards before the nineteenth century.

The disease reached global significance with the pandemic of 1817-23. It originated in Lower Bengal but soon became the source of monsoon Asia, spreading eastwards to China and Japan as well as westwards through

Mesopotamia (Iraq) to the shore of the Mediterranean and south-westwards across the Indian Ocean to the east coast of Africa. The infection spread both by sea and by old overland routes and left a terrible trail of death in China, Ceylon, Burma and Persia (Iran) before subsiding, having failed to reach north-west Europe.

Britain became involved in the second and greatest pandemic. This flared up in the valley of the Ganges in India in 1826, advanced rapidly through the Punjab, Afghanistan and Persia into south-eastern Europe. Soon it spread to all parts of the western world (Fig. 11.2).

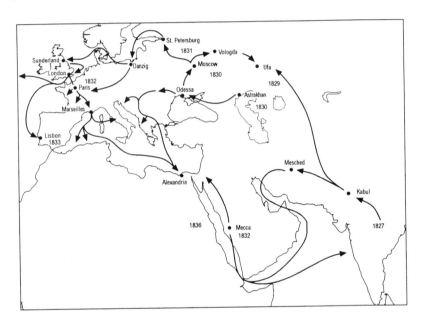

Fig. 11.2 Progress of the cholera epidemic from India to Britain, 1827–31 (adapted from E. Rodenwaldt, *Welt-Seuchen Atlas*)

When William IV opened Parliament on 21 June 1831 he declared: 'It is with deep concern that I have to announce to you the continued progress of a formidable disease in the eastern parts of Europe.'

The advance of the epidemic westward was noted by people in Britain with fear and trepidation. The epidemic reached Moscow by 1830 and survived and continued through a very severe winter. It reached Berlin in August 1831 and Hamburg two months later. As Hamburg was, at that time, a mere thirty-six hours away from England by steamship, the occurrence of cholera there provoked considerable public concern in Britain. Ministers were urged in the House of Commons to impose stricter

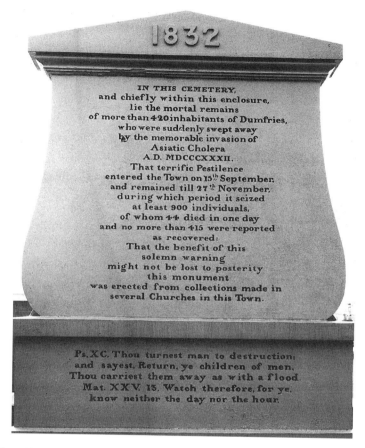

IN THIS CEMETERY,
and chiefly within this enclosure,
lie the mortal remains
of more than 420 inhabitants of Dumfries,
who were suddenly swept away
by the memorable invasion of
Asiatic Cholera
A.D. MDCCCXXXII.
That terrific Pestilence
entered the Town on 15ᵗʰ September,
and remained till 27ᵗʰ November,
during which period it seized
at least 900 individuals,
of whom 44 died in one day
and no more than 415 were reported
as recovered:
That the benefit of this
solemn warning
might not be lost to posterity
this monument
was erected from collections made in
several Churches in this Town.

Ps. XC. Thou turnest man to destruction:
and sayest, Return, ye children of men.
Thou carriest them away as with a flood.
Mat. XXV. 13. Watch therefore, for ye.
know neither the day nor the hour.

Plate 13: Tombstone in St Michael's Kirkyard, Dumfries, to 420 victims of cholera in 1832 (by permission of Lise Moore)

quarantine and to set up a Board of Health. On 18 October 1831, the Privy Council issued a set of *Instructions and Regulations regarding Cholera*, prepared for them by the Board of Health.

It was in Sunderland, on 19 October 1831, that cholera made its first appearance in Britain, and the first case was diagnosed on 4 November. From Sunderland it moved on to Tynemouth, Newcastle and Gateshead, and to villages within a few miles of them on both banks of the Tyne. The disease then spread northwards through Northumberland into Scotland, arriving at Haddington, East Lothian, in December, Hawick, Roxburgh and Edinburgh in January 1832, Glasgow early in February, and thence northwards into the Scottish Highlands. The heaviest death toll in Scotland occurred in Glasgow where there were 3,166 deaths and as many as 228 in one week in August 1831. Another wave of the disease moved southwards to engulf in turn Leeds

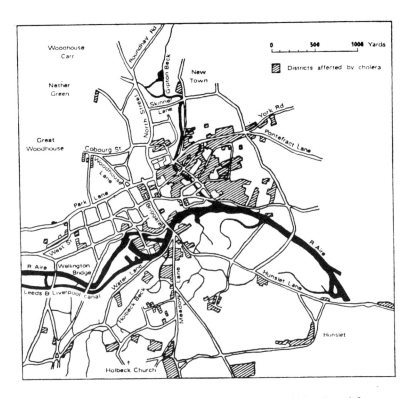

Fig. 11.3 Robert Baker's 'cholera plan' of Leeds, 1833 (adapted from
E. W. Gilbert, 'Pioneer maps of health and disease in England')

(700 deaths, Fig. 11.3), York (200 deaths), Liverpool (1,500 deaths), and
Manchester-Salford (900 deaths). London was reached by February but was
free of cholera by the autumn, the official figure of deaths for the year being
just under 5,300. The Midlands suffered a heavy attack in June with over
2,000 deaths by the end of November. The disease was rampant amid the
shacks and hovels of the new industrial districts. There was a brief outbreak
in Sheffield from early July to the last week in August during which 400
people died. The West Country received the epidemic in mid-July. Cornwall
had a death toll of just over 300, Somerset rather less, but in Devon cholera
took off nearly 2,000 people (Fig. 11.4).

Dr Thomas Shapter's[25] first-hand account of the epidemic in Exeter
affords a vivid picture of the ravages of the disease and its effect upon the
life of that city.

This inadequate water supply combined with the deficiency of drainage, is
of itself sufficient evidence, that the necessary accommodation for the daily

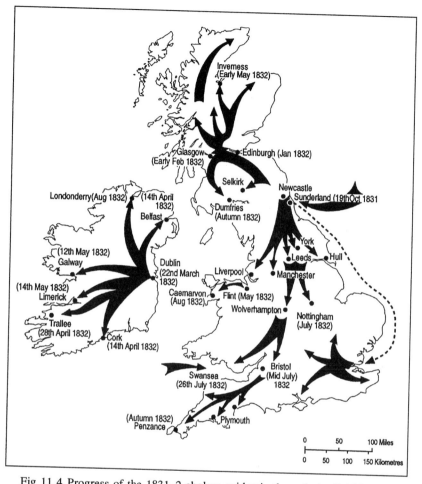

Fig 11.4 Progress of the 1831–2 cholera epidemic through the British Isles (based on C. Creighton, *A History of Epidemics in Britain*, and N. Longmate, *King Cholera*)

usages of the population must have been very limited ... they speak of dwellings occupied by from five to fifteen families huddled together in dirty rooms with every offensive accompaniment, slaughter-houses in the Butcher Row, with their putrid heaps of offal, of pigs in large numbers kept throughout the city ... poultry kept in confined cellars and outhouses; of dung-heaps everywhere.

Such were the conditions prevailing in the lower-lying and neglected portions of Exeter, and 'Amid this desolation, the profligacy and drunkenness of the lower orders increased to such an alarming extent as to become a matter of public remark and censure.'

The epidemic began in the second half of July but was almost over by the autumn. In that time, however, there were over 400 deaths in the city out of a population of 28,242. The story of cholera in Exeter could apply equally to several other towns in the early nineteenth century; it was, in microcosm, the story of cholera in Britain.

Cholera reached Flint in north Wales early in May 1832 and spread quickly to Holywell (49 deaths), and widely into north Wales by late July. It occurred in Caernarfon during August and the early part of September causing thirty deaths. 'The terror and dismay which reigned in this town during the prevalence of the disease can never be forgotten by its inhabitants' (*Caernarvon Herald*, 22 September 1832). In south Wales the towns of the coalfield experienced severe outbreaks of the disease, both in 1832 and in the subsequent epidemic years of 1849, 1854 and 1866. It appeared in Newport on 24 June 1832, and independently in Swansea on 26 July when the *Mary Ann* called at the port with two of her crew dying from the disease. The disease continued thence to Llanelli, Neath, Haverfordwest, Merthyr Tydfil, and Builth Wells. Merthyr Tydfil had 160 deaths from cholera during the 1832 epidemic and Swansea 152 deaths.[26]

In Ireland the first undisputed cases of cholera were reported in Dublin in March 1832. Thereafter it spread throughout the whole country and caused great terror among the populace (Fig. 11.5). Ireland was not to be free until well into 1834 by which time it had suffered 25,378 deaths out of a population of 7,800,000. In England and Wales, the death toll was 21,882 out of a total population of almost 14 million; Scotland lost 9,592 of its 2,300,000 people.

The Cholera Acts were rushed through an agitated British Parliament but cholera came again and again. For ten years Britain remained immune from the disease, then the assault was renewed with a brief but very severe epidemic in the south of Scotland in mid-winter 1848–9 (Fig. 11.6). It arrived at Leith and Edinburgh at the beginning of October and reached Glasgow by December, casting a blight upon Hogmanay celebrations. Edinburgh suffered 450 deaths, Glasgow 3,800 and Scotland as a whole 7,000–8,000.

The epidemic in Scotland was over before the disease really began in England. It started in London, probably reintroduced into the country by a seaman, John Harrold from Hamburg. It spread first south of the River Thames in the Lambeth and Southwark areas. During 1849 it raged practically the length and breadth of England causing 52,293 deaths. The East Riding of Yorkshire, Lancashire, Northumberland and Durham,

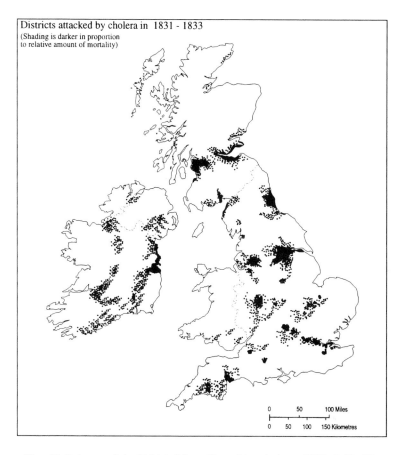

Districts attacked by cholera in 1831 - 1833
(Shading is darker in proportion to relative amount of mortality)

0   50   100 Miles
0   50   100   150 Kilometres

Fig. 11.5 Areas of the British Isles affected by cholera, 1831–3 (A. H. Petermann, *A Cholera Map of the British Isles*)

Staffordshire, Devon and south Wales suffered severely. In south Wales the distress among the people of Merthyr Tydfil attracted particular attention. At this time the town, with about 50,000 people, was the largest in Wales and, like Aberdare, Rhymney, Tredegar, and Ebbw Vale along the northern edge of the coalfield, had experienced a mushroom growth as an iron-smelting centre. Rows of cottages had been erected in haste to house the vast influx of workers. The result was a huge labour camp. The town lacked practically every amenity, and conditions for men and women were sordid. 'The body and habits of the people [of Merthyr Tydfil] are almost as dirty as the town and houses in which they swarm; the people are savage in their manner, and mimic the repulsive rudeness of those in authority over them.' Such was the comment of a government commissioner in 1847.

Fig 11.6 Principal locations in the British Isles affected by cholera, 1848–9 (based on C. Creighton, *A History of Epidemics in Britain*, and other sources)

The town was, without question, unsalubrious and typified the worst excesses of mid-Victorian squalor.

Cholera had broken out on the coast at Cardiff in May 1849 and caused almost 400 deaths.[27] In subsequent months it made enormous ravages in the mining valleys of south Wales. It broke out in places as far apart as Newport, Swansea, and in Holyhead in north Wales, but it was Merthyr Tydfil, twenty miles north of Cardiff, which suffered most. Cholera appeared in the town on 21 May, and from then on until well into

November the epidemic raged and 'hardly an house escaped without feeling the lash of this scourge', by which time 1,400 of the citizens of Merthyr had died.

It is not strictly part of the 'period-picture' to which this chapter is devoted, but mention must be made of the 1853–4 visitation of cholera, since it was this epidemic, beginning on Wearside, which stimulated the second edition of John Snow's essay 'On the mode of communication of Cholera' in 1855. This edition makes special mention of the Soho (London) epidemic of cholera and includes a map of the distribution of cholera deaths in the Broad Street (now called Broadwick Street, Soho) district in 1854 (Fig. 11.7). The Revd Henry Whitehead, vicar of St Luke's, Berwick Street, in Soho, wrote of the epidemic as 'limited in its extent, brief in its duration, continually on the wane from the moment of its appearance'. The 'cholera field' as Snow called it, had its centre at the pump in Broad Street, near Golden Square, and the 'field' was bounded roughly by Great Marlborough Street, Dean Street, Brewer Street and King Street. Within this small area over 500 people died from cholera in the ten days from 1 to 10 September 1854. Snow demonstrated that most of these deaths occurred among those who consumed water from a pump in Broad Street, whereas those living in the same neighbourhood but using other water supplies escaped. He insisted that an engineer examine the well below the pump and established that the water had become contaminated by seepage from a leaking cesspool or drain. It was arranged to have the pump handle removed. The numbers of new and subsequently fatal cases during the critical fortnight of August–September 1854, as given by Snow, suggest that the outbreak was already limiting itself and that the value of removing the pump handle was largely symbolic. The weight of positive evidence of the source of the disease was that of the distribution map, aided by such sidelights as the case of the woman who lived at a distance but had her water brought from the Broad Street pump (because she liked the taste) and caught cholera.[28]

Pulmonary tuberculosis (phthisis) was the most widespread and persistently deadly disease of the nineteenth century. Under the name 'consumption' it had appeared in the Bills of Mortality of the seventeenth century and was certainly prevalent in the eighteenth. However, it was in the nineteenth century in association with overcrowding in factories and slums that it thrived. It was a dreaded disease and not well understood. Diagnostic precision was lacking, and it was frequently confused with other diseases. Yet the first analysis by the Registrar-General[29] for England and Wales in 1839 revealed that identifiable consumption alone accounted for 17.6 per cent of all deaths.

On the basis of information in the London Bills of Mortality, Brownlea[30]

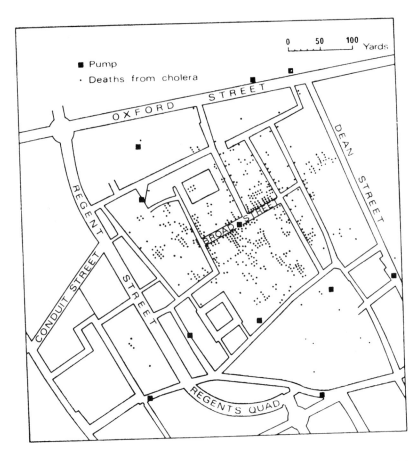

Fig. 11.7 Deaths from cholera in the Soho district of London, September 1854

shows that the proportion of all deaths due to tuberculosis in London rose throughout the eighteenth century, reached a peak in the fifty years between 1780 and 1830, and fell steadily thereafter. Other researchers put the effective turning-point in tuberculosis mortality near 1850. Be that as it may, it is clear that tuberculosis was overwhelmingly the most important single cause of death in the 1830s. The disease had a long epidemic cycle.

Tuberculosis is caused by the *Mycobacterium tuberculosis*, discovered by Robert Koch in 1882. The two types, human and bovine, can cause disease in humans. The disease may be contracted either by drinking infected milk from tubercular cows or by inhaling the bacilli when a person with the disease coughs or spits. Bovine tuberculosis was particularly common in nineteenth-century Britain but the relationship with cows' milk was not known. The conditions under which cows were kept then made it highly

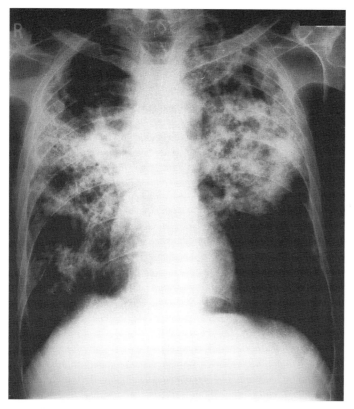

Plate 14: Radiograph of cavitated pulmonary tuberculosis
(by permission of Llandough Hospital and Community NHS Trust)

probable that every drop of milk was heavily charged with the organisms responsible for bovine tuberculosis.

Unsightly scrofulous glands were a frequent sight in people suffering from tuberculosis. The Revd Patrick Brontë, father of Charlotte, Emily and Anne, was so afflicted. The disease thrived in deprived bodies, its allies were undernourishment, debilitation, unventilated homes and working accommodation, and squalor. Such circumstances were ever-present among certain of the working population[31] in early nineteenth-century Britain, particularly among the vast army of spinners and handloom weavers in the cotton and woollen industries, the frame-work knitters of Nottinghamshire and Leicestershire, the silk workers of Coventry, the nail-makers of Birmingham, the lace workers, shoemakers, together with general labourers and porters.

The staple diet of the manufacturing populations is potatoes and wheaten bread, washed down by tea or coffee. Milk is but little used. Meal is consumed to some extent, either baked into cakes, or boiled up with water, making a porridge at once nutritious, easy of digestion and easily cooked. Animal food forms a very small part of their diet and that which is eaten is often of an inferior quality. In the class of fine spinners and others, whose wages are very liberal, flesh meat is frequently added to their meals. Fish is brought to some extent, though by no means largely, and even this is not till it has undergone slight decomposition, having first been exposed in the markets, and being unsaleable, is then hawked about the back streets and alleys where it is disposed for a mere trifle. Herrings are eaten not unusually; and though giving a relish to their otherwise tasteless food, are not very well fitted for their use. The process of salting, which hardens the animal fibre, renders it difficult of digestion, dissolving slowly, and their stomachs do not possess the most active or energetic character. Eggs, too, form some portion of the operatives' diet. The staple is, however, tea and bread. Little trouble is required in preparing them for use; and this circumstance joined to the want of proper domestic arrangements, favours their extensive use among a class so improvident and careless as the operative manufacturers.[32]

Burnett[33] points out that town life had important effects on food habits. It necessarily meant a greater dependence on professional services of bakers, brewers and food retailers, partly because living conditions were generally overcrowded and ill-equipped for the practice of culinary arts, and because many wives worked at factory or domestic trades and had little time or energy for cooking. 'The kind of food which most commended itself was, therefore, that which needed little preparation, was tasty, and if possible, hot, and for these reasons bought bread, potatoes boiled or roasted in their jackets, and bacon which could be fried in a matter of minutes, became the mainstays of urban diets. Tea was also essential because it gave warmth and comfort to cold, monotonous food.'

The first half of the nineteenth century was a time of unprecedented malnutrition. It was a hungry half-century. The diet of the majority of town-dwellers was at best stodgy and monotonous, at worst hopelessly deficient in quality and nutriment. Agricultural labourers fared little better, although those in the northern counties of England and in Scotland seem to have been more fortunate than those in the south. In the north oatmeal was made palatable by the addition of milk, which was rarely available to the southern labourer who had no cow pasture of his own. Potatoes were a popular item of diet in Scotland, Cumberland, Westmorland and in the northernmost counties generally, where 'the children of our gentry prefer potatoes to bread', but they were regarded with considerable scorn by labourers in the south of England. In many respects it might be said that the agricultural labourer and his family lived near to or on the verge of starvation.

Living conditions in the towns, have already been referred to (pp.159ff). The description by Dickens of 'the neighbourhood beyond Dockhead in the Borough of Southwark (London)' is as grim as anything Chadwick or Engels ever wrote:

> ... a maze of close, narrow and muddy streets ... tottering house fronts, projecting over the pavement, dismantled walls that seem to totter as he passes, chimneys half crushed half hesitating to fall ... Crazy wooden galleries common to the backs of half-a-dozen houses, with holes from which to look upon the slime beneath; windows broken and patched, with poles thrust out, on which to dry the linen that is never there; rooms so small, so filthy and squalor which they shelter; wooden chambers thrusting themselves out above the mud, and threatening to fall in – as some have done; dirt-besmeared walls and decaying foundations; every repulsive lineament of poverty, very loathsome indication of filth, rot and garbage.[34]

It was under such conditions that tuberculosis thrived. Tubercular infection was rife among the ill-fed poor, and a great many cripples owed their misfortune to this. It was considered part of life, apparently inevitable and accepted mutely. Hobson[35] suggests that much of the dramatic poetry and drama written in the nineteenth century would never have been created but for the stimulus of tuberculosis. 'Probably the diminished physical vigour brought about by disease increases the urge to mental activity.' Certainly the ideal of feminine beauty at that time was a languorous pale creature, lying upon her couch, dressed in white, flimsy drapery. How far this was because of the prevalence of tuberculosis, or the cult among the 'ladies' of keeping themselves out of the sunlight so as to appear 'genteel' is difficult to assess.[36]

The nineteenth century set no great premium on infant life. Child deaths were inevitably most frequent in the dreadful environment of the slums of towns. Of the one-roomed houses of the slum backlands of the industrial towns it is said that one in every five of all children born in them never saw the end of their first year, and of those who so prematurely died one-third were never seen by a doctor in the course of their illness. One out of every five children who survived infancy died before they were fifteen. Ferguson[37] tells that 'in the new industrial world, children were apt to be a nuisance, a drag on their parents, until they came to be old enough to earn a wage' and refers to infanticide and near-infanticide, and to the administration of opiates to the young in the Lancashire cotton towns (a dose of 'quietness' was given to the child to prevent it being troublesome while the mother was out to work) with disastrous effects. Infant mortality was excessive not only in the towns but also in the countryside where 'herded together in cottages which by their imperfect arrangements, violated every sanitary law, generated all kinds of disease ... [men were] compelled by insufficient wages to expose their wives to the degradation of field labour, and to send their children to work as soon as they could crawl.'[38]

Children suffered severely from bronchitis, pneumonia, summer diarrhoea, the common infectious diseases of childhood and rickets (Plate 16). Previously rickets had been more common in the upper social class because of the large families, the habit of wet-nursing, over-emphasis on meat, with a diminished intake of milk, together with the practice of protecting babies from sunshine. It was now common in the poorer classes, and not only among those who had insufficient food; families were larger, and with increased income more attention was given to the consumption of meat and less to milk and cheese. Diarrhoea was associated with general and domestic uncleanliness, just as diseases of the respiratory organs were due to conditions of the atmosphere and typhus to overcrowding and vermin. The common infectious diseases such as scarlet fever, measles and whooping cough were of a relatively mild character, it was the complication rather than the original disease which caused death and disability. For example, death from measles was often due to a secondary broncho-pneumonia. Rickets was a national scourge, with thousands of infants suffering from bent limbs and curved spines. Faulty diets were to blame, not least the proprietary baby foods. The latter were preponderantly farinaceous and consisted of flour starch, malted flour and similar materials. They were deficient in protein, in fat and in most of the vitamins. Proprietary baby foods were responsible for appalling amounts of malnourishment and sickness.

12

Late Victorian Times

The main theme in the history of the Victorian era was that of economic and social change and the cultural response to it. Consequently the late Victorian period contrasted markedly with early Victorian times. By the end of the nineteenth century Britain had lost her industrial and commercial supremacy to such countries as Germany and the USA. She was no longer 'the workshop of the world'. The pace of her economic growth had slackened and readjustment was taking place. The Corn Laws had been repealed, cheap North American and Russian wheat was flooding the market, and those branches of agriculture concerned with the growing of cereals were depressed. Yet the population of the country continued to increase. It doubled within the two-thirds of a century of Queen Victoria's reign. The 16.3 millions in 1831 rose to 23.1 millions by 1861 and 33 millions by 1891. By the 1890s, 70 per cent of the population dwelt in towns. Birth rates remained high and death rates continued to decline, although after about 1880 there were indications that the birth rate was beginning to fall (Fig. 12.1).

The late Victorian era experienced the last of the cholera epidemics (1866), an epidemic of smallpox (1871), and a pandemic of influenza (1889). It also embraced a developing social conscience, the 'ages' of Chadwick and Simon, and inspired such eminent Victorians as Lord Shaftesbury (Young Men's Christian Association), Dr Barnardo (Homes for waif children) and General Booth (Salvation Army) to seek to improve the lot of their suffering fellow citizens.

Edwin Chadwick (1800–90),[1] author of the *Report on the Sanitary Conditions of the Labouring Population of Great Britain* (1842) (see p. 146), was Secretary of the Poor Law Commission. The statement on the general condition of the dwellings of the labouring classes or of workmen's lodging houses, the sanitation of their homes and places of work, and the domestic habits affecting the health of the labouring classes contained in his *Report* demonstrated the need for national action and was instrumental in forcing questions of public health into politics. Chadwick waged war against dirt and disease, and has been called 'Father of the Sanitary Idea'. The Public Health Act, passed in 1848, was very much linked with him,

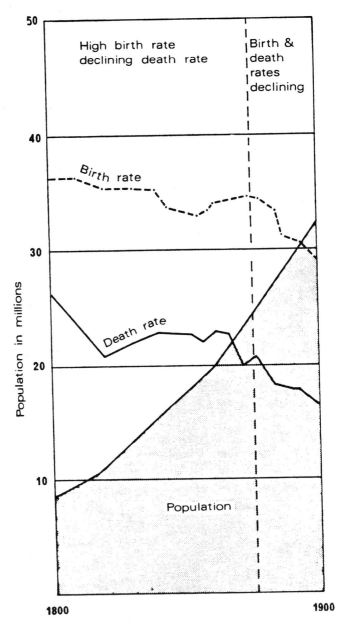

Fig. 12.1 Birth rates, death rates and population totals in Britain, 1800–1900

and his co-workers, Dr Southwood Smith, Dr Neil Arnott, Dr J. P. Kay and Dr John Snow.

John Simon (1816–1904), Medical Officer of Health for the City of

London and later at the Office of the Privy Council, was the first public-health pioneer after Chadwick and drew heavily on his work. He promoted several inquiries into the incidence and mortality of diseases in different areas of the country, which had an enormous influence in promoting sanitary reform. At this same time William Farr was Compiler of Abstracts at the General Register Office. It was he who analysed the available data relating to life and death in Britain which were used to such effect by both Chadwick and Simon in their crusade against insanitary conditions.

The late nineteenth century was a time when the role of micro-organisms in the causation of disease had yet to be demonstrated. Many diseases were still thought of as being initiated by the diffusion of gaseous material from poisons in the soil, usually of putrefactive origin, from decomposing animal and vegetable substances, from damp and filth, and from close and overcrowded dwellings. Odours and emanations (miasmas) were considered the responsible agents.

Until late in the nineteenth century medical men knew little more than had their Greek forebears about actual causes of plague, fever and pestilential scourges. By the end of Pasteur's career, near the end of the century the rudimentary germ theory of infectious diseases had been proved and was no longer seriously contested; the patterns of many infective diseases were understood; methods had been devised for preventing or combating some of the most serious infections; conditions under which surgical procedures were carried out had been revolutionized, and the sciences of bacteriology and preventive medicine had been launched.

Hieronymus Frascatorius (see p.106), Marcus Antonius von Plenaz and others had earlier approached the correct explanation of the nature and causation of infectious disease, but they were incapable of providing the necessary proof. The development of the microscope in the seventeenth century made it possible to demonstrate the existence of living unicellular organisms by actual observation, but it was Louis Pasteur (1822–95) and Robert Koch (1843–1920) who provided indisputable proof of the existence of germs, of their modes of reproduction, and of their specificity in causing disease. This work culminated in preventive inoculation against rabies (*hydrophobia*) in 1885. Pasteur prophesied that microbes could produce disease, but it was Robert Koch who provided the proof. Koch isolated the tubercle bacillus (*Mycobacterium tuberculosis*) in 1882 and identified it as the specific organism of pulmonary tuberculosis (consumption, phthisis). By the end of the century the organisms causing diphtheria, lobar pneumonia, erysipelas, Malta fever, cerebro-spinal meningitis, tetanus, plague, botulism, cholera, dysentery and wound infection had been identified, isolated and proved to be responsible for the diseases with which they were associated. Equally important was knowledge of the usual sources of the

PUNCH, OR THE LONDON CHARIVARI.—July 21, 1855.

FARADAY GIVING HIS CARD TO FATHER THAMES;

And we hope the Dirty Fellow will consult the learned Professor.

Plate 15: *Punch* cartoon of 1855 (by permission of *Punch* Ltd)

organisms and the routes by which they travelled. Not until the closing years of the nineteenth century was the part played by insects (ticks, flies, fleas, etc.) in the transmission of disease discovered. Armed with such knowledge, ways and means for blocking the routes and preventing further infections were made possible.

Influenza had been present in Britain in fairly severe epidemic form during the nineteenth century (1803, 1831, 1833, 1837, 1847–8), but Greenwood,[2] writing in 1935, said: 'In 1889 this country had been free

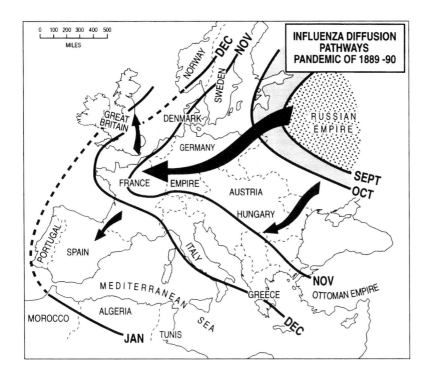

Fig. 12.2 Diffusion pathways of the influenza pandemic of 1889–90. Considered by many authorities to be the first of our 'modern' influenza pandemics, the disease spread rapidly through Europe's centre in 1889, along the extensive network of late nineteenth-century railway connections
(after Pyle and Patterson, 1983)

from pandemic influenza for more years than in any previous epoch since the middle of the seventeenth century.' That year, however, saw the beginning of a pandemic which was to last until 1894, with recurrences in 1895, 1900 and 1908, until it culminated once again in the pandemic of 1918–19. Though its source was in doubt, the pandemic of 1889 seemed to have originated in south-west Siberia in what was then Russian Turkestan (now Turkmenistan, Uzbekistan, Tajikistan, Kyrgyzstan and Kazakhstan), and to have spread rapidly westwards to western Europe, reaching Britain by January 1890. By February it had spread throughout the whole of the British Isles (Fig. 12.2). It was a mild form of influenza and did not cause the high mortalities experienced in many countries on the Continent. This epidemic of 'Russian influenza' was followed by three more waves, which had 'peaks' in May 1891, January 1892 and December 1893. The first (1890), was nation-wide, the second (which began in Hull and on the Welsh Border) and third (first reported in the west of Cornwall and in the east of

Scotland) were more localized and more desultory or prolonged. The revival of the epidemic in three successive seasons made the late nineteenth-century invasion of the disease unique, since no similar sequence had been recorded in the previous history of the disease in Britain. Many authorities have considered it to be the first of our 'modern' influenza pandemics.

Influenza is caused by viruses that have the ability both to drift and to shift in genetic composition. There are three known antigenic types, A, B and C. Influenza viruses A and B have been implicated in several major epidemics. Sporadic cases or localized outbreaks of influenza C are the rule. Influenza virus is transmitted by direct contact and droplet infection. The virus of the 1889 epidemic was due to a sudden mutation of the virus type A, rendering it slightly different from, and more virulent than, the strain which had previously been prevalent in Britain. Such a mutation enabled the virus to produce infection among individuals who would have escaped prior to the alteration. Having acquired no immunity, people were only able to put up the feeblest of resistance to the epidemic in 1889.

Influenza is a winter disease as a rule (Fig. 12.3), and it requires relatively low temperatures for its propagation. It also needs a low level of immunity in large numbers of the population and the presence of a suitable type of virus at the time to enable the epidemic to occur. Evidently these environmental conditions were present in combination in Britain in 1889.

Pneumonia was frequently associated with influenza during the 1918–19 pandemic. Indeed there might have been a concurrent epidemic of pneumonia in Britain at the time. As a disease in its own right, pneumonia in 1900 was the fourth major cause of death in Britain after heart disease, tuberculosis and bronchitis. For any person to be in poor health was an invitation to pneumonia. Pneumonia, inflammation of the lungs, usually results from *Pneumococci*, or other organisms already present in the throat or inhaled from outside sources, spreading down and multiplying widely in the substance of the lung. As with influenza, it is most common in cold months. Evidently at the time of the influenza pandemic, the whole population was also susceptible to pneumonia. There were, in addition, viral pneumonias and a haemolytic streptococcal form present as complications of the influenza. Young children were particularly vulnerable, and pneumonia, after diarrhoea was probably the second most important cause of death of children under five.

Undernourishment was a possible contributory cause of the influenza and pneumonia epidemics of 1918–19. Food shortages and rationing were fairly severe during the First World War following the 1917 German U-boat campaign. There was not the same attention given by the government

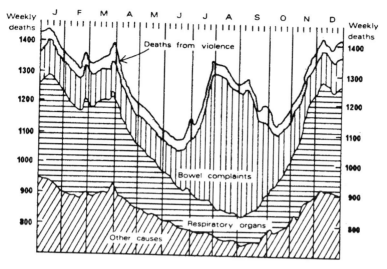

Fig. 12.3 Seasonal trends of deaths in London, 1845–74 (after A. Buchanan and A. Mitchell, 1973–5)

of the day to the provision of bread of high nutritive value, to milk supplement for expectant and nursing mothers and all children up to the age of fifteen years, and to fortifying margarine with vitamins A and D, as during the Second World War.

Bronchitis, the name given in the early nineteenth century by Charles Badham[3] to 'the more chronic pectoral (chest) complaints, especially those of people advanced in life', flourished in Britain at the end of the Victorian era, particularly in the damp and smoky atmospheres of the new industrial areas. It was a disease of the industrial towns of Lancashire, the West Riding of Yorkshire, the Midlands, the Black Country, South Wales and Clydeside. Bronchitis is essentially inflammation of the mucous membranes of the bronchi. A cold environment predisposes to the disease as it does to pneumonia and other respiratory infections, and inflammation is liable to be set up by a sudden change from warm to cold air. Air polluted by toxic substances, inhaled with a humid atmosphere, also irritates the respiratory passages. Acute bronchitis may be precipitated by excessive atmospheric pollution; chronic bronchitis refers to long-standing inflammation of the bronchi. Whatever the conditions, the possible causes (including viral or bacterial infection) were not known at the start of the century – indeed they are elusive even in the latter half of the twentieth century.

In the 1830s scarlet fever took over the mortality trail which until then had been blazed by cholera, influenza and smallpox. For a long time it was

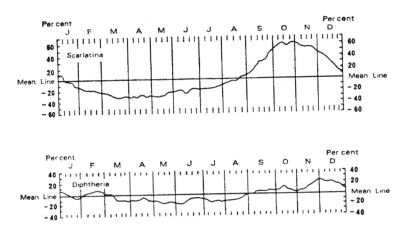

Fig. 12.4 Seasonal trends in deaths from scarlatina and diphtheria in London, 1845–74 (after A. Buchanan and A. Mitchell, 1973–5)

impossible to differentiate it from diphtheria,[4] because both diseases had, in common, the symptom of a sore throat. Typically, however, scarlet fever had, in addition to the sore throat, the rash; in diphtheria, the sore throat was sometimes associated with paralysis (especially of the soft palate) and the obstruction of the larynx. During the middle years of the nineteenth century scarlet fever (scarlatina) was the leading cause of death among the infectious diseases of childhood and during 1863 – the year with the highest mortality – the death rate for children under fifteen was 3,966 per million. There were over 30,000 deaths from scarlet fever in 1863 (Fig. 12.4). Scarlet fever is the result of infection with *Streptococcus haemolyticus*, which may remain quiescent for a long time in dust or clothing but which reproduces rapidly in organic substances, notably milk. From its peak in the 1860s, scarlet fever showed a marked decline, which continued to the end of the century and in fact, to the present day. Why it changed from being a dreaded children's disease to a mild illness affecting older age groups – a change which long preceded the use of antibiotics – is still obscure. It may have been due to a reduction in the virulence of the various types of beta-haemolytic streptococci.

At first diphtheria was overshadowed by scarlet fever, but a wave of prevalence started in the mid-nineteenth century which brought it very much to the fore. The outbreak of 1856–9 was part of a sudden uprising of the disease throughout the world. Creighton[5] tells of fatalities from 'inflammation of the throat', 'putrid sore throat', 'malignant sore throat', 'disease of the throat' in Cornwall (Launceston, Liskeard, Truro), Lincolnshire (Spalding), Kent

(Ash), Oxfordshire (Thame), Essex (Billericay, Maldon) and Derbyshire (Chesterfield). The distribution of the epidemic suggested that diphtheria might have been a country disease, since agricultural counties appear to have had somewhat more than their usual share of an infective mortality than the industrial centres. After the initial outburst, the apparent rural preference of the disease disappeared, but a high death rate of about 800 per million population persisted until about 1900.

Table 12.1 Main causes of death at the end of the Victorian era

	%
Heart disease	12.8 (largely old age)
Phthisis (tuberculosis)	10.4
Bronchitis	9.2
Pneumonia	7.5
Vascular lesions of nervous system	7.0 (largely old age)
Cancer	4.5
Accidents	3.1
Infant mortality (measles, whooping cough, diphtheria, scarlet fever)	23.5
All others	22.5

Figures 12.5–12.8 show, for England and Wales only, the areal, spatial or geographical distribution of average death rates for all causes, zymotic diseases, phthisis and infant mortality respectively in 1901. Living conditions in the late nineteenth century improved in ways which quite certainly influenced the cause of infectious diseases. Accumulated knowledge of the conditions of life among the industrial poor and of the part which environmental conditions played in predisposing to the disease stimulated sanitary endeavour. Better housing, cleanliness, ventilation, disinfection, control of nuisances, improved water supplies and improved refuse and sewage disposal were some of the measures which were applied successfully, although with no significant improvement in mortality rates until after 1871.[6] Preventive measures did not rest on knowledge of the mechanism of infection but derived empirically from noting the association between sickness and bad living conditions. The effectiveness of the measures was later explained rationally by the science of bacteriology.

Against no disease did the sanitary improvements of the late nineteenth century win greater triumphs than typhus, unassisted by bacteriological research or by knowledge of the bionomics of vermin. There were sharp falls in the death rates and probably in the incidence of typhus and enteric fevers (typhoid and paratyphoid). Cholera had virtually disappeared, so had smallpox after the implementation of the Vaccination Act of 1861

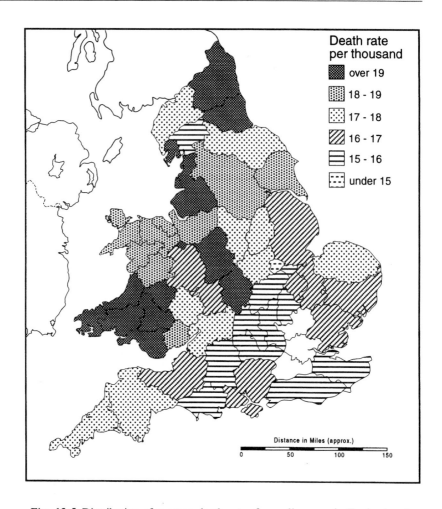

Fig. 12.5 Distribution of average death rates from all causes in England and Wales, 1901 (adapted from J. G. Bartholomew (ed.), *Bartholomew's Gazetteer of the British Isles*)

(Fig. 12.6). The risk of epidemic and crowd diseases fostered by poor sanitation and overcrowding was decreasing, but in the towns there was a high risk of degenerative disease resulting from the harder wear and tear of factory employment and urban discomfort. The census of 1901 disclosed that about 16 per cent of the population of London lived in overcrowded conditions. Higher proportions existed in Dudley (17 per cent), Devonport (17 per cent), Plymouth (20 per cent), Sunderland (30 per cent), Newcastle-upon-Tyne (30 per cent), Tynemouth (31 per cent), South Shields (32 per cent) and Gateshead (34 per cent).

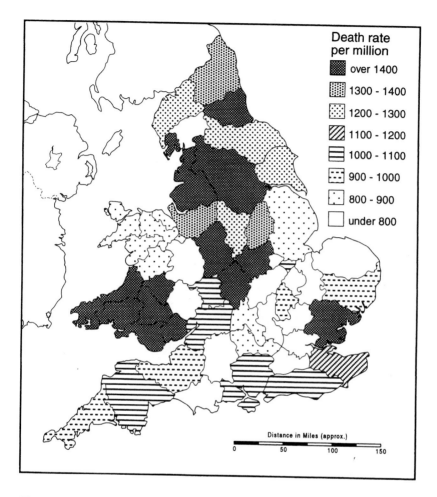

Fig. 12.6 Distribution of average death rates from zymotic (i.e. infectious and contagious) diseases in England and Wales (adapted from J. G. Bartholomew (ed.), *Bartholomew's Gazetteer of the British Isles*)

Tuberculosis, the *white plague* ('where youth grows pale, and spectre thin, and dies')[7] was still a much dreaded disease (Fig. 12.7). Infant mortality, too, continued at a high rate (172 per 1,000 during the period 1891–1900), but there was a change in the relative importance of the fatal diseases. Scarlet fever, previously the most fatal of the common infectious diseases of childhood, was, by the end of the century, fourth after measles, whooping cough, and diphtheria.

The end of the Victorian era was a time of declining birth and death rates. The crude birth rate in 1901 was 29 per 1,000, and the crude death

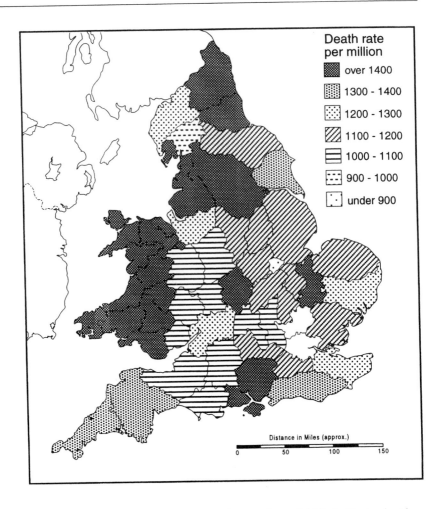

Fig. 12.7 Distribution of average death rates from phthisis in England and Wales, 1901 (adapted from J. G. Bartholomew (ed.), *Bartholomew's Gazetteer of the British Isles*)

rate 17 per 1,000. Expectation of life at birth was 43.7 years for men and 47.2 years for women during the period 1881–90, and 44.1 years for men and 47.8 years for women in the period 1891–1900. It can probably be said that there was a gain of ten or more years in the expectation of life at birth during the course of the nineteenth century, indicative of progress towards healthier living conditions and greater facilities for combating disease rather than any material modification in inborn characteristics of the population itself. In some respects there was a decline in the overall physique of the workers. Seemingly the forces which had produced a

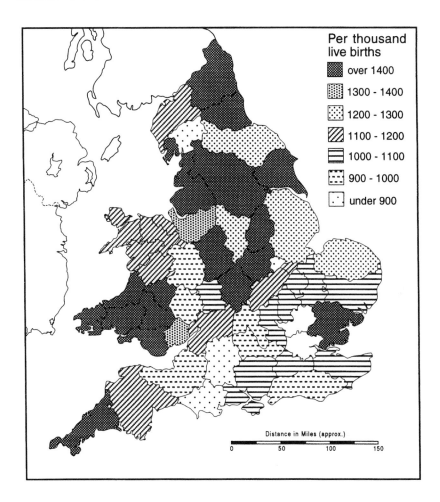

Fig. 12.8 Distribution of average infant mortality rates in England and Wales, 1901 (adapted from J. G. Bartholomew (ed.), *Bartholomew's Gazetteer of the British Isles*)

reduction in the death rate had not operated equally throughout every section of the population. Some sections were being missed, as was evidenced by the Recruiting Returns of the South African War. Appreciable defects in physique, health and efficiency were disclosed. Rejection of army recruits was as high as 60 per cent in some areas, and over the whole country nearly 40 per cent. The chief grounds for rejection were bad teeth, heart affections, poor sight or hearing, and deformities. Indeed the extent of defects among volunteers for the South African War shook the public conscience. The material progress of the nineteenth century had been purchased seemingly at the cost of a general deterioration in health of the population. Drummond says: 'It is no exaggeration to say that the opening of the twentieth century saw malnutrition more rife in England than it had been since the great dearths of medieval and Tudor times.'[8] Burnett disagrees and considers Drummond's statement 'almost certainly untrue'.[9] An Inter-Departmental Committee, set up to investigate the extent of the physical deterioration of the population, reported in 1904[10] and substantiated what had been amply demonstrated by Seebohm Rowntree[11] for York in 1900 and Booth[12] for London in 1902. The committee's comprehensive survey of the possible causes of the poor physique and ill-health of the labouring population of the towns made special mention of such factors as overcrowding, bad sanitation, alcoholism, factory conditions and ignorance. Drummond says that the survey failed to give due regard 'to what was by far the most important cause, semi-starvation due to sheer poverty', and highlights the deficiencies of white bread and the diet of children. Even so the Inter-Departmental Committee Survey did pay considerable attention to the defective diet of babies and young children. Attention was given to the rapid decline in breast-feeding, due partly to the employment of married women in industry, but more importantly to the chronic ill-health of mothers, which rendered many of them incapable of providing the necessary milk. The usual substitute in working-class homes was sweetened condensed skimmed milk, rich in sugar but almost wholly devoid of fat. When older, poor children passed to a diet consisting essentially of bread, margarine and jam. The 1904 Inter-Departmental Committee Report found that 33 per cent of all children were undernourished in the sense that they actually went hungry. Two years earlier, a survey of Leeds had shown that in the poorest areas of the city, 50 per cent of the children had marked rickets and 60 per cent had carious teeth. It comes as no surprise, therefore, to learn that at the beginning of the twentieth century twelve-year-old boys at public or private (fee-paying) schools were, on average, 5 inches taller than those in local authority or council schools. It was this growing concern for the health of children, fortified by the complaints of teachers that hungry scholars were uneducable, that culminated in the passing of the Education Act (Provision of Meals) in 1906 and the Medical Inspection Act in 1907.

The end of the Victorian era was a time of paradox. For some it was an age of affluence and well-being, but for too many it was a time of pauperism and fearful mortality.[13] Even so, the modern growth of population which started in the eighteenth century continued apace into the nineteenth century (Fig. 12.9). McKeown and his co-authors have discussed possible reasons for this rise of population.[14] They draw attention to the decline in mortality between 1840 and 1900 and show that 'five

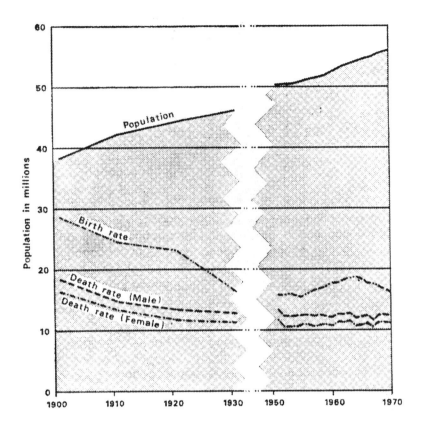

Fig. 12.9 Birth rates, death rates and population totals in Britain, 1900–70
(Registrar-General's Statistical Reviews of England and Wales)

Table 12.2 Expectation of life in years at birth in selected localities in Britain, 1841
and 1881–90 (extracted in part from D. V. Glass)

Period		London	Liverpool	Manchester	Surrey	Selected healthy districts in England	Glasgow
1841	Males	35	25	24	44		
	Females	38	27		46		
1881	Males			29		51	35.2
–90	Females			33		54	44.3

diseases or groups of diseases were responsible for it: tuberculosis for a little less than half; typhus, typhoid and continued fever for about a fifth; scarlet fever for a fifth; cholera, dysentery and diarrhoea for nearly a tenth; and smallpox for a twentieth.' They further suggest that in order of relative importance the influences responsible for the reduction in mortality were '(a) a rising standard of living, of which the most significant feature was possibly improved diet (responsible mainly for the decline of tuberculosis and, less certainly and to a lesser extent, of typhus); (b) hygienic changes, particularly improved water supplies and sewage disposal, introduced by sanitary reformers (responsible for the decline of the typhoid and cholera groups); and (c) a favourable trend in the relationship between infectious agent and human host (which accounted for the decline of mortality from scarlet fever and may have contributed to that from tuberculosis, typhus and cholera). The influence of specific prevention or treatment of disease in the individual was restricted to smallpox and made little contribution to the total reduction of the death rate.'

13

Modern Times – Morbidity

The grosser environmental defects of past ages such as lack of safe water supplies and sanitation have been remedied. This, combined with general improvements in nutrition and living standards since the mid-nineteenth century and developments in modern medicine and drug therapy have resulted in the virtual elimination of communicable disease as a major cause of morbidity and mortality.

Smallpox has been eradicated from the world[1] and several other diseases almost eliminated. Mortality from diphtheria has virtually disappeared. A diphtheria anti-toxin was first produced in 1890 and the diagnostic Schick test and active immunization date from the 1940s. The results were impressive. Notification in England and Wales declined from nearly 50,000 a year to an annual average of 287 in the 1950s, and to less than five each year in the 1980s. In 1992, 1993 and 1994 notifications were 8, 6 and 9 respectively. By the 1950s immunization against diphtheria was combined with protection against whooping cough and tetanus (DPT).

The hygiene and sanitation of modern society indirectly *inhibits* the growth and development of immunity against poliomyelitis. In Britain improved sewage systems, the eradication of insanitary living conditions and greater care over infant feeding contributed to this process. The population became vulnerable and in 1947 almost 8,000 cases of paralytic disease were notified, compared with fewer than 1,000 in any one year for the previous thirty-five years. Between 1947 and 1958 over 50,000 persons contracted the disease, and deaths averaged 350 a year. The majority of the victims were young adults. Vaccinations with the Salk vaccine started on a small scale in 1956, and then with the Sabin vaccine in 1962. Since then notifications of the disease have declined, and in the 1990s poliomyelitis has become even more rare than diphtheria. International studies of the effects of poliomyelitis vaccine suggest that the decline can be directly attributed to the vaccination campaign. Poliomyelitis vaccine is given orally.

Tetanus is now a rarity, as are anthrax (an industrial zoonosis, usually associated with exposure to contaminated wool hair, hides and bone meal), brucellosis (an occupational zoonosis affecting persons in the dairy industry) and bovine tuberculosis (from infected milk).

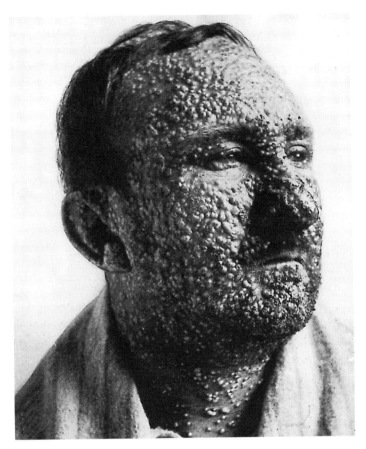

Plate 16: A victim of smallpox, Gloucester, 1896
(from The Jenner Museum collection)

Tuberculosis was made statutorily notifiable in 1913, when there were over 117,000 notifications of all types and nearly 5,000 deaths in England and Wales. In 1994 there were 4,587 notifications and fewer than 350 deaths. The incidence remains high in susceptible groups such as immigrants from Asia. Tuberculosis may be rising in persons infected with the human immunodeficiency virus (HIV).

Vaccination for measles, introduced in 1968, has brought about a reduction in notifications from an average of over 91,000 per annum for the period 1980–5 to 14,888 per annum for 1991–1994. Higher levels of vaccination could result in the virtual elimination of the disease. Scarlet fever, a manifestation of acute haemolytic streptococcal infection, declined from almost 120,000 notifications in 1943 to just over 7,000 in 1988. There was a rise in notifications to 10,386 in 1989, but a subsequent fall to 8,031 in

1994. Reasons for the decline are obscure. The waxing and waning of the incidence and severity of scarlet fever in the past suggests that streptococcal infection may again increase in virulence and in incidence.

Typhoid and paratyphoid fevers are currently rare diseases, reflecting the high standards of sanitation, of hygiene, of drinking water and food supplies in this country, and also the control of hospital infections. Eighty-five per cent of the 300–400 cases a year are imported.

Bacillary dysentery due to *Shigella sonnei* increased in incidence during the Second World War and a large outbreak took place in the 1950s. Notifications reached a peak of nearly 50,000 in England and Wales. After that the incidence declined to under 3,000 in 1979 and 1980, but rose again between 1981 and 1984 to a peak in excess of 8,000. A peak to 11,506 in 1991 and 20,620 in 1992 has been followed by a fall to 7,539 in 1994. Reasons for the recrudescence of the disease remain obscure.

Meningococcal infection appeared in epidemics after the First World War, in the 1930s and in a very large epidemic during the Second World War. Occasional localized outbreaks continue to occur: one such in Yorkshire in December 1995 was caused by the particularly virulent C strain of meningococcus.

Chronic rheumatic heart disease, caused by rheumatic fever, has diminished as rheumatic fever has declined in severity and incidence. This has been due largely to improvements among the socially and economically disadvantaged groups. Rheumatic fever itself is caused by streptococcal throat infections. The control of these infections by anti-bacterial therapy contributed substantially to the rapid fall in mortality from rheumatic heart disease since the late 1930s.

Over the past fifty or so years diabetes has changed from a progressive or rapidly fatal disease into a controlled chronic disorder with mortality confined mainly to old age. The new picture dates from the isolation of insulin in 1922.

Food poisoning diseases are increasing. They are due either to *Salmonella* bacteria (various strains, e.g. *Salmonella enteritidis* (in eggs and poultry) which cause vomiting and diarrhoea closely related to typhoid), *Campylobacter* (ubiquitous in raw, poorly cooked food, including unpasteurized milk), *Yersinia* or *Staphylococcus aureus* or *Escherichia coli* (*E. coli*). These germs are common in foods such as cooked meats, poultry, gravy and stock, dairy products, raw eggs, shellfish and other seafood, and cooked rice.

The world-wide and nation-wide transportation and distribution of foods means that microbes that survive in food once localized become widespread. Because food from any one particular source finds its way to many different places throughout the country a disease can spread as quickly as food is distributed. Furthermore new methods of food preparation often mean that food is dispatched only half-prepared, which, in turn, provides more opportunities for microbes to become more active.

Contemporary shopping and living habits (cooking food too quickly, preparing large quantities for later eating but not refrigerating them, not re-heating food at high enough temperatures to kill bacteria etc.) have been implicated in what has become a food-poisoning plague. Food poisoning rarely impinges on public consciousness unless a large number of people die, as in the outbreak at the Stanley Royd Hospital, Wakefield, in 1984, which killed nineteen elderly patients. A large outbreak of *E. coli* in Lanarkshire in November and December 1996 resulted in 318 people showing symptoms of food poisoning, 184 confirmed cases and the deaths of 19 elderly persons. Food poisoning notifications have risen from 23,237 in 1984 to 86,894 in 1994.

Influenza, 'the unchanging disease due to a changing virus', continues to make periodic visitations. Taken in its global context, the disastrous 1918–19 pandemic, the so-called 'Spanish influenza', was one of the most destructive pandemics in history, ranking with the Great Pestilence (Black Death) as one of the severest holocausts of disease ever encountered. Though commonly thought of as a disease of the colder part of the year, the first wave of prevalence of this pandemic in Britain came in May, June and July 1918. The second wave came in October and November and was much more severe than the first. It tended to kill the young rather than the elderly. A third and final wave occurred in February 1919. There were, all told, about 150,000 influenza deaths in England and Wales during the epidemic; in Scotland there were 3,776 deaths in Glasgow alone.

A strain of influenza virus different from previous visitations was involved in the 1957–8 pandemic, popularly called 'Asian flu'. The new strain bypassed the immunity in the world's population acquired from exposure to previous strains of the virus. It arrived in Britain in June 1957 and diffused first in the north of the country mainly from such ports as Hull, Middlesbrough and Liverpool (Fig. 13.1). By October it was beginning to wane there and shifted rapidly to invade southern England and Wales.

The last influenza pandemic was in 1968. The last serious epidemic was in 1975–6 and minor ones occurred in 1993 and 1995. Epidemics are associated with changes in the antigenic structure of influenza A virus, and these are most unpredictable. Timing of another antigenic shift in the virus and a consequent pandemic cannot be foretold.

Accompanying the environmental changes of the twentieth century have been impressive advances in medical standards and skills. Chemotherapy and a wide range of antibiotics have further contributed to changes in the patterns of disease. A century ago tuberculosis was the most fatal of all

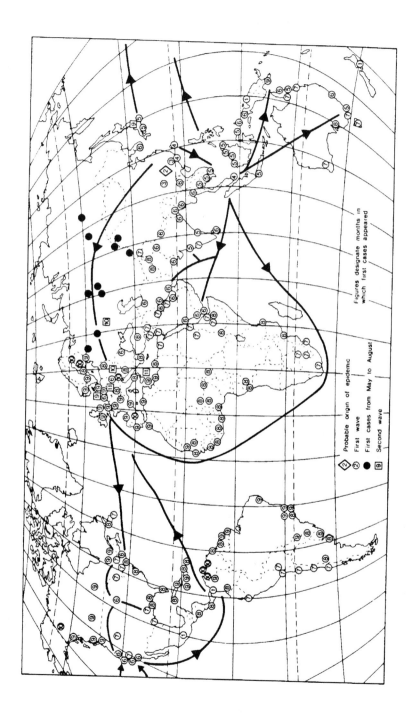

Fig. 13.1 Diffusion of 'Asian' influenza, February 1957 to January 1958 (after A. D. Langmuir, 'Epidemiology of Asian influenza. International Conference on Asian Influenza', *American Review of Respiratory Diseases*, 83 (1961), 2

diseases in Britain; it is now twenty-fifth in the ranking of the leading causes of death.

Many factors have contributed to these results: better housing; better diets; earlier diagnosis through mass X-rays; the prevention of infection through cows' milk (bovine tuberculosis); the combined success of antibiotics and chemotherapeutics, streptomycin, PAS (para-amino-salicylic acid) and INAH (Isoniazid), and later, Ethambutol with Pyrazinamide in the clinical treatment of the disease; and the BCG vaccination campaign. Tuberculosis is no longer the killer disease it was in the past, but sadly there is growing resistance to first- and second-line drugs.

The recorded death rates for pneumonia rose steadily during the second half of the nineteenth century but have fallen steadily since the first part of the twentieth. As with tuberculosis, the steady decline to the 1930s can be ascribed to rising standards of medicine and public-health measures. Rates fell steeply from the late 1930s until the mid-century, since when they have remained relatively constant. It is reasonable to attribute the greater part of this abrupt improvement in death rates to the introduction of sulphonamides in 1935, penicillin a few years later and the broad-spectrum antibiotics in the late 1940s and early 1970s. Even so, pneumonia continues to account for upwards of 31,000 of the 650,000 or so deaths in Britain each year.

The extended life expectancies for both sexes, the virtual eradication of diphtheria and poliomyelitis, and the dramatic reduction in the prevalence of respiratory tuberculosis, tetanus, anthrax, typhoid, measles, whooping cough and other infectious diseases means that the great majority of people now survive to become liable to chronic conditions associated with advancing age. Whereas in 1851 only a million people were over the age of sixty-five, a century later the number had risen to five million, by 1981 to eight million, and to 9.2 million by 1991. By the year 2021 there are expected to be almost 11 million people over sixty-five, or more than 18 per cent of the projected total population. As the figures imply, people are living longer than previously, from 40–5 years in the mid-nineteenth century to over 75 years now. For every twenty people of working age there are at present twelve who are either over retirement age or under fifteen years of age. Sadly, senior citizens suffer from the poorest health of any sector of the population, have the highest morbidity and mortality rates and make ever-increasing demands on the National Health Service and on care services generally. The extra years of life gained by the elderly are usually extra years with a disability. The consequences of demographic changes are of the greatest bearing on social and economic life in contemporary Britain.

Arguably the mental illnesses represent the leading cause of disability in contemporary Britain. Three major classes of mental disorder are recognized by the World Health Organization. The most severe are the psychoses. These are conditions in which impairment of mental functions has developed to a degree that interferes grossly with insight, ability to meet some of the ordinary demands of life, or adequate contact with reality. The second category embraces a wide variety of milder handicaps – neuroses, personality disorders and psychophysiological disorders. Learning disability is the third class of mental disorders, a condition of arrested or incomplete development of mind that is especially characterized by subnormality of intelligence.

Existing investigations of the aetiology of mental illnesses still mainly provide only guidelines rather than firm evidence of the operation of clearly defined causal mechanisms. Apart from a person's genetic endowment, unfavourable physical and social environmental factors are implicated. These include climatic variables, population density and crowding, environmental pollution, socio-economic status (e.g. the disabling mental illness schizophrenia – the largest single group in mental hospitals – is more frequent towards the lower end of the social scale), ethnic minorities (the incidence of mental illness is higher among minority groups than among the population at large) and poverty. In Britain, as in other economically-advanced nations, both the incidence and the prevalence of mental disorders increase with advancing age; particularly the dementias. The elderly mentally ill constitute the fastest-growing group in mental hospitals.

The health of children generally has improved, though substantial differences due to social class, locality and housing persist. This is in marked contrast to a century or so ago, when, in Glasgow, for example, the incidence of but one disease, rickets, gave children 'legs so misshapen and soft … that they were helpless as babies as far as locomotion was concerned.'[2] Rickets then was associated exclusively with urban malnutrition and atmospheric pollution, being virtually unknown in the countryside.

Present-day children are also growing up earlier. Puberty is coming earlier and growth stopping sooner. The most obvious change has been a steady increase in the height of children which, since the start of the twentieth century, has amounted to half an inch per decade in five- to seven-year-olds and about an inch per decade in ten- to fourteen-year-olds. Today's five-year-olds are generally taller than five-year-olds in 1905. In eleven-year-olds and indeed thirteen-year-olds, the difference is nearer four inches (Fig. 13.2). In girls the age of menarche (the first menstrual period) is an accurate indication of the onset of puberty. The menarcheal age has fallen from sixteen or seventeen years in the middle of the nineteenth century to around twelve or thirteen years in the late 1990s.[3] Adults too

Plate 17: A group of Glasgow children with rickets, *c.* 1910
(by permission of Greater Glasgow Health Board)

have been growing taller, but with social-class differences probably reflecting continuing contrasts both in nutrition and social-class determinants of height such as smoking in pregnancy, hygiene and housing. Many people question whether the early maturity in children is, at the present time, desirable, and wonder what the educational, social and economic implications will be of any further lowering of the age of maturity.

Ever-increasing amounts of alcohol are being consumed in Britain, and alcoholism is a major health hazard. Defined as 'one extreme of a continuum of drinking behaviour rather than a distinct and separate pathological entity', alcoholism displays not only the alcohol-dependence syndrome (addiction) but a whole series of problems which may be attributed wholly or in part to excessive drinking. They include many disabling and sometimes physical, behavioural and psychological conditions together with a significant proportion of road traffic accidents. Alcoholic drinks are now more easily available than in the past. Supermarkets sell beers, wines and spirits and soft drinks, some of which have a higher alcohol content than ordinary beers; public houses have been made more attractive and acceptable to women and younger people, and licensing hours have been extended

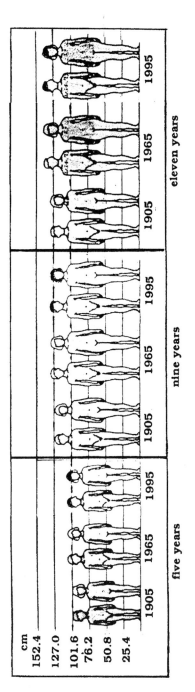

Fig. 13.2 Heights of children, 1905–95

50th centile increase 1965–1995

age	1965	1995	cm increase	% increase
Girls				
5	107.2	108.67	1.47	1.37
9	130.6	132.57	1.97	1.50
11	142.7	143.84	1.14	0.79
Boys				
5	108.3	109.67	1.37	1.26
9	131.6	133.16	1.56	1.18
11	141.9	143.24	1.34	0.94

The approx. 1 per cent increase in growth over the last thirty years is not particularly evident in the illustration, but the comparative decrease in secular trend of the last thirty years from the previous sixty is of interest. (Data from the Child Growth Foundation.)

(11 a.m. to 11 p.m.). Advertising on radio, television and in newspapers has further enhanced the overall consumption of alcohol.

Certain types of occupation are conventionally associated with heavy drinking. These include those associated with the drink trade, those with ready access to free or cheap alcohol (as on expense accounts, or in the armed forces), salesmen and journalists. The environment within which an individual develops also moulds his attitude towards alcohol. Several authors have commented on the high incidence of problem drinking among Irish and Scots who migrate to the industrial areas of England. Cirrhosis of the liver is often associated with alcoholism (see pp.65-6). A life-style which involves drinking alcohol at high levels impairs health, with attendant problems of the liver, heart, brain or pancreas, among other organs, tending to develop insidiously over a long period of time. R. E. Kendell in a perceptive and much-quoted article regards alcoholism as an environmental, political and social problem to which medicine *per se* has little to offer.[4]

Cancer is one disease for which nation-wide morbidity data are available. Regional cancer registries throughout the UK record each new case of cancer as it is diagnosed. The registries monitor the incidence of cancer and its treatment, trace inferences about the aetiology of the cancers in the different parts of the country, prepare survival statistics of patients registered and assist in the evaluation of the health services in the areas concerned. Comparable data from these registries, published in *Cancer Incidence in Five Continents VI* (1992)[5] have been used to show the relative importance of the several cancer sites in different parts of the country 1983-7 (Figs. 13.3, 13.4). Incidence maps for the period 1974-7 are given in Howe, *Global Geocancerology*.

A 1983-7 study[6] which examined the relation between cancer and social factors such as areas of residence, marital status, fertility history, and five different measures of 'socio-economic position' concluded that 'the association of cancer risk with socio-economic position is relatively robust'. In men the incidence of lung cancer and stomach cancer were lowest in Social Class I and increased progressively in the lower social classes. In women there were similar trends in cancer of the stomach and cervix. In men the highest incidence of the large intestine (colon) was in Social Classes I and II, the lowest in Social Class V (Fig. 13.5).

Diseases which cause most distress, dislocation of human endeavour, loss of efficiency in work and of working hours are not necessarily the killing diseases. For this reason death rates no longer provide suitable indices of the general health of the population.

Other indicators provide a guide to the health or morbidity status of the population. The *Annual Abstract of Statistics*[7] contains data on the number

Fig. 13.3 Registries reporting cancer incidence in 1987

of days of incapacity due to illness. In 1993, for example 35.7 per cent of
the days of incapacity in the population were due to circulatory diseases,
25.4 per cent to the musculo-skeletal system, 5.8 per cent to mental
diseases and 5.3 per cent to diseases of the nervous system.[8] Twelve per
cent of the male population and 18 per cent of the female population
consulted their general practitioners during the year, with males averaging

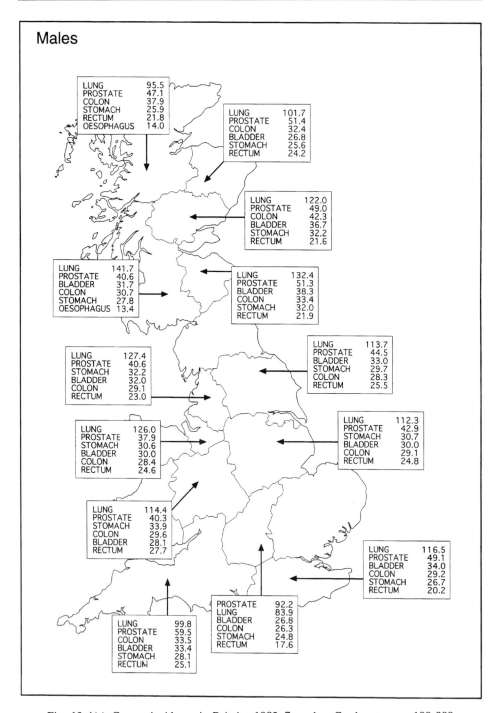

Fig. 13.4(a) Cancer incidence in Britain, 1983–7, males. Crude rates per 100,000

Females

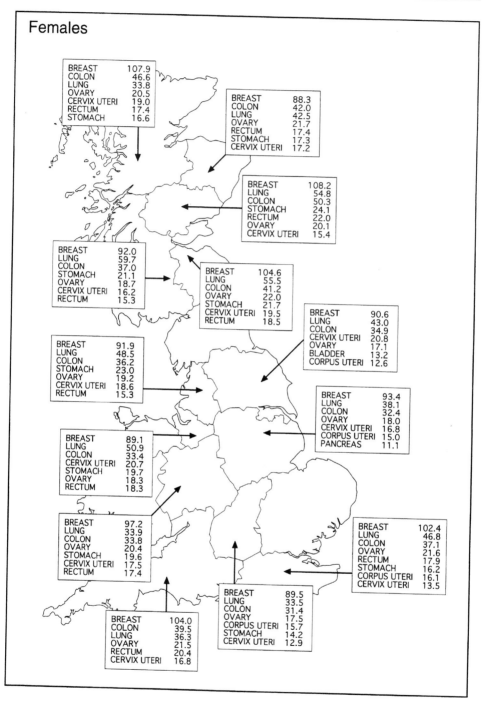

BREAST	107.9
COLON	46.6
LUNG	33.8
OVARY	20.5
CERVIX UTERI	19.0
RECTUM	17.4
STOMACH	16.6

BREAST	88.3
COLON	42.0
LUNG	42.5
OVARY	21.7
RECTUM	17.4
STOMACH	17.3
CERVIX UTERI	17.2

BREAST	108.2
LUNG	54.8
COLON	50.3
STOMACH	24.1
RECTUM	22.0
OVARY	20.1
CERVIX UTERI	15.4

BREAST	92.0
LUNG	59.7
COLON	37.0
STOMACH	21.1
OVARY	18.7
CERVIX UTERI	16.2
RECTUM	15.3

BREAST	104.6
LUNG	55.5
COLON	41.2
OVARY	22.0
STOMACH	21.7
CERVIX UTERI	19.5
RECTUM	18.5

BREAST	90.6
LUNG	43.0
COLON	34.9
CERVIX UTERI	20.8
OVARY	17.1
BLADDER	13.2
CORPUS UTERI	12.6

BREAST	91.9
LUNG	48.5
COLON	36.2
STOMACH	23.0
OVARY	19.2
CERVIX UTERI	18.6
RECTUM	15.3

BREAST	93.4
LUNG	38.1
COLON	32.4
OVARY	18.0
CERVIX UTERI	16.8
CORPUS UTERI	15.0
PANCREAS	11.1

BREAST	89.1
LUNG	50.9
COLON	33.4
CERVIX UTERI	20.7
STOMACH	19.7
OVARY	18.3
RECTUM	18.3

BREAST	97.2
LUNG	33.9
COLON	33.8
OVARY	20.4
STOMACH	19.6
CERVIX UTERI	17.5
RECTUM	17.4

BREAST	102.4
LUNG	46.8
COLON	37.1
OVARY	21.6
RECTUM	17.9
STOMACH	16.2
CORPUS UTERI	16.1
CERVIX UTERI	13.5

BREAST	89.5
LUNG	33.5
COLON	31.4
OVARY	17.5
CORPUS UTERI	15.7
STOMACH	14.2
CERVIX UTERI	12.9

BREAST	104.0
COLON	39.5
LUNG	36.3
OVARY	21.5
RECTUM	20.4
CERVIX UTERI	16.8

Fig. 13.4(b) Cancer incidence in Britain, 1983–7, females. Crude rates per 100,000

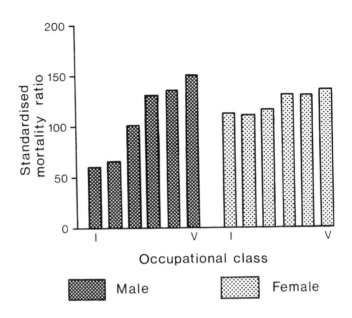

Fig. 13.5 Occupational class and mortality from malignant neoplasms (men and married women, by husband's occupation)

four consultations and females six. Thirty-one per cent of the male population and 33 per cent of the female population reported chronic (long-standing) ill-health, and 18 per cent of the men and 20 per cent of the women reported acute ill-health. Findings from the *Fourth National Study* for the year 1991–2[9] conducted by members of the College of General Practitioners (excluding Scotland and Northern Ireland) revealed that men (but not women) living in the north of England, the Midlands and Wales were more likely to consult their doctors than those living in the south of England. People living in urban areas were more likely to consult their doctors than those living in rural areas, and a higher proportion of council-house tenants and those living in other rented accommodation consulted than people living in owner-occupied dwellings. By marital status widowed and divorced people were more likely to consult than those who were single or married. A higher proportion of people in social classes IV and V (defined by occupation) consulted than those in Classes I and II, with a general gradient between these two extremes. Some 78 per cent of patients consulted at least once during the year, rates being highest among small children. A higher proportion of people consulted for respiratory conditions than for diseases of the nervous system or the sense organs. Some 14 per cent of the people consulted at least once for infectious and parasitic diseases, e.g. mycoses (fungi), particularly for moniliasis (thrush) and chicken-pox caused by a virus among small children, and herpes zoster (shingles) among the elderly.

Some diseases have increased in incidence during the present century, some have decreased, others have risen and declined. Measles (*morbilli*), whooping cough (pertussis), and rubella (German measles) in pregnancy continue to cause disability and death, but recent decades have witnessed a noticeable downward trend in respiratory tuberculosis, poliomyelitis, diphtheria, 'scarlet fever', acute rheumatic fever, appendicitis, peptic ulcer, pleurisy and anaemia as causes of sickness absence from work. This same period has witnessed an increase in mental illnesses, accidents, salmonellosis, asthma,[10] Legionnaire's disease and the sexually transmitted diseases. Since the beginning of the 1980s the acquired immune deficiency syndrome (AIDS) has become a nation-wide problem. Heart disease is now declining among the 35–55 age group, but diabetes is showing an increase among men. Few if any diseases have a constant incidence: for the most part they display ever-changing patterns. Yet it could well be that in these changing patterns lie clues to causation and hence to methods of prevention.

14

Modern Times – Mortality

As noted in chapter 13, raised standards of hygiene, the provision of pure and adequate water supplies, the efficient disposal of sanitary waste, improved housing and nutrition, health legislation and therapeutic advances have brought about improvements in general health and a marked decline in mortality from most infectious or communicable diseases. People are living longer and enjoy physically healthier lives than ever before. Indeed, most live out their natural biological lifespan. Whereas the major disease problems were once acute illnesses with a fairly abrupt onset and a finite duration, the major ones now are chronic illnesses of indefinite duration. Virtually all the severely disabling and killing communicable diseases, endemic during pre-industrial and industrial times, have been eliminated. Instead Britain, like the USA, Benelux, France, Germany, Scandinavia, Australasia and other industrialized countries, is scourged now by a cruel and deadly family of chronic, non-infectious diseases which includes the circulatory diseases (coronary artery disease, stroke, etc.), cancer, respiratory diseases (chronic bronchitis, emphysema, asthma), mental illnesses, accidents and violence (road accidents, accidents in the home, suicide) (Fig. 14.1). Such infectious diseases as tuberculosis, scarlet fever, measles, typhoid, gastro-enteritis and diphtheria have been brought under control, but influenza ('the last plague') and pneumonia continue to present major problems[1] as do certain diseases of early infancy.

Of deaths before age five, most are due to congenital anomalies. Accidents (mainly involving motor vehicles) and violence account for a large percentage of deaths in young males between the ages of five and thirty-five and females between five and thirty. Circulatory diseases become and remain the major causes of death in both sexes from about thirty-five years. Cancer strikes at most ages, but at an earlier age among women. Many of the chronic diseases are a consequence of ageing and, as the numbers of survivors into old age increase, so do cases of chronic disease. Those of the population over sixty or sixty-five years of age may be considered vulnerable with respect to heart and circulatory disease, to cancer, diabetes and certain bone diseases such as Paget's and osteoporosis (Fig. 14.2).

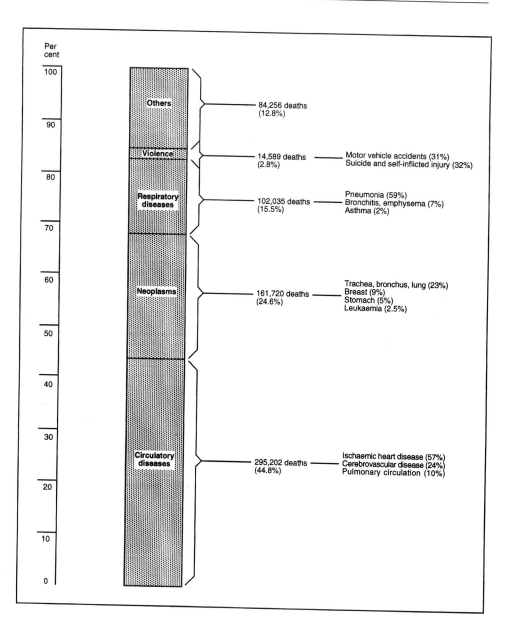

Fig. 14.1 Deaths in Britain analysed by disease groups, 1993
(*Source: Annual Abstract of Statistics*)

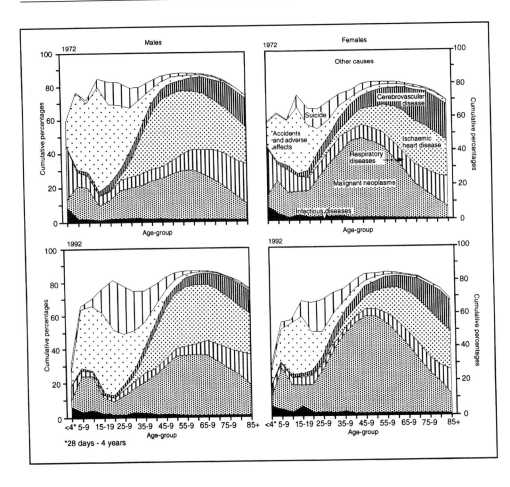

Fig. 14.2 Causes of death by age groups, England and Wales, 1972 and 1992
(*Source*: *Population Trends*)

Table 14.1 shows, for both sexes combined, deaths by major disease groups in 1993.[2] Circulatory diseases account for just under half of all deaths, cancer about a quarter, and respiratory disease for just over 15 per cent. Motor-vehicle and other accidents and suicide account for just over 2 per cent. Other causes make up the remainder. Average annual deaths over the six-year period 1979–84 and for the year 1993 for selected causes are shown in Table 14.1.

Table 14.1 Deaths in Britain analysed by cause, 1979–84 and 1993

Cause	Average Annual Deaths 1979–84	Deaths 1993
Circulatory Disease (44.8%)		
Ischaemic Heart Disease (ICD Nos 410–414)	178700	167602
Cerebrovascular Diseases (ICD Nos 430–438)	81000	713287
Cancer (24.6%)		
Malignant neoplasm of the trachea, lung and bronchus (ICD No 162)	40000	37714
Malignant neoplasm of the female breast (ICD No. 174)	14000	14737
Malignant neoplasm of the stomach (ICD No 151)	12000	8307
Respiratory Diseases		
Pneumonia (ICD Nos 480–486)	60000	60906
Bronchitis, emphysema, asthma (ICD Nos 490–493)	21000	8644

Total deaths of all ages and causes in the UK in 1993 were 657852 (317393 males, 340459 females)

Source: HMSO, *Annual Abstract of Statistics*, 1996

Circulatory diseases (including heart attacks and strokes) are the main causes in both sexes. Lung cancer and bronchitis, emphysema and asthma are rather more severe for men than women. The substantial number of female deaths from breast cancer, cancer of the ovaries and mental disorders tends to redress the balance between the sexes. Lung cancer deaths in women have increased in recent years and may soon overtake breast cancer as a leading cause of death. In Scotland this took place in 1984.

Deaths in old age have an overwhelming impact on total figures and consequently obscure the relative significance of those deaths which are considered untimely or premature, i.e. those which come before the biblical 'three score years and ten'. For instance, in 1995, practically 78 per cent of all male deaths and 87 per cent of all female deaths occurred beyond sixty-five years. On the other hand it is the *early* deaths which reflect adversely on the health status of the nation, and also affect social and economic development in the country. Premature deaths can be properly assessed only if they are separated from overall mortality statistics. For this reason the analysis of geographical or spatial patterns of mortality which follows (pp.202ff.) directs attention to age group 15–64 years. In 1991 this group comprised 63.9 per cent of the total UK population of 57.8 million.[3] The lower limit of fifteen is selected since accidents are the major cause of death during childhood and early adult life; the upper limit of sixty-four years since, as noted earlier, 78 per cent of deaths occur after this age. By restricting the analysis to this age group, emphasis is directed to the spatial incidence, inequalities and variations of premature death in the UK and to possible genetic and/or environmental relationships.

Appropriate sex-specific and age-specific mortality data[4] for the years 1980–2[5] inclusive, centring on the accurate age-structure of local populations at the time of the 1981 census have been used to complete standardized mortality ratios (SMRs)[6] for over 400 administrative districts embracing the whole of the UK (Fig. 14.3 and Appendix). Standardized mortality ratios rather than crude death rates are used on the maps (Figs. 14.3–14.5, 14.7, 14.10, 14.12–14.16) since they allow for the fact that some areas have more than the average number of older people in their populations, while other areas have comparatively youthful populations. Computed SMRs recorded in succinct form on demographic base maps,[7] which are simplified versions,[8] illustrate the spatial distribution and spatial relationships of the areas with favourable and unfavourable mortality experience relative to the UK average. Such maps dispense with pages of statistics or verbal description, aid analysis, stimulate ideas and assist in the formulation of working hypotheses relating to explanation and/or aetiology. On the other hand they are silent on the physical, biological and social processes of the areas they depict. In such cases local knowledge is a desirable prerequisite.

Circulatory diseases (ICD Nos. 390–459)

These diseases comprise a group of closely related conditions including atherosclerotic heart disease (commonly presenting as heart attack or angina), cerebro-vascular disease (otherwise known as stroke), hypertensive disease (high blood pressure) and peripheral vascular disease. Loosely called degenerative disease of arteries, they account for more deaths in Britain than any other condition (51 per cent in 1970; 45 per cent in 1993). Two processes are involved in the development of these conditions, viz. either ischaemia or haemorrhage, or both. Ischaemia is the reduction of the blood supply caused by a narrowing of the lumen of the arteries through the process of furring up (atheroma, atherosclerosis), clotting (thrombosis) or sudden blockage (embolus). Haemorrhage occurs when blood leaks through weakened vessel walls into the surrounding tissue. A blood clot obstructing the coronary artery results in a heart attack; obstruction of the cerebral arteries causes stroke or cerebral thrombosis.

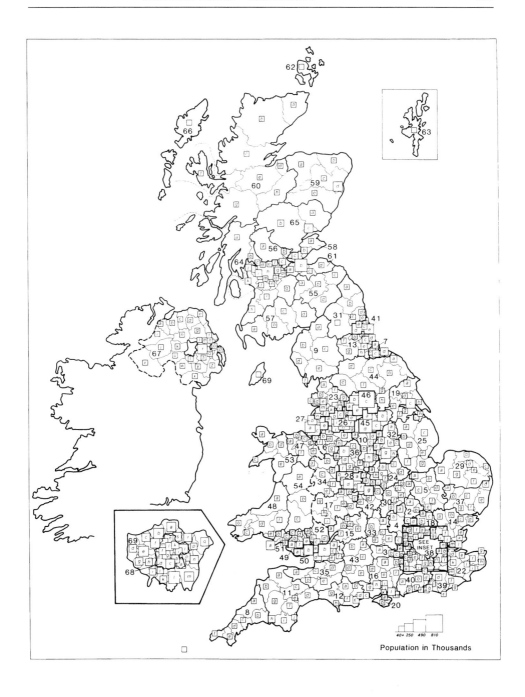

Fig. 14.3 Administrative districts of the UK, as used in chapter 14
(For key, see Appendix A)

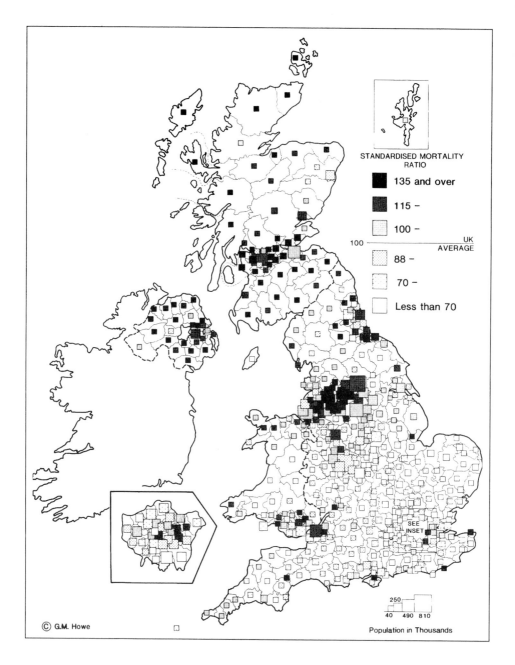

Fig. 14.4 Mortality from acute myocardial infarction in the UK, 1980-2, males aged 15-64 years

Coronary heart disease (acute myocardial infarction) (ICD nos. 410–14)

This is the most important form of vascular disease and the single most common cause of untimely male deaths in Britain. During the period of study average annual deaths from coronary heart disease (CHD) for men under the age of sixty-five was 24,434. Although most fatal attacks occur in old people, one man in eleven can currently expect to have a fatal attack before sixty-five. Figure 14.4 shows the geographical distribution of premature male deaths from acute myocardial infarction. There are considerable regional variations but a pronounced south-east–north-west gradient is evident. The areas with the lowest risk or most favourable mortality experience are in the more affluent and economically favoured south-east of England, mainly south-east of a line from the head of the Bristol Channel to the estuary of the Humber. Areas where men are particularly vulnerable to the disease, or are at the highest risk (i.e. areas where SMRs exceed the UK average of 100), lie in many northern districts of England (e.g. the north-east, Greater Manchester, Merseyside), in Scotland,[9] Northern Ireland and south Wales. But risks vary greatly from place to place.

Spatial variations or inequalities are evident also at the intra-urban scale. Take, for example, London. Men living in Camden, Islington, Hackney, Tower Hamlets, Newham, Hammersmith, Fulham, Greenwich, Redbridge, Barking, Dagenham and Ealing are seemingly more liable to heart attacks than men living elsewhere in the metropolis (Fig. 14.4, inset). Inequalities occur also at the enumeration-district or postal-district scale. Glasgow city, for instance, has an overall SMR which is a third above the average for the UK and yet there are parts of the city where the mortality ratios greatly exceed that figure. Nation-wide, regionally and locally, dramatic and alarming variations occur in the incidence of untimely deaths. It would appear that 'place' or location, either of residence or work, and its associated uniqueness in terms of environment, is important in this context (i.e. a place can be 'better' or 'worse' than the UK average with respect to risk of incurring premature death from this particular cause).

Of course there is always genetic susceptibility or the operation of chance whereby only certain individuals in a community may be stricken by, be predisposed to, or be at risk of a fatal heart attack when others would appear immune. Many people would not sustain certain activities any more than would soldiers at war, criminals or racing drivers if they did not take an optimistic view of risk and probability. Avoiding the ecological and aggregative fallacy[10] (i.e. attributing community or average conditions to individuals, and vice versa), the maps reveal some quite startling geographical variations in the incidence of premature male death from acute myocardial infarction within the UK.

Table 14.2 Ranking by SMRs (1980–2) of selected districts in the UK with low and high risk of premature death from acute myocardial infarction: males

District	SMR relative to UK aver. 100
Low risk	
South Norfolk	35
Suffolk coastal	42
Mid-Suffolk	45
Huntingdon (Camb.)	46
Dinefwr (Dyfed)	50
Aylesbury Vale (Bucks.)	50
Coventry (West Midlands)	50
Wychavon (Hereford & Worcester)	51
Chichester (West Sussex)	51
Sutton (London)	51
UK average SMR 100	
High risk	
Afan (West Glamorgan)	169
Hamilton (Strathclyde)	170
Omagh (Northern Ireland)	171
Motherwell (Strathclyde)	174
Western Isles	178
Inverclyde (Strathclyde)	179
Monklands (Strathclyde)	186
Dungannon (Northern Ireland)	194
Lochaber (Highland)	195
Tweeddale (Borders)	197
Caithness (Highland)	209

The distribution of SMRs for women is similar to that for men (Fig. 14.5), although the actual rate of premature death attributable to this cause is less for women than for men. Women tend not to develop the disease until after the menopause. Central Scotland, Northern Ireland, the north-east of England, Merseyside, Greater Manchester, South and West Yorkshire, north and south Wales are the areas of greatest risk. In the metropolis, risk is greatest in Camden, Islington, Hackney, Tower Hamlets, Newham, Redbridge, Greenwich, Barking, Dagenham and Ealing (Fig. 14.5, inset).

Despite a National Health Service (NHS) which sets out to be 'a publicly sponsored service ... available to all who want to use it'[11] (which would make it not unreasonable, therefore, to expect uniformity or homogeneity in the distribution of premature mortality from CHD throughout the whole of Britain) marked disparities are evident between different parts of the

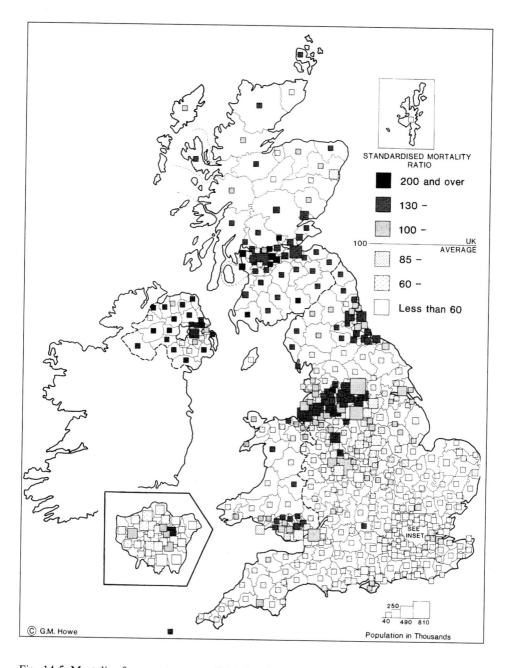

Fig. 14.5 Mortality from acute myocardial infarction in the UK, 1980–2, females aged 15–64 years

Table 14.3 Ranking by SMRs (1980–2) of selected districts in the UK with low and high risk of premature death from acute myocardial infarction: females

District	SMR relative to UK aver. 100
Low risk	
South Cambridgeshire	18
North Norfolk	19
North Shropshire	24
East Northamptonshire	25
Mid-Suffolk	29
Epsom and Ewell (Surrey)	30
Wimborne (Dorset)	30
Fareham (Hampshire)	31
Elmbridge (Surrey)	32
Wansdyke (Avon)	32
UK average SMR 100	
High risk	
Hamilton (Strathclyde)	209
Inverclyde (Strathclyde)	214
Cumbernauld and Kilsyth	219
Annandale and Eskdale	238
Burnley (Lancashire)	242
Cookstown (Northern Ireland)	245
Wigtown (Dumfries and Galloway)	245
Omagh (Northern Ireland)	250
Londonderry (Northern Ireland)	251
Motherwell (Strathclyde)	261
Monklands (Strathclyde)	267

country, between different cities and towns, and between different parts of the same city. Such variations must surely reflect the presence or absence of certain local environmental risk or predisposing factors.

Health care, diagnostic practices and medical services under the NHS may vary from one part of the UK to another, but CHD being such a common cause of death the spatial variations in deaths shown in Figs. 14.4 and 14.5 must be substantially real. Why, then, with comparatively few exceptions, is there the divide in mortality experience between Scotland, Northern Ireland and Wales on the one hand, and south-east England on the other?

CHD is a multifactorial and complex disease, and its causes have yet to be fully identified. Environmental (mainly social) risk factors appear to be more important than heredity (though a positive family history of CHD is not infrequent among patients with CHD). Risk factors include cigarette-smoking, raised serum cholesterol concentration (linked with the intake of animal (saturated) fats in the diet), hypertension (high blood pressure), diabetes, obesity, inactivity (lack of physical exercise) and stress. The effects of more than one of these risk factors on the mechanisms (fats and cholesterol, blood clotting etc.) which cause the majority of CHD deaths are synergistic, i.e., the combined influence of the separate risk factors is greater than the sum of the influences of each risk factor alone.

Smoking or eating (dietary) habits in different parts of the country have not been studied sufficiently to be implicated in the geographical distribution of premature deaths shown in Fig. 14.2 (but see pp.64–5). It is known, however, that male heavy smokers under the age of forty-five have ten to fifteen times the risk of a fatal heart attack compared with that of non-smokers of the same age. Heavy smoking and smoking practices generally are much higher among manual groups than non-manual groups. Overall, some 24 per cent of the CHD deaths in men and 11 per cent in women are attributable to smoking.

Manual groups tend also to eat more red meats and processed meats, fried foods (e.g. chipped potatoes, eggs and bacon), cheese and butter, all of which are high in saturated fats. Saturated fats predispose to a general thickening, narrowing and blocking of the arteries with fatty streaks of low-density lipoprotein cholesterol. Over the years these streaks get bigger and thicker, forming patches or 'plaques' on the artery walls. This process, called atherosclerosis, causes damage or malfunction of the heart, chest pains or a heart attack ('coronary'). Polyunsaturated margarines or spreads, skimmed milk and fibre-rich foods (fresh vegetables, wholemeal bread and salads) all of which are low in saturated fats, are also less popular with men. A common assumption with many manual workers is that a high-calorie diet is warranted because they work hard physically; they tend to ignore the evidence that a high-calorie intake tends to lead to obesity, which is itself a significant contributory risk factor.

Hypertension puts an abnormal strain on the heart and arteries, and this can lead to heart failure, rupture of artery walls, stroke, haemorrhage and kidney failure. Such strain may be aggravated by excessive amounts of salt in food, by the kind of fat consumed, by excess alcohol, anxiety, stress, lack of exercise, obesity and other factors. The precise way in which hypertension develops is not understood.

The human body is physically suited to an active life, but with the progressive automation of industry and the consequent elimination of physical effort, work is becoming increasingly sedentary. Exercise taken in leisure time provides the physical activity necessary to compensate for the lack of exercise associated with many sedentary occupations. Any possible relationship between CHD and physical activity – or lack of it – is, however, complicated by measurement problems and associations with other risk factors. Those under stress, for example, are often those who take little exercise; obesity, exercise and diet are themselves all interrelated.

Stress involves environmental, emotional and social factors. It can be caused by physical hazards in the workplace, interpersonal relationships, problems at work, financial worries, fear of redundancy, unemployment, death of a partner or a host of other factors. On the other hand emotional stress for some provides a challenge for others. Individuals classified according to behaviour patterns as Type A, with high levels of competitiveness and time urgency, are thought to be coronary-prone and experience double the incidence of CHD compared with individuals of personality Type B, who are characterized by their low levels of competitiveness and time urgency.

Britain is, in no way, uniform or homogeneous (see chapters 2–5). No part of the country is the same as another, no two places are alike. Any one particular locality is unique in terms of its environment, its people and their occupations, their local culture, social make-up, lifestyles, social history, social structure and class relations. May not the geographical variations in premature death from CHD reflect or relate to the variety of human life in these local environments and the health hazards or benefits they embrace? Occupational or social class (see pp.59–60) would appear to be significant since premature deaths from CHD vary according to class.[12] CHD deaths are more common among unskilled manual workers (Class V) than among those in the professions (Class I), with a noticeably steeper gradient among women than men. This is nothing new, for even in the mid-nineteenth century the differential life expectations of men classified as gentry, tradesmen and labourers ranged from 35 years to 15 years in Liverpool, and 50 to 33 years in Wiltshire (p.151). Occupation itself is directly correlated with such variables as income, housing, nutrition, education and a range of other health indicators (or hazards!) including cigarette-smoking and/or drinking alcohol to excess. The cumulative impact on health of the advantages and disadvantages of class differences and some of their associated variables (affluence and deprivation) is very evident.

In Britain the total hardness of the public water supply is higher in most areas south and east of a line from the Humber to the Mersey, then to the Severn estuary and thence southwards to near Weymouth. Premature deaths from acute myocardial infarction are certainly lower in these areas and some medical researchers have suggested a link between the two. On the other hand, a detailed study in Glasgow, which has a soft water supply throughout, revealed some wards with mortality experience greatly in excess of the national average while others had experience 20 per cent or more *below* the average.

In spite of what governments have done over the years, regional and local variations or inequalities in premature deaths from CHD (and indeed other causes) continue to exist or indeed persist. One may speculate whether the life-style, attitudinal, behavioural or material factors of individuals within a social class or within a particular locality or heredity account for or cause mortality differentials. Such considerations apart, premature deaths from heart attacks, and heart attacks generally have been falling in recent years (Fig. 14.6). Standardized mortality ratios (SMRs) for ischaemic heart disease have decreased for both men and women, with SMRs in 1993 19 per cent lower for men and 13 per cent lower for women than in 1984.

Cerebro-vascular disease (stroke), ICD nos. 430–8

Bearing in mind likely inaccuracies associated with the clinical diagnosis and certification of the particular kind of stroke, taken as a single category, stroke is the third commonest cause of death after CHD and cancer. Stroke mortality experience increases from the south-east of Britain to the north and west. Unlike ischaemic heart disease in general or acute myocardial infarction in particular, where there is a pronounced preponderance of premature male deaths, in the case of cerebro-vascular disease there is no apparent sex differential. Even so, the regional inequalities in the mortality experience of these two major causes are strikingly similar, except that in the case of stroke the high SMRs extend further south into Staffordshire and the West Midlands. The similarity in geographical distribution between stroke and CHD is not surprising since both high blood pressure and atherosclerosis play a part in each of these conditions.

The incidence of premature deaths in men from stroke exceeds the UK average in central Scotland, Northern Ireland, Tyne and Wear, Cleveland, Merseyside, Greater Manchester, South and West Yorkshire, Derbyshire, the West Midlands, Staffordshire, south Wales, and in much of Inner London (Fig. 14.7).

Population-based studies show that hypertension is an important disposing factor in all types of stroke, the risk increasing with increasing blood pressure. High blood pressure is a widespread disorder which affects between one in five and one in ten of the population, particularly in middle age. It is the result of many influences or factors (p.209). Drugs for reducing high blood pressure are available and successful treatment is available for reducing strokes and other cardiovascular complications. Even so, cerebro-vascular disease, like coronary artery disease, is one of multiple-

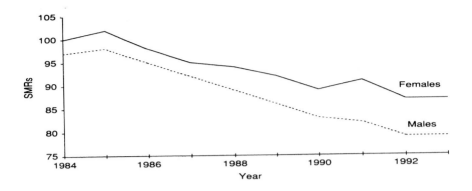

Fig. 14.6 Standardized mortality ratios (SMRs) for ischaemic heart disease
1984–93 (1980–2 = 100)
Source: OPCS

Table 14.4 Ranking by SMRs (1980–2) of selected districts in the UK with low
and high risk of premature death from stroke: males

District	SMR relative to UK aver. 100
Low risk	
Windsor and Maidenhead (Berkshire)	52
Brighton (East Sussex)	60
Barnet (Outer London)	64
Harrow (Outer London)	65
Thurrock (Essex)	66
Tendring (Essex)	67
UK average SMR 100	
High risk	
Sedgefield (Durham)	164
Middlesbrough (Cleveland)	165
Allerdale (Cumbria)	171
Falkirk (Stirling)	177
Manchester (Lancashire)	177
Motherwell (Strathclyde)	178
Glasgow (Strathclyde)	185
Inverclyde (Strathclyde)	186
Banff and Buchan (Grampian)	192
Preseli (Dyfed)	217
Cunninghame (Strathclyde)	265

A selection of districts with high and low SMRs for females is given in
Table 14.5.

Table 14.5 Ranking by SMRs (1980–2) of selected districts in the UK with low and high risk of premature death from stroke: females

District	SMR relative to UK aver. 100
Low risk	
Broadland (Norfolk)	47
North Norfolk	48
South Oxfordshire	51
Beverley (Yorkshire)	52
North Hertfordshire	59
Guildford (Surrey)	59
Northampton (Northamptonshire)	61
Southampton (Hampshire)	64
UK average SMR 100	
High risk	
Renfrew (Renfrewshire)	186
Glasgow (Strathclyde)	190
Tameside (Greater Manchester)	208
Cunninghame (Strathclyde)	233
Falkirk (Central)	241
Inverclyde (Strathclyde)	260
Motherwell (Strathclyde)	262

factor aetiology in which atherosclerosis affecting blood vessels in the brain, alcohol, diet, tobacco-smoking and social class have been implicated. In the UK mortality from this disease is certainly higher among the lower social classes, though it is not known to what extent this reflects differential exposure to aetiological factors or to variations in the uptake of preventive services. In 1993, the SMRs for stroke among men had decreased by 29 per cent and among women by 26 per cent compared with the 1984 level (Fig. 14.8).

Cancer (malignant neoplasms), ICD Nos. 140–208

The term cancer (malignant neoplasms, MN) refers to any one of 200 or more different diseases which, as a group, are second only to the circulatory diseases as a cause of human death in Britain and a considerably higher proportion of human misery. Cancer results when the process of cell division, usually well ordered, gets out of control, leading to the development of malignant cells, i.e. cells that tend to grow to excess if uncorrected. These cells multiply in an uncontrolled and inappropriate fashion, independently of the body's normal growth mechanisms, to form

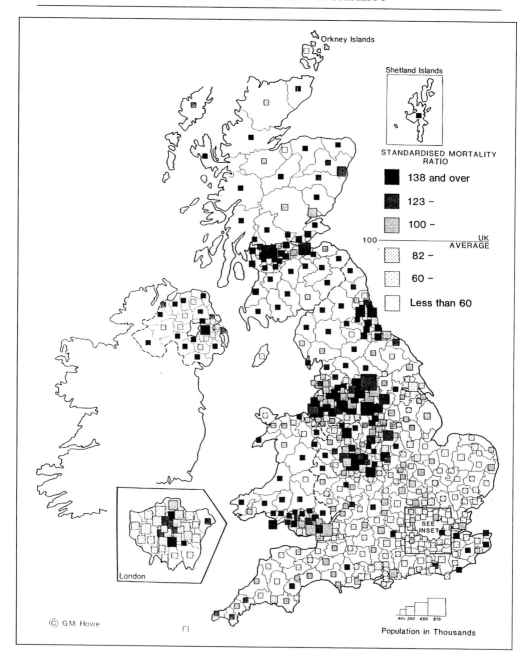

Fig. 14.7 Mortality from cerebro-vascular disease (stroke) in the UK, 1980–2, males aged
15–64 years

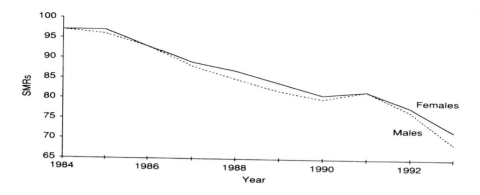

Fig. 14.8 Standardized mortality ratios (SMRs) for cerebro-vascular disease
(stroke) 1984–93 (1980–2 = 100)
(*Source*: OPCS)

a tumour.[13] With virtually all cancer the cause is unknown. The disease
can affect almost any part of the body, including the blood (as in
leukaemia). Statistics for 1993 reveal that 24.6 per cent of all ages of the
population die of cancer (20 per cent in 1970) (Fig. 14.1), and the loss of
life to those dying of the disease averages sixteen years. Cancer now
accounts for 13.5 per cent of all male deaths in age group 15–39 years,
24.3 per cent in age group 40–64 and 31 per cent in age group 65–79. In
women cancer accounts for 33 per cent in age group 15–39 years and 51.8
per cent in age group 40–64 years, and 30.6 per cent in age group 65–79.
The percentages in both sexes decrease with subsequent ageing, but the
death rates in general continue to rise.

Of the many cancer sites the lung is undoubtedly the most important for
men, accounting overall for one in every four of those registered (28 per
cent), though locally (e.g. in Glasgow) as many as one in every two (49
per cent). Breast cancer ranks first for women, accounting for one in every
five of those registered (22 per cent), but (as happened in Scotland in 1984)
cancer of this site seems likely to be overtaken by lung cancer, which is
now rising rapidly, especially among young women. Skin cancers (excluding melanoma) are probably the commonest cancers of all for both sexes,
accounting for one in every ten registered. Only a relatively small proportion of those that occur are reported. Thereafter the most common sites
for men are prostate (8 per cent), stomach (7 per cent), bladder (6 per
cent), colon (large intestine) (6 per cent) and rectum (5 per cent). For
women they are the lung (9 per cent), colon (9 per cent), stomach (5 per
cent), ovary (5 per cent), rectum (5 per cent), cervix uteri (4 per cent) and
corpus uteri (4 per cent) (Fig. 14.9).

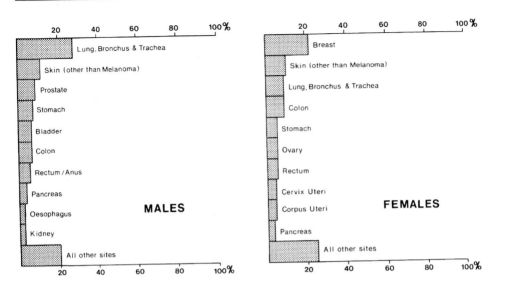

Fig. 14.9 Most commonly registered cancer sites in the UK

Cancer of the trachea, lung and bronchus, ICD nos. 162, 163, 164

For many years cancer of the trachea, lung and bronchus has been the commonest cancer in men, and it may soon overtake breast cancer to become the commonest cause of cancer mortality in women. The geographical distribution or spatial variability of premature deaths caused by lung cancer in males is shown in Fig. 14.10. That deaths vary greatly from place to place is very evident. Why should this be so? The overall pattern highlights west central Scotland, Tyne and Wear, Durham, Cleveland, Humberside, Merseyside, Greater Manchester, Staffordshire and the West Midlands as areas where the standardized mortality ratios exceed the national (UK) average. In Inner London (Fig. 14.10, inset) there is a cluster of boroughs embracing Camden, Southwark etc., which represents a high-risk area. Outer London, with SMRs below the national average, has a more favourable mortality experience. A core–periphery pattern of incidence is well marked in the metropolis. Glasgow's mortality from lung cancer is among the highest in the world.[14] The city, as a whole, has a mortality ratio 82 per cent above the UK average, but in parts of the north and east of the city the incidence is more than twice the national average. That Glasgow has been dubbed the 'Cancer Capital of the World'[15] seems not altogether inappropriate.

Of interest are the generally low ratios among men in industrial south Wales where premature mortality from other causes is high. Traditionally

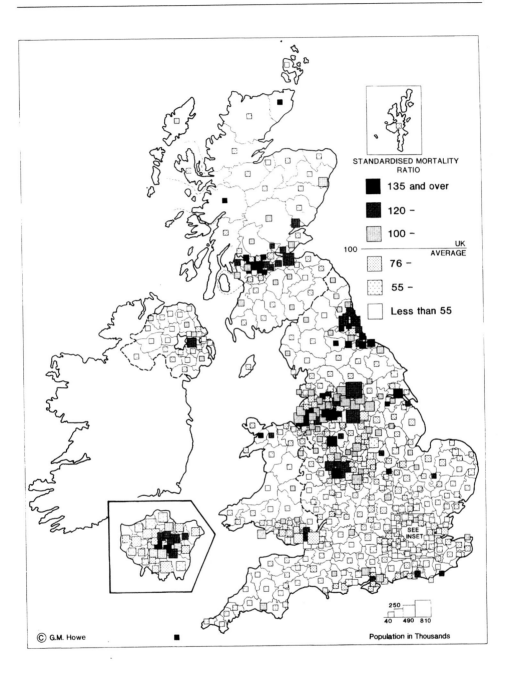

Fig. 14.10 Mortality from lung–bronchus cancer in the UK, 1980–2, males aged 15–64 years

(though not since the late 1980s when the majority of the collieries were closed) south Wales was a mining community and miners were not allowed to smoke underground. If, as is generally thought, cigarette-smoking is the chief, though not the sole cause of lung cancer, eight hours at least a day without a cigarette could possibly help explain the lower lung cancer deaths here. On the other hand the question then arises whether men living in Outer London necessarily smoke fewer cigarettes than those in Inner London to account for the significant geographical gradient in the disease pattern already noted within the metropolis. Cities and towns like Belfast, Plymouth, Southampton, Portsmouth, Brighton and Aberdeen also embrace clusters of high ratios.

Table 14.6 Ranking by SMRs (1980–2) of selected districts in the UK with low and high risk of premature death from lung cancer: males

District	SMR relative to UK aver. 100
Low risk	
Stroud (Gloucestershire)	45
Elmbridge (Surrey)	50
Chiltern (Buckinghamshire)	50
Waverley (Surrey)	52
Reigate and Banstead (Surrey)	53
Woodspring (Avon)	54
Harrow (Greater London)	56
UK average SMR 100	
High risk	
Stoke-on-Trent (Staffordshire)	161
Hartlepool (Cleveland)	164
Southwark (Greater London)	165
Middlesbrough (Cleveland)	167
Knowsley (Merseyside)	179
Glasgow City (Strathclyde)	182

The worst areas for women and those with the best prospects of surviving are given in Table 14.7, though it should be appreciated that of the lung cancer victims, two-thirds are men and one-third women.

Though not exclusively so, there is a decided urban pattern to the geographical distribution of premature death from lung cancer in much of Britain. On the other hand, experience in Outer London, Bristol and several other towns appears to belie an association between urban living and an increased risk of dying from lung cancer, and calls into question the assumed causal association of lung cancer and cigarette-smoking. It seems highly unlikely that the level of cigarette consumption in, say, Inner

Table 14.7 Ranking by SMRs (1980–2) of selected districts in the UK with low and high risk of premature death from lung cancer: females

District	SMR relative to UK aver. 100
Low risk	
West Wiltshire	26
Lichfield (Staffordshire)	34
Lisburn (Antrim)	37
Mendip (Somerset)	42
Northavon (Avon)	45
Newcastle-under-Lyme (Staffordshire)	49
High risk	
Sunderland (Tyne and Wear)	134
Edinburgh (Midlothian)	136
Salford (Great Manchester)	138
Gateshead (Tyne and Wear)	140
Belfast (Antrim)	141
Southwark (Inner London)	141
Lewisham (Inner London)	142
Aberdeen (Aberdeenshire)	147
Manchester (Lancashire)	160
North Tyneside (Northumberland)	164
Liverpool (Merseyside)	175
Glasgow (City of, Strathclyde)	200
Newcastle (Tyne and Wear)	204
Middlesbrough (Cleveland)	216

London, is higher than it is in Outer London, or higher in Liverpool than in Bristol or higher in Walsall than in Oxford to account for their different death ratios. Findings suggest the north of England, Yorkshire, Humberside and Wales as having the highest cigarette consumption for males, and the north, Yorkshire, Humberside and the north-west for females.

Cigarette-smoking, a self-imposed risk, has been strongly implicated in the incidence of lung cancer (enhanced by self-specific habits such as inhaling the tobacco smoke, which obviously increases exposure to the carcinogens in cigarette smoke). Indeed 86 per cent of all male lung-cancer deaths and 69 per cent of all female are thought to be attributable to smoking tobacco. Yet, it seems unlikely that the inter-regional, inter-city and intra-urban variations in premature death from the disease reflect only the distribution of heavy cigarette-smokers. Is it a reflection of socio-economic groupings with heavy cigarette-smoking greatest in unskilled and

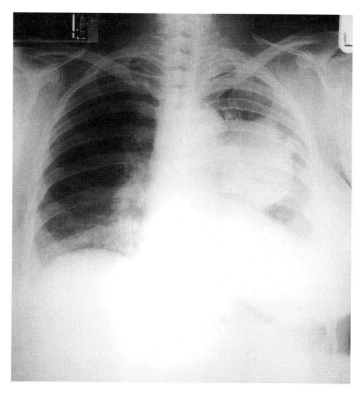

Plate 18: X-ray photograph of a female chest showing a carcinoma in the middle
of the left lung (by permisson of University Hospital of Wales, Cardiff)

manual occupations? The aetiological indictment of cigarette-smoking in
the context of lung cancer may well be an over-simplification of what is
essentially a multifactoral situation. Research has shown that 80 per cent
of the cancers may be caused by environmental (including life-style) factors
and therefore may be preventable. Genetic factors are thought to play only
a minor role. The geographical inequalities in lung-cancer mortality in the
UK probably reflect synergistic relations between a number of risk factors
which include cigarette-smoking, occupational (e.g. asbestos) exposure,
atmospheric pollution by man-made chemicals, radiation from radon gas,
and other, as yet unknown or unsuspected environmental carcinogens associated with urban living – i.e. the 'urban factor'. The rate for lung cancer
among men in 1993 was 23 per cent lower than in 1984, whereas among
women, the rate for lung cancer was 12 per cent higher than in 1984 (Fig.
14.11).

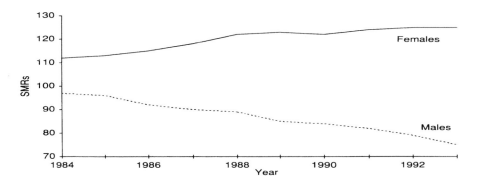

Fig. 14.11 Standardized mortality ratios (SMRs) for lung cancer 1984–93
(1980–2 = 100) (*Source*: OPCS)

Cancer of the female breast (ICD nos. 174–5)

Cancer of the breast is one of the most serious manifestations of cancer in women in Britain. It accounts for 5 per cent of all deaths in women and about 20 per cent of cancer deaths in total. More than 14,000 women die from the disease in Britain every year, 6,000 or more under the age of sixty-five years. Figure 14.12 shows geographical variation and inequalities in the incidence of premature deaths from this cause. No particular trend or regional pattern is evident. There are, instead, clusters of areas with low ratios and clusters with high ratios scattered in apparent random fashion throughout the country. Not infrequently there are low- and high-risk areas in adjacent districts, such as the Isle of Wight and Bournemouth-Poole, Anglesey and Arfon, Harborough and Rutland. Clusters of high and low ratios occur also in London. Camden, Redbridge, Sutton and Bromley are among the boroughs where premature deaths from breast cancer are most likely to occur. Other cities have clear intra-urban variations. Glasgow, for example, has ratios 10 per cent or more above the UK average in the north and west of the city but 5–10 per cent below in the south-west and east. Whether these clusters or distributions are due to chance, to some external cause or to treatment is not immediately obvious. Usually women in the upper social classes are more prone to breast cancer than are those in the lower classes. Among the several factors thought to be implicated are the age of menarche (start of menstruation), length of a woman's reproductive life and age at menopause (last menstrual period). The earlier a woman starts menstruation and the later she reaches the menopause the greater the risk.[16] Additional factors include late first full-term pregnancy and raised post-menopausal weight. Diets rich in fat and animal protein are

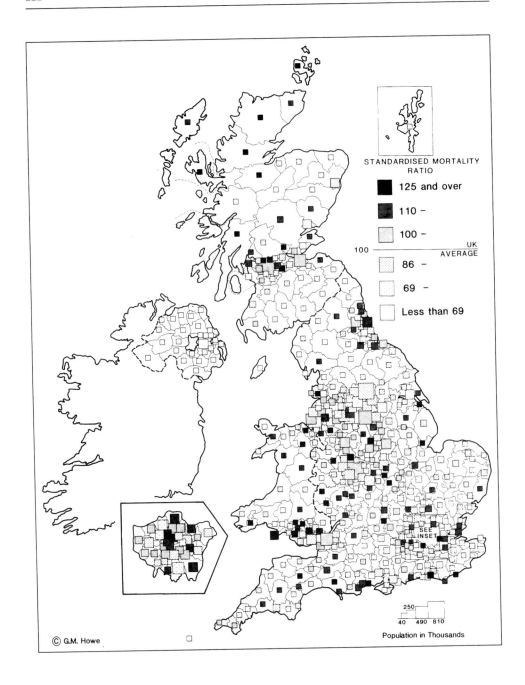

Fig. 14.2 Mortality from cancer of the female breast, 1980–2, 15–64 years

also strongly implicated. About 5 per cent are thought to be related to a strong inherited predisposition. Two breast-cancer genes, BRCA1 and BRCA2, are considered critical factors for those families with a history where breast cancer develops in relatives.

Table 14.8 Ranking by SMRs (1980–2) of selected districts in the UK with low and high risk of premature death from cancer of the female breast

District	SMR relative to UK aver. 100
Low risk	
Durham	53
Watford (Hertfordshire)	53
Wansdyke (Avon)	57
Copeland (Cumbria)	59
Barrow-in-Furness (Cumbria)	61
New Forest (Hampshire)	68
Dundee City (Tayside)	70
Preston (Lancashire)	70
UK average SMR 100	
High risk	
Motherwell (Strathclyde)	140
Swansea (West Glamorgan)	141
Epsom and Ewell (Surrey)	142
Christchurch (Dorset)	144
Clackmannan (Central)	145
Cynon Valley (Mid Glamorgan)	149
Boston (Lincolnshire)	150
Hereford	150
Bearsden and Milngavie (Strathclyde) ·	157
Harborough (Leicestershire)	157

Stomach (gastric) cancer, ICD no. 151

Stomach cancer is a disease of its lining cells. It starts in the stomach but may spread (metastasize) to the liver and occasionally to other parts of the body. The causes are not known, though the bacterium *Helioblaster pylori* is thought to be implicated. Unusual among the tumours, its incidence, globally and within the UK, has tended to decline over the past forty to fifty years. It is thought that the decreasing reliance upon foodstuffs that have been stored or preserved in traditional ways (e.g. pickling and salting) and the increasing use of refrigeration, which has led to people eating more fresh vegetables and fruit, may have contributed to the decrease. The less nutritious the diet the greater the risk (pp.49–51).

The geographical pattern for deaths from stomach cancer (Figs. 14.13, 14.14) differs markedly from that for lung cancer (Fig. 14.9). This is not unexpected since, as already noted, the term cancer relates not to a single disease but is a generic (umbrella) term embracing many different malignant neoplasms, each with its own pathology and aetiology.

With the exception of certain of the London boroughs (Barking, Greenwich, Newham, Southwark) the remainder of the south-east of Britain enjoys favourable mortality experience from stomach cancer. Most high risk areas include south-east London, Gloucester, Newport (Gwent), West Bromwich, Stoke-on-Trent and other towns in Staffordshire, Oldham, Salford, Bury, Bolton, Warrington, Bootle, Teesside, Hartlepool, Sunderland, Gwynedd, Belfast, Dundee and parts of Lanarkshire, Renfrewshire, Ayrshire and Fife. Standardized mortality ratios in these areas exceed the national average by more than 40 per cent. High-risk areas occur in both urban and rural situations (witness the unfavourable areas in parts of north Wales and Scotland) with no particular regional pattern.

A range of factors has been postulated as being associated with the disease in different parts of the world. These include trace elements in soil and water, nitrosamines and blood-group type. The spoil heaps and old workings of defunct lead, zinc and copper mines contain residual amounts of these metals, generally as sulphides. These are changed to more soluble form by aerial oxidation. Rivers in spate in the vicinity of mine dumps (bings, tips) in parts of Wales (e.g. Rheidol River) and Scotland (e.g. Leadhills area and the River Clyde) are often polluted by mine effluent containing these metals. Small amounts of lead or zinc (e.g. 3 ppm) in the rivers and streams have been shown to be fatal to fish life. Other metals such as selenium, silver, bismuth, arsenic and antimony are also found with galena, the main source of lead. The evidence, such as it is, suggests that the lead in water and zinc-copper in soils act as possible co-factors rather than complete determinants in the genesis of stomach cancer. In this same context the action of plumbo-solvent water on domestic lead pipes in certain of the older properties throughout the country (e.g. Glasgow) is not without significance. Alternatively, it may be that the factors responsible for high incidence and death from gastric cancer tend to move in parallel with lead pollution of drinking-water or the zinc-copper ratio in the soil and food chain, both being themselves not strictly relevant.

Statistical evidence has suggested an association with blood group A, i.e. that individuals of this blood group experience an incidence of stomach carcinoma greater than individuals of the other ABO blood groups. In Britain, the inherited element does not appear to be responsible since the eastern parts of the country, known to have the highest proportion of people of blood group A, have some of the lowest SMRs for gastric cancer. This

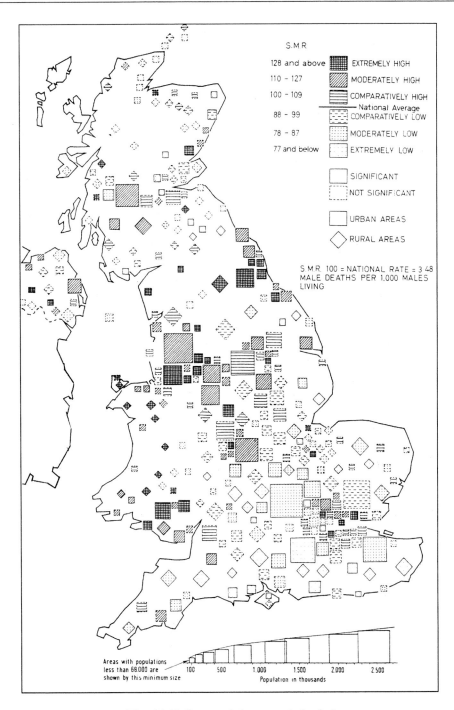

Fig. 14.13 Cancer of the stomach (males)

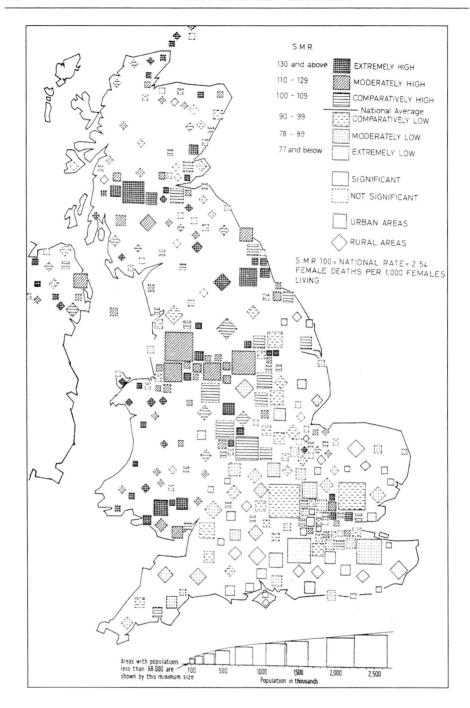

Fig. 14.14 Cancer of the stomach (females)

spatial pattern would lend further support to the importance of environmental factors in the aetiology of gastric cancer.

Cancer of the cervix, ICD no. 180

This disease, responsible for *c.* 1,600 female deaths a year, appears to be associated with sexual intercourse and poor hygiene (in both sexes). It is commoner in women who start sexual activity at a young age, with the frequency of intercourse and with the number of partners. It is more common among the lower socio-economic groups and among prostitutes ('call-girls'). On the assumption that cancer of the cervix is caused by a virus transmitted during sexual intercourse Doll et al.[17] have suggested that the women at greatest risk are those with male partners who make use of prostitutes. The infectious theory is based on the rarity of the disease in nuns and its relative frequency among prostitutes.

Other malignant neoplasms

Other common cancer sites include the prostate, colon, rectum and skin. *Prostate* cancer, common in older men, is uncommon before the age of sixty. It is currently the second commonest cause of cancer in men after lung cancer, and responsible for something like 14,000 cases and up to 10,000 deaths each year. This is four times as many men as cervical cancer in women. There is some evidence to suggest that diet may play a part in the development of *colo-rectal cancer*, and that a high-fibre and vegetable diet may reduce the risk of developing these tumours. An excess of meat and animal fats is thought to increase the risk. Cancer can appear on any area of the *skin*, but most commonly develops on the parts of the body exposed to the sun. The most important causal influence is excessive exposure to the ultraviolet rays of the sun. As such it is almost entirely preventable (p.27). The popularity of sunshine holidays has led to a big increase in the number of people developing skin cancer, which now kills around 1,800 people each year. It strikes affluent people (socio-economic groups 1 and 2) in the age-range 40–60 who can afford foreign holidays more than the relatively poor (socio-economic classes IV and V) – a reverse of the norm. In the 1990s the age profile for the disease is getting younger, not older – possibly reflecting the gradually increasing exposure of the body by successive generations. The death rate from *malignant melanoma* has increased remarkably in the last twenty to thirty years. The most important single cause of this most serious form of skin cancer is exposure to strong sunlight (over-exposure to ultraviolet rays and on sunbeds). It is twice as likely to develop in women as in men, with

fair-skinned, freckled individuals most at risk. In Britain there is about one
new case per 6,000 people each year. Nuclear radiation is not a proven
cause of malignant melanoma, but it is linked to the two other forms of
skin cancer – squamous cell carcinoma and rodent ulcers. At this point it
is of interest to comment on a change of fashion which has taken place
within the last century. Whereas in the 1990s a bronzed body is considered fashionable, in Victorian times the ideal of feminine beauty was 'a
languorous pale creature' who kept herself out of the sunlight so as to
appear 'genteel'. Sensible people are now reverting to the Victorian practice and protecting themselves from excess sunshine.

Leukaemia, sometimes known as cancer of the blood, is the most
common form of childhood cancer. About 600 children are diagnosed as
having the disease (acute lymphoblastic leukaemia) every year but as yet,
the cause is not known.

Respiratory diseases, ICD Nos. 480–93

Bronchitis, emphysema and asthma, ICD nos. 490–3

The distribution of premature deaths from chronic bronchitis (see p.173)
and emphysema (sometimes used as an alternative diagnosis to chronic
bronchitis) varies substantially by geographical area (Figs. 14.15, 14.16).
Asthma is excluded since only a very small percentage of mortality is due
to this diagnosis. Even so it is increasing at such a rate that now one in
ten children and one in twenty adults is thought to be affected.

Bronchitis, the so-called 'English disease', because of its prevalence and
seriousness in Britain is, after heart disease, stroke and lung cancer, the
most potent killer. No single factor is readily identifiable as the prominent
influence in promoting the disease; rather, a combination of factors is
implicated in its aetiology (causation). Three main groups of environmental factors, physical, social and biological, are recognized as incorporating
both causative and predisposing elements. The influence of short-term
weather conditions and longer-term climate is particularly important. The
national pattern of the disease may well reflect regional variations in
climate with incidence higher in the cool and more humid areas of the
north-west of the country. Seasonality is also significant with a maximum
incidence in the winter months. Another factor is atmospheric pollution
which many authorities consider to be the most important causative agent.
Bronchitis is an urban disease, since almost every town in the country
stands out worse than the surrounding countryside. Pollution builds up in
towns and cities where it can become trapped between buildings. In the

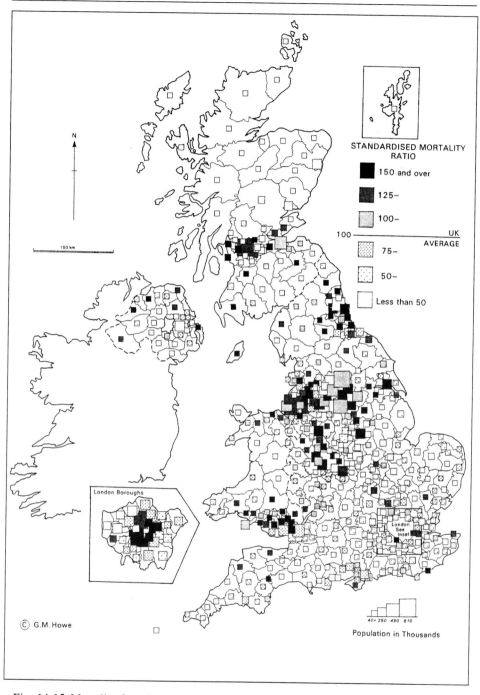

Fig. 14.15 Mortality from bronchitis, emphysema and asthma, 1980–2, males aged 15–64 years

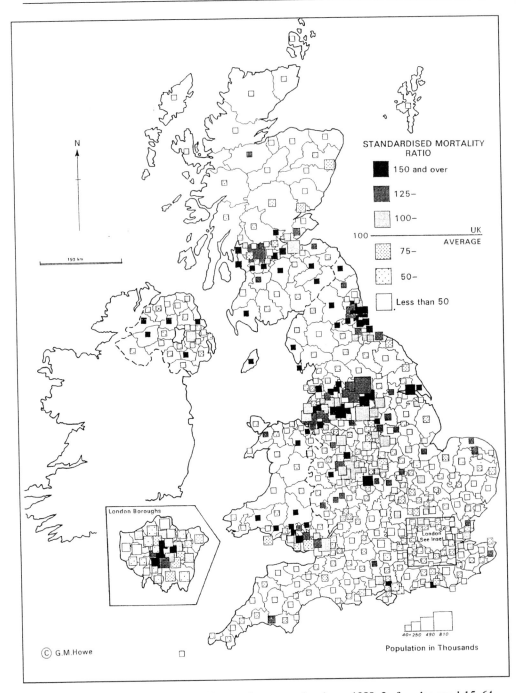

Fig. 14.16 Mortality from bronchitis, emphysema and asthma, 1980–2, females aged 15–64
years

great London smog of December 1952 (p.55) most of the 3,500–4,000 deaths were due to chronic bronchitis and heart disease. The worst air pollution in London subsequent to the 1952 episode was one week in December 1991 when hourly average levels of nitrogen dioxide reached over 420 parts per billion, twice the safe limit recommended by WHO. The lethal 'cocktail' of nitrogen dioxide and the fine particles of smut in black smoke (i.e. particulates) resulting from unusually still weather was responsible for more deaths or illness from respiratory ailments and heart disease.

It is a matter of some regret that industrialization, urbanization and ever-increasing vehicular traffic appear to negate advantages accruing from concerted remedial action. Of the social environmental factors implicated, the habit of cigarette-smoking has to be cited. This practice, which Sir George Godber rightly called 'the most lethal instrument devised by man for peaceful use', may be regarded as the single most significant contributory factor. Passive or involuntary smoking, where non-smokers inhale the smoke of others who are smoking, also contributes. Furthermore, there is an increased risk of contracting bronchitis in certain occupational groups (coal-miners, foundry workers and operatives in certain sectors of the chemical industry) where the operatives are exposed to moderate to high levels of dust and gaseous contaminants. The chances of unskilled manual workers and their wives (socio-economic group V) dying from bronchitis are four to five times greater than among the professional classes (socio-economic group I).

Biological influences relate primarily to predisposition or susceptibility of the individual to the disease. It is doubtful whether hereditary or genetic factors have a role, but age and sex are certainly important determinants. Of the male mortality, over 70 per cent occurs in the over-sixty-five-years category, and there are almost three times more male deaths than there are female deaths from chronic bronchitis.

Pneumonia, ICD nos. 480–6

The bacteria *pneumococci*, which commonly cause pneumonia, are comensal organisms colonizing the back of the throat and nose. When environmental factors alter the anatomical habit of the *pneumococci*, they may descend into the lungs and cause pneumonia or ascend and cause severe, and often fatal, meningitis (inflammation of the membranes that cover the brain and spinal column). Influenza often provides an opening for several kinds of bacteria and viruses to cause pneumonia. Chronic bronchitis is also frequently implicated as an important predisposing factor for the onset of the disease. Sir William Osler (1849–1919), the distinguished Canadian physician, called the pneumococcus 'the old

Table 14.9 Ranking by SMRs (1980–2) of selected districts in the UK with low and high risk of premature death from chronic bronchitis–emphysema–asthma (ICD nos. 490–3): males

District	SMR relative to UK aver. 100
Low risk	
Canterbury (Kent)	41
Barnet (Outer London)	42
Bournemouth (Hampshire)	46
Wycombe (Buckinghamshire)	47
Redbridge (Outer London)	60
Ealing (Outer London)	61
Harborough (Leicestershire)	63
Southend-on-Sea (Essex)	69
Bromley (Outer London)	73
Blackpool (Lancashire)	75
High risk	
Manchester	190
Wandsworth (Inner London)	198
Barnsley (Yorkshire)	206
Hackney (Inner London)	207
Stoke-on-Trent (Staffordshire)	207
Tower Hamlets (Inner London)	215
Inverclyde (Inverclyde)	219
Rhondda (Mid Glamorgan)	232
Taff-Ely (Mid Glamorgan)	243
Cannock Chase (Staffordshire)	246
Afan (West Glamorgan)	268
Burnley (Lancashire)	298

man's friend', and it is still common for the elderly to succumb to terminal pneumonia despite the many antibiotics that are available. There is always greater danger to the elderly, especially those deprived and living alone in cold, damp and poorly heated houses. An abnormal reduction in the body temperature – hypothermia – is easily brought about in old people living in a cold house during severe winter months. Hypothermia makes the individual susceptible to pneumococcal infections, and many old people die alone in their homes as a result. Similarly, very young babies within weeks of their birth, can die as a result of hypothermic pneumonia if neglected by their parents and left alone in a cold room. Regrettably, even in present-day society with its many welfare services, this outcome is not uncommon.

Table 14.10 Ranking by SMRs (1980–2) of selected districts in the UK with low and high risk of premature death from chronic bronchitis–emphysema–asthma (ICD nos. 490–3): females

District	SMR relative to UK aver. 100
Low risk	
Waltham Forest (Outer London)	39
Wycombe (Buckinghamshire)	41
Ealing (Outer London)	46
Barnet (Outer London)	51
Merton (Outer London)	55
Solihull (West Midlands)	56
Richmond upon Thames (Outer London)	57
Bromley (Kent)	59
Stockport (Greater Manchester)	62
Derby (Derbyshire)	64
Redbridge (Outer London)	69
High risk	
Kingston-upon-Hull (Yorkshire)	189
Barnsley (Yorkshire)	189
Wakefield (Yorkshire)	189
Tameside (Greater Manchester)	193
Wandsworth (Inner London)	202
Derwentside (Durham)	235
Rhondda (Mid Glamorgan)	236
Hartlepool (Durham)	262
Burnley (Lancashire)	312

Accidents and violence, ICD nos. E810–19

Of the many kinds of fatalities from accidents, those resulting from road traffic accidents loom large. They represent a major twentieth-century scourge and have reached epidemic proportions. The latest data published by the Department of Transport are for 1993. They show a fall in total deaths from the record of over 9,000 in 1941 (attributed to the blackout restrictions imposed during the Second World War years and to inexperienced drivers of armed service vehicles) to 5,934 in 1982 and 4,668 in 1993. Deaths of car drivers and their passengers account for almost half of road deaths, and one in ten deaths are motor cyclists or their passengers. Pedal-cyclist casualty rates and child-pedestrian deaths have increased. The redistribution of injury from motor-vehicle driver to pedestrian, and from older age groups to lower age groups, is a major cause of concern. Significant also is the gender gap with greater death rates from road accidents in young male adults.

Seat-belts, air bags, laminated windscreens, head-rests and impact-absorbing engineering features have been introduced in vehicles nation-wide, and small-scale engineering solutions (road markings, route indicators, etc.) implemented to remove accident black spots, have had the effect of reducing serious casualties and fatalities. Human factors, including carelessness, alcoholic drink-driving and self-imposed risks generally, continue to be responsible for a significant number of deaths. As with the other causes of death considered, there are significant geographical variations in the incidence of fatal road accidents, and one wonders why some areas are more prone to, or some groups of people more threatened than others, by road accidents.

Figure 14.17 (after Whitelegg)[18] shows the spatial variation in fatal and serious road accidents. There is a rate of serious outcomes ranging from 2.01 persons per 1,000 vehicles in Cheshire to 5.83 per 1,000 vehicles in Lothian. Considerable bunching occurs in the range 2.4–3.6 per 1,000 vehicles. The map shows a clear Scottish bias, with the highest rates occurring in Lothian (5.83), Borders (5.1), Strathclyde (5.18) and Highland Region (4.74). Of the English counties only North Yorkshire intrudes into this group. Large tracts of rural areas with well-defined market towns seem to characterize this high-risk group. This vulnerability is reflected in some Welsh counties, such as Dyfed (4.41) and Powys (4.06), but even these are lower than the Scottish regions. The lower end of this distribution, those with a low vulnerability in terms of this measure, is a mixed group which includes West and South Glamorgan, West Sussex and Hertfordshire, with Cheshire the best performer of all at 2.01 fatal and serious accidents per 1,000 vehicles.[19] Modifying human behaviour through education seems to have limited effectiveness, and Whitelegg[20] argues that 'this view absolves system design and grossly under-estimates the importance of spatial factors, movement and interaction – which can be influenced by policy rather more effectively than human behaviour under the range of conditions experienced by motorists, pedestrians and other road users.'

Traditionally, causal factors for road traffic accidents have focused on the vehicle or the human agents or the immediate road environment as cases for treatment. The fact that there is a geography of road traffic accidents, that accident fatalities vary so markedly both regionally and locally, suggests a need for detailed study of a much wider spatial system which will itself influence the pattern of accident causation. Whitelegg is of the opinion that 'solutions to problems posed by road traffic accidents may involve measures at some remove from the accident and its principal

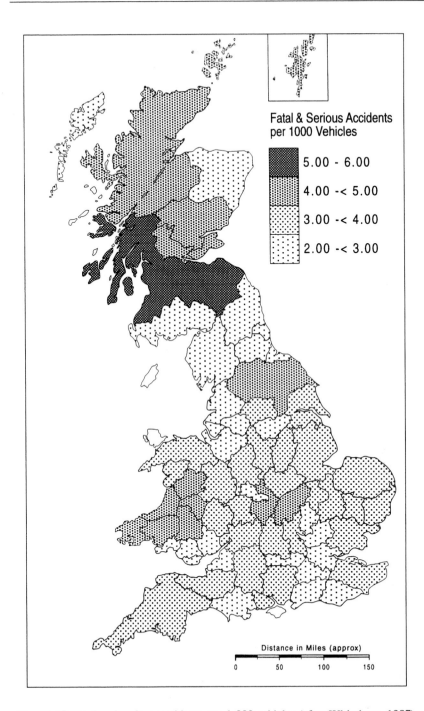

Fig. 14.17 Fatal and serious accidents per 1,000 vehicles (after Whitelegg, 1987)

actors.'[21] Road traffic accidents, especially for children, are essentially urban in their distribution.

Accidents in the home are no less serious than road traffic accidents. They result in over 4,000 deaths each year. Falls, burning (involving uncontrolled fire), and poisoning/inhalation are the main causes, with stairs/steps, food and drink and fire (controlled heat) the articles most frequently involved.

Suicide, ICD nos. E950–9

The calculated act of self-destruction is the most tragically preventable of deaths. It is a specifically human behavioural attribute, with about 90 per cent of the victims suffering from some form of mental illness at the time of committing suicide. Incidence is particularly high among abnormal personalities, especially psychopaths (persons suffering from an emotional disorder). No single cause of suicidal behaviour can be identified but a strong, positive correlation between the incidence of suicide and alcoholism has frequently been demonstrated. About 30 per cent of people who kill themselves abuse alcohol. It is for this reason that alcoholism has been described with considerable justification, as 'chronic suicide'. Rates are particularly high (over 20 per 100,000) in Orkney and Shetland, rather less in the Highlands and elsewhere in Scotland. Inner London, parts of Tyne and Wear, Merseyside, Greater Manchester, West and South Yorkshire in England record significantly high rates. In Wales Gwynedd, Clwyd, Powys and Dyfed have high SMRs for men.[22]

Stress resulting from unemployment, is proving a major contributory factor in suicide among young men in their twenties. In suicide, as with a wide range of illnesses, men suffer more than women at every stage in life (Fig. 14.18).

Infant Mortality

The twentieth century has witnessed a truly spectacular fall in infant deaths under one year. Table 14.11 provides details of the downward trend, which has been shared by every region in the country. Rates have varied appreciably from one region to another, the most pronounced reductions being in Northern Ireland, East Anglia and Wessex.

Although it only measures how many children die before the age of one year, the infant mortality rate is often taken as an indicator of the general health and well-being of the nation. The remarkable improvement in infant mortality rates has been associated with improvements in the socio-

Rates per 100,000 population

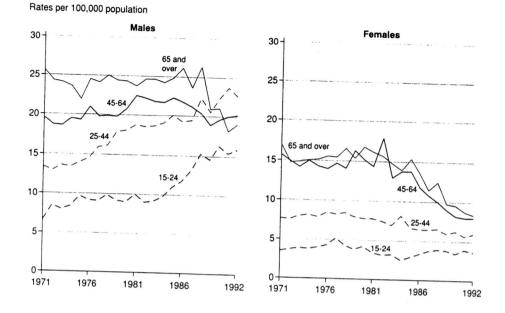

Fig. 14.18 Death rates from suicide in England and Wales, by sex and age
(*Source*: Office of Population Censuses and Surveys)

Table 14.11 Infant deaths (under one year) and death rates per 1,000 live births

	000s	per 1,000 live births
1900–2	156.0	142.5
1920–2	83.4	81.9
1930–2	49.9	66.5
1940	42.8	61.0
1950	25.6	31.2
1960	20.7	22.5
1970	16.7	18.5
1980	9.1	12.1
1985	7.0	9.4
1990	6.0	7.2
1993	5.0	5.9

economic environment in combination with improved surveillance and care
during infancy, together with the availability of antimicrobial drugs such as
DTP (diphtheria, tetanus and pertussis triple immunization) and MMR
(measles, mumps and rubella). The slight rise in the infant mortality rate
in recent years has been of concern to health-service planners.

Besides the regional variations in infant mortality, there are those associated with social (occupational) class. Numbers and rates have declined for all social classes in the UK, but differences in rates between Class I and Class V remain almost constant, possibly even widening. At birth and during the first month of life, the risk of death in Class V (unskilled manual workers) is double the risk in Class I (professional workers). From the end of the first month to the end of the first year, class differentials in infant mortality reach a peak of disadvantage. For the death of every male in Class I there are four deaths in Class V. Among female infants these ratios are even more disadvantageous to the offspring of manual workers.[23]

Perinatal mortality, (the death rate for babies under a week of age and an accepted indicator of good health *care*) varies notably. The worst regional rate, 11.6 per 1,000 live births against a UK average of 9.9 per 1,000 live births, is found in the West Midlands. The lowest mortality rate, 8.8, is in East Anglia, and the second lowest, 9.1, is in the south-east of England.

Premature Deaths from All Causes

From the foregoing analyses of the major causes of premature mortality, and mindful of the ecological or aggregative fallacy (p.205), it is obvious that, in terms of life expectancy and/or the avoidance of premature death, some areas of the country have above-average mortality rates for certain complaints and other areas have below-average rates for the same complaints. Overall the favoured parts of the country for men lie in the south and east of England (south-east of a line from Gloucester to Whitby), together with north Yorkshire, Cumbria, Northumberland, Wales (except for 'the Valleys' in the south) and the Borders, Tayside and Grampian regions of Scotland. Areas where the ratios for premature mortality are high, include Strathclyde, Lothian and Fife regions of Scotland, and Mid Glamorgan in Wales, most of Northern Ireland; in England, Tyne and Wear, Merseyside, Greater Manchester, south Lancashire, Staffordshire, the West Midlands and certain of the Inner London boroughs (Fig. 14.19 and Table 14.12). There are a few slight variations in detail for women, but the overall geographical pattern of premature mortality experience is similar to that for men, except that men are twice as likely as women to die before the age of sixty-five. The main reason is that men have a much higher risk of dying from heart disease (which kills four times as many men as women) and stroke. Overall, men tend to live less healthy lives than women.

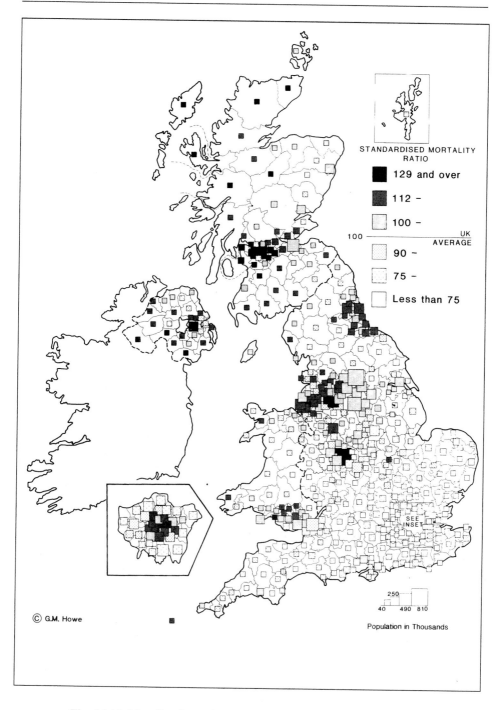

Fig. 14.19 Mortality from all causes, 1980–2, males aged 15–64 years

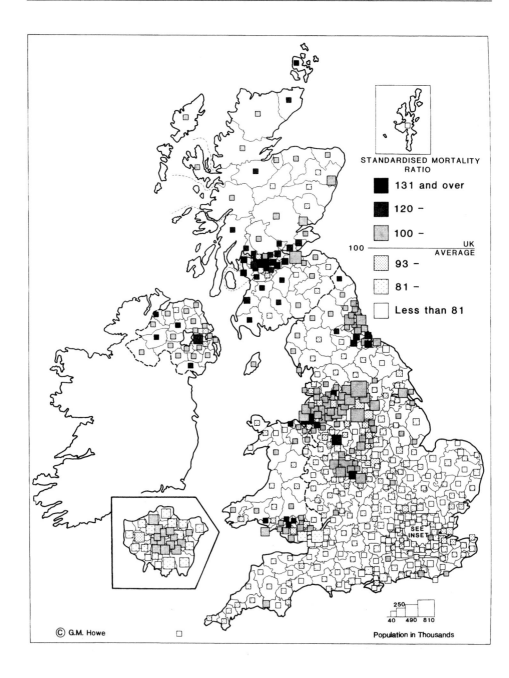

Fig. 14.20 Mortality from all causes, 1980–2, females aged 15–64 years

Table 14.12 Ranking by SMRs (1980–2) of selected districts in the UK with low and high risk of premature death from all causes: males

District	SMR relative to UK aver. 100
Low risk	
Hart (Hampshire)	59
Rochford (Essex)	61
South Norfolk	65
Elmbridge (Surrey)	66
Surrey Heath	67
Wansdyke (Avon)	68
Blaby (Leicestershire)	69
South Cambridge	70
Mid-Devon	70
South Shropshire	70
Wokingham (Berkshire)	71
UK average SMR 100	
High risk	
Clydebank (Strathclyde)	143
Western Isles (Scotland)	145
Kilmarnock and Loudon (Strathclyde)	148
Caithness (Highland)	149
Sutherland (Highland)	149
Badenoch and Strathspey (Highland)	151
Inverclyde (Strathclyde)	152
Glasgow City (Strathclyde)	154
Skye and Lochalsh	169
Lochaber (Highland)	182

The finality and majesty of death remain part of the common human condition.

> No man is an Island, intire of its selfe; every man is a peece of the Continent, a part of the maine; if a clod be washed away by the Sea, Europe is the less, as well as if a Promonterie wer, as well as if a Mannor of thy friends or if thine own were; any man's death diminishes me, because I am involved in Mankinde; And therefore never send to know for whom the bell tolls; It tolls for thee. (John Donne, *Devotions*)

The geographical patterning of premature death from the major causes for both men and women in Britain (Figs. 14,19, 14.20) has revealed variations and contrasts between the different parts of the country. For any one specific cause of death, some areas show premature death to be either unduly common or unexpectedly infrequent; for other causes the same

Table 14.13 Ranking by SMRs (1980–2) of selected districts in the UK with low and high risk of premature death from all causes: females

District	SMR relative to UK aver. 100
Low risk	
Tweeddale (Borders)	53
East Cambridgeshire	62
Rutland (Leicestershire)	66
Vale of White Horse (Oxfordshire)	67
Surrey Heath	67
Wansdyke (Avon)	68
Tewkesbury (Gloucestershire)	69
West Somerset	69
Mole Valley (Surrey)	69
North Norfolk	70
UK average SMR 100	
High risk	
Londonderry (Northern Ireland)	136
Cumnock and Doon Valley (Strathclyde)	136
Omagh (Northern Ireland)	137
Cunninghame (Strathclyde)	138
Middlesbrough (Cleveland)	138
Orkney	143
Monklands (Strathclyde)	144
Glasgow City (Strathclyde)	146
Inverclyde (Strathclyde)	153
Motherwell (Strathclyde)	154

areas may well display something quite different. Locality obviously plays a crucial role in disease mortality. Comment has been made concerning certain of the observed distributional or spatial patterns for generating hypotheses about the causation of premature death, but it is not possible, in the light of present knowledge, to explain the reasons for the variations. Interpretation of the differences is complicated by a range of problems related to local details of the environment, differences in social class composition, geographical or social mobility etc. The range of factors thought to be aetiologically implicated require testing by cohort, case-control or correlation studies, or by case-characteristic types of investigation before they are accepted.

When death is premature it is of special concern, the more so when deaths from particular causes appear to occur more frequently in some parts of the country than in others. One wonders why, in spite of everything that governments have done over the last brief century – the introduction of the NHS in 1948, with the injection of vast sums (£41 billion in 1995-6) into health care, that regional and local variations or inequalities in both morbidity and mortality not only exist but persist. Do these inequalities represent maladaptation to local environmental factors or do they reflect internal migration within the country? Have the healthier, possibly more dynamic and ambitious members of society moved to the south-east of England, with its greater economic potential, and left behind those who are less fit and less ambitious? Or is there a relationship with blood groups and genetic inheritance?

The study of disease patterns and the highlighting of spatial variations in risk has considerable potential for aiding understanding of the causes or aetiology of the deadly diseases like heart disease, stroke and the cancers which scourge contemporary society. It is claimed that the geographical and environmental perspective provides a valuable alternative approach to the anthropocentric viewpoint of most medical scientists. It is accepted that some of the *risk* factors for the circulatory diseases, the cancers and the respiratory diseases are known, but the real *causes* have yet to be discovered. In the mean time long-term prevention of disease seems most likely to be achieved through environmental, social and economic management rather than by an exclusively biological approach or through medical intervention.

The natural environment itself is not benign; it is under constant interference or threat by human populations. Witness the effect of chlorofluorocarbons (CFCs) on the layer of stratospheric ozone which shields the earth from the most dangerous of the sun's rays, the effects of carbon dioxide and other atmospheric pollutants causing so-called 'acid rain' and the 'greenhouse effect', nitrates affecting ground-water supplies, or of the sewage, heavy metals and radio isotopes being poured into the oceans etc. Some of the changes being wrought by society are imperceptible and insidious, others are blatantly obvious. What is beyond doubt is that twentieth-century populations are altering the balance of a relatively stable system – the whole ecology of life – by their actions. The ecology of life on this planet is being radically changed. From the health point of view some of the changes may be good, some may be harmful, while others could well prove catastrophic. That there are no precise views of the impact of the changes being wrought in the balance of the great natural forces and of the new environments being created is cause for serious concern. It is palpably unwise to continue to interfere with the environment without, at the same time, striving to determine the real and lasting effects of such actions on human health and general well-being. To ignore these effects may lead to the extinction of life on this planet and the death of tomorrow. Unless action is taken to prevent further environmental spoilation the prognosis for human life on this planet is indeed bleak.

But I shall let the little I have learnt go forth into the day in order that someone better than I may guess the truth and in his work may prove and rebuke my error. At this I shall rejoice that I was yet a means whereby this truth has come to light. (Albrecht Dürer)

15

Retrospect and Prospect

In chapters 6–14 the ways in which populations, environment and disease have interacted throughout the ages have been examined in some detail. It seems not inappropriate now to engage in some historical speculation with a brief study of the impact of disease on the history of Britain. Many of the fateful diseases discussed in the corpus of the book suggest a perspective on events that is not often found in the treatment of British history. Bubonic plague in the mid-fourteenth century, for instance, was a death-dealing disease for many of Britain's communities. With ten-to-twelvefold increases in deaths, it cut heavily into Britain's population. Such was the demographic impact of these excessive deaths on the population that the earlier expansion of England into the Celtic fringe was seriously curtailed and her territorial designs in France aborted. Not until the reign of Elizabeth, in the second half of the sixteenth century, was the strength inherent in a growing population sufficient to cause expansionist schemes to be revived. During the plague years of the seventeenth century (1664–6) when 'Many died frequently in the streets suddenly without any warning' (Defoe), the disease caused serious repercussions on trade, as British ships were not allowed into any ports of France, the Netherlands, Spain or Italy, for fear of spreading the disease to those countries.

Throughout the eighteenth century smallpox (variola) was a conspicuous disease, and smallpox deaths among the reigning families of Europe twice affected British public life in important ways. 'In 1700 Queen Anne's son and sole surviving direct heir died of smallpox, thus opening afresh the question of succession to the English throne. Scarcely had the union of England and Scotland and the Hanoverian succession been agreed upon than another smallpox death in 1711, this time in the Imperial Hapsburg House disastrously disrupted plans among the powers allied against France in the war of the Spanish succession. These two events, coming so close to each other, and sharply altering the course of British political history, alerted the ruling classes of Britain to the dangers of smallpox.'[1]

Typhus ('fever') outbreaks in early Victorian times had devastating effects. Conveyed by the common louse, the disease, one of overcrowding and poverty, depopulated jails, poor houses and urban slums (pp.150–3).

Among the deprived and poverty-stricken peasants of Ireland, following the potato famine of 1846-7, the disease caused widespread terror and death (p.152). Typhus, together with dysentery, assailed the Irish with particular intensity and caused probably ten times as many deaths as were caused by starvation. The impact of the fever epidemic and famine disease, together with the actions of some unscrupulous English landlords evicting peasant tenants, resulted in the movement of peasants out of Ireland to America and Britain. 'It was the famine emigrants leaving their country with hatred in their hearts for the British and the British Government – who built up communities across the ocean, above all in the United States, where the name of Britain was accursed, and whose descendants continued to be Britain's powerful and bitter enemies, exacting vengeance for the sufferings their forebears endured.' Perhaps two million emigrants from Ireland crossed the Atlantic to North America during the years of the potato blight[2] and there was an even larger emigration across the Irish Sea to Great Britain, to Liverpool, Glasgow and the ports of south Wales.

In the mid-nineteenth century the several outbreaks of cholera resurrected the spectre of the Black Death and promoted sanitary reforms throughout the country (pp.167-9). Pure water supplies were provided and sewer systems installed. A Central Board of Health was set up in 1848. Key public health legislation resulted in sharp reductions not only in cholera and typhoid but also in several other less serious water-borne infections. It may be noted as an aside that in the Crimean War (1854-6), ten times as many British soldiers died from dysentery as were killed by Russian weapons. Half a century later, in the South African (Boer) War (1899-1902) British deaths from typhoid accounted for twice as many deaths as were inflicted by the enemy. The outcome was the routine inoculation of all army recruits against a range of such common infections as typhoid, smallpox and tetanus.

Phthisis (pulmonary tuberculosis) was, without doubt, one of the most dreaded diseases of the nineteenth and early twentieth centuries. Recorded as 'consumption', it showed no epidemic pattern but was common to the industrial towns with poor housing and low levels of hygiene, where people ate food of indifferent nutritional value. It was a widespread infection, often leading to chronic and increasing disablement and high fatalities (p.161). The disease was of considerable economic importance because of its particular impact on men and women of working and reproductive ages. Sanatoria and special houses were built for tubercular patients. Given better nutrition, improved housing and reduced overcrowding, people became less susceptible to infection by the TB bacillus, and with the advent of chemotherapy and BCG immunization, sanatoria were closed or adapted for other purposes. For some time now the one-time scourge has been 'under control'. Often referred to popularly as 'the white plague' or 'the captain of the men of death', the disease was often considered fashionable in the early decades of the nineteenth century in both literary and aesthetic circles. In recent years there has been a disturbing upsurge in the incidence of tuberculosis. Venereal or sexually transmitted diseases (STDs) attained epidemic proportions among British troops during the First World War and were a source of continued anxiety to the government of the day. There was considerable incapacity (estimated by some at 25 per cent of soldiers) at various stages of the conflict, with consequent serious effects on the war effort.

The several epidemics of influenza have had devastating effects. That of 1556–60 caused an estimated 20 per cent mortality rate.[3] Pandemics of the disease occurred in 1580 ('Spanish Flu'), 1729–30, 1732–33 ('Russian Flu'), 1782, 1847–8 and 1889–90 ('Chinese distemper', 'Calais Sweat', 'Scottish Rant'), but it was the so-called 'Spanish Influenza' of 1918–20 which proved particularly catastrophic. It was part of a pandemic and in many ways was comparable to the Black Death. New strains of the influenza virus occurred which proved unusually destructive. Mortality in the 20–40 age group was enormous. In the country as a whole there were over 200,000 deaths and as many as 3,776 deaths in the city of Glasgow alone. The resources of the medical profession throughout the country were taxed to the utmost. The potential life and productive work lost through the epidemic was immense, and the post-war economic recovery was severely curtailed. Further pandemics occurred in the period 1957–68 ('Asian flu') (Fig. 13.1) and 1968–76 ('Hong Kong' flu), the latter, however, of less severity in terms of mortality and morbidity than the former. The outbreak of 1968–70 produced some 25 million lost working days during the period December 1969 to March 1970; this was approximately 7 per cent of the total lost working days for all causes during the whole year.[4]

From the few foregoing examples, and with the benefit of hindsight, it is clear that aspects of the environment have influenced, and continue to have a profound influence on human health and well-being.

Solving the problem of cold with caves, houses and clothes led to rabies and bed bugs; solving the problem of the meat supply through the domestication of animals led to smallpox, helminthic disease and possibly tuberculosis; solving the problem of food storage and advancing civilization through occupational specialization led to a settled way of life, to towns and cities and to plagues. Today, 10,000 years later, enjoyment of excessive sunshine leads to skin cancer, heat conservation in homes to accumulation of radon and lung cancer, and widespread travel, personal contact, and tolerance among people of all races to the escape of a virus, that causes the acquired immune deficiency syndrome (AIDS), whose peculiar features would have doomed it to extinction 10,000 years ago.[5]

Rats, fleas, lice,[6] ticks, mites, polluted drinking-water, inclement weather, inadequate housing, insanitary living conditions, overcrowding, contaminated food, hazardous occupations, poor nutrition, contaminated milk, viruses, bacteria, spores, fungi etc. have, over the centuries, all played a role in disease occurrence in Britain and in its history. Environmental influences such as these are all external to the human body, and an individual has little or no control over them. Of themselves individuals cannot ensure that foods, water supplies, drugs, etc. are safe and uncontaminated, that the health hazards of air, water and noise pollution are controlled, that the spread of infectious diseases is prevented, that effective sewage and refuse disposal is carried out, or that the social environment does not have harmful effects on health.

But an examination of the essential causes or risk factors of morbidity, mortality and disability in Britain at the present time reveals many over which the individual, to a large extent, *does* have control. They are, in effect, self-imposed risks and are thus preventable. They include a high intake of animal fat (possibly contributing to atherosclerosis and coronary heart disease), cigarette-smoking (causing chronic bronchitis, emphysema and lung cancer, and aggravating coronary artery disease), alcohol addiction (leading to cirrhosis of the liver and malnutrition), abuse of drugs (leading to drug dependence, suicide, murder, malnutrition and accidents), social excess of alcohol (leading to motor vehicle accidents and obesity), over-eating (leading to obesity), fad diets (leading to malnutrition), careless driving (leading to accidents and resultant deaths and injuries) and promiscuity (leading to sexually transmitted diseases, including syphilis, gonorrhea and AIDS). When such deleterious self-imposed risks result in illness or death, the victim's life-style (itself part of the social environment) can be said to have contributed to, or caused, his or her illness or death.

In summary it may be noted how infectious diseases fell rapidly with rising economic status. Increasing life expectancy then unmasked chronic diseases which occur in a distinctive pattern. Initially deaths from trauma (shock) increase. Next comes a rise in coronary heart disease. Coronary heart disease emerges after diabetes, and cancer five years after the others have emerged. This symphony of change is orchestrated by the environment interacting with the genetic susceptibility or predisposition of people.

When the impact of the physical, biological and socio-cultural environments and the influence of the genetic endowment (susceptibility or immunity) have been assessed, there can be no doubt that the traditional way of equating the health status of the population with the availability of physicians and surgeons, nurses and hospitals etc. is inadequate. The art or science of medicine is not, as is generally perceived, the fount from which all improvements in health have flowed. Indeed, before the eighteenth century, the demographic impact of the medical profession remained negligible, and it was not until the years after 1850 that the practice of medicine and the organization of medical services was able to make large-scale differences in human survival rates and population growth. Admirable though Britain's National Health Service (introduced in 1948) is, despite all its failings, in comparison with the health service of many other countries, there is little doubt that it is essentially a national sickness or illness service, oriented more to the treatment or cure of existing illnesses or disability than a national health or disease-prevention service.

Thomas McKeown,[7] then Professor of Social Medicine in the University of Birmingham, through an analysis of mortality trends since the mid-nineteenth century, demonstrated that the general improvement in health in the UK in fact pre-dated the introduction of the various immunization programmes, sulphonamides and antibiotics. He clearly established that the decline in mortality from most infectious diseases was a consequence of raised standards of hygiene – improved sanitation, the provision of pure water supplies – and a general overall improvement, rather than of advances in medical technology. The NHS would appear generally to be of only marginal relevance to the nation's health, and especially to the inequalities in the distribution of untimely deaths. Future improvements in the health status of the people of the UK must lie largely in protecting and improving the environment (the provision of adequate housing, sound nutritional diets etc.), and in moderating self-imposed risks (not least the abuse of such addictive substances as tobacco, alcohol, prescribed psychotropics and illegally acquired drugs). Nowhere is the moderating of self-imposed risks more relevant than in respect of the acquired immune deficiency syndrome (AIDS) which, rightly, attracted much attention. By December 1996 there were 13,720 reported cases of AIDS in the UK (12,644 in England, 172 in Wales, 73 in Northern Ireland and 831 in Scotland) of whom 70.5 per cent are known to have died. A total of 28,447 HIV-1 infected individuals had been reported by the same date.[8] The number of cases and deaths from what is invariably proving a lethal disease remain, as yet, relatively small. Nevertheless, in the absence of a cure, it poses a significant threat to the well-being of the UK community not altogether different from the prospect of nuclear war. AIDS represents a major and urgent health crisis and, in the view of one Chief Medical Officer of England and Wales, constitutes 'an issue of prime importance to the future of the nation' (Acheson).

To date, almost 90 per cent of the cases in the UK have occurred among homosexual/bisexual (gay) males and intravenous drug abusers (IVDA), and most of these are in the four Thames regions of the NHS (Figs. 15.1, 15.2). Effective vaccines and treatments do not yet exist. It follows that if further human immunodeficiency virus (HIV) and related disorders are to be avoided and the spread of the infection into the general population prevented, behavioural change in sexual activities and substantial modification of the life-style of these high-risk groups is an essential prerequisite. Apart from haemophiliacs (p.41) unfortunate enough to be infected by blood transfusions, AIDS is a self-imposed disease and, as such, is preventable. Sadly, fuelled considerably by the spread of HIV and AIDS, there has been an increase in tuberculosis and concern for drug resistance to *Mycobacterium tuberculosis*. Until the late 1980s tuberculosis had been in steady decline in Britain for over forty years, but between 1982 and 1993 there were around 6,000 cases of tuberculosis notified annually in England and Wales alone.

What of the future? Poised on the threshold of the twenty-first century, at a time of great change, how is the vexing genes-versus-environment issue in relation to disease likely to unfold? Prediction is notoriously difficult in a dynamic world, and what follows can represent but a few carefully selected issues.

At the outset, it must be recognized that quite extraordinary advances are being made in the field of human molecular genetics. The genetic element in inherited disease is becoming increasingly well known. Inherited diseases result from 4,000 or more known genetic defects. It is now considered likely that within the next few decades the entire set of human genes will become available as a giant computer listing. In fact, a veritable genetic revolution is currently under way. Screening for genetic defects for cancer, heart disease, Alzheimer's Disease, tendencies to schizophrenia, obesity, extroversion, or even extreme shyness is likely to become commonplace. Screening for insurance purposes so as to prevent fraud now seems highly likely.[9] Genetic modification involving the adding of human genes to the hearts and kidneys of pigs for subsequent transplants has been reported. Human genes have also been added to sheep, cows, rabbits, mice and fish. Indeed, more than 60,000 genetically modified organs are currently being made in Britain every year, and there is a scramble by commercial firms to try to patent any genes or gene fragments which may, on the basis of future research, yield a commercial return (gene therapy, diagnostic tests, vaccines etc.). Several social, moral and ethical issues are likely to be raised by transplants using pigs' or other animals' organs altered by human genes. That apart, there remains one fundamental obstacle – that of the human body's immune system. The immune system is the most effective and complex system known to science. Despite

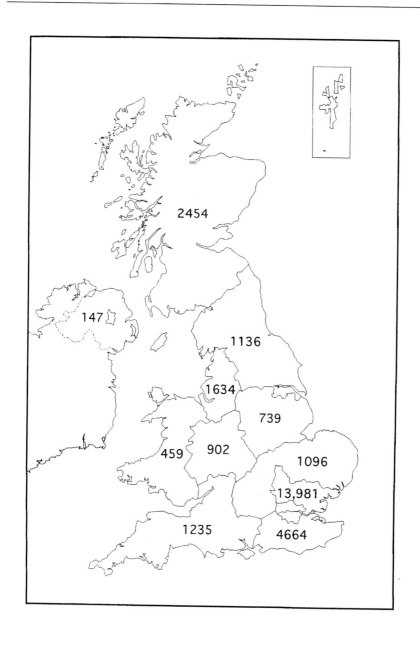

Fig. 15.1 Distribution of HIV-1 infected persons as at the end of December 1996 (*Source*: Public Health Laboratory Service (Communicable Disease Surveillance Centre))

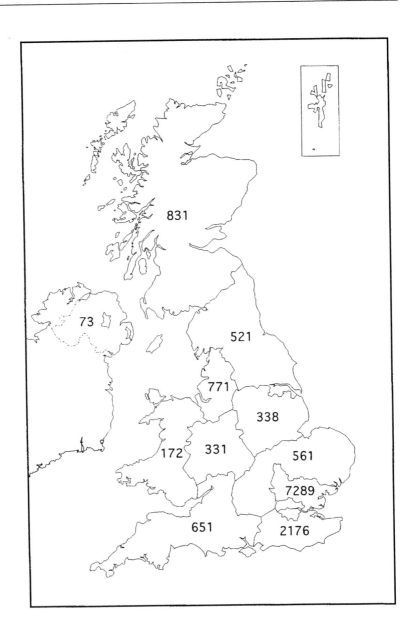

Fig. 15.2 Distribution of AIDS cases as at the end of December 1996
(*Source*: Public Health Laboratory Service (Communicable Disease Surveillance
Centre))

years of research, the mechanism whereby it can differentiate between such foreign cells as bacteria or transplanted organs, or discriminates between 'self' and 'non-self' has yet to be unravelled. Even so the advent of the drug Cyclosporin in 1985 has helped to stop the body rejecting alien tissue.

Ageing is of paramount importance. Life expectancy has increased, largely through the supply of wholesome food, healthy diets, safe water supplies, effective waste disposal, pollution controls and improved housing. At the beginning of this century life expectancy at birth was 46 years for men and 49 for women. It has now reached 74.4 years for men and 79.7 for women.[10] By the year 2001 men can expect to live to 75 years and women to 80 years (Fig. 1.1).

There have been certain triumphs of endurance, such as that of Madame Jeanne Calment in France who, on 4 February 1997 was 122 years old, and the 120 years and 237 days of Shigechiyo Izum of Japan who died in 1986. They are sufficiently rare to suggest that the maximum human life-span is likely to be about 120 years. With average life expectancy currently less than 80 in Britain (and differences of a few years between men and women) the question arises as to the reasons for the forty-year gap between the French lady and the Japanese gentleman and the rest of society? Diet, exercise, controlling blood pressure, avoidance of smoking certainly matter, though new research into the biological basis of ageing is beginning to reveal the mechanisms that underlie such differences in longevity. In the long term, such research could yield treatments that can delay senescence and its accompanying low quality of life, and contribute to a healthier old age. Meantime more and more people in Britain are heading for a life of miserable ill-health in their extra final years from diseases associated with ageing, like diabetes mellitus, a greatly increased risk of coronary heart disease, stroke, renal disease, visual impairment, osteoporosis, neuropathy, dementia and its most common type, Alzheimer's Disease. The elderly and infirm account for an increasing proportion of the population (Fig. 15.3), and in consequence incur rising costs for their care at a time when the working population is shrinking.[11]

Britain now finds itself in a post-industrial era dominated by technology. The traditional nuclear family of half a century or so ago, with husband at work and wife at home with their children, is no longer the basic unit of society. Gone, too, are the strong sense of community and the traditional values and social intimacies of that period. Such isolating technologies as cars, telephones, radios, televisions, videos, mobile telephones, faxes, computers, transistors, robots, inchoate Internet, space missiles and virtual-reality techniques now dominate and militate against an intimate society. The leisurely pace of former times has been replaced long since

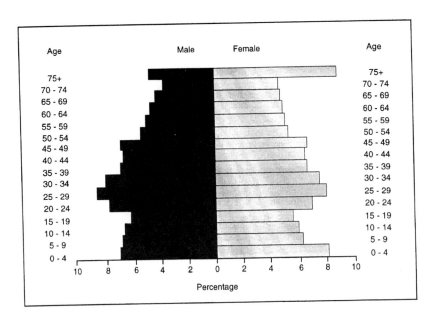

Fig. 15.3 Age–sex structure of the UK population in mid-1993
(*Source*: Office of Population Censuses and Surveys)

by hectic daily routines in which it would seem that every moment needs
to be accounted for.

Marriages have slumped to their lowest level for fifty years, and the
number of divorces has risen to an all-time high. Forty per cent of marriages
now end in divorce. Women are choosing to have fewer children, while one
in five conceptions ends in abortion. Twenty per cent of mothers with dependent children are lone mothers.[12] Single-parent families are commonplace.
Children of such single parents are thought to suffer a measurable disadvantage, emotionally, financially, educationally and otherwise, while the
parent suffers stress, anxiety, debilitation, depression and mental illness.

Life-styles tend to be passive and to lack physical activity. Children and
adults spend many hours watching television or videos, listening to radios,
compact discs or tapes or playing computer games. In 1993 people watched
for an average 25 hours and 41 minutes a week. In sport, the majority are
mainly interested observers rather than active participants. Children now
are less fit than they were ten years ago, and large numbers are overweight
and showing signs of obesity. It is the view of the National Forum for
Coronary Heart Disease Protection[13] that active children are ten times
more likely than inactive children to become active adults. In 1991–2 just
over half of adult men and over two-fifths of women were either overweight

or obese.[14] Sedentary life-styles and sedentary occupations, inactivity, lack of physical exercise and consistent overeating, often of processed foods, are responsible for the increasing number of overweight people.

The resultant obesity increases the risk of various fatal diseases such as stroke, cancer of the colon, rectum and prostate in men and breast, uterine and cervical cancer in women. Many families are seeking a healthier life-style. Diets are slowly switching from red meats to leaner white meats and fish, full-fat dairy products are being replaced by lower-fat varieties, and there is a switch from saturated fats like butter and lard to polyunsaturated spreads and oils. More fruit, vegetables and cereals are being eaten, and less salt and sugar. Several of these dietary trends are in line with recommendations contained in *The Health of the Nation*,[15] which, it is thought, should lead to lower levels of disease, fewer cancers and a virtual end to constipation. On the other hand the ever-increasing consumption of high-fat fried potato products like chips and crisps, and a steady climb in the consumption of sugary soft drinks and fatty sugary snacks means that significant amounts of fat, sugar and salt are being added back into our diet. Most obesity is non-genetic in origin.

One further aspect of modern society is the misuse of drugs, especially by teenagers. Heroin, cannabis, cocaine and crack, Ecstasy, amphetamines, anabolic steroids, hallucinogens and solvents are but a selection of a large range of drugs with effects that can prove dangerous and even fatal. Regular heroin use (usually by smoking) leads to drowsiness and slurred speech, constipation and, among women, an interrupted menstrual cycle. One of the main dangers of cannabis use is the degree of intoxication involved, resulting in an inability to drive a vehicle, cross roads or operate machines. The long-term dangers include paranoid and psychological disturbance, bronchitis and lung cancer. The unpleasant side-effects of amphetamines (speed, uppers, sulphate) include disturbed sleep, loss of appetite, uncomfortable itching, acute anxiety and paranoia. The effects and longer-term consequences of cocaine and crack include convulsions, depression and weight loss. Ecstasy (MDMA), classed as a hard drug, has a calming effect but at high doses the user may feel anxious and confused. The most commonly used hallucinogens are LSD (acid) and 'magic mushrooms'. With these drugs experiences vary. Users can feel confused and disorientated for some time. Those with mental illness can be damaged, or a psychotic response may be triggered. Tranquillizers are the most commonly misused prescription drugs. Most of those dispensed belong to the group of drugs known as benzodiazapines – the best known examples being Valium and Ativan. Prescribed only for a few weeks these help a patient to cope with a specific period of anxiety or tension. Taken over a long period, they bring the danger of withdrawal convulsions and physical and psychological dependence.

Solvents (aerosol sprays, glues, butane gas etc.) are the substances young people are most likely to experiment with. The effects of sniffing ('huffing') solvents are similar to being drunk on alcohol. They can be lethal or cause long-term damage by affecting the heart or by being poisonous; as they are inflammable, there is always the risk of fire. Steroids are potent and potentially dangerous. Misused by athletes and bodybuilders to increase muscle size and stimulate aggression they can also have side-effects which include muscle wasting, diabetes, raised blood pressure, excessive weight gain and thinning of the bones.[16]

Alcohol is a primary cause of accidents, including fire and drowning and is a common factor in suicides. Heavy drinking causes liver damage (in extreme cases cirrhosis), increased susceptibility to various cancers, pancreatitis, gastritis, duodenal ulcers and a range of other disorders. Consumed to excess or at the wrong time, alcohol can cause significant physical, psychological and social harm. On the other hand there are those who enjoy moderate drinking, and claim certain beneficial effects such as a reduction in the susceptibility to heart attack from consuming wines and spirits.[17] Consumption of alcohol has increased in recent years from, for example, 3.7 litres a year for the average Briton in 1950 to 7.5 litres in 1990.

Drug misuse and excessive consumption of alcohol represent major social problems locally and nationally. In addition to ill-health, accidents and death, they also represent major factors in law-and-order problems and contribute to family breakdown and industrial inefficiency.

The steady improvement in housing and nutrition during the nineteenth and twentieth centuries has witnessed a steady decline in the incidence of tuberculosis. From the 1950s this decline was accelerated by antibiotics. Nevertheless the disease is still present in Britain and continues to be linked with poverty and poor housing and malnutrition.

Lung cancer is the main respiratory disease in contemporary Britain, and smoking (nicotine addiction) is the principal causal factor. Sadly, the consequences of smoking tobacco reach beyond the lungs. They include an increased likelihood of heart disease, stroke, bronchitis, emphysema, thrombosis, lung cancer and cancer of several other anatomical sites. Smoking mothers run the risk of having premature, low-birth-weight babies, and of infant mortality. Some encouragement may be gained from the fact that smoking rates among men fell by almost a half between 1971 and 1992, and the rates for lung cancer fell to almost a half during that same period.[18] Men in manual occupations are three times more likely to smoke than those in the professions (Table 15.1). During that same period (1971–1992) lung cancer rates among females increased by a sixth. The *Health of our Children*[19] study reveals that in 1990 16 per cent of the children in England aged 11 to 15 were regular or occasional smokers. In Scotland the figure was 20 per cent and in Wales 15 per cent. Of 16- to 19-year-olds in Britain as a whole 30 per cent smoked. Smoking represents the largest single preventable cause of mortality, and it behoves everyone to refrain from smoking and prevail on those contemplating smoking to desist.

Table 15.1 Cigarette-smoking (percentages), 1972, 1982, 1992, by gender and socio-economic group (Great Britain)[1]

	1972	1982	1992
Males			
Professional	33	20	14
Employers and managers	44	29	23
Intermediate and junior non-manual	45	30	25
Skilled manual	57	42	34
Semi-skilled manual	57	47	39
Unskilled manual	64	49	42
All aged 16 and over	52	38	29
Females			
Professional	33	21	13
Employers and managers	38	29	21
Intermediate and junior non-manual	38	30	27
Skilled manual	47	39	31
Semi-skilled manual	42	36	35
Unskilled manual	42	41	35
All aged 16 and over	41	33	28

[1] Adults aged 16 and over, except for 1972 which relates to those aged 15 and over
(Source: Office of Population Censuses and Surveys)

Another respiratory disease, this time showing a striking increase in incidence is asthma. It is the only common chronic disease that has become progressively more common in recent decades. Reasons for the increase in incidence remain unclear and continue to elude researchers. The inhalation of substances circulating inside our homes, factories and offices (house dust, mites, cat hair etc.) and pollutants in the external environment (nitrogen oxide, hydrocarbons, diesel exhaust particles, grass pollen, dust from grain) would appear to contribute to what is fast becoming an epidemic, but to date, there is little reliable evidence to support links between pollutants and the disease.[20]

In the overall context of people, their environments and associated disease, there are two longer-term prospects, viz. global warming and the destruction of the stratospheric ozone layer. Both warrant consideration. There is now a virtual consensus among scientists studying global warming that there has been an increase in global mean temperatures by 0.3°C and 0.6°C since the middle of the nineteenth century (i.e. beyond the historic range of climate variation). The Intergovernment Panel on Climate Change (IPCC) is certain that emissions resulting from human activities are substantially increasing the atmospheric concentrations of the greenhouse gases. These increases will enhance the greenhouse effect, resulting on average, in additional warming of the earth's surface. Global average temperatures are expected to increase between 1.0°C and 3.5°C by 2100.[21]

IPCC says, 'it is unlikely to be entirely due to natural causes'.[22] In the UK warmer summers and milder, wetter winters are expected, with an increase in the frequency of extremely warm years. The unequivocal detection of global warming is unlikely for at least ten years.[23] Even so, it is noteworthy that August 1995 was the hottest, sunniest and driest August since records began in the seventeenth century, and that 1995 as a whole was the warmest year since 1659 when temperature readings began.

The direct effects on human health will be related to the effects of temperature. Warming should bring about a slight reduction in the usual winter increase in mortality associated with cold weather and fuel poverty, but on balance the impact is likely to be negative. Indirect effects could well include changes in the incidence of communicable diseases. Since insect vectors and the pathogens they transmit are sensitive to temperature, it seems likely that diseases found in tropical latitudes could spread to Britain.

A Greenpeace document[24] which reviews the potential impact of climate change on health provides the following list of insect-associated diseases which may appear or increase in Britain – leishmaniasis, malaria, rickettsiosis, viral encephalitis, bubonic plague, cutaneous myiasis, asthma, food-borne and water-borne diseases such as cryptosporidiosis, paratyphoid fever, gastro-enteritis and bacillary dysentery.

Ten or more years have elapsed since the world was alerted to the depletion of the high-altitude ozone layer over the Antarctic. The rate of fall of the ozone levels there in July and September 1995 was the fastest on record, as were the levels over Europe in spring 1996.

Because of exceptionally cold weather, the destruction of the ozone layer over the Arctic reached record levels. The ozone layer over Britain suffered the worst damage on record during the winter of 1995–6. Since the ozone layer screens out harmful ultraviolet rays, a reduction in ozone levels will increase the danger of skin cancer, cataracts and immuno-suppressive disorders.

Predictions of all kinds are notoriously fallible, and those of changing life-styles, societal mores, advances in knowledge of genetics, of climate change, or of microbes evolving and adapting in response to changing environmental conditions are no exception. Today's doctors are able to treat diseases caused by most known microbes and assess those who will suffer diseases caused by genetic defects. There are new vaccines and treatments such as heart transplants, heart bypass surgery, hip replacements, cataract surgery, lens replacement, keyhole surgery, radiotherapy and chemotherapy, and the prospect of routine virtual-reality surgery, all of which increase people's expectation of enhanced health and longevity. Yet medical technology in its turn can lead to new infections (staphylococci etc.) through its use of invasive procedures such as keyhole surgery, implanting pacemakers, introducing catheters through a vein in the heart. Medical science will continue to improve its detection and treatment of existing ailments within the UK but the 'global village' or 'one-world' concepts created by today's frequent air travel are not just phrases. They highlight the fact that germs are able to spread globally and at great speed (Fig. 15.4). The prospect of new emerging infectious diseases, or the resurfacing of others spreading to Britain by mutating microbes and viruses is ever-present.[25] And, as though to compound the situation, forms of the bacteria responsible for such diseases resistant to antibiotics are developing rapidly. Multiple resistance is a possible future scenario. Control and prevention of such diseases represents a major health problem at the dawn of the new millennium.

In a broad sense every human disease is caused either by environmental factors or by genetic factors and the interaction of people and their environments, nature and nurture, persists throughout life. It follows no pre-ordained evolutionary programme. Diseases remain hidden in the recesses of the human genome and the infinite subtleties of the all-embracing environment with an intimacy and complexity yet to be unravelled or understood.

In reality there are few if any individuals who die a natural death led there by the inability to continue living. All are constantly exposed to causes of destruction against which they fight with a greater or lesser degree of success depending on their strength. (...) With regard to the human species, an understanding of the probability of dying is not only of the utmost importance for the physician, the administrator and the economist, but is also of the greatest importance for each of us. It may help us in the usual conduct of our lives to temper exaggerated fears or expectations; it may facilitate our submission to the severe laws of nature. (Antoine Augustin Cournot, *Exposition de la théorie des chances et des probabilités* (On the theory of chance and probability), 1843).

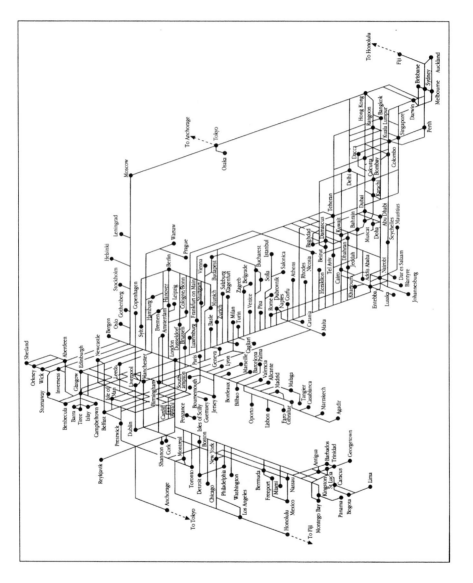

Fig. 15.4 The UK as a focus of airline links with the rest of the world (*Source*: British Airways)

Appendix A

Administrative Districts of the United Kingdom
(until April 1996)

ENGLAND

AVON (1)
a. Northavon
b. Bristol
c. Kingswood
d. Woodspring
e. Wansdyke
f. Bath

BEDFORDSHIRE (2)
a. North Bedfordshire
b. Mid Bedfordshire
c. South Bedfordshire
d. Luton

BERKSHIRE (3)
a. Newbury
b. Reading
c. Workingham
d. Bracknell
e. Windsor and
   Maidenhead
f. Slough

**BUCKINGHAMSHIRE
(4)**
a. Milton Keynes
b. Aylesbury Vale
c. Wycombe
d. Chiltern
e. Beaconsfield

**CAMBRIDGESHIRE
(5)**
a. Peterborough

b. Fenland
c. Huntingdon
d. East Cambridgeshire
e. South
   Cambridgeshire
f. Cambridge

CHESHIRE (6)
a. Warrington
b. Halton
c. Ellesmere Port and
   Neston
d. Vale Royal
e. Macclesfield
f. Chester
g. Crewe and Nantwich
h. Congleton

CLEVELAND (7)
a. Hartlepool
b. Stockton-on-Tees
c. Middlesbrough
d. Langbaurgh

CORNWALL (8)
a. North Cornwall
b. Caradon
c. Restormal
d. Carrick
e. Kerrier
f. Penwith

CUMBRIA (9)
a. Carlisle
b. Allerdale
c. Eden

d. Copeland
e. South Lakeland
f. Barrow-in-Furness

DERBYSHIRE (10)
a. High Peak
b. West Derbyshire
c. North East
   Derbyshire
d. Chesterfield
e. Bolsover
f. Amber Valley
g. Erewash
h. Derby
i. South Derbyshire

DEVON (11)
a. North Devon
b. Torridge
c. Tiverton
d. East Devon
e. Exeter
f. Teignbridge
g. West Devon
h. Plymouth
i. South Hams
j. Torbay

DORSET (12)
a. North Dorset
b. Wimborne
c. Christchurch
d. Bournemouth
e. Poole
f. Purbeck

g. West Dorset
h. Weymouth and
   Portland

DURHAM (13)
a. Chester-le-Street
b. Derwentside
c. Durham
d. Easington
e. Sedgefield
f. Wear Valley
g. Teesdale
h. Darlington

ESSEX (14)
a. Uttesford
b. Braintree
c. Colchester
d. Tendring
e. Maldon
f. Chelmsford
g. Epping Forest
h. Harlow
i. Brentwood
j. Basildon
k. Rochford
l. Southend-on-Sea
m. Castle Point
n. Thurrock

GLOUCESTERSHIRE (15)
a. Forest of Dean
b. Gloucester
c. Tewkesbury
d. Cheltenham
e. Cotswold
f. Stroud

HAMPSHIRE (16)
a. Basingstoke
b. Hart
c. Rushmoor
d. Test Valley
e. Winchester
f. East Hampshire
g. New Forest
h. Southampton
i. Eastleigh

j. Fareham
k. Gosport
l. Portsmouth
m. Havant

HEREFORD and WORCESTER (17)
a. Wyre Forest
b. Bromsgrove
c. Redditch
d. Wychavon
e. Worcester
f. Malvern Hills
g. Leominster
h. Hereford
i. South Herefordshire

HERTFORDSHIRE (18)
a. North Hertfordshire
b. Stevenage
c. East Hertfordshire
d. Broxbourne
e. Welwyn Hatfield
f. St Albans
g. Dacorum
h. Three Rivers
i. Watford
j. Hertsmere

HUMBERSIDE (19)
a. North Wolds
b. Holderness
c. Kingston upon Hull
d. Beverley
e. Boothferry
f. Scunthorpe
g. Glanford
h. Grimsby
i. Cleethorpes

ISLE OF WIGHT (20)
a. Medina
b. South Wight

ISLES OF SCILLY (21)
a. Islands Council

KENT (22)
a. Dartford

b. Gravesham
c. Medway
d. Gillingham
e. Swale
f. Canterbury
g. Thanet
h. Dover
i. Shepway
j. Ashford
k. Maidstone
l. Tonbridge and
   Malling
m. Sevenoaks
n. Tunbridge Wells

LANCASHIRE (23)
a. Lancaster
b. Wyre
c. Blackpool
d. Fylde
e. Preston
f. Ribble Valley
g. Pendle
h. Burnley
i. Rosendale
j. Hyndburn
k. Blackburn
l. Chorley
m. South Ribble
n. West Lancashire

LEICESTERSHIRE (24)
a. North West
   Leicestershire
b. Charnwood
c. Melton
d. Rutland
e. Harborough
f. Oadby and Wigston
g. Leicester
h. Blaby
i. Hinckley and
   Bosworth

LINCOLNSHIRE (25)
a. West Lindsey
b. Lincoln
c. East Lindsey

d. North Kesteven
e. Boston
f. South Kesteven
g. South Holland

MANCHESTER, GREATER (26)
a. Wigan
b. Bolton
c. Bury
d. Rochdale
e. Oldham
f. Tameside
g. Stockport
h. Manchester
i. Salford
j. Trafford

MERSEYSIDE (27)
a. Wirral
b. Sefton
c. Liverpool
d. Knowsley
e. St Helens

MIDLANDS, WEST (28)
a. Walsall
b. Wolverhampton
c. Dudley
d. Sandwell
e. Birmingham
f. Solihull
g. Coventry

NORFOLK (29)
a. West Norfolk
b. North Norfolk
c. Great Yarmouth
d. Broadland
e. Norwich
f. South Norfolk
g. Breckland

NORTHAMPTON-SHIRE (30)
a. East Northamptonshire
b. Corby

c. Kettering
d. Daventry
e. Wellingborough
f. Northampton
g. South Northamptonshire

NORTHUMBER-LAND (31)
a. Berwick-upon-Tweed
b. Alnwick
c. Castle Morpeth
d. Wansbeck
e. Blyth Valley
f. Tynedale

NOTTING-HAMSHIRE (32)
a. Bassetlaw
b. Mansfield
c. Newark
d. Ashfield
e. Gedling
f. Broxtowe
g. Nottingham
h. Rushcliffe

OXFORDSHIRE (33)
a. Cherwell
b. West Oxfordshire
c. Oxford
d. Vale of White Horse
e. South Oxfordshire

SHROPSHIRE (34)
a. Oswestry
b. North Shropshire
c. Shrewsbury and Atcham
d. The Wrekin
e. South Shropshire
f. Bridgnorth

SOMERSET (35)
a. West Somerset
b. Taunton Deane
c. Sedgemoor
d. Mendip
e. Yeovil

STAFFORDSHIRE (36)
a. Newcastle-under-Lyme
b. Stoke-on-Trent
c. Staffordshire Moorlands
d. Stafford
e. East Staffordshire
f. South Staffordshire
g. Cannock Chase
h. Lichfield
i. Tamworth

SUFFOLK (37)
a. Forest Heath
b. St Edmundsbury
c. Mid Suffolk
d. Waveney
e. Suffolk Coastal
f. Ipswich
g. Babergh

SURREY (38)
a. Spelthorne
b. Runnymeade
c. Surrey Heath
d. Woking
e. Elmbridge
f. Epsom and Ewell
g. Reigate and Banstead
h. Tandridge
i. Mole Valley
j. Guildford
k. Waverley

SUSSEX, EAST (39)
a. Hove
b. Brighton
c. Lewes
d. Wealden
e. Eastbourne
f. Rother
g. Hastings

SUSSEX, WEST (40)
a. Chichester
b. Horsham

c. Crawley
d. Mid Sussex
e. Adur
f. Worthing
g. Arun

TYNE AND WEAR (41)
a. Newcastle-upon-
   Tyne
b. North Tyneside
c. South Tyneside
d. Gateshead
e. Sunderland

WARWICKSHIRE (42)
a. North Warwickshire
b. Nuneaton
c. Rugby
d. Warwick
e. Stratford-on-Avon

WILTSHIRE (43)
a. Thamesdown
b. North Wiltshire
c. Kennet
d. West Wiltshire
e. Salisbury

YORKSHIRE, NORTH (44)
a. Scarborough
b. Ryedale
c. Hambleton
d. Richmondshire
e. Craven
f. Harrogate
g. York
h. Selby

YORKSHIRE, SOUTH (45)
a. Barnsley
b. Doncaster
c. Rotherham
d. Sheffield

YORKSHIRE, WEST (46)
a. Calderdale

b. Bradford
c. Leeds
d. Wakefield
e. Kirklees

WALES

CLYWD (47)
a. Colwyn
b. Rhuddlan
c. Delyn
d. Alyn and Deeside
e. Wrexham-Maelor
f. Glyndwr

DYFED (48)
a. Ceredigion
b. Preseli
c. South Pembrokeshire
d. Carmarthen
e. Llanelli
f. Dinefwr

GLAMORGAN, MID (49)
a. Ogwr
b. Rhondda
c. Cynon Valley
d. Merthyr Tydfil
e. Rhymney Valley
f. Taff-Ely

GLAMORGAN, SOUTH (50)
a. Vale of Glamorgan
b. Cardiff

GLAMORGAN, WEST (51)
a. Swansea
b. Lliw Valley
c. Neath
d. Afan

GWENT (52)
a. Blaenau Gwent
b. Islwyn
c. Torfaen
d. Monmouth
e. Newport

GWYNEDD (53)
a. Ynys Môn–Isle of
   Anglesey
b. Arfon
c. Dwyfor
d. Aberconwy
e. Meirionnydd

POWYS (54)
a. Montgomery
b. Radnor
c. Brecknock

SCOTLAND

BORDERS (55)
a. Tweeddale
b. Ettrick and
   Lauderdale
c. Berwickshire
d. Roxburgh

CENTRAL (56)
a. Stirling
b. Clackmannan
c. Falkirk

DUMFRIES and GALLOWAY (57)
a. Wigtown
b. Stewartry
c. Nithsdale
d. Annandale and
   Eskdale

FIFE (58)
a. North-East Fife
b. Kirkcaldy
c. Dunfermline

GRAMPIAN (59)
a. Moray
b. Banff and Buchan
c. Gordon
d. Aberdeen City
e. Kincardine and
   Deeside

HIGHLAND (60)
a. Caithness
b. Sutherland

c. Ross and Cromarty
d. Nairn
e. Inverness
f. Skye and Lochalsh
g. Lochaber
h. Badenoch and
   Strathspey

LOTHIAN (61)
a. West Lothian
b. Edinburgh City
c. Midlothian
d. East Lothian

ORKNEY (Islands
Council) **(62)**

SHETLAND (Islands
Council) **(63)**

STRATHCLYDE (64)
a. Argyll and Bute
b. Dumbarton
c. Clydebank
d. Bearsden and
   Milngavie
e. Strathkelvin
f. Cumbernauld and
   Kilsyth
g. Monklands
h. Glasgow City
i. Renfrew
j. Inverclyde
k. Cunninghame
l. Kilmarnock and
   Loudoun
m. Eastwood
n. East Kilbride
o. Hamilton
p. Motherwell
q. Lanark
r. Cumnock and Doon
   Valley
s. Kyle and Carrick

TAYSIDE (65)
a. Angus
b. Perth and Kinross
c. Dundee City

**WESTERN ISLES
(66)**
(Islands Council)

**NORTHERN
IRELAND**

Districts (67)
a. Londonderry
b. Limavady
c. Coleraine
d. Ballymoney
e. Moyle
f. Larne
g. Ballymena
h. Magherafelt
i. Strabane
j. Omagh
k. Cookstown
l. Antrim
m. Newtonabbey
n. Carrickfergus
o. North Down
p. Ards
q. Castlereagh
r. Belfast
s. Lisburn
t. Craigavon
u. Dungannon
v. Fermanagh
w. Armagh
x. Newry and Mourne
y. Banbridge
z. Down

LONDON

INNER LONDON (68)
a. Lewisham

b. Southwark
c. Lambeth
d. Wandsworth
e. Hammersmith and
   Fulham
f. Kensington and
   Chelsea
g. City of Westminster
h. City of London
i. Tower Hamlets
j. Newham
k. Hackney
l. Islington
m. Camden
n. Haringey

**OUTER LONDON
(69)**
a. Enfield
b. Barnet
c. Harrow
d. Hillingdon
e. Ealing
f. Brent
g. Hounslow
h. Richmond upon
   Thames
i. Kingston upon
   Thames
j. Merton
k. Sutton
l. Croydon
m. Bromley
n. Bexley
o. Greenwich
p. Barking and
   Dagenham
q. Havering
r. Redbridge
s. Waltham Forest

Appendix B

International Classification of Diseases (ICD), Ninth Revision

ICD chapter	ICD number	Diseases
I	(001–139)	Infectious and parasitic diseases
II	(140–239)	Neoplasms
III	(240–79)	Endocrine, nutritional and metabolic diseases and immunity disorders
IV	(280–9)	Blood and blood-forming organs
V	(290–319)	Mental disorders
VI	(320–89)	Nervous system and sense organs
VII	(390–459)	Circulatory system
VIII	(460–519)	Respiratory system
IX	(520–79)	Digestive system
X	(580–629)	Genito-urinary system
XI	(630–76)	Complications of pregnancy, childbirth etc.
XII	(680–709)	Skin and subcutaneous tissue
XIII	(710–39)	Musculo-skeletal system
XIV	(740–59)	Congenital anomalies
XV	(760–79)	Certain conditions originating in the perinatal period
XVI	(780–99)	Signs, symptoms and ill-defined conditions
XVII	(800–999)	Injury and poisoning
EXVII	(E800–E999)	External causes of injury and poisoning
VII	410–14	Ischaemic heart disease
VII	430–8	Cerebro-vascular disease
II	162	Malignant neoplasm of trachea, bronchus and lung
VIII	480–6	Pneumonia
VII	415–29	Diseases of pulmonary circulation and other forms of heart disease
II	174–5	Malignant neoplasm of breast
II	151	Malignant neoplasm of stomach
III	250	Diabetes mellitus
VIII	490–2	Bronchitis, emphysema
IX	531–3	Ulcer of stomach and duodenum
EXVII	E810–E825	Motor-vehicle accidents

ICD chapter	ICD number	Diseases
EXVII	E950–E959	Suicide and self-inflicted injury
II	204–8	Leukaemia
IX	571	Chronic liver disease and cirrhosis
VII	401–5	Hypertensive disease
II	179–82	Malignant neoplasm of uterus
VII	393–8	Chronic rheumatic heart disease
IX	550–3, 560	Hernia of abdominal cavity and other intestinal obstruction
X	580–9	Nephritis, nephrotic syndrome and nephrosis
VIII	493	Asthma
II	210–29, 239	Benign and unspecified neoplasms
IV	280–5	Anaemias
VIII	487	Influenza
X	600	Hyperplasia of prostate
I	010–12	Tuberculosis of respiratory system
I	013–18, 137	Other tuberculosis, including late effects
VI	320–2	Meningitis
I	036	Meningococcal infection
IX	540–3	Appendicitis
III	260–9	Nutritional deficiencies
XV	767–70	Birth trauma, hypoxia, birth asphyxia and other respiratory conditions
I	090–7	Syphilis
I	084	Malaria
XI	630–9	Abortion
I	055	Measles

Source: ICD 9th Revision, WHO

Glossary of Terms

To be used in conjunction with the index. Some of the terms are not, or only partially, explained in the text.

Medical

Aetiology (Etiology) The science of the causes of disease.

'Ague' Sometimes used as synonymous with malaria although not all agues were malarial. The term ague originally meant any acute fever and later was often applied specifically to typhus ('burning ague').

AIDS The acronym for acquired immune deficiency syndrome. A group of illnesses caused by the human immunodeficiency virus (HIV).

Alcoholism A chronic illness, psychic, somatic or psychosomatic, which manifests itself as a disorder of behaviour.

Alzheimer's Disease A particular type of degenerative disease leading to dementia (serious impairment or loss of mental capacity).

Anaemia A disorder of the blood in which the oxygen-carrying red cells are fewer than normal or have less red-pigment haemoglobin than normal.

Angina Pectoris A sudden and violent pain in the chest which is usually precipitated by exertion in patients with diseased coronary arteries.

Anopheles Genus of mosquitoes, several species of which transmit the agents of malaria, the so-called *Plasmodia*.

Antibody Substance produced in the blood as a normal response to poisons and germs (bacteria, viruses or a fungus) when they enter the body.

Antibiotics Substances extracted from fungi which kill or inhibit the growth of organisms causing disease.

Antigen A substance that stimulates the body to make antibodies (i.e. a poison or a germ).

Arthritis Any disease or disability in which there is a degenerative change in a joint.

Asbestosis An occupational disease of the lungs which may develop in those exposed to inhalation of asbestos fibres.

Asthma An allergic lung condition associated with shortness of breath. If the condition is the result of obstructed airways it is said to be *bronchial asthma*. If red cells fail to carry oxygen away from the lungs it is *cardiac asthma*.

Atheroma A fatty deposit of cholesterol which forms in the inner layer of the artery wall leading to narrowing and reduction in the flow of blood.

Atherosclerosis A disease of the innermost coat (intima) of the aorta and of its main branches. The disease is characterized by modular patchy fatty degeneration resembling porridge in appearance (athere, porridge).

BCG vaccination (in tuberculosis). Consists of a live though harmless bacillus originally produced by Calmette and Guerin in 1906 (hence the initials BCG). The strain is mild and does not produce active tuberculosis but it establishes resistance.

Bacteria Single-celled organisms (without nuclei). They are among the smallest living creatures known and because of their minute size are often termed micro-organisms.

Becquerel (Bq) measures the amount of radioactivity present in an item.

Botulism A serious type of food poisoning caused by a toxin produced by the micro-organism *Clostridium botulinum*.

Brain Tumour Growth of abnormal tissue – either benign or malignant – in the brain.

Bronchitis Essentially inflammation of the mucous membrane which lines the bronchi leading from the windpipe to the lungs and down which passes the air in breathing. *Acute Bronchitis* refers to a brief attack of inflammation. *Chronic Bronchitis* refers to long-standing inflammation of the bronchi and is often associated with fibrosis, emphysema, asthma, and chronic sinusitis.

Broncho-Pneumonia See **Pneumonia**.

Calorie A measure of energy (or heat), including the energy content of food.

Cancer (Malignant Tumour, Malignant Neoplasm) An abnormal proliferation of new growth in cells and tissues that produces harmful and often fatal effects. The basic cause, i.e. the 'carcinogens', is unknown. Common cancers include cancer of the skin, cancer of the lung, cancer of the stomach, cancer of the breast, cancer of the pancreas, cancer of the prostate and cancer of the cervix.

Cancer of the Lung and Bronchus See **Cancer**. The aetiology of lung-bronchus cancer, as indeed of any other cancer, is not yet understood, but the causal relationship with smoking is now well established.

Carcinogen A cancer-producing substance.

Cardio-vascular Disease Disease associated with the heart and arteries.

Cell The smallest unit of life capable of surviving and reproducing independently.

Cerebrospinal Fever (Epidemic Meningitis) See **Meningitis**.

Cerebrovascular Disease (Stroke, Shock) Disease following an interruption of the blood supply to part of the brain caused by bleeding in the brain tissue accompanying a burst blood vessel or the blocking of a blood vessel by a clot.

Chemotherapy The cure of disease by the administration of chemical substances which kill the organisms causing it without at the same time damaging the body.

Chloramphenicol (Chloromycetin) An antibiotic substance used in the treatment of many infectious diseases.

Cholera (Asiatic Cholera) A disease caused by the *Comma bacillus* (*Vibrio cholerae*) (discovered in 1883 by Koch) and its toxins. The bacilli are ingested in contaminated water and food, and lead to diarrhoea, vomiting and dehydration of the body.

Cholesterol One of the types of fat or lipids found in bile, gallstones, types of fat or brain, blood cells, plasma, egg yolk, seeds and animal tissues etc. The amount of saturated fat (largely from meat and dairy produce) in the diet is one of the determinants of the blood cholesterol level.

Chromosome A thread-like structure in the cell nucleus which contains the genetic information.

Consumption See **Pulmonary Tuberculosis**.

'Continued Fever' ('Putrid Malignant Fever') See **Typhus** and **Typhoid**.

'Convulsions' See **Infantile Diarrhoea**.

Coronary Heart Disease Narrowing of the arteries on the surface of the heart.

Coronary Thrombosis (Myocardial Infarct, Heart Attack) A sudden collapse with severe chest pain due to a part of the heart muscle being deprived of blood because of a blood clot in one of the main coronary arteries.

Dental Caries Decay of the teeth.

Deoxyribonucleic acid (DNA) The material that carries genetic information (i.e. hereditary material).

Derbyshire Neck See **Goitre**.

Diabetes Mellitus A disease associated either with a breakdown of the body's own supply of insulin through damage to the pancreas or with a change in the sensitivity of the body's response to insulin.

Diphtheria ('Croup') An acute contagious throat infection with possible fatal outcome. It is caused by the diphtheria bacillus and its chemical toxin.

Dysentery An acute form of diarrhoea with spasms in the bowels and bloody excretion, called 'bloody flux' by our forebears. It is caused by either the dysentery bacilli (bacillary dysentery) or the dysentery amoebas (amoebic dysentery).

Emphysema A respiratory disease associated with overdistension of the lungs.

Endemic The term applied to a disease which is permanently present within a community.

'English Sweat' ('Sweating Sickness') A mysterious and deadly disease which affected England in 1486, 1507, 1518, 1529 and 1551. See also **Influenza**.

Enteric Fever ('Slow Nervous Fever', 'Continued Fever') See **Typhoid and Paratyphoid**.

Epidemic The term applied to a disease not permanently present within a community but affecting a large proportion of the population occasionally.

Epidemiology The study of disease occurrence in human populations and the factors that influence these patterns.

Erysipelas (St Anthony's Fire) An acute bacterial infection of the skin, usually of the face, in which the affected parts are of a deep red colour.

Escherichia coli Bacterium, normally resident in the colon, of which certain types are pathogenic.

Factor VIII A substance derived from donated blood that assists blood clotting in people with haemophilia. All Factor VIII is heat-treated to kill HIV.

'Farmer's Lung' ('Allergic Alveolitis') A disease of the lungs resulting from the handling of a variety of dusty, mouldy, organic materials such as mouldy hay.

The pulmonary condition results from the inhalation of fungal spores, especially of actinomycetes (*Thermopolyspora polyspora*).

Gastric and Duodenal Ulcer (Peptic Ulcer) Localized defect in the lining of the stomach or duodenum.

Gastro-Enteritis Inflammation of the stomach and of the intestines usually produced by some of the Salmonella group of bacteria.

Gene The basic unit of heredity present in the chromosome.

Gene therapy Treatment of a disease by manipulating the genetic material.

Genome The entire genetic material of one individual organism or species.

Goitre (Derbyshire Neck) A thyroid enlargement, thought to be due to, or closely linked with, iodine deficiency.

'Griping of the Guts' See **Infantile Diarrhoea**.

Haemophilia An inherited disorder in which blood fails to clot slowly. Treatment is possible with Factor VIII – the blood-clotting agent missing in haemophilia. During the 1980s the same treatment of haemophilia became capable of transmitting the AIDS virus (HIV). All blood donations in the UK are now tested for HIV and all clotting factors are treated to eliminate viruses.

Hay Fever (Allergic Rhinitis) Disease of the nose associated with any allergen such as dust, eye-grass, or ragweed and characterized by impaired nasal breathing. Symptoms are similar to those for a head cold (common cold).

Heart Attack See **Coronary Thrombosis**.

HIV (Human Immunodeficiency Virus) The virus which leads to AIDS. Previously called HTLV-III or LAV.

Homeostasis The concept of self-regulation, in which an organism or a system exhibits an ability to maintain a balance or state of equilibrium.

Hookworm Disease (Ancyclostomiasis) A disease of tropical climates, but may be encountered in cooler regions, particularly in mines and tunnels. It is caused by a parasitic roundworm and causes severe anaemia, debilitation and lowered efficiency.

Hypertension A state of abnormally high blood pressure.

Hyperthermia A state of abnormally high body temperature.

Hypothermia A state of abnormally low body temperature.

Incidence (of a disease) The number of people suffering from a disease during a given period of time.

Infantile Diarrhoea ('Summer Diarrhoea', 'Convulsions') A definite epidemiological entity, due either to a bacterium or a virus, which reached its zenith in Britain in the later years of the eighteenth century. It was then a nation-wide scourge in every hot summer.

Infective Hepatitis (Catarrhal Jaundice) Inflammation of the liver cells caused by a virus.

Influenza ('New Disease', 'Hot Ague', 'New Ague', 'New Fever', 'New Pestilence') An acute infectious respiratory disease caused by a virus. Whether the so-called 'Sweating Sickness' (q.v.) that swooped on Britain in the fifteenth century and the first half of the sixteenth century was a form of influenza or a distinct disease remains an unsolved mystery.

Ischaemic Heart Disease A heart disease resulting from a decreased blood supply to the heart. This may be due to narrowing or occlusion of the coronary arteries.

Legionnaire's Disease A form of bacterial pneumonia.

Leprosy (Hansen's Disease) A chronic infectious disease of the skin and nerves causing mutilations and deformities. The disease, called *zara'ath* in the Bible, usually translated as 'leprosy', is a generic term referring probably to several skin diseases of which true leprosy (caused by *Mycobacterium leprae*) may be one.

Leukaemia A disease usually regarded as a type of cancer in which there is an abnormally large number of white blood cells (leucocytes) in the blood and in the blood-forming tissues. Cancer of the blood.

Lipids A general term that includes fats and fat-like compounds.

Malaria ('Lencten Adl', 'Spring Ill') Now thought of as a 'hot-country' (tropical) disease but it was at one time endemic in certain marshy districts of Britain such as the Fens, the Isle of Sheppey, south-east Kent, and Somerset Levels. It is due to a group of protozoa, with complicated life histories, which are carried from infected to uninfected persons by anopheline mosquitoes. The word 'ague' (q.v.) once a popular name for malaria, was merely an acute fever rather than an intermittent or paroxysmal one.

Measles (Morbilli, 'Mezils') A disease caused by a virus. In the Middle Ages the term 'measles' was used as a generic sense to designate every chronic skin disease, and it was not until the sixteenth century that measles was distinguished from smallpox and/or scarlet fever.

Meningitis Infection of the membranes which surround the brain. It is of several forms and occurs usually in the wake of other general infections, e.g. tuberculosis or septicaemia caused by streptococci or staphylococci. Only meningococcal meningitis (cerebrospinal fever, spotted fever) occurs in epidemic form.

Mental Ill-health Includes neurotic disorders or neuroses (excessive anger, anxiety, fear, hate, jealousy etc.), psychoses (manic depressive psychosis, schizophrenia), mental depression, psychosomatic disorders and senile dementia due to Alzheimer's Disease (q.v.).

Mesothelioma A malignant tumour of the membrane that lines the chest cavity and covers the lungs (i.e the pleura). There is an increased incidence of mesothelioma in people exposed to asbestos dust.

Metabolism An inclusive term which applies to virtually all the active processes in living organisms.

Morbidity Disease incidence in a community.

Mortality Death frequency of a particular disease in a certain population.

Mutation Broadly defined as any genetic change in an organism. Mutations form the new material for evolution.

Myocardial (Cardiac) Infarction See **Coronary Thrombosis**.

Oncogene A defective version of growth-regulating genes which forces the human 'cell' in which it resides to grow in a cancerous fashion.

Osteo-Arthritis Degenerative joint disease is the preferred term for this disease because it describes the underlying degenerative process in contrast to the inflammatory process which accompanies rheumatoid arthritis (q.v.).

Pandemic An epidemic spreading over a whole country or continent.

Paratyphoid Fever See **Typhoid and Paratyphoid**.

Penicillin The first antibiotic, discovered by Fleming, which revolutionized the treatment of many infectious diseases having a bacterial aetiology.

Peptic Ulcer See **Gastric and Duodenal Ulcer**.

Pernicious Anaemia A nutritional deficiency disease. The basic defect is the absence of a gastric intrinsic factor without which vitamin B12 cannot be absorbed.

Pestilence A word used in a generic sense much like 'the plague', 'fever', 'measles' etc. It referred to any kind of acute epidemic. The bubonic plague which invaded Britain in the fourteenth century was called 'The Great Pestilence' by contemporary chroniclers.

Phthisis See **Pulmonary Tuberculosis**.

Pituitary Adenoma A simple tumour of the pituitary gland. This gland controls the thyroid, adrenals, ovaries etc., and an adenoma may stimulate these to excessive activity.

Plague A term formerly used loosely to apply to every epidemic resulting in high mortality. Later used exclusively to define the particular epidemic which, recognized by specific clinical, epidemiological and bacteriological characteristics, is now called plague. There are three forms of plague: (*a*) bubonic plague ('botch') with such characteristic symptoms as swelling of the lymph nodes in the groin and armpits, (*b*) pneumonic (pulmonary) plague in which the victims appear blue-black, and (*c*) septicaemic plague in which the organisms proliferate in the bloodstream.

Pneumoconiosis Lung disease due to inhalation and retention in the lungs of industrial dusts, with the production of fibrosis.

Pneumonia There are two types, Lobar pneumonia (pneumococcal) and Bronchopneumonia. *Lobar pneumonia* is due to infection with pneumococci and is a severe, occasionally fatal, disease if untreated. The disease responds dramatically to sulphonamides, penicillin and other antibiotics. *Broncho-pneumonia* is characterized by a gradual spread of infection from the bronchi to the lungs. The infection may be caused by a variety of organisms and the response to therapy is less dramatic.

Poliomyelitis A febrile disease affecting mainly the spinal chord of the central nervous system. It carries the risk of permanent paralysis. It is caused by three types of virus referred to as Types I, II and III.

Prevalence (of a disease) The number of people suffering from a disease at a given point in time without any distinction between new and old cases.

Psycho-Neurotic Disorders Disorders associated with anxieties of one kind or another.

Psychoses A group of serious mental disorders characterized by primary disturbance of emotional feeling, acute depression, mania, delusions of persecution etc.

'Quinsy' Severe inflammation of the throat or tonsils, usually following tonsillitis.

Relapsing Fever Caused by *Spirochaetes*, is characterized by anything between two and ten relapses. It is transmitted by human head lice (*Pediculus humanus corporis*) and by ticks.

Rheumatic Heart Disease (Rheumatic Fever) A generalized disease manifest by inflammation of the heart but mainly affecting the valves. The exact cause of rheumatic heart disease is not yet known.

Rheumatism A general descriptive term meaning discomfort, pain and stiffness in or around muscles and joints. The term **Arthritis** (q.v.) is used when there is pathological change in a joint.

Rheumatoid Arthritis A chronic, generally progressive disease, involving inflammation of several joints.

Rhinitis Acute and chronic disease of the nose characterized chiefly by impaired nasal breathing. In its acute form, such as a head cold, rhinitis is accompanied by a profuse watery discharge.

Rickets (Rachitis) A deficiency disease which is invariably due to a shortage of vitamin D in the body. This may result from inadequate intake of this vitamin or lack of sunshine.

Rickettsiae Minute micro-organisms which resemble very small bacteria or large viruses. Some cause important diseases in humans such as Typhus (q.v.), Trench Fever and Q.Fever.

St Vitus's Dance (Chorea) A nervous manifestation of that process which usually results in rheumatic heart disease (q.v.).

Scarlet Fever (Scarlatina) A reaction to a streptococcol infection. It is characterized by a throat infection, high temperature and red rash.

Scurvy A deficiency disease caused chiefly by the lack of fresh vegetables and fruit, more particularly of the vitamin C (ascorbic acid) they contain.

Sibbens See **Syphilis**.

Sievert (Sv) measures the dose that is received from a given exposure to radiation. A millisievert (mSv) is a thousandth of a sievert.

Silicosis A severe lung disease which occurs as a result of inhalation of fine particles of quartz and particles of silicon-containing rock.

Smallpox (Variola, 'The Pox') A deadly and contagious disease caused by a virus. It was widespread and common in eighteenth-century Britain but diminished following the introduction of vaccination.

Spirochaetes Small corkscrew-like organisms which correspond more closely to protozoa than bacteria.

Sporozoite The form of the malaria parasite in which it is transferred to humans by the mosquito.

Streptococcus A micro-organism which is round and arranged in chains. It may cause such conditions as acute tonsillitis, erysipelas etc.

Syphilis ('Great Pox' or 'French Pox') One of the major venereal diseases. The causative organism – a spirochaete, the *treponema pallidum* – is usually acquired during sexual intercourse with an infected person. Such diseases as pinta and yaws are caused by similar organisms.

Tetanus (Lockjaw) A disease characterized by muscular rigidity and spasms and caused by the bacillus *B. tetani* and its exotoxin.

Toxaemia of Pregnancy An undesirable complication of pregnancy associated with high blood pressure, accumulation of fluid and disturbances of the urinary and nervous systems.

Toxins Poisonous substances.

Trauma Injury Either physical (bruise, fracture, sprain) or emotional (shock or experience that makes a profound impression on the mind).

Trench Fever A rickettsial disease caused by *Rickettsia quintana* and transmitted from person to person by the body louse. Symptoms include rapid onset of fever, accompanied by headache, varying degrees of mental clouding, prostration and rash.

Tuberculosis (Consumption, Phthisis) The result of an infection of various organs with a bacillus known as the tubercle bacillus, *Mycobacterium tuberculosis*. Many different organs can be affected but disease of the lungs is by far the most common form.

Tumour A swelling on or in a part of the body, resulting from abnormal growth of tissue. Tumours may be non-cancerous, benign or cancerous (malignant).

Typhoid (Enteric) and Paratyphoid Fever An acute infectious disease of man caused by a bacterium *Salmonella typhosa*. Paratyphoid fever closely resembles typhoid, though usually milder, caused by *Salmonella* organisms of other species.

Typhus ('Gaol Fever', 'Ship's Fever', 'Hospital Fever', 'Synochus') A disease of famines, characterized by high fever, headache, numbness, and by the so-called petechiae, i.e. red spots on the skin resembling flea bites (hence 'petechial typhus'). In its classic form it is caused by *Rickettsia prowazekii* and is transmitted by lice from person to person.

Venereal Diseases A group of infections which have in common the same means of transmission. The causative organisms are usually acquired during sexual intercourse with an infected person. The major venereal diseases are syphilis (q.v.) and gonorrhoea.

Viruses Infectious self-producing agents which are smaller than bacteria and which multiply only within living cells. They are responsible or potentially responsible for a wide range of infectious diseases including measles and influenza.

Whooping Cough (Chin-Cough, Pertussis) An acute, highly communicable respiratory disease characterized in its venal form by bouts of coughing, followed by a long-drawn inhalation or 'whoop'. It is caused by bacilli, *Haemophilus pertussis*.

Yellow Fever An acute infectious disease of tropical and subtropical regions which is capable of invading the temperate zones. It is caused by a virus transmitted by a domestic mosquito *Aedes aegyptii*.

Zoonosis A disease or infection transmitted to humans from an infected animal.

Geographical

Acid rain Precipitation in a polluted environment where the raindrops become contaminated by either sulphur oxides or by a combination of sulphur dioxide and nitrogen oxide.

Adaptation A genetically controlled characteristic that enhances a person or organism's chances to survive and reproduce in the environment in which it resides.

Aerosols Suspended minute particles (solid or liquid) of dust, sea, salt, carbon, lead and aluminium compounds.

Age-Structure The composition of a population according to age and/or sex.

Air Mass An area of the lower atmosphere with similar properties of temperature and moisture in the horizontal field.

Air Pollution Episode A period in which air-pollution concentrations reach levels that are hazardous to human health.

Areal Differentiation The differences in the different areas of the earth's surface.

Asbestos A term for the fibrous varieties of several distinct mineral species, all of which are silicates.

Biometeorology (Bioclimatology) The study of weather (climate) in relation to the living organisms (plants, animals and humans).

Carbon dioxide An atmospheric gas (CO_2) capable of absorbing radiation. It prevents excessive loss of terrestrial radiation and accompanying heat loss.

Cartography The art and science of map and chart construction.

Census The process of collecting, compiling and publishing demographic, economic and social data pertaining to all persons in a defined territory at a specified time.

Choropleth Map A thematic map utilizing areally based data and tonal shadings proportional to density by aerial units.

Climate The average weather conditions at a specific place over a lengthy period of time (thirty-plus years).

Class A large aggregate of individuals of similar status, income and culture, broadly sharing the same position in the division of labour.

Cold Front The leading edge of a mass of advancing cold air that is undercutting and displacing slower-moving warm air, thus forcing it to rise.

Conurbation A continuous built-up area formed by the coalescing of once-separate settlements into a continuous built-up area.

Demographic Transition A pattern of change in birth rates and death rates related to industrialization and common in developed countries in which a decline in the death rate is followed by a decline in the birth rate.

Depression A low-pressure system (meteorology).

Diffusion The spread of a phenomenon (e.g. a disease) over space and through time.

Ecological Fallacy The problem of inferring individual characteristics from aggregate population data, which are used in much geographical work.

Ecology The study of relationships of organizations or groups of organizations to their environments.

Ecosystem A functioning, interacting system composed of one or more living organisms and their physical, biological and chemical environments.

Eutrophication The state of a body of water when it has an excess of plant nutrients derived from agricultural fertilizers, from neighbouring farming activities and from other human activities.

Environmental Hazard Any risk to humans encountered in the physical, biological or human (man-made) environment.

Genetic Make-Up The genetic information possessed by an individual.

Greenhouse Effect Describes the process whereby incoming sunlight (short-wave solar radiation) passes easily through the atmosphere to reach and warm the earth's surface whereas outgoing longer-wave terrestrial (infra-red) radiation cools it down. However, some infra-red radiation is trapped by certain gases – principally water vapour, carbon dioxide, methane and nitrous oxide – acting like a blanket, and this keeps heat in the lower atmosphere. The greenhouse effect, increased by the burning of fossil fuels and the destruction of rainforest, leads to global warming.

Hazard A perceived event which threatens the life or the well-being of an organism, especially humans.

Hypothermia A condition of abnormally low human-body core temperature (c. 32°C/c. 90°F) which sometimes results in coma and possibly death, following exposure to severe weather conditions.

Life Expectancy The average number of years to be lived, calculated from birth or from a particular age.

Little Ice Age A name applied to the climate cooling in the Northern Hemisphere between the mid-sixteenth and the mid-nineteenth century AD during which time Britain experienced a preponderance of cold winters.

Malthusian Theory Population tends to increase faster than the means of subsistence, thus absorbing all economic gains unless controlled by 'preventive' and 'positive' checks.

Mortality Together with fertility and migration, death is an essential determinant of population structure and growth. Geographers are interested in the role of mortality in population change; in the influence of environment on mortality; in the ways in which particular diseases are diffused; and in the spatial pattern of mortality and its relationships with physical, economic and social conditions.

Mutagen A chemical substance or physical agent (such as radiation) capable of producing a change in an individual's genetic make-up.

Ozone The triatomic form of oxygen (O_3) created when ultraviolet rays irradiate O_2). It is found in minute quantities at high levels in the atmosphere (20–5 km). Since ozone readily absorbs most of the shorter waves of the sun's radiation it prevents the shorter lethal ultraviolet waves from reaching the earth's surface but allows through the more beneficial ultraviolet radiation with longer wavelengths.

Photochemical Fog A state of poor visibility caused by the chemical reaction of sunlight on hydrocarbons (petroleum, methane, paraffin etc.).

Pollution The condition of being physically unclean or impure. Atmospheric pollution is caused by the emission of aerosols (combustion of coal, oil, etc.), which can lead to health hazards (smog). Freshwater pollution is caused by disposal of effluents from industry, domestic buildings and farming. Salt-water (moving) pollution is caused by oil spillages, sewage outfalls and industrial wastes. Noise pollution comes from machinery, aircraft, loud music (karaoke, etc.).

Population density The number of people in relation to the space occupied by them (e.g. the number of people per square mile or per square kilometre).

Smog Literally a contraction of 'smoke-fog'.

Thematic Map A map that depicts statistical variations of abstract objects in space, e.g. population density, disease incidence.

Trace Elements Those elements in the earth's crust which occur in very small quantities.

Warm Front The boundary in a depression between an advancing mass of warm air where it is overriding and rising above a mass of colder air which it is slowly overtaking.

Windchill The effects upon humans and other living creatures of cold winds. The stronger a cold wind is blowing the more rapid will be the rate of heat loss from a person. This can lead to a lowering body temperature and the onset of hypothermia.

Notes

Notes to Chapter 1: Introduction

1. World Health Organization (WHO, 1985). *Targets for Health for All: Targets in support of the European Regional Strategy for Health for All* (European Health for All Series no. 1, Copenhagen, WHO Regional Office for Europe).
2. This was the main emphasis of medical geography up to the time when the first edition of this book was published (1972). Since the mid-1970s, however, medical geographers have been giving increasing attention to the spatial analysis of health-care services and their utilization.
3. 'An ecosystem is a functioning interacting system composed of one or more living organisms and their effective environment, both physical and biological' (F. R. Fosberg, 'The island ecosystem', in H. R. Fosberg (ed.), *Man's Place in the Island Ecosystem: A Symposium* (Honolulu, 1963), 1–6).
4. See R. Clarke, *We All Fall Down: The Prospect of Biological and Chemical Warfare* (London, 1968) and idem, *The Science of War and Peace* (London, 1971).
5. *The Practitioners* (World Health Organization News Bulletin, June 1965).
6. For further consideration of 'normality' see E. T. Renbourn, 'Normality in relation to human reactions', *Proceedings of the Ninth International Congress on Industrial Medicine* (London, 1948).

Notes to Chapter 2: People in Britain

1. Offa's Dyke was an embankment and ditch built along the border hills from Prestatyn to Chepstow. It was an agreed frontier between King Offa of Mercia and the Welsh princes.
2. H. J. Fleure, *A Natural History of Man in Britain* (London, 1971).
3. See F. Vogel, 'ABO blood groups and disease', *American Journal of Human Genetics*, 22 (1970), 464–75; and D. Brothwell, 'Disease, micro-evolution and earlier populations: an important bridge between medical history and human biology', in E. Clarke (ed.), *Modern Methods in the History of Medicine* (London, 1971).
4. A. S. Weiner, 'Blood groups and disease', *American Journal of Human Genetics*, 22 (1970), 476–83.

Notes to Chapter 3: Health Hazards of the Physical Environment

1. C. E. A. Winslow and L. P. Herrington, *Temperature and Human Life* (Princeton UP, London UP, 1949); S. W. Tromp, *Biometeorology* (London, 1980).
2. Hypothermia occurs when the body temperature falls below 35°C (95°F). It is not known which are the more harmful, prolonged cold spells or sudden temperature changes.
3. B. B. Waddy, 'Climate and respiratory infections', *Lancet*, 2 (1952), 674–7.
4. J. T. Boyd, 'Climate, air pollution and mortality', *British Journal of Social and Preventive Medicine*, 14 (3) (1960), 123.
5. Ions are atom-sized particles in the atmosphere which carry a positive or negative electrical charge. The theory is that exposure to negative ions in the purer air on mountains, at the seaside and in the countryside results in a feeling of well-being. On the other hand, cities and towns contain more positive ions because of pollution (car fumes and other pollutants absorb negative ions) and studies suggest that high levels of positive ions may lead to colds, headaches, fatigue and low morale.
6. C. E. P. Brooks, *The English Climate* (London, 1954); new edition by H. H. Lamb (1964); T. J. Chandler and S. Gregory (eds.), *The Climate of the British Isles* (London, 1976).
7. E. Hawkins, *Medical Climatology of England and Wales* (London, 1923).
8. Many places in Britain are thought traditionally to possess a 'bracing' quality at some time or another of the year. Examples are:
In the spring, Rhyl, Blackpool, Cheltenham, Skegness
In the summer, Tunbridge Wells, Harrogate, Thanet
In the autumn, Buxton, Cromer
In the winter, Bournemouth, Felixstowe
   The selection of places with a 'relaxing' or 'sedative' climate is more difficult but would include:
In the spring, the Cornish Riviera
In the summer, the New Forest
In the autumn, the Severn Valley
In the winter, South Devon and Cornwall
9. See W. F. Tyler 'Bracing and relaxing climates', *Quarterly Journal of the Royal Meteorological Society*, 61 (1935), 209–15.
10. See R. Reiter, 'Neuere Untersuchungen zum Problem der Wetterabhängigkeit des Menschen', *Archiv für Meteorologie, Geophysik und Bioklimatologie*, Ser. B, 4 (Vienna, 1953), 327–77.
11. H. C. Darby (ed.), *An Historical Geography of England before 1800 AD* (Cambridge 1936, 1969).
12. Ozone is a blue, pungent gas made of oxygen molecules (triatomic oxygen, i.e. oxygen molecules with three atoms). The layer of ozone, located between twelve and thirty miles above the earth's surface, screens 99 per cent of the harmful ultraviolet radiation coming from the sun. In 1984 the British Antarctic Survey announced it had found a thinning in the ozone layer over

the Antarctic. CFCs and HCFCs from aerosol propellants in refrigerators and for blowing foam such as polystyrene decrease the concentration of ozone. An increase in ultraviolet light levels on the earth will raise the incidence of skin cancer and blindness.

13. E.g. the notorious winter of 1962–3 gave the longest unbroken spell of frost and snow since reliable recording began about 150 years ago. Historical documents indicate that it was almost certainly the coldest winter since 1740 although it was still not as bad as the notable winter of 1684 described in *Lorna Doone* by R. D. Blackmore which was published in 1869. The winters of 1981–2, 1984–5 and 1985–6 were also notably cold. Gales of hurricane force, with gusts exceeding 90 mph, which swept across southern England on 16 October 1987 were responsible for the deaths of eighteen people, many injuries and considerable environmental damage.

14. See *New Scientist*, no. 1599, 11 February 1988, and 1631, 22 September 1988, 24. The health hazards of radon were first discovered half a century ago during investigations into why half the uranium miners in the Ore Mountains of Czechoslovakia died of lung cancer. The Environmental Protection Agency (EPA) in America has put radon on the same footing as cigarettes and toxic wastes: an immediate hazard demanding 'quick action' ('Concern about radon grows in Britain and America', 1631 (*New Scientist* (2 September 1988), 24.

15. H. V. Warren, R. E. Delavault and C. H. Cross, 'Possible correlations between geology and some disease patterns', *Annals of the New York Academy of Science*, 136 (1967), 657–710; G. M. Howe, 'Disease patterns and trace elements', *Spectrum*, 77 (1970), 2–8.

16. Goitre is an abnormal enlargement of the thyroid gland due to lack of thyroid hormone (thyroxine). Though dubbed 'Derbyshire neck' it was equally severe, if not more so, in Oxfordshire, Gloucestershire and Dorset. It was the content of iodine in the drinking-water which was a determining factor in the distribution of endemic goitre. At the outbreak of the Second World War it was realized that iodine had a beneficial effect on the health and yield of milk herds, and it was subsequently added to cattle feed. The combination of increased intake and higher milk iodine levels almost certainly accounted for the subsequent disappearance of goitre in areas where it was previously common. Iodine-deficiency diseases are now controlled by iodized salt, used by all sections of society.

17. M. D. Crawford, M. J. Gardner and J. N. Norris, 'Mortality and hardness of local water supplies', *Lancet*, 1 (1968), 827–83.

18. H. A. Schroeder, 'Relation between mortality from cardiovascular disease and treated water supplies', *Journal of the American Medical Association*, 172 (17) (1960), 1902–8.

19. G. M. Howe, 'The geographical distribution of cancer mortality in Wales, 1947–53', *Transactions and Papers, Institute of British Geographers*, 28 (1960), 190–215. See also G. M. Howe, 'Disease patterns and trace elements', *Spectrum*, 77 (1970), 2–8.

20. Closed in 1978, when it was discovered that its water was contaminated with amoeba, but reopened in 1983 following the sinking of a new bore hole which delivers uncontaminated hot spring water under artesian pressure.

21. The UK government is proposing to ban the use of artificial fertilizers containing nitrates in several parts of the country or to introduce treatment of water in some other areas to remove nitrates.

Notes to Chapter 4: Health Hazards of the Biological Environment

1. See Ch. 1, note 3.
2. The American molecular biologist Peter Duesberg of the University of California, Berkeley, maintains that since the human immuno-deficiency virus does not fulfil R. Koch's postulates, it does not cause AIDS. 'No known virus or microbe discriminates between men and women nor between homosexuals and heterosexuals' (see *Cancer Research*, 49 (1987), 119).
3. It is difficult to estimate the extent of malaria in Britain during early times, because the term 'ague' was applied indiscriminately to many fevers. See M. Dobson, 'Marsh fever – the geography of malaria in England', *Journal of Historical Geography*, 6 (1980), 359–89, 'When malaria was an English disease', and 'Malaria in England: a geographical and historical perspective', *Parassitologia*, 36 (1994), 1313–14.
4. See V. B. Wigglesworth, *The Principles of Insect Physiology* (sixth edn, London, 1965), for details.
5. The development of powerful chemical pesticides based on organophosphorous and chlorinated hydrocarbons revolutionized chemical warfare against insects and other pests which constitute a threat to the health of humans and their crops. Many of these chemicals, however, may be lethal, and DDT dieldrin, aldrin and related substances persist in soils and accumulate in animal and body fat. On 28 March 1969, Sweden announced a ban on DDT and other chlorinated hydrocarbons, aldrin, dieldrin and lindane, to take effect from 1 January 1970. The Swedish Poisons Board, which motivated the ban, said that the insecticides were dangerous to animal and plant life and were long-term health risks for humans. A similar ban has been effected in the USA, and the United Kingdom. There are reports now of farmers working with organophosphorous sheep dips experiencing neurological problems.
6. See R. G. Will, J. W. Ironside, M. Zeidler et al., 'A new variant of Creutzfeldt-Jakob disease in the UK', *Lancet*, 347 (1996), 921–5, and A. J. M. Michael, 'Bovine spongiform encephalopathy: its wider meaning for population health', *British Medical Journal*, 312, 7042 (1996), 1313–14.

Notes to Chapter 5: Health Hazards of the Human Environment

1. E. Chadwick, *Report on the Sanitary Conditions of the Labouring Population of Great Britain, 1842*, New edn, edited and with an introduction by M. W. Flinn (Edinburgh, 1965).
2. J. Yudkin and J. C. McKenzie, *Changing Food Habits* (London 1964).

3. Cyclamate sweeteners were banned in Britain in October 1969.
4. The Report of the Swann Committee (November 1969) recommended that the use of penicillin and the tetracyclines in animal feedstuffs should be prohibited and the use of antibiotics restricted. The recommendations were accepted by the government. The use of growth-promoting hormones in beef cattle has been banned in Britain and in the European Union but is permitted in the USA.
5. Ground-water pollution by leaching of nitrate fertilizers is serious in south Lincolnshire and Norfolk. Nitrate levels have increased because of the use of fertilizers to boost production.
6. See *Water Pollution from Farm Waste* (Water Authority Association Publication, 1987).
7. The temperature of the air generally gets lower with increasing height but occasionally the reverse is the case, and when the temperature *increases* with height there is said to be an 'inversion'. This leads to the formation of a high layer of warm air. Inversions of temperature are commonly experienced in hollows and valleys, especially in winter on calm, clear nights.
8. See R. Lynn, *Personality and National Character* (Oxford, 1971).
9. Department of Health and Social Security, *Inequalities in Health. Report of a Research Working Group* (London, 1980). There are conflicting views on ways to improve the health of those in the lower socio-economic groups. A reduction in the inequalities might be achieved through commitment to welfare policies, e.g. by closing the income gap between the rich and the poor. Another solution might lie in the generating of wealth through economic progress for the benefit of all social groups. See also in this context, A. Smith and B. Jacobson (eds.), *The Nation's Health: A Strategy for the 1990's* (King Edward's Hospital Fund, 1988), and *The Health of the Nation*: A Consultative Document for Health in England (London, 1991).
10. Entries in Earl of Malmesbury, *Memoirs of an Ex-Minister* (London, 1885), for the year 1858 read as follows:

> June 21st – The heat of this last month has been quite exceptional, the thermometer constantly rising to 84°...
> June 23rd – The pestilential smell from the Thames is becoming intolerable, and there has been a question of changing the locality of Parliament. Nothing can be done during this heat ...
> June 27th – We have ordered large quantities of lime to be thrown into the Thames, for no works can begin until this hot weather is over. The stench is perfectly intolerable, although Madame Ristori, coming back one night from a dinner at Greenwich by Lord Hardwicke, sniffed the air with delight, saying that it reminded her of her dear Venice ...

11. Department of the Environment and the Welsh Office, *River Quality in England and Wales* (London, 1988).
12. N. Wald et al. (eds.), *UK Smoking Statistics* (Oxford, 1988); *Cigarette Smoking 1972 to 1986* (OPCS Monitor SS88/1, London, 9 February 1988). See also N. Wald and N. Nicolaides-Bouman, *UK Smoking Statistics*, 2nd edn. (Oxford, 1991).

13. HMSO (Central Statistical Office), *Social Trends*, 25 (London, 1995).
14. Said to affect half the hospitals in Britain (BBC *Panorama* programme, 15 January 1996).

Notes to Chapter 6: Pre-Norman and Norman Times

1. W. G. Hoskins, *The Making of the English Landscape* (London 1963).
2. The Antonine Wall was a turf wall erected between the Forth and Clyde; Hadrian's Wall was built along the Solway–Tyne Gap (Bowness to Wallsend). The latter defended the northern frontier of the Roman province of Britain; between it and the Antonine Wall was a frontier zone.
3. H. J. Fleure, *A Natural History of Man in Britain* (London, 1951; rev. edn, 1971), 521.
4. C. Fox, *The Personality of Britain* (National Museum of Wales, Cardiff, 1932, 1938, 1947). Recent archaeological excavations suggest that the picture of seventh- and eighth-century England may have to be redrafted. Digs at Southampton's Saxon town Hamwic, for example, show evidence of the earliest post-Roman planned street layout in north-west Europe, of a town trading on a large scale with European ports as early as AD 700 and of an industrial centre with iron, bronze, leather, bone and textile production. Such findings would tend to dispel the image of Britain as a cultural and trading backwater during the 'Dark Ages'.
5. Hoskins, op. cit.
6. Palaeopathology 'examines the evolution and progress of disease through long periods of time and examines how humans adapted to changes in their environment'. See Charlotte Roberts and Keith Manchester, *The Archaeology of Disease* (second edn, 1995), for recent developments in the study of palaeopathology.
7. W. P. MacArthur, 'Some notes on old-time leprosy in England and Ireland', *Journal of the Royal Army Medical Corps*, 45 (1925), 414–22.
8. A leper house was endowed at Canterbury by Lanfranc, the first Norman archbishop of that see. Others were founded later at Westminster, Southwark, Highgate and other places in London, and there were numerous other hospitals throughout England. See C. Creighton, op. cit., 86, and J. Y. Simpson, 'Archaeological Essays', vol. 11, p. 19, for a list of over a hundred leper establishments in England.
9. J. D. Comrie, *History of Scottish Medicine to 1860*, vol. 1 (Wellcome Historical Medical Museum, London 1932), 43.
10. C. Creighton, *A History of Epidemics in Britain* (1894), second edn with additional material by D. E. C. Eversley, E. A. Underwood and L. Ovenall (London, 1965). This great work of scholarship is the only book which deals systematically with the history of epidemic disease in Britain. It is an inexhaustible store of information and has been referred to frequently during the preparation of this book. Nevertheless Creighton's data and interpretations must always be handled with care. He did not believe in the germ theory of disease, and some of his material was selected, if not to disprove it, at least not to support it. He believed in the localist-miasmatic theory of disease causation.

11. W. Bonser, *The Medical Background of Anglo-Saxon England*, The Wellcome Historical Medical Library (London 1963).

12. Adamnan, *Life of St Columba*, ed. W. Reeves (1874).

13. J. F. D. Shrewsbury, 'The yellow plague', *Journal of the History of Medicine and Allied Sciences* (1949) 14.

14. W. P. MacArthur, 'The identification of some pestilences recorded in the Irish Annals', *Irish History Studies*, 6 (1949), 172. See Bonser, *Medical Background of Anglo-Saxon England*, 64–70, for discussion.

15. Pelusium is now represented by two large mounds close to the coast and the edge of the desert, twenty miles east of Port Said. The easterly distribution of the Nile on which it was sited has long since been silted up.

16. Procopius of Caesarea, *De bello Persico* (550) (Works of Procopius of Caesarea, vol 2), tr. H. B. Dewing (Loeb Classics), quoted by L. F. Hirst, *The Conquest of Plague* (Oxford 1953), 11.

17. The Venerable Bede, *Ecclesiastical History*, iii. 27. The discovery in the 1980s of the remains of black rats at Romano-British sites in London, York and Wroxeter in Shropshire would appear to confirm that the pestilence mentioned by Bede which raged in England in the seventh century was, in fact, bubonic plague.

18. C. F. Mullet, *The Bubonic Plague and England: An Essay in the History of Preventive Medicine* (Lexington, Kentucky, 1956).

19. Comrie, op. cit., 49.

20. Creighton, op. cit., 15–17.

21. W. P. MacArthur, 'A brief story of English malaria', *British Medical Bulletin*, 8 (1) (1951), 76–9. See also W. D. L. Smith, 'Malaria and the Thames', *Lancet*, 270 (1956), 433–6.

22. Creighton, op. cit., 13–14.

Notes to Chapter 7: Medieval Times

1. J. F. D. Shrewsbury, *A History of Bubonic Plague in the British Isles* (London, 1970).

2. See R. S. Roberts, 'The use of literary and documentary evidence in the history of medicine' (Reference 25), in E. Clarke (ed.), *Modern methods in the history of medicine* (London, 1971).

3. L. F. Hirst, *The Conquest of Plague: A Study in the Evolution of Epidemiology* (Oxford, 1953).

4. Many ports of southern England were in frequent contact with the Continent or with the Channel Islands. The plague may have been brought from Calais or else from Jersey and Guernsey, which were suffering badly from disease at this time. See P. Ziegler, *The Black Death* (London, 1968), 119–22.

5. Creighton, op. cit., 116.

6. Ziegler, op. cit., 136.

7. W. Rees, 'The Black Death in England and Wales, as exhibited in manorial documents', *Proceedings of the Royal Society of Medicine (History of Medicine)*, 16 (1923), 27.

8. W. F. Skene (ed.), *Chronicle of the Scottish Nation* (Edinburgh, 1872).

9. D. Laing (ed.), *Cronykil of Andrew of Wyntoun* (Edinburgh, 1872), vol.11, p.482.

10. Rees, op. cit.

11. The mortality figures for Britain were paralleled on the Continent, which lost at least a quarter of its population between 1348 and 1350. Florence was reduced in population from 90,000 to 45,000 and Siena from 42,000 to 15,000. Hamburg apparently lost about two-thirds of its inhabitants.

12. Narrow, ill-cleansed streets, ditches and streams filled with household garbage and sweepings, a virtual absence of sewage disposal, and insanitary conditions generally typified the larger towns in the fourteenth century.

13. J. M. W. Bean, 'Plague, population and economic decline in the late Middle Ages', *Economic History Review*, 2nd ser. 15 (1963), 423–38.

14. J. W. Thompson, 'The aftermath of the Black Death and the aftermath of the Great War', *American Journal of Sociology*, 16 (1920–1), 565. See also C. H. Talbot, *Medicine in Medieval England* (1967), 163–4; and W. L. Langen, 'The Black Death', *Scientific American*, 210, 2 (1964), 114–21. Other aspects of human behaviour in the face of the plague are considered in connection with the plague of 1665 (p.112).

15. For a dramatic account of a twentieth-century visitation by plague and its impact on the population of one city, Oran in Algeria, see *La Peste* (The Plague) by Albert Camus (first published in France in 1947) in *The Collected Fiction of Albert Camus* (9th impression, London, 1985).

16. Shrewsbury, op. cit.

17. W. Langland (c. 1332–c. 1400), supposed English author of fourteenth-century poem *Piers Plowman*.

18. Talbot, op. cit., 162.

Notes to Chapter 8: Tudor Times

1. E. H. P. Brown and S. V. Hopkins, 'Seven centuries of the prices of consumables compared with builders' wage-rates', *Economica*, NS, 23 (1956), 296.

2. J. C. Drummond and A. Wilbraham (revised by D. Hollingsworth), *The Englishman's Food: A History of Five Centuries of English Diet* (London, 1957).

3. The effects of the climatic deterioration from about AD 1300 to 1500–1600 and after have commonly been ignored, presumably because they were heavily overlaid by the Black Death of 1349–50 and the recurring ravages of the plague thereafter. See Lamb, op. cit.

4. J. Saltmarsh, 'Plague and economic decline in the later Middle Ages', *Cambridge Historical Journal*, 7 (1941), 23–41.

5. The Company of Parish Clerks was granted a charter in the thirteenth century. At this time its function was connected with church music.

6. J. Graunt, *Natural and Political Observations ... made upon the Bills of Mortality* (London, 1662).

7. J. Caius, *A Boke or Conseill against the Disease called the Sweate, or Sweatying Sicknesse* (London, 1552).

8. The epidemic of syphilis in England was used to discredit the Romish

mass-priest, the monasteries, and orders of friars. The scandalous lives of priests, monks and friars made the strongest argument for the policy that Henry VIII had adopted against papal supremacy and in favour of Reformation.

9. Creighton, op. cit., 415.

10. A. Hirsch, *Handbook of Geographical and Historical Pathology* (1881, in German). English translation by C. Creighton (London, 1883–6), 92–8.

11. W. Clowes, *A Short and Profitable Treatise touching the Cure of the Disease called Morbus Gallicus by unctions* (London, 1579).

12. J. F. D. Shrewsbury, 'Henry VIII: a medical study', *Journal of the History of Medicine and Allied Sciences*, 7 (2) (1952), 141–85.

13. Hippocrates (460–c. 377 BC) and Hippocratic writers gave general descriptions of the weather and climate associated with various diseases prevalent in the island of Thasos, off the coast of Thrace. Atmospheric conditions were grouped under four constitutions (katastases). The first constitution, marked on the whole by cool, dry weather, was related to mumps, and pulmonary illness. The humid and warm fourth constitution was one described as 'pestilential' by Galen (AD 130–200). Galen developed the idea of miasmatic corruption of the air.

14. Drummond and Wilbraham, op. cit., 133.

Notes to Chapter 9: Stuart Times

1. An epidemic in London in 1563 left 17,000 dead out of a population of 93,000, plus a further 2,700 deaths in Westminster, which was then a separate city. There were further epidemics in London in 1575 and 1593 (with more than 20,000 deaths).

2. There are 'plague pits' close to the city marked on present-day Ordnance Survey maps.

3. *Lachiymae Londinenses Or, London Tears and Lamentations, for God's Heavie Visitation of the (sic) Plague of Pestilence* (London. Printed [by B. Alsop and T. Fawcet] for H. Holland and G. Gibbs, 1626).

4. S. Pepys, *Pepys' Diary*, ed. J. P. Kenyon (London, 1963).

5. D. Defoe, *A Journal of the Plague Year*, introduction by D. J. Johnson (London, 1966).

6. L. F. Hirst, *The Conquest of Plague: A Study in the Evolution of Epidemiology* (Oxford, 1953), 53.

7. R. Mead, *A Discourse on the Plague* (London, 1720), vol.I, p.290.

8. Quoted from C. R. Batho, 'The plague of Eyam: a tercentenary re-evaluation', *Derbyshire Archaeological Journal*, 84 (1964), 88–9. On p.86 he writes: 'It is just conceivable that the Plague of Eyam had its origin in Derby. The village wakes, held on the first Sunday after the festival of St. Helen to whom Eyam Church was dedicated (18 August), are said by the oral tradition to have been visited by a larger number than usual in 1665. The Victorians speculated that it was premonition of impending doom for the village which brought the crowds; a more likely explanation is that it was the unusually fine weather … One of these visitors might have been a friend or relative from Derby, unwittingly transporting a flea bearing the fatal bacillus.'

9. Creighton, op. cit., I, 684.

10. Quoted by T. Ferguson, *The Dawn of Scottish Social Welfare* (London, 1948), 106.

11. Until 1900 when, following a sea-borne infection, it appeared in a densely peopled district of Glasgow. There were forty-eight cases and sixteen deaths from the disease.

12. Langer, op. cit., 114-21.

13. In an epidemic in 1563 Queen Elizabeth took refuge in Windsor Castle and had a gallows erected on which to hang any one who had the temerity to go to Windsor from plague-ridden London.

14. See I. Opie and P. Opie, *Oxford Dictionary of Nursery Rhymes* (Oxford, 1957).

15. G. Thomson, *Loimotamia, or the Pest Anatomized* (London, 1666). Quoted by L. F. Hirst, op. cit., 2, who also cites several other remedies and magical measures resorted to in an attempt to cope with plague.

16. *Mycobacterium tuberculosis* was first recognized by Robert Koch in 1882.

17. J. Brownlea, 'The history of the birth and death rates in England and Wales taken as a whole from 1570 to the present time', *Public Health*, 29 (1916).

18. Thomas Willis, *Diatribae duae medico-philosophicae, quarum prior agit de fermentatione sive de motu intestino particularum in quovis copore; altera de febribus, sive de motu earundem in sanguine animalium* (London, 1659), 171-5.

19. It was the epidemic of 1670 which gave Thomas Sydenham (1624-89), the 'English Hippocrates', the opportunity to write his classical description of measles.

20. W. Harris, *Tractatus de morbis acutis infantum* (London, 1689); English translation by Cockburn (1693). Quoted by Creighton, op. cit., 750.

21. Pepys also noted that in the winter of 1666 the River Thames was emptied of its traffic by 'a most furious storm', and the streets made too dangerous to walk by bricks and tiles being pitched from houses and buildings, and London Bridge tottering.

22. Creighton, op. cit., vol.II, pp.313-39.

23. In 1658 Oliver Cromwell died unexpectedly from 'ague' at the relatively early age of 59. The disease was either influenza or malaria.

24. Willis, op. cit.

25. Cited by Creighton, op. cit., vol.II, p.338.

26. J. Evelyn, *Fumifugium, or the Inconvenience of the Aer and Smoake of London Dissipated* (London, 1661), vii.

27. A certain Mr Corbyn Morris.

28. T. J. E. Rogers, *The history of agriculture and prices in England* (1866-7), V. As illustration of the last of the periods mentioned by Rogers the following entries have been extracted from 'Calendar of Historic Weather Events since 1500', in Lamb, op. cit., Appendix 2:

21 April 1695   Strong SW winds and rain ended exceptionally long severe and snowy winter, almost the first rain for several months near London. NE and E. winds have been almost continuous since 21 March ...' (This April and May the greatest extension of the Arctic sea ice ever known was spreading around the entire coast of Iceland.)

21 August 1695   North winds and night frost at the end of a cold summer

with continual rain and westerly gales. 'Greater frosts were not always seen in winter' (John Evelyn at Wotton, Surrey). (This summer was one of the first of a sequence of disastrous harvests in Scotland where famine ensued.)

18 August 1696   End of the rains in the South, where westerly winds brought mostly fair weather over the next month: dearth of food becoming serious in Scotland.

11 December 1696   East wind brought in spell of snowy weather lasting till February 1697.

7 June 1697   Uncommonly wet spring in England and Ireland with frequent rain and hail.

14 May 1698   Weather mostly poor till 20 August.

19 May 1698   Deep snow in Shropshire.

29. Drummond and Wilbraham, op. cit., 101.
30. The consumption of alcohol in Britain reached an all-time high between 1684 and 1750, with an average consumption of five units of alcohol a day (see ch.13, note 8). – equivalent to two and a half pints of beer for every man, woman and child in the country. Today it is barely 3.5 units.
31. T. C. Smout, *A History of the Scottish People 1560–1830* (London, 1973), 144.
32. Mentioned by Ferguson, op. cit., 110.

Notes to Chapter 10: Hanoverian Times

1. Sufferers from gout have large quantities of uric acid circulating in their bloodstreams. Gout and uric acid levels are controlled by several factors, of which the social-class factors responsible for gout are quite distinct from those which affect the level of uric acid. See R. M. Acheson, 'Social class gradients and serum uric acid in males and females', *British Medical Journal*, 4 (1969).
2. Dr (the Revd) Alexander Webster was minister of the Tolbooth Church of Edinburgh.
3. Three possible causes of a reduction in the death rate from infectious diseases are: (1) specific medical therapy, (2) changes in the balance between the virulence of the infective organism and its host, (3) improvements in the environment. These causes are examined by T. McKeown and R. G. Brown, 'Medical evidence related to English population changes in the eighteenth century', *Population Studies*, 9 (2) (1955), 119–41, who conclude that the improvement resulted from an improvement in economic and social conditions. See also H. J. Habbakuk, 'English population in the eighteenth century', *Economic History Review*, 2nd ser., 6 (1953), 117–33, and G. T. Griffith, *Population Problems of the Age of Malthus* (Cambridge, 1926).
4. The Kirk Records of Aberdeen, quoted by Thomas Ferguson, in *The Dawn of Scottish Social Welfare* (London, 1948).
5. Inoculation against smallpox is usually known as vaccination. The practice of inoculation was first introduced into Britain by Lady Mary Wortley Montague (1689–1762).
6. E. Ashworth Underwood and A. M. G. Campbell, *Jenner: The Man and his*

Work (Bristol, 1967). There is a tombstone in Worth Matravers church, Dorset, with the inscription '(Sacred) to the Memory of Benjamin Jesty (of Downshay) who departed this Life April 16th 1816 aged 79 years. He was born at Yetminster in the County, and was an upright honest man; particularly noted for having been the first person (known) that introduced the cow pox by inoculation, and who, from his great strength of mind made that experiment from the (cow) on his wife and two sons in the year 1774.' This experiment was performed twenty-two years before Jenner made his first vaccination. See 'Who discovered smallpox vaccination? Edward Jenner or Benjamin Jesty?', *Transactions of the American Clinical and Climatological Association*, 90 (1978), and E. Marjorie Wallace, 'The first vaccinator: Benjamin Jesty of Yetminster Worth Matravers and his family' (1981).

7. Typhus and typhoid were listed together in the General Register Office up to 1869. Synonyms for typhus (tuphos = fog) included epidemic fever, spotted fever, putrid fever, gaol fever, camp fever, fourteen-days fever, malignant fever and petechial fever.

8. It was possible to hold a 'frost fair' and carnival on the frozen River Thames. There were six such occasions in the 1700s.

9. Generally through imported foods, as at Bournemouth, Poole and Christchurch in 1936, Croydon in 1937, and Aberdeen in 1964.

10. J. Fothergill, *An Account of the Sore Throat attended with Ulcers* (London, 1748).

11. J. Huxham, *An Essay on Fevers* (London, 1750).

12. The winter of 1739–40 was one of intense frost (see note 7) and the beginning of a two-year sickly period in which typhus and dysentery reached heights unprecedented in the eighteenth century. See Creighton, op. cit., vol.XI, p.693.

13. Creighton, op. cit., vol.II, p.645.

14. Drummond and Wilbraham, op. cit., 244. Creighton considers that diarrhoea of infants in London was probably at its worst in the period 1720–40 during the era of cheap gin. This opinion may have been influenced by the fact that Creighton himself was teetotal.

15. Griffith, op. cit.

16. T. McKeown and R. G. Record, 'Reasons for the decline of mortality in England and Wales during the nineteenth century', *Population Studies*, 16 (1962), 94–122.

Notes to Chapter 11: Early Victorian Times

1. The birth rates among the less well-off families reached levels hitherto present only in the aristocracy.

2. The end of the Salt Tax made possible the commercial production of synthetic soda, which ended the burning of seaweed to produce kelp on the coasts of the Islands and Highlands of Scotland, an industry which had supported a larger population than was possible by agriculture alone.

3. See T. H. Elkins, 'National characteristics of industrial landscapes', *Mélanges de géographie* (Gembloux, 1967).

4. P. Gaskell, *The Manufacturing Population of England: Its Moral, Social and Physical Conditions and the Changes which have arisen from the use of the Steam Machinery* (London, 1833).

5. J. P. Kay, *The Moral and Physical Condition of the Working Classes Employed in the Cotton Manufacture in Manchester* (Manchester, 1832).

6. *Parliamentary Papers*, XVIII (1845).

7. From a Report on the State of the Public Health in Birmingham by a Committee of Physicians and Surgeons, *Parliamentary Papers*, XIV (1843).

8. Report on the Sanitary Condition of Bradford by James Smith of Deanston, *Parliamentary Papers*, XVIII, 2, Appendix (1895).

9. J. C. Symons, *Parliamentary Papers*, XIV, E.11 (1843).

10. Report by James Smith, *Parliamentary Papers*, XVIII (1845).

11. Report by J. R. Martin, *Parliamentary Papers*, XVIII (1845).

12. Report by the Revd Whitwell Elwin, *Parliamentary Papers*, XXVI (1842).

13. Report by Dr Laurie, *Parliamentary Papers*, Lords, XXVI (1842).

14. In Reports from Assistant Hand-Loom Weavers' Commissioners for the South of Scotland by J. C. Symons, *Parliamentary Papers*, XLII (1839).

15. William Cobbett, *Rural Rides* (for 7 November 1821), 1830 (1835 edn).

16. W. A. Guy, *First Report of the Health of Towns Commissioners*, I, p.82 (1835 edn.).

17. Gaskell, op. cit.

18. Frederick (Frederich) Accum (1769–1838) exposed the adulteration of food in his *Treatise on the Adulteration of Food and Culinary Poisons* (London, 1820). Accum became the subject of a bitter campaign of abuse on the part of those whom he had ruthlessly exposed. Unfortunately he himself provided them with the opportunity for revenge. Seemingly he tore pages from certain books in the library of the Royal Institution in London, which obtained a bill of indictment against him. Before the case was heard Accum fled to Germany and forfeited £200 bail.

19. The laws which prevented the general public from hunting and fishing in the forests still existed. Moreover it was illegal for anyone to buy or sell game.

20. Chadwick, op. cit., 220.

21. Previous to July 1837, no distinction was made in published tables between typhus fever and enteric fever.

22. A. K. Chalmers, *The Health of Glasgow, 1818–1925: An Outline* (Glasgow, 1930), 2–3.

23. Chalmers, op. cit., 4.

24. J. Currie, *Medical Reports* (Liverpool, 1797), 204.

25. T. Shapter, *The History of Cholera in Exeter in 1832* (London, 1841).

26. G. P. Jones, 'Cholera in Wales', *National Library of Wales Journal*, 10 (1957–8), 281–99.

27. A hospital for cholera cases was built on the small island of Flat Holm in the Bristol Channel to which sailors suffering from cholera were admitted prior to landing. There was another such hospital off the coast of Devon.

28. See A. D. Cliff and P. Haggett, *Atlas of Disease Distributions: Analytical Approaches to Epidemiological Data* (Oxford, 1988), for a series of maps prepared from data relating to the epidemics of Asiatic cholera which affected London in 1848–9 and 1854.

29. First Report of the Registrar-General, Appendix (London, 1839).

30. J. Brownlea, 'An investigation into the epidemiology of phthisis in Great Britain and Ireland', *Medical Research Journal*, Special Reports Series, no. 18, Table XXV (1918).

31. The range of earnings among wage-earners in the early nineteenth century was so large that it is impossible to speak of a single 'working class'.

32. Gaskell, op. cit.

33. J. Burnett, *Plenty and Want: A Social History of Diet in England from 1815 to the Present Day* (London and Edinburgh, 1966).

34. C. Dickens, *Oliver Twist* (London, 1838). *Oliver Twist* and *Bleak House* bear the impress of the close relationship between Dickens and Dr Southwood Smith (see p.168), the Unitarian physician who devoted his life to the betterment of the poor, especially the sick poor. In their pages occur passages which are taken almost verbatim from one of Smith's reports to Parliament.

35. W. Hobson, *World Health and History* (Bristol, 1963). He cites Keats, Shelley, Stevenson and others.

36. Young ladies of the upper social class, with their tightly fitted corsets, liked to look pale and delicate. When the pallor was marked, a slightly yellow tinge was apparent. They had a tendency to faint, and when they were seen by the doctor a diagnosis of 'chlorosis' (a form of anaemia) was often made. They were almost certainly anaemic, and the probable cause was iron deficiency. A hearty appetite was considered undignified.

37. T. Ferguson et al., 'Public health in Britain in the climate of the nineteenth century', *Public Health and Urban Growth*, Report no. 4, Centre for Urban Studies, University College (London, 1964).

38. R. E. Prothero, speaking of the standard of life from 1800 to 1834 in *The Pioneers and Progress of English Farming* (London, 1888).

Notes to Chapter 12: Late Victorian Times

1. See S. E. Finer, *Sir Edwin Chadwick* (London, 1952); also R. A. Lewis, *Edwin Chadwick and the Public Health Movement, 1832–48* (London, 1952).

2. M. Greenwood, *Epidemics and Crowd Diseases: An Introduction to the Study of Epidemiology* (London, 1935).

3. C. Badham, *Observations on the Inflammatory Affections of the Mucous Membranes of the Bronchia* (London, 1808).

4. Although it was recognized and described as a sharply defined disease by P. Bretonneau in 1826, the term 'diphtheria' was first introduced by B. Godfrey in 1857. It is of interest in the context of disease classification to recall the contribution of Miss Florence Nightingale. Cecil Woodham-Smith reminds us that in 1859 each hospital followed its own method of naming and classifying diseases, and Miss Nightingale embarked on a campaign for uniform hospital statistics. With the help of Sir James Page and Sir James Clarke she drew up a standard list of diseases and drafted model hospital statistical forms which would, she wrote, 'enable us to ascertain the relative mortality of different hospitals, as well as of different diseases and injuries at the same and at different ages, the relative frequency of different diseases and injuries among the classes which enter

hospital in different countries and in different districts of the same countries' (C. Woodham-Smith, *Florence Nightingale, 1820–1910*, 335).

5. Creighton, op. cit. XI, 739.
6. B. Benjamin, 'Urban background to public health changes', in T. Ferguson et al., *Public Health and Urban Growth*, Centre for Urban Studies, University College, Report no. 4 (London, 1964), 16.
7. J. Keats, 'Ode to a Nightingale'.
8. Drummond and Wilbraham, op. cit., 403.
9. Burnett, op. cit., 214.
10. Report of the Inter-Departmental Committee on Physical Deterioration (London, 1904).
11. S. B. Rowntree, *Poverty: A Study of Town Life* (London, 1901).
12. C. Booth, *Life and Labour of the People of London*, 17 vols. (London, 1902).
13. Charles Dickens (1812–70) provides hard-hitting portraits of the slum housing, harsh working conditions, vermin and disease in his *Hard Times* (1854).
14. McKeown and Brown, op. cit.; T. McKeown and R. G. Record, 'Reasons for the decline in mortality in England and Wales during the nineteenth century', *Population Studies*, 16 (1962), 94–122; T. McKeown, 'Medical issues in historical demography', in E. Clarke (ed.), *Modern Methods in the History of Medicine* (London, 1971), 57–74.

Notes to Chapter 13: Modern Times – Morbidity

1. Smallpox was eliminated from the World Health Organization's list of infectious diseases in 1979, and on 8 May 1980 was announced the global eradication of the disease.
2. William Mitchell, *Rescue the Children* (London, 1886), 84.
3. J. W. Tanner, 'Early maturation in man', *Scientific American*, 218 (1968), 21, 7; R. J. Rona, A. V. Swan, D. G. Altman, 'Social factors and height of primary schoolchildren in England and Scotland', *Journal of Epidemiology and Community Health*, 32 (1978), 147–54, and 42 (1988), 299–303; personal communication from Child Growth Foundation, London.
4. R. E. Kendell, 'Alcoholism: a medical or political problem?', *British Medical Journal*, 1 (1979), 367–71.
5. D. M. Parkin, C. S. Muir, S. L. Whelan, Y.-T. Gao, J. Ferlay and J. Powell (eds.), *Cancer Incidence in Five Continents*, VI, IARC Scientific Publication no. 120 (Lyon, 1992).
6. HMSO (1988).
7. HMSO, *Annual Abstract of Statistics* (London, 1993).
8. Alcoholism is not given as a reason for absence from work, but earlier reports (*A Survey of Alcoholism in an English County* by M. C. Moss and Beresford Davies (1968) and *A Study of the Prevalence, Distribution and Effects of Alcoholism in Cambridgeshire* by Griffith Edwards) implicate this 'widespread killing, largely preventable disease which has a devastating effect on family life and is causing heavy losses to industry every year in frequent lateness at work and Monday morning absenteeism.' See *Health Update. 3. Alcohol.* Health Education Authority (London, 1993).

9. A. McCormick, D. Fleming and J. Charlton (eds.), *Morbidity Statistics from General Practice: Fourth National Study 1991–2* (London, 1995).

10. Asthma is currently responsible for as many as 5 million days off work or school. It affects more than 3 million people in Britain and kills almost 2,000 each year. The cause of asthma is still not fully understood.

Notes to Chapter 14: Modern Times – Mortality

1. The common cold is still a major communicable disease. It seems safe to assume that there will be at least one episode of cold for each person in the UK per annum, which would amount to over 56 million episodes in a normal year.

2. Office of Health Economics (OHE) (R. S. B. Chew), *Compendium of Health Statistics, 1987*, 6th edn, p.11 (London, 1988) and 9th edn (1995).

3. OHE, op. cit.

4. Since the fact of death is incontrovertible, mortality statistics are of more use than equivocal statistics of morbidity. The medical certificate of the cause of death is laid out so that several conditions may be listed in sequence, the first being termed the underlying cause of death. Its use for medical, geographical, geomedical or epidemiological research is of necessity limited by the accuracy of the stated cause of death (see M. R. Alderson, R. I. S. Bayliss, C. A. Clarke, A. G. W. Whitfield, 'Death certification', *British Medical Journal* (1983), 287, 444–5. Mortality indices provide a measure of incidence for those diseases for which there is a high fatality rate. For those in which the fatality rate is low, for example 'rheumatoid arthritis', they are, of necessity, almost meaningless.

5. Mortality data for a more recent period, centring on the 1991 census, were not available when this chapter was being prepared.

6. The index used for mapping is the 'Standardized Mortality Ratio' (SMR). As its name implies, the SMR is a ratio not a rate. This ratio makes due allowance for differences in the local age-structure of populations relative to the UK age-structure by a process of 'indirect standardization'. The SMR, a single measure of mortality, provides a means of comparing the mortality of any local area with that of the UK as a whole, and is a more reliable index than is the crude death rate. A local rate equal to the national (UK) expectation or rate is 100. Ratios over 100 indicate a higher-than-average death rate; ratios under 100 indicate a lower-than-average death rate.

7. Demographic base maps, in which the areas of the squares are proportional to the populations of the places they represent, are used for the presentation of the SMRs in preference to geographical base maps since they relate the SMRs to the local populations 'at risk' rather than to the areas in which the people live.

8. The figures are simplified versions of maps prepared by the author for his Presidential Lecture ('Does it Matter Where I Live?') delivered at the annual conference of the Institute of British Geographers in January 1986, and published in *Transactions of the Institute of British Geographers*, NS 11 (1986), 387–414.

9. Attention must be drawn to the different medico-legal systems in Scotland compared with elsewhere in the UK. Where post-mortem diagnosis is not available, the tendency is to diagnose acute myocardial infarction, whereas a post-mortem diagnosis tends to be coronary atheroma or coronary occlusion. There are far fewer forensic necropsies carried out in Scotland than in England and Wales. In one year, for example, in England and Wales 71 per cent of the coronary deaths in men and 67 per cent of those in women were ascribed to acute myocardial infarction. In the same year in Scotland the corresponding figures were 81 and 77 per cent. The result is that acute myocardial-infarction deaths appear proportionately commoner in Scotland than in England.

10. M. Susser, *Causal Thinking in the Health Service* (New York and London, 1973).

11. Great Britain, *A National Health Service* (London, 1944).

12. DHSS (Department of Health and Social Security), *Inequalities in Health Report of a Research Group* (London, 1980).

13. Molecular biologists say that 'a series of co-operatively acting genes', the *oncogenes* control cell division, which is the essential cause of the process leading to cancer.

14. G. M. Howe, *Global Geocancerology (A World Geography of Human Cancers)* (London and Edinburgh, 1986).

15. I. Kemp, P. Boyle, M. Smans and C. Mair (eds.), *Atlas of Cancer in Scotland, 1975–1980: Incidence and Epidemiological Perspective* (Lyon, 1985).

16. B. Ramazzini (1743) was the first to suspect an association with reproductive factors when he demonstrated that nuns in Padua (Italy) had excess rates of mortality from breast cancer. See his *De morbis artificum, diatriba*, Venice, 1743.

17. R. Doll, D. C. G. Skegg, P. A. Corwin and C. Paul. 'Importance of the male factor in cancer of the cervix', *Lancet*, 2 (1982), 581–3.

18. J. Whitelegg, 'A geography of road traffic accidents', *Transactions of the Institute of British Geographers*, NS 12 (2) (1987) 161–76.

19. Whitelegg, op. cit., 167.

20. J. Whitelegg, 'Road safety: defeat, complicity and the bankruptcy of science', *Accident Analysis and Prevention*, 15 (1984), 153–60.

21. Whitelegg, 'Geography of road traffic accidents', 163.

22. M. J. Gardner, P. D. Winter and D. J. P. Barker, *Atlas of Mortality from Selected Diseases in England and Wales, 1968–78* (Chichester, 1984).

23. DHSS, *Inequalities in Health*, 35.

Notes to Chapter 15: Retrospect and Prospect

1. W. H. McNeill, *Plagues and People* (New York, 1976), 224–5.

2. C. Woodham-Smith, *The Great Hunger: Ireland 1845–49* (London, 1962). Forty million Americans claim Irish descent.

3. F. J. Fisher, 'Influenza and infection in Tudor England', *Economic History Review*, 2nd ser., 18 (1965), 120–9.

4. G. C. Child, 'Influenza', in G. Melvyn Howe (ed.), *A World Geography of Human Diseases* (London, 1977).

5. T. R. E. Southwood, 'The natural environment and disease: an evolutionary perspective', *British Medical Journal*, 294 (1987), 1,087.

6. When martyr Thomas à Becket (killed by Henry II's knights at Canterbury on 29 December 1170) was undressed after his murder, a contemporary observer recorded that his innermost garments of haircloth seethed with lice 'like water simmering in a cauldron' (quoted by T. R. E. Southwood, op. cit., 1,087).

7. T. McKeown, 'Medical History and Care', in *A Historical Appraisal of the Medical Task* (Oxford, 1971), *The Modern Rise of Population* (London, 1976) and 'Looking at disease in the light of human development', *World Health Forum*, 6 (Geneva), 70–5.

8. Communicable Disease Surveillance Unit, Communicable Disease Report, March 1997.

9. Patrick Dixon, *The Genetic Revolution* (London, 1995).

10. *Social Trends* (1995 edn) (London).

11. Age Concern

12. *Marriage and Divorce Statistics: England and Wales* (1992) (London).

13. National Forum for Coronary Heart Disease Protection.

14. *Social Trends* (1995). A suppressed report (September 1995) by the Government's Nutritional and Physical Activity Task Forces predicted that by the year 2005 a quarter of British women and 18 per cent of British men will be obese.

15. *The Health of the Nation: A Consultative Document for Health in England* (London, 1991).

16. The information on drugs is taken from a series of booklets published by the Institute for the Study of Drug Dependence (ISDD).

17. R. Doll, R. Peto et al., 'Mortality in relation to consumption of alcohol: 13 years' observations on male British doctors', *British Medical Journal*, 309, 911 (October 1994). But see R. Jackson and R. Beaglehote, 'Alcohol consumption guidelines: relative safety vs absolute risks and benefits', *Lancet*, 396 (1995), 716.

18. *Social Trends* (1995).

19. *The Health of our Children*, OPCS (London, 1995).

20. A. J. Newman Taylor, 'Environmental determinants of asthma', *Lancet*, 345 (1995) 296–9. See also *MRC News* (Medical Research Council), no. 67 (Summer 1995), 22–5.

21. The Intergovernment Panel on Climate Change (IPCC), World Meteorological Office, *Climate Change: The IPCC Impacts Assessment* (UNEP, 1990).

22. E. Friis-Christensen of the Danish Meteorological Institute, Lyngby, and others cite sunspot 'maxima' coinciding with increased solar radiation. The increase is very slight, no more than a fraction of 1 per cent, but it is enough to cause a noticeable increase in average global temperatures on earth (*Journal of Atmospheric and Terrestrial Physics*, June 1995).

23. The European Remote Sensing Satellite, ERS 2, the European Space Agency's most complex satellite to date, launched by an Ariane rocket in April 1995 will record temperatures during a three-year mission in space. If the temperatures it records match those predicted by computer models there will be little doubt that climate change has begun. But see J. Emsley (ed.), *The Global Warming Debate* (The European Science and Environment Forum, London,

1996), in which a number of scientists dissent from the consensus on global warming. In the context of global warming it may not be inappropriate to consider the direct warming influence of the human body. In the 1920s the global population was around 2 billion. It is now in excess of 6 billion, with a few hundred thousand born every day. With its intrinsic heat of 37°C and its emissions is the global population itself not a continuing contributory factor?

24. Greenpeace, *Potential Impacts of Climate Change on Health in the UK*, London (1994). See also M. G. M. Rowland, 'Climate Change and human health: possible communicable disease consequences in the United Kingdom', *Medicine and War*, 11, no. 4 (1995), 188–94, and the quarterly journal *Emerging Infectious Diseases* from the National Centre for Infectious Diseases, Atlanta, USA, first published in January 1995. Its goals are to promote the recognition of new and re-emerging infectious diseases and to improve the understanding of factors involved in disease emergence, prevention, and elimination.

25. See Laurie Garrett, *The Coming Plague: Newly Emerging Diseases in a World out of Balance* (New York, 1995) in which the author predicts the end of the world by mutant viruses. The following figures show domestic and international passengers passing through all British airports: 1981 – 43,731,000; 1991 – 72,786,000; 1994 – 96,359,000 (*Source*: Civil Aviation Authority. From *Social Trends* (London, HMSO, 1996).

Selected Bibliography

Abbott, D. C. and Thomson, J., 'Pesticide residue analysis', *World Review of Pest Control*, 7(2) (1968), 70–83.

Accum, Frederick (Friedrich), *Treatise on the Adulteration of Foods and Culinary Poisons* (London, 1820).

Acheson, E. D., 'Record linkage and identification of long-term environmental hazards', *Proceedings of the Royal Society of London*, B., 205 (1979), 165–78.

Acland, H. W., *Memoir of the Cholera at Oxford in the year 1854* (London, 1856).

Alderson, M. R., *International Mortality Statistics* (London, 1981).

—— 'The geographical distribution of cancer', *Journal of the Royal College of Physicians*, 16 (1982), 245–51.

—— *An Introduction to Epidemiology* (second edn, London, 1983).

Alderson, M. R., Bayliss, R. I. S., Clarke, C. A. and Whitfield, A. G. W., 'Death certification', *British Medical Journal*, 287 (1983), 444–5.

Allan, T. M., and Dawson, A. A., 'ABO blood groups and ischaemic heart disease in men', *British Heart Journal*, 30 (1968), 377–82.

Allen-Price, E. D., 'Uneven distribution of cancer in West Devon', *Lancet*, 1 (1960), 1235–8.

Anderson, W. F., 'Human gene therapy', *Science*, 256 (1992), 808–13.

Appleby, A. B., 'The disappearance of plague: a continuing puzzle', *Economic History Review*, 2nd ser., XXXIII (1980), 161–73.

Arbuthnot, J., *An Essay concerning the Effects of Air on Human Bodies* (London, 1733).

Ashby, Sir Eric, *Royal Commission on Environmental Pollution: First Report* (London, 1971).

Badger, G., 'Environmental factors in human cancer', *Search*, 12 (1981), 22–9.

Badham, C., *Observations on the Inflammatory Affections of the Mucous Membranes of the Bronchia* (London, 1808).

Baker, H. T., 'Human adaptations to the physical environment', in S. Jones, R. Martin and D. Albeam (eds.), *The Cambridge Encyclopaedia of Human Evolution* (Cambridge, 1992).

Baker, R., *Report of the Leeds Board of Health* (Leeds, 1833).

Banks, A. L., 'The study of the geography of disease', *Geographical Journal*, 125(2) (1959), 199–216.

Bartholomew, J. G. (ed.), *Bartholomew's Gazetteer of the British Isles* (Edinburgh, 1902).

Batho, C. R., 'The plague of Eyam: a tercentenary re-evaluation', *Derbyshire Archaeological Journal*, 84 (1964), 81–91.

Bayliss, J. H., 'The extinction of bubonic plague in Britain', *Endeavour* 4(2) (1980), 58–66.

Bean, J. M. W., 'Plague, population and economic decline in the later Middle Ages', *Economic History Review*, 2nd ser., 15 (1963), 423–38.

Bede, The Venerable, Leo Sherley-Price, *A History of the English Church and People*, trs. and intro. (London, 1955).

Behbehani, A. M., 'The smallpox story: life and death of an old disease', *Microbiological Reviews*, 47 (1983), 455–509.

Belasco, J. E., 'Characteristics of air masses over the British Isles', *Geophysical Memoirs*, 87 (London, 1952).

Bell, W. G., *The Great Plague of London in 1665*, rev. edn (London, 1951).

Bentham, G., 'Motor vehicle accidents: a rural epidemic?' IBG/AAG Symposium in medical geography (University of Nottingham, 1985).

Beresford, S. A. A., 'Is nitrate in the drinking water associated with the risk of cancer in the urban United Kingdom?', *Internat. J. Epidem.*, 14 (1985), 57–63.

Black, D., *'The Plague Years': A Chronicle of AIDS, the Epidemic of Our Times* (London, 1986).

Bonser, W., 'Epidemics during the Anglo-Saxon period', *Journal of the British Archaeological Association*, 3rd ser., 9 (1944), 48–71.

—— *The Medical Background of Anglo-Saxon England* (Publications of the Wellcome Historical Medical Library, NS, no. 3) (London, 1963).

Booth, C., *Life and Labour of the People of London* (London, 1889–97).

Boyd, J. T., 'Climate, air pollution and mortality', *British Journal of Social and Preventive Medicine*, 14(3) (1960), 123–35.

Bozzo, S. R., Novak, K. M., Galdos, F., Hakoopian, R. and Hamilton, L. D., 'Mortality, migration, income and air pollution', *Social Science and Medicine*, 13(D) (1979), 95–110.

Brash, J. C., 'The Anglo-Saxon cemetery at Bidford-on-Avon, Warwickshire: notes on the cranial and other skeletal characters', *Archaeologia*, 73 (1923) 106.

Briggs, A., 'Cholera and society in the nineteenth century', *Past & Present*, 19 (1961), 76–96.

Brockington, F., *World Health* (Harmondsworth, 1958).

Brooks, C. E. P., *The English Climate* (London, 1954).

Brothwell, D. R., 'The palaeopathology of early British man: an essay on the problems of diagnosis and analysis', *Journal of the Royal Anthropological Institute*, 91(2) (1961), 318–44.

—— *Digging up bones* (Brit. Museum, Natural History) (London, 1963).

Brothwell, D. R. and Sandison, A. T. (eds.), *Disease in Antiquity* (Springfield, Ill., 1967).

Brown, E. H. P. and Hopkins, S. V., 'Seven centuries of the prices of consumables compared with builders' wage-rates', *Economica*, NS, 23 (1956), 296.

Brown, E. S., 'Distribution of the ABO and rhesus (D) blood groups in the North of Scotland', *Heredity*, 20 (1965), 289–303.

Brownlea, J., 'The history of the birth and death rates in England and Wales taken as a whole from 1570 to the present time', *Public Health*, 29 (1916), 211–22 and 228–38.

—— 'An investigation into the epidemiology of phthisis in Great Britain and

Ireland', *Medical Research Council, Special Reports Series*, 18 (1918).

Brunt, D., 'Some physical aspects of the heat balance of the human body', *Proceedings of the Physics Society*, 59 (1947), 713–26.

Buchanan, A. and Mitchell, A., 'The influence of the weather on mortality from different diseases and at different ages', *Journal of the Scottish Meteorological Society*, 4 (1873–5), 187–265.

Bulloch, W., *The History of Bacteriology* (London, 1938).

Burnet, M. and White, D. O., *Natural History of Infectious Disease* (fourth edn, Cambridge, 1972).

Burnett, J., *Plenty and Want: A Social History of Diet in England from 1815 to the Present Day* (London and Edinburgh, 1966).

Caius, J., *A Boke or Conseill against the Disease called the Sweate, or Sweatying Sicknesse* (London, 1552).

Calder, R., *The Life Savers* (London, 1961).

Camus, A., *La peste* (The Plague). In *The Collected Fiction of Albert Camus* (London, 1960; 9th impression, 1985).

Cardiovascular Review Group (Report), Committee on Medical Aspects of Food Policy, *Nutritional Aspects of Cardiovascular Disease* (London, 1994).

Carpentier, E., 'Autour de la peste noire: famines et épidémies dans l'histoire du XIVe siècle', *Annales, Économies, Sociétés, Civilisations*, 17 (1962), 1062–92.

Catford, J. C. and Ford, S., 'On the state of public health: premature mortality in the United Kingdom and Europe', *British Medical Journal* 24, 289 (1984), 1668–70.

Cavalli-Sforza, L. L., Menozzi, P. and Piazza, A., *The History and Geography of Human Genes* (Princeton, NJ, 1993).

Central Statistical Office, *Social Trends*, 24 (London, 1994).

Chadwick, E., *Report on the Sanitary Condition of the Labouring Population of Great Britain, 1842*, ed. and intro. by M. W. Flinn (Edinburgh, 1965).

Chalmers, A. K., *The Health of Glasgow, 1818–1925: An Outline* (Glasgow, 1930).

Chandler, T. J., *The Climate of London* (London, 1965).

Chilvers, C. and Adelstein, A., 'Cancer mortality: the regional pattern', *Population Trends*, 12 (1978), 4–9.

Christie, A. B., 'Smallpox', in G. M. Howe (ed.), *A World Geography of Human Diseases* (London, 1977), 255–70.

—— 'Plague: a review of ecology', *Ecology of Disease*, 2 (1982), 111–15.

Citron, K. M., Raynes, R. H. and Borrie, J. R. H., *Tuberculosis Today* (London, 1981).

Clare, R. H. and Southwood, T. R. E., 'Risks from ionizing radiation', *Nature*, 338 (1989), 197–8.

Clark, J., *The Influence of Climate in the Prevention and Cure of Chronic Diseases, more particularly of the Chest and Digestive Organs* (London, 1830).

Clarke, E. (ed.), *Modern Methods in the History of Medicine* (London, 1971).

Clarke, R., *We All Fall Down: The Prospect of Biological and Chemical Warfare* (London, 1968); *The Science of War and Peace* (London, 1971).

Clegg, A. G. and Clegg, P. C., *Man against Disease* (London, 1987).

Clements, F. W. and Rogers, J. F., *Diet in Health and Disease* (Sydney, 1966).

Clemow, F. G., *The Geography of Disease* (Cambridge, 1903).

Cliff, A. D. and Haggett, P., *Atlas of Disease Distributions: Analytical Approaches to Epidemiological Data* (Oxford and New York, 1988).

Clough, P. W. L., 'Nitrates and gastric carcinogens', *Minerals and the Environment*, 5 (1983), 91–5.

Clowes, W., *A Short and Profitable Treatise touching the Cure of the Disease called Morbus Gallicus by Unctions* (London, 1579).

Cobbett, L., 'The decline of the death rate of diphtheria compared with that of scarlet fever', *British Medical Journal*, 2 (1933), 139–40.

Cobbett, W., *Rural Rides* (London 1830; 1835 edn).

Coleman, D. and Sult, J., *The British Population: Patterns, Trends and Processes* (Oxford, 1992).

Commission of the European Communities (CEC), Health effect assessment COST 613/2, Report Series on Air Pollution Epidemiology, Report 2 (Brussels 1992).

Communicable Diseases Scotland Unit, *Communicable Diseases Scotland*, Weekly Reports (Glasgow, Scottish Centre for Infection, 1967 to date).

Comrie, J. D., *History of Scottish Medicine to 1860*, 2nd edn, 2 vols. The Wellcome Historical Medical Museum (London, 1932).

Cook, G. C., *Communicable and Tropical Diseases* (London, 1988).

Copeman, W. S. C., *Doctors and Disease in Tudor Times* (London, 1960).

Court-Brown, W. M., Spiers, F. W., et al., 'Geographical variation in leukaemia mortality in relation to background radiation and other factors', *British Medical Journal*, 1 (1960), 1753–9.

Cousens, S. H., 'The regional pattern of emigration during the great Irish famine, 1846–51', *Transactions of the Institute of British Geographers*, 28 (1960), 11–34.

—— 'Regional death rates in Ireland during the great famine', *Population Studies*, 19 (1960), 55–73.

Crawford, M. D., Gardner, M. J. and Morris, J. N., 'Mortality and hardness of local water supplies', *Lancet*, 1 (1968), 827–83.

Crawfurd, R., 'Contributions from the history of medicine to the problem of the transmission of typhus', *Proceedings of the Royal Society of Medicine*, 6 (1913), 6–17.

Creighton, C., *A History of Epidemics in Britain* (1894), 2 vols., 2nd edn, with additional material by D. E. C. Eversley, E. A. Underwood and L. Ovenall (London, 1965).

Currie, J., *Medical Reports* (Liverpool, 1797).

Darby, H. C. (ed.), *An Historical Geography of England before 1800 AD: Fourteen studies* (Cambridge, 1936, 1948, 1957, 1969).

Davidson, S. and Passmore, R., *Human Nutrition and Dietetics*, 3rd edn (London, 1966).

Defoe, D., *A Journal of the Plague Year, 1722*, Intro. by D. J. Johnson (London, 1966).

Department of Health and Social Security (DHSS), *Inequalities in Health*. Report of a Research Working Group chaired by Sir Douglas Black (London, 1980).

—— *On the State of the Public Health for the year 1984* (London, 1986).

—— *On the State of the Public Health for the year 1985* (London, 1986).

—— *On the State of the Public Health for the year 1986* (London, 1987).

Department of the Environment and the Welsh Office, *River Quality in England and Wales, 1985: A Report of the 1985 Survey* (London, 1988).

Departmental Committee of Enquiry, *Report on the Aberdeen Typhoid Epidemic* (Edinburgh, 1964).

Dickens, C., *Oliver Twist* (London, 1836) and *Hard Times* (London, 1854).

Dixon, P., *The Genetic Revolution* (London, 1995).

Dobson, M., 'Marsh fever' – the geography of malaria in England', *Journal of Historical Geography*, 6 (1980), 357–89.

—— 'When malaria was an English disease', *Geographical Magazine*, 54 (1982), 94–9.

Doll, R. (ed.), *Methods of Geographical Pathology*. Report of Study Group. International Organisations of Medical Sciences (Oxford, 1959).

—— (ed.), *The Geography of Disease* (London, 1984).

—— 'Major epidemics of the 20th century: from coronary thrombosis to AIDS', *Journal of the Royal Statistical Society*, Series A, 150 (1988), Part 4. Reprinted in *Social Trends*, no. 18 (London, 1988).

Doll, R. and Hill, A. B., 'Lung cancer and other causes of death in relation to smoking', *British Medical Journal*, 2 (1956), 1071.

Doll, R., Peto, R. et al., 'Mortality in relation to consumption of alcohol: 13 years' observations on male British doctors', *British Medical Journal*, 309 (October 1994), 911.

Dorling, D. I. (and Simpson, S.), *A New Social Atlas of Britain* (London, 1995).

Drummond, J. C. and Wilbraham, A., *The Englishman's Food: A History of Five Centuries of English Diet* (London, 1939; revised and edited with a new chapter by Dorothy Hollingsworth, 1957).

Dublin, L. I., Lotka, A. J. and Spiegler, M., *Length of Life: A Study of the Life Table*, rev. edn (New York, 1949).

Dubos, R., *Mirage of Health* (New York, 1959).

Durey, M., *The Return of the Plague: British Society and the Cholera, 1831–2* (Dublin, 1979).

Elkins, T. H., 'National characteristics of industrial landscapes', in J. A. Sporek and B. Schoumaker (eds.), *Mélanges de géographie physique, humaine, économique, appliquée, offerts à M. Omer Tulippe* (Gembloux, 1967).

Engels, F., *The Condition of the Working Class in England in 1844* (London, 1892).

Evans, H. J., 'Mutation as a cause of genetic disease', *Philosophical Transactions, Royal Society, London*, Series B 319 (1988), 325–90.

Evelyn, J., *Fumifugium, or the Inconvenience of the Aer and Smoke of London Dissipated* (London, 1661).

Eyler, J. M., *Victorian Social Medicine* (Baltimore, 1979).

Eyles, J., *The Geography of the National Health* (London, 1987).

—— and Woods, K. J., *The Social Geography of Medicine and Health* (London, 1983).

Ferguson, T., *The Dawn of Scottish Social Welfare* (London, 1948).

Ferguson, T., Benjamin, B. et al., *Public Health and Urban Growth*, Report no. 4, Centre for Urban Studies, University College (London, 1964).

Fiennes, R. N. T., 'Stress in a crowded world', *New Society* (1963), 357.

Finer, S. E., *The Life and Times of Sir Edwin Chadwick* (London, 1952).

Fisher, F. J., 'Influenza and inflation in Tudor England', *Economic History Review*, 2nd ser., 18 (1965), 120–9.

Fleure, H. J., *A Natural History of Man in Britain* (London, 1951; rev. edn 1971).

Forbes, D., 'Water-borne typhoid', *Lancet*, 1 (1938), 567–8.

Forman, D., Al-Dabbagh, S. and Doll, R., 'Nitrates, nitrites and gastric cancer in Great Britain', *Nature*, 313 (1985), 620–5.

Fosberg, F. R. (ed.), *Man's Place in the Island Ecosystem: A Symposium* (Honolulu, 1963).

Fothergill, J., *An Account of the Sore Throat attended with Ulcers* (London, 1748).

Fox, A. J. and Goldblatt, P. O., 'Longitudinal study: socio-demographic mortality differentials, 1971–75', OPCS Series LS., no. 1 (London, 1982).

Fox, C., *The Personality in Britain*, National Museum of Wales (Cardiff, 1947).

Fracastoro, G., *Syphilis sive morbus gallicus* (Verona, 1530).

—— *De Contagione* (Venice, 1546).

Frost, W. H. and Richardson, B. W., *Snow on Cholera* (reprint of two papers) (London, 1936).

Fussell, C. E., 'Agricultural and economic geography in the eighteenth century', *Geographical Journal*, 74 (1929), 170–7.

Galbraith, N. S., Forbes, P. and Mayon-White, R. T., 'Changing patterns of communicable disease in England and Wales', *British Medical Journal*, 281 (1980), 427–30, 489–92, 546–9.

—— and Barrett, N. J., 'Changing patterns of communicable disease', *Health and Hygiene*, 8 (1987), 102–17.

Gale, A. H., *Epidemic Diseases* (Harmondsworth, 1959).

Gardner, M. J., Winter, P. D., Taylor, C. P. and Acheson, E. D., *Atlas of Cancer Mortality in England and Wales, 1968–78* (Chichester, 1983).

—— and Barker, D. J. P., *Atlas of Mortality from Selected Diseases in England and Wales, 1968–78* (Chichester, 1984).

Garrett, L., *The Coming Plague: Newly Emerging Diseases in a World out of Balance* (New York, 1995).

Gaskell, P., *The Manufacturing Population of England: Its Moral, Social and Physical Conditions and the Changes which have arisen from the Use of the Steam Machinery* (London, 1833).

Gatenby, P. C., 'Patterns of cardiovascular disease mortality in the Glasgow region', *Ecology of Disease*, 1 (1982), 75–85.

General Register Office (Scotland), *Occupation Mortality, 1969–1973* (Edinburgh, 1981).

Gerrard, N., 'The tuberculosis environment', *Geographical Magazine*, 53 (1981), 641–4.

Giggs, J., 'Mental health and the environment', in G. M. Howe and J. Lorraine (eds.), *Environmental Medicine* (London, 1980), 281–305.

Gilbert, E. W., 'Pioneer maps of health and disease in England', *Geographical Journal*, 124 (1958), 172–83.

Glass, D. V., 'Some indicators of differences between urban and rural mortality in England and Wales and Scotland', *Public Health and Urban Growth*, Centre for Urban Studies, University College, Report no. 4 (London, 1964).

Glass, D. V. and Eversley, D. E. C. (eds.), *Population in History: Essays in Historical Demography* (London, 1965).

Goad, J., *Astro-Meteorologica or Aphorisms and Discourses of the Bodies Celestial, their Nature and Influences ... and other Secrets of Nature* (London, 1686).

Godber, G., Third World Conference on Smoking and Health (New York, 1976).

Gould, P., *The Slow Plague: A Geography of the AIDS Pandemic* (Oxford, 1993).

Graunt, J., *Natural and Political Observations ... made upon the Bills of Mortality* (London, 1662).

Great Britain, *A National Health Service* (London, 1944).

Greaves, J. P. and Hollingsworth, D. F., 'Trends in food consumption in the United Kingdom', *World Review of Nutrition and Diet*, 6 (1966), 34–89.

Greenwood, M., 'The epidemiology of influenza', *British Medical Journal*, 2 (1918), 563–6.

—— *Epidemics and Crowd Diseases: An Introduction to the Study of Epidemiology* (London, 1935).

Gregory, S., 'Water supply maps for England and Wales', *Town Planning Review*, 28 (1957), 145–63.

Griffith, G. T., *Population Problems of the Age of Malthus* (Cambridge, 1926).

Habakkuk, H. J., 'English population in the eighteenth century', *Economic History Review*, 2nd ser., 6 (1953), 117–33.

Handschin, E., 'The effect of soil temperature on the behaviour and the migration of soil fauna', in *Report on Agricultural Meteorological Conference, 1928* (London, 1928).

Hare, R., *Pomp and Pestilence: Infectious Disease, its Origins and Conquest* (London, 1954).

Harris, R. J. C., 'Cancer and the environment', *International Journal of the Environment*, 1 (1970), 59–65.

Harris, W., *Tractatus de morbis acutis infantum* (London, 1689), English translation by Cockburn, 1693).

Harvey, G., *The Disease of London or a New Discovery of the Scurvy* (London, 1675).

Haviland, A., *The Geographical Distribution of Heart Disease and Dropsy, Cancer in Females and Phthisis in Females in England and Wales* (London, 1875).

—— *Geographical Distribution of Disease in Great Britain*, 2nd edn. (London, 1892).

Hawkins, E., *Medical Climatology of England and Wales* (London, 1923).

Haynes, R., *The Geography of the Health Services in Britain* (Beckenham, 1987).

Henschen, F., *The History and Geography of Diseases*, tr. J. Tate (New York, 1967).

Hill, A. B. and Mitra, K., 'Enteric fever in milk-borne and water-borne epidemics', *Lancet*, 2 (1936), 589–94.

Hirsch, A., *Handbook of Geographical and Historical Pathology* (1881 in German), 3 vols. with English translation by C. Creighton (London, 1883–6).

Hirst, L. F., *The Conquest of Plague: A Study in the Evolution of Epidemiology* (Oxford, 1953).

Hobson, W., *World Health and History* (Bristol, 1963).

Hobson, W. and Pavanello, R., 'Air pollution in Europe', *New Scientist*, 268 (1962), 34–6.

Hodgkin, R. H., *A History of the Anglo-Saxons*, 3rd edn, I (London, 1959), 2; 1959 edn.

Hollingsworth, T. H., *Historical Demography* (London, 1969).

Hort, E. C., 'Typhus fever', *British Medical Journal*, 1 (1915), 673–5.

Hoskins, W. G., *The Making of the English Landscape* (London, 1958).

—— *Local History in England* (London, 1959).

Hoyle, F. and Wickramasinghe, C., *Diseases from Space* (London, 1979).

Howe, G. M., 'The geographical distribution of cancer mortality in Wales, 1947–53', *Transactions and Papers, Institute of British Geographers*, 28 (1960), 190–210.

—— 'Windchill, absolute humidity and the cold spell of Christmas, 1961', *Weather*, 17 (1962), 349–58.

—— 'Computing the chilling effects of winter winds', *New Scientist*, 17 (1963), 276.

—— *A National Atlas of Disease Mortality in the United Kingdom* (London, 1963; 2nd rev. and enl. edn 1970).

—— 'Last month's cold snap', *New Scientist*, 28 (1965), 742.

—— 'The geography of death', *New Scientist*, 38 (1968), 612–14.

—— 'Disease patterns and trace elements', *Spectrum*, 77 (1970), 2–8.

—— 'Geography looks at death', *Spectrum*, 71 (1970), 5–7.

—— 'The geography of life in Britain in the mid-twentieth century', *Update*, 3 (1971), 429–41.

—— 'The geography of lung-bronchus and stomach cancer in the United Kingdom', *Scottish Geographical Magazine*, 87 (1971), 202–20.

—— 'The mapping of disease in history', in E. Clarke (ed.), *Modern Methods in the History of Medicine* (London, 1971).

—— *Man, Environment and Disease in Britain: A Medical Geography through the Ages* (Newton Abbot, 1972; Harmondsworth, 1976).

—— 'Some aspects of social malaise in South Wales', *International Journal of Environment Studies*, 4 (1972), 9–20.

—— 'London and Glasgow: a comparative study of mortality patterns', *International Geographical Union* (IGU) (Toronto, 1972), 1214–17.

—— 'Disease and the environment in Britain', *Journal of the Royal College of Physicians*, 8(2) (1974), 127–39.

—— 'Environmental factors in disease', in J. Lenihan and W. W. Fletcher (eds.), *Environment and Man* (Glasgow, 1976), 1–29.

—— (ed.), *A World Geography of Human Diseases* (London, 1977).

—— 'Death in London', *Geographical Magazine*, LI (4) (1979), 284–9.

—— 'Mortality from selected malignant neoplasms in the British Isles: the spatial perspective', *Geographical Journal*, 145(3) (1979), 401–15; reprinted in *Social Science and Medicine*, 15D (1981), 199–211.

—— 'London and Glasgow: a spatial analysis of mortality experience in contrasting metropolitan centres', *Scottish Geographical Magazine*, 98(2) (1982), 119–27.

—— 'Does it matter where I live?', *Transactions of the Institute of British Geographers*, NS, 11 (1986), 387–414.

Howe, G. M. (ed.), *Global Geocancerology* (London, 1986).

—— and Lorraine, J. (eds.), *Environmental Medicine* (London, 1973, 1980).

—— *Global Geocancerology* (Edinburgh, 1986).

Huckstep, R. L., *Typhoid and Other Salmonella Infections* (Edinburgh, 1962).

Humphreys, G., 'Housing quality', one of several maps published by the Population Studies Group, *Transactions of the Institute of British Geographers*, 43 (1968).

Hutt, M. S. R. and Burkitt, D. P., *The Geography of Non-Infectious Diseases* (Oxford, 1986).

Huxham, J., *Observationes de Aere at Morbis Epidemicis ab anno MDCCXXVIII ad finem Anni MDCCXXXVII, Plymuthi factae. His accedit opusculum de morbis colicis damnoniensi auctore* (London, 1739). Translated from the Latin original: '*Observations on the Air and Epidemic Diseases from 1728–1737 inclusive by Dr. Huxham at Plymouth, together with a short Dissertation on the Devonshire Colic*, 2 vols. (London, 1738–59).

—— *An Essay on Fevers* (London, 1750); 8th edn (Edinburgh, 1779).

Illich, I., *Medical Nemesis* (New York, 1975).

Inglis, B., *The Diseases of Civilisation* (London, 1981).

Isle of Man, Chief Registrar, *Annual Report and Statistic Review of Births, Marriages and Deaths in the Isle of Man*, 1980, 1981 and 1982 (Isle of Man, 1981, 1982, 1983).

James, S. P., 'The disappearance of malaria from England', *Proceedings of the Royal Society of Medicine*, 23 (1929), 1–18.

Jones, G. P., 'Cholera in Wales', *National Library of Wales Journal*, 10 (1957–8), 281–99.

Jones, H., *Population Geography* (London, 1990).

Jones, K. and Moon, G., *Health, Disease and Society: An Introduction to Medical Geography* (London, 1987).

Jones, S., *The Language of the Genes* (London, 1993).

Kay, J. P., *The Moral and Physical Condition of the Working Classes Employed in the Cotton Manufacture in Manchester* (Manchester, 1832).

Keller, E. F., 'Nature, nurture and the human genome project', in D. J. Kevles and L. Hood (eds.), *The Code of Codes: Scientific and Social Issues in the Human Genome Project* (Cambridge, Mass., 1992).

Kemp, I., Boyle, P., Smans, M. and Muir, C. (eds.), *Atlas of Cancer in Scotland 1975–1980: Incidence and Epidemiological Perspective*, LARC Publication no. 72 (Lyon, 1985).

Kiple, K. F. (ed.), *The Cambridge World History of Disease* (Cambridge, 1993).

Kopec, A. C., 'Blood groups in Great Britain', *Advancement of Science*, 51 (1956), 200–3.

—— *The Distribution of the Blood Groups in the United Kingdom* (Oxford, 1970).

Krause, J. T., 'Changes in English fertility and mortality, 1781–1850', *Economic History Review*, 2nd ser., 2 (1958–9), 52–70.

Krause, R. M., 'The origin of plagues, old and new', *Science* 257 (1992), 1073–8.

Laidlaw, P., *Virus Diseases and Viruses* (London, 1938).

Lamb, H. H., 'Our changing climate, past and present', *Weather*, 14 (1959), 299–318.

—— *The English Climate* (London, 1964).

Lancaster, H. O., *Expectations of Life* (London, 1990).

Langer, W. L., 'The Black Death', *Scientific American*, 210(2) (1964), 114–21.

Langmuir, A. D., 'Epidemiology of Asian influenza', *American Review of Respiratory Diseases*, 2 (1961), 83.

Lawther, P. J., 'Climate, air pollution and chronic bronchitis', *Proceedings of the Royal Society of Medicine*, 51 (1958), 262–4.

Lawther, P. J., Martin, A. E. and Wilkins, E. T., *Epidemiology of Air Pollution: Report on a Symposium*, Public Health Papers, no. 15 (Geneva, 1962).

Lawton, R., 'Historical geography: the Industrial Revolution', in J. W. Watson with J. B. Sissons (eds.), *The British Isles: A Systematic Geography* (London, 1964).

Learmouth, A., *Disease Ecology* (Oxford, 1988).

Lewis, W. P. D., 'Mortality from fog in London', *British Medical Journal*, 1 (1956), 722.

Lloyd, O. Ll., Williams, F. L. R., Berry, W. G. and Florey, C. du V., *An Atlas of Mortality in Scotland* (London, 1987).

Longmate, N., *King Cholera: The Biography of a Disease* (London, 1966).

Lynn, R., *Personality and National Character* (Oxford, 1972).

MacArthur, W. P., 'Some notes on old-time leprosy in England and Ireland', *Journal of the Royal Army Medical Corps*, 45 (1925), 414–22.

—— 'Old-time typhus in Britain', *Transactions of the Royal Society of Tropical Medicine and Hygiene*, 20 (1926–7), 487–503.

—— 'Some medical references in Pepys', *Journal of the Royal Army Medical Corps*, 50 (1928), 321–35.

—— 'The identification of some pestilences recorded in the Irish Annals', *Irish History Studies*, 6 (1949), 172.

—— 'A brief story of English malaria', *British Medical Bulletin*, 8(1) (1951), 76–9.

—— 'Medieval "leprosy" in the British Isles', *Leprosy Review*, 24 (1953), 8–19.

McCluer, J. W. and Kammerer, C. M., 'Dissecting the genetic component to coronary heart disease', *American Journal of Human Genetics*, 49 (1991), 1139–44.

McConkey, E. H., *Human Genetics: The Molecular Revolution* (Boston and London, 1993).

McCormick, A., Fleming, D. and Charleton, J., *Morbidity Statistics from General Practice: Fourth National Study, 1991–1992* (London, 1995).

McCracken, K. W. J., 'Analysing geographic variations in mortality', *Area*, 13 (1981), 203–10.

McDowall, M., 'William Farr and the study of occupational mortality', *Population Trends*, 31 (1983).

McGlashan, N. D. and Blunden, J. R., *Geographical Aspects of Health* (London, 1983).

McIntosh, M. J., Moore, M. R., Goldberg, A., Fell, G. S., Cunningham, C. and Halls, D. J., 'Studies of lead and cadmium exposure in Glasgow, UK', *Ecology of Disease*, 1 (2/3) (1982), 177–184.

McKeown, T., 'Medical issues in historical demography', in E. Clarke (ed.), *Modern Methods in the History of Medicine* (London, 1971).

—— *The Modern Rise of Population* (London, 1976).

—— *The Role of Medicine: Dream, Mirage or Nemesis?* (Oxford, 1979).

McKeown, T., *The Origins of Human Disease* (Oxford and New York, 1988).

McKeown, T. and Brown, R. G., 'Medical evidence related to English population changes in the eighteenth century', *Population Studies*, 9(2) (1955), 119–41.

McKeown, T. and Record, R. G., 'Reasons for the decline of mortality in England and Wales during the nineteenth century', *Population Studies*, 16 (1962), 94–122.

McKie, R., 'Genetic patchwork of an island nation', *Geographical Magazine*, LXV, 6 (1993), 25–8.

McNalty, A., 'Indigenous malaria in England', *Nature*, 17 April 1943, 440.

McNeill, W. H., *Plagues and Peoples* (New York, 1976).

Maitland, F. W., *Domesday Book and Beyond: Three Essays in the Early History of England* (London, 1960).

Malmesbury, Earl of, *Memoirs of an Ex-Minister* (London, 1885).

Manley, G., *Climate and the British Scene* (London, 1952).

Marshall, H., 'Sketch of the new geographical distribution of diseases', *Edinburgh Medical and Surgical Journal*, 38 (1832), 330–5.

Maunder, W. J., *The Value of the Weather* (London, 1970).

May, J. M., *Studies in Medical Geography: The Ecology of Disease*, vol. 1 (New York, 1958).

—— *The Ecology of Malnutrition in the Far and Near East* (New York, 1961).

—— *Studies in Disease Ecology* (New York, 1961).

Mead, R., *A Discourse on the Plague* (London, 1720).

Medical Research Council, *Assay of Strontium 90 in Human Bone in the United Kingdom* (London, 1969).

Medical Research Council, Environmental Epidemiology Unit, *Maps and Cancer*, Scientific Report no. 3 (Southampton, 1984).

—— Institute for Environment and Health (IEH). *Air Pollution and Health: Understanding the Uncertainties*, Report R1 (Leicester, 1994).

Meetham, A. R. et al., *Atmospheric Pollution: Its Origins and Prevention*, third rev. edn (London, 1964).

Mercer, A., *Disease, Mortality and Population in Transition* (Leicester, 1990).

Meteorological Office, *Report on Agricultural Meteorological Conference, 1928* (London, 1928).

Ministry of Agriculture, Fisheries and Food, 'Domestic food consumption and expenditure', *Report of the National Food Survey Committee* (London, 1963–5).

Ministry of Health, 'Report on the pandemic of influenza, 1918–19', *Report on Public Health and Medical Subjects*, no. 4 (1920).

Mitchell, W., *Rescue the Children* (London, 1886).

Morris, J. N., *Use of Epidemiology*, second edn (London, 1960).

Morris, R. J., 'Cholera: the social disease', *New Society* (July 1971), 52–6.

Mourant, A. E., Kopec, A. C. and Domaniewska-Sobczak, K., *Blood Groups and Diseases: A Study of Association of Diseases with Blood Groups and Other Polymorphisms* (Oxford, 1978).

Mulligan, R. C., 'The basic science of gene therapy', *Science*, 260 (1993), 926–32.

Mullett, C. F., *The Bubonic Plague and England: An Essay in the History of Preventive Medicine* (Lexington, Kentucky, 1956).

National Food Survey Committee, *Household Food Consumption and Expenditure 1987*, Annual Report (London, 1988).

Office of Health Economics, *Stroke* (London, 1988).

—— *Diabetes* (London, 1989).

—— *Mental Health in the 1990s* (London, 1989).

—— *Asthma* (London, 1990).

—— *Cholesterol and Coronary Heart Disease* (London, 1991).

—— *Drug Misuse* (London, 1992).

—— *Obesity* (London, 1994).

—— *Compendium of Health Statistics*, ed. R. S. B. Chew (9th edn, London, 1995).

Office of Population Censuses and Surveys (OPCS) *Mortality Statistics: Area 1980, 1981–93*.

—— (Series DH5, nos. 7, 8–18) (London, 1982, 1983–95).

—— *Occupational Mortality, 1970–72* (London, 1978).

—— *Area Mortality, 1969–73* (Series DS no. 4) (London, 1981).

—— *1841–1980 Mortality Statistics, Serial Tables* (London, 1985).

—— *Occupational Mortality, 1979–80, 1982–83* (London, various years).

—— *Decennial Supplement* (London, 1986).

—— *Cigarette Smoking 1972 to 1986*, Monitor SS 88/1 (London, 1988).

—— *General Household Survey* (London, various years) (Series GHS) (London, 1995).

—— *Mortality and Geography* (Series DS no. 9) (London, 1995).

Open University (UK) Course U205, *Health and Disease*, in eight books (Milton Keynes, 1985).

Opie, I. and Opie, P., *Oxford Dictionary of Nursery Rhymes* (Oxford, 1955).

Osborne, R. H., 'Population', in J. W. Watson with J. B. Sissons (eds.), *The British Isles: A Systematic Geography* (London, 1964).

Pacione, M. (ed.), *Medical Geography: Progress and Prospect* (London, 1986).

Parkin, D. M., Muir, C. S., Whelan, S. L., Gao, Y.-I., Ferlay, J. and Powell, J. (eds.), *Cancer Incidence in Five Continents*, vol. VI, IARC Scientific Publication no. 120 (Lyon, 1992).

Parliamentary Papers (Commons), Hand-Loom Weavers: Assistant Commissioners' Reports, 1839 (159), 42, 511.

—— (Lords), Report of the Poor Law Commissioners to the Secretary of State, on an Inquiry into the Sanitary Condition of the Labouring Population of Great Britain, 1842, xxvi, 1 (Reports by the Revd W. Elkin and Dr Laurie).

—— (Commons), Reports by J. Smith and J. R. Martin in the Second Report of the Commissioners for Inquiring into the State of Large Towns and Populous Districts, 1845 (602)(610), 18, 1, 299.

Patrick, A., 'A consideration of the nature of the English sweating sickness', *Medical History*, 9 (1965), 272–9.

Patterson, K. D., 'Pandemic and epidemic influenza 1830–48', *Social Science and Medicine*, 21 (1985), 571–80.

Pelling, M., *Cholera, Fever and English Medicine, 1825–1865* (Oxford, 1978).

Pepys, S., *Pepys' Diary*, ed. J. P. Kenyon (London, 1963).

Percival, T., *Observations on the State of the Population in Manchester* (Manchester, 1773).

Perring, F. H. and Mellanby, K., *Ecological Effects of Pesticides* (London, 1977).

Petermann, A. H., *Cholera Map of the British Isles, showing the Districts*

Attacked in 1831, 1832, and 1833. Constructed from Official Documents (London, 1852).

Peto, J., 'Radon and the risks of cancer', *Nature*, 345 (1990), 389–90.

Pinching, A. J., Weiss, R. A. and Miller, D., *AIDS and HIV Infection: The Wider Perspective* (Edinburgh, 1988).

Pirie, N. W., 'Gluttony', *New Scientist*, 423 (1964), 838–41.

Plant, M. A., *Drugs in Perspective* (London, 1987).

Pocock, S. J., Cook, D. G. and Shaper, A. G., 'Analysing geographic variations in cardiovascular mortality', *Journal of the Royal Statistical Society Series A*, 145 (1982), 313–41.

Pollitzer, R., *Plague* (Geneva, 1954).

Prothero, R. E., *The Pioneers and Progress of English Farming* (London, 1888).

Public Health Laboratory Service (PHLS) Communicable Disease Surveillance Centre, *Communicable Disease Reports*, weekly editions (London).

Pyle, G. F., *Applied Medical Geography* (New York, 1979).

—— and Patterson, K. D., 'Influenza diffusion in European history: patterns and paradigms', *Ecology of Disease*, 2 (1983), 173–84.

Ramazzini, B., *De morbis artificum, diatriba* (Venice, 1743).

Rawstron, E. M. and Coates, B. E., *Regional Variations in Britain* (London, 1971).

Reader's Digest Association, *Complete Atlas of the British Isles* (London, 1965).

Redmayne, P., *Britain's Food: The Changing Shape of Things* (London, 1963).

Rees, W., 'The Black Death in Wales', *Transactions of the Royal History Society*, 3 (1920), 115–36.

—— 'The Black Death in England and Wales, as exhibited in manorial documents', *Proceedings of the Royal Society of Medicine* (Hist Med) 16 (1923), 27.

Reiter, R., 'Neuere Untersuchungen zum Problem der Wetterabhängigkeit des Menchen', *Archiv fur Meteorologie, Geophisik und Bioklimatologie*, ser. B, 4 (Vienna) (1953), 327–77.

Renbourn, E. T., 'Normality in relation to human reactions', *Proceedings of the Ninth International Congress on Industrial Medicine* (London, 1948).

Richie, J., 'Enteric fever', *British Medical Journal*, 2 (1937), 160–3.

Roberts, C. and Manchester, K., *The Archaeology of Disease* (Stroud, 1995).

Roberts, R. S., 'A consideration of the nature of the English sweating sickness', *Medical History*, 9 (1965), 385–9.

—— 'The use of literary and documentary evidence in the history of medicine', in G. Clarke (ed.), *Modern Methods in the History of Medicine* (London, 1971).

Rodenwaldt, E., *Welt-Seuchen Atlas. Weltatlas der Seuchenverbreitung und Seuchenbewegung* (World Atlas of Epidemic Diseases. World Atlas of the Distribution and Spread of Epidemic Diseases), parts I and II (Hamburg, 1952, 1956).

Rogers, T. J. E., *The History of Agriculture and Prices in England*, vol. V (London, 1866–7).

Rolleston, J. D., 'The history of scarlet fever', *British Medical Journal*, 2 (1928), 926–9.

Rona, R. J., Swan, A. V. and Altman, D. G., 'Social factors and heights of primary schoolchildren in England and Scotland', *J. Epidemiol. Community Health*, 32 (1978), 147–54, and 42 (1988), 299–303.

Rose, G., 'Environmental factors and disease: the man-made environment', *British Medical Journal*, 294 (1987), 963-5.

Rowland, A. J. and Cooper, P., *Environment and Health* (London, 1983).

Rowntree, S. B., *Poverty: A Study of Town Life* (London, 1901).

Russell, J. C., *British Medieval Population* (Albuquerque, 1948).

Russell, W. T., 'The epidemiology of diphtheria during the last forty years', *Medical Research Council, Special Reports Series*, 247 (1943).

Saltmarsh, J., 'Plague and economic decline in the later Middle Ages', *Cambridge Historical Journal*, 7 (1941), 23-41.

Schroeder, H. A., 'Relationship between mortality from cardiovascular disease and treated water supplies', *Journal of the American Medical Association*, 172 (17) (1960), 1902-8.

Scott, H. H., *Some Notable Epidemics* (London, 1934).

Shannon, G. W. and Cromley, R. G., 'The great plague of London', *Urban Geography*, 1 (1980), 254-70.

Shapter, T., *The History of the Cholera in Exeter in 1832* (London, 1841).

—— *Sanitary Measures and Their Results: Being a Sequel to the 'History of Cholera in Exeter'* (London, 1853).

Shaw, M. B., 'A short history of the sweating sickness', *Annals of Medical History*, 5 (1933), 246-73.

Shrewsbury, J. F. D., 'The yellow plague', *Journal of the History of Medicine and Allied Sciences*, 4 (1949), 5-47.

—— 'Henry VIII: a medical study', ibid., 7(2) (1952), 141-85.

—— *A History of Bubonic Plague in the British Isles* (Cambridge, 1970).

Siegfried, A., *Germs and Ideas: Routes of Epidemics and Ideologies*, tr. J. Henderson and M. Claraso (Edinburgh and London, 1965).

Singer, C., *A Short History of Medicine* (Oxford, 1928).

Slack, P., 'The disappearance of plague: an alternative view', *Economic History Review*, 34 (1981), 469-76.

—— *The Impact of Plague in Tudor and Stuart England* (London, 1985).

Smith, A. (ed.), *Recent Advances in Community Medicine*, no. 3 (Edinburgh, 1985).

Smith, A. and Jacobsen, B. (eds.), *The Nation's Health: A Strategy for the 1990s* (King Edward's Hospital Fund, 1988, 2nd edn. 1991).

Smith, K., *Environmental Hazards* (London, 1991).

Smith, W. D. L., 'Malaria and the Thames', *Lancet*, 270 (1956), 433-6.

Snow, J., *On the Mode of Communication of Cholera* (London, 1849; 2nd edn., 1855).

Spiers, F. W., *The Hazards to Man of Nuclear and Allied Radiations*, report by a committee appointed by the Medical Research Council (London, 1956).

—— *The Hazards to Man of Nuclear and Allied Radiations*, II, a second report to the Medical Research Council (London, 1960).

Stamp, L. D., *The Geography of Life and Death* (London, 1964).

Stocks, P., *Regional and Local Differences in Cancer Death Rates* (Studies in Medical and Population Subjects) (London, 1947).

Susser, M., *Causal Thinking in the Health Sciences* (London, 1973).

Swedlow, A. and I. dos Santos Silva, *Atlas of Cancer Incidence in England and Wales, 1968-85* (Oxford, 1993).

Talbot, C. H., *Medicine in Medieval England* (London, 1967).

Tanner, J. W., 'Earlier maturation in man', *Scientific American*, 218 (1968), 21–7.

Thackrah, C. T., *The Effects of Arts, Trades, and Professions and of Civic States and Habits of Living on Health and Longevity* (London, 1831).

Thomas, R., *Geomedical Systems: Intervention and Control* (London, 1992).

Thompson, J. W., 'The aftermath of the Black Death and the aftermath of the Great War', *American Journal of Sociology*, 16 (1920–1).

Thomson, D., 'Whooping cough: a review', *Monthly Bulletin of the Ministry of Health* 12 (1953), 92–100.

Thomson, G., *Loimotamia, or the Pest Anatomized* (London, 1666).

Thomson, J. and Abbott, D. C., 'Pesticide residues: history, alternatives and analysis', *Royal Institute of Chemistry*, Lecture Series no. 3, 1966 (London, 1967).

Thring, M. W. (ed.), *Air Pollution*, based on papers given at a conference in the University of Sheffield, 1956 (London, 1957).

Tobacco Research Council, *Statistics of Smoking in the United Kingdom* (Research Paper 1) (seventh edn, London, 1976).

Trevelyan, G. M., *English Social History: A Survey of Six Centuries, Chaucer to Queen Victoria* (third edn, London, 1961).

Tromp, S. W., *Medical Biometeorology* (London, 1963).

Tromp, S. W. and Weihe, W. H. (eds.), *Biometeorology* (London, 1967).

Tucker, G. S. I., 'English pre-industrial population trends', *Economic History Review*, 2nd ser., 16 (1963), 205–18.

Tyler, W. F., 'Bracing and relaxing climates', *Quarterly Journal of the Royal Meteorological Society*, 61 (1935), 309–15.

Tyndall, R. M., 'Patterns of cardiovascular disease mortality in Greater Glasgow', unpublished PhD thesis, University of Strathclyde, Glasgow, 1984.

Underwood, E. A., 'The history of cholera in Great Britain', *Proceedings of the Royal Society of Medicine* (1948), 165–73.

United Nations, *Demographic Year Book, 1967* (New York, 1968).

Varmus, H. E. and Weinberg, R. A., *Genes and the Biology of Cancer* (New York, 1993).

Vogel, F., 'ABO blood groups and disease', *American Journal of Human Genetics*, 22 (1970), 464–75.

Waddy, B. B., 'Climate and respiratory infections', *Lancet*, 2 (1952), 674–7.

Wald, N., *UK Smoking Statistics* (Oxford, 1988). See *Key Data, National Statistics, 1996* (Government Statistical Service, London, 1996) for more recent data.

Wald, N. and Nicolaides-Bouman, A., *UK Smoking Statistics*, 2nd edn. (Oxford, 1991).

Warren, H. V., 'Geology and health', *Science Monthly*, 78(6) (1954), 339–45.

—— 'Geology and multiple sclerosis', *Nature*, 184 (1959), 561.

Warren, H. V., Delavault, R. E. and Cross, C. H., 'Possible correlations between geology and some disease patterns', *Annals of the New York Academy of Science*, 136 (1967), art. 22, 657–710.

Water Authority Association, *Water Pollution from Farm Waste* (London, 1987).

Waterhouse, J. A. H., Muir, C. S., Shanmugaratnam, K. and Powell, J. (eds.), *Cancer Incidence in Five Continents*, IARC Scientific Publication no. 42 (Lyon, 1982).

Watson, J. W. with Sissons, J. B. (eds.), *The British Isles: A Systematic Geography* (London and Edinburgh, 1964).

Watt, R., *Treatise on the History, Nature and Treatment of Chin-Cough* (Glasgow, 1813).

Weiner, A. S. 'Blood groups and disease', *American Journal of Human Genetics*, 22 (1970), 476–83.

Wells, C., *Bones, Bodies and Disease* (London, 1964).

Whitelegg, J., 'A geography of road traffic accidents', *Transactions of the Institute of British Geographers*, NS, 12 (1987), 161–76.

Wigglesworth, V. B., *The Principles of Insect Physiology* (sixth edn, London, 1965).

Williams, E. M., 'Genetic studies of Welsh gypsies', in P. S. Harper and E. Sutherland (eds.), *Genetic and Population Studies in Wales* (Cardiff, 1986).

Willis, T., *Diatribae duae medico-philosophicae* (London, 1659).

Wilson, F. P. (ed.), *The Plague Pamphlets by Thomas Dekker* (Oxford, 1925).

—— *The Plague in Shakespeare's London* (Oxford, 1927).

Winslow, C. E. A. and Herrington, L. P., *Temperature and Human Life* (London, 1949).

Wise, M. E., 'Human radiation hazards', in N. Rashevsky (ed.), *Physico-mathematical Aspects of Biology* (New York, 1962).

Woodham-Smith, C., *Florence Nightingale, 1820–1910* (London, 1950).

—— *The Great Hunger: Ireland 1845–49* (London, 1962).

Woods, H. M., 'Epidemiological study of scarlet fever in England and Wales since 1900', *Medical Research Council, Special Reports Series*, 180 (1933).

Woods, R. and Woodward, J., *Urban Disease and Mortality in Nineteenth Century England* (London, 1984).

World Health Organization, *Endemic goitre* (Geneva, 1960).

—— *Basic documents* (16th edn, Geneva, 1965).

—— *Manual of the International Statistical Classification of Diseases, Injuries and Causes of Death*, ninth revision (Geneva, 1977).

Wrigley, E. A. and Schofield, R. S., *The Population History of England 1541–1871: A Reconstruction* (London, 1981).

Yudkin, J. and McKenzie, J. C. (eds.), *Changing Food Habits* (London, 1964).

Ziegler, P., *The Black Death* (London, 1968).

Zinsser, H., *Rats, Lice and History* (London, 1935).

Index of People

References to maps, graphs and tables are distinguished by italic type in each index.

This index does not include the names of authors whose work is cited in the chapter references, the bibliography or acknowledged in captions to figures

Index of Places

General Index